JOHANN GEORG HAMANN AND THE ENLIGHTENMENT PROJECT

ROBERT ALAN SPARLING

Johann Georg Hamann and the Enlightenment Project

UNIVERSITY OF TORONTO PRESS
Toronto Buffalo London

©University of Toronto Press Incorporated 2011
Toronto Buffalo London
www.utppublishing.com
Printed in Canada

ISBN 978-1-4426-4215-7

Library and Archives Canada Cataloguing in Publication

Sparling, Robert Alan, 1975–
Johann Georg Hamann and the enlightenment project / Robert Alan Sparling.

Includes bibliographical references and index.
ISBN 978-1-4426-4215-7

1. Hamann, Johann Georg, 1730–1788.   I. Title.

B2993.S63 2011   193   C2010-906222-1

This book has been published with the help of a grant from the Canadian
Federation for the Humanities and Social Sciences, through the Aid to
Scholarly Publications Program, using funds provided by the Social Sciences
and Humanities Research Council of Canada.

University of Toronto Press acknowledges the financial assistance to its
publishing program of the Canada Council for the Arts and the Ontario Arts
Council.

 Canada Council   Conseil des Arts
for the Arts   du Canada

 ONTARIO ARTS COUNCIL
CONSEIL DES ARTS DE L'ONTARIO

University of Toronto Press acknowledges the financial support of the
Government of Canada through the Canada Book Fund for its publishing
activities.

Contents

Preface

The work of Johann Georg Hamann has been at once the steady object of admiration and neglect. Historians of ideas are well aware of his significance in late eighteenth-century German thought, and many philosophers have expressed wonder at the degree to which he appears to 'anticipate' modern developments, notably the linguistic turn in philosophy, the emphasis on aesthetics, and the insistence on the concerned nature of philosophy that so captivated Nietzsche, Kierkegaard, later so-called existentialists, and postmodern analysts of power. Yet for all that Hamann looked forward to the main trends of twentieth-century thought, he also looked backward to the authority of the divine word, the *Heilsgeschichte* of the Old and New testaments, and to a view of the world as divine language. Thus, Hamann opposed the Enlightenment with weapons that appear to us as both pre- and postmodern. For every aspect of Hamann's thought that appears tailor-made for our era there are equally important elements that jar, that disturb, or that evoke incomprehension.

This is a study of Hamann's significance for political philosophy. It attempts both to contextualize his thought and to indicate the enduring significance of his position. The study is framed around the eighteenth-century movement known as the Enlightenment and the trans-historical battles over the Enlightenment Project. Hamann saw himself as an opponent of his age and its ideals; the first chapter of this work will defend and define these widely used and widely contested terms, the *Enlightenment* and the *Enlightenment Project*. Before we begin, however, it is worthwhile to make several preliminary remarks about the method and intent of this work.

Hamann is not an easy writer to read, but the difficulties that one encounters in his texts are distinct from those encountered in many philosophers said to be difficult. Systematic writers like Hegel or Kant employ a series of philosophical terms of art that one must master as one proceeds – slow, attentive reading suffices. In the case of oracular writers like the late Heidegger, one must make great effort to break through their purposely opaque vocabulary. Unlike the systematic or the oracular writers, Hamann's method is ironic and allusive. He only employs *other people's* terms of art, and his intent is invariably to alter their meaning. The 'ironic' and occasional nature of his works presents certain difficulties that can be overcome only by attending to their con- texts (both literary and historical). The other aspect of his writing that renders it difficult is its density. Any given sentence from a Hamannian piece usually *implies* several arguments by way of numerous allusions (usually humorously rendered) to the Bible, to the text(s) he is attacking, and, more often than not, to some other work that would appear to be related only tangentially to the matter at hand. He juxtaposes radically different thoughts in wild non sequiturs, and the argument is to be found in the space between. He overlays the vocabulary of one text onto the grammatical construction of another and leaves the reader to piece together the meaning. We will discuss at some length the signifi- cance of these stylistic oddities in chapter 2; for the moment, I wish merely to indicate the difficulties in proceeding. Given the occasional and allusive nature of Hamann's writing, no discussion of his work can avoid extensive textual exegesis, but such exegesis always runs the danger of overwhelming the analysis of the works. Thus, while making ample use of the now-sizeable exegetical literature on the subject, I will attempt to refrain from a tendentious *Entstehungsgeschichte* so as not to lose our way in the labyrinth of references.

I have written this work in the awareness of Hamann's relative ob- scurity, and I have thus never assumed familiarity with his oeuvre. However, I have not attempted to write an introduction to Hamann's thought. In the German academy, this job has already been accom- plished by such writers as Sven-Aage Jørgensen and Oswald Bayer.[1] For *la Francophonie*, the job was amply done by Jean Blum's interpretive biography.[2] The English-speaking academy is surprisingly well served, containing several brief, readable accounts of Hamann's life and work.[3] Isaiah Berlin's *The Magus of the North*, with which I find fault, is none- theless a brisk and lively treatment. More substantive but equally read- able introductory works have been penned by James O'Flaherty and

W.M. Alexander. Gwen Griffith-Dickson offers a thorough exegesis of many of Hamann's more important works, placing helpful emphasis on the 'relational' nature of Hamannian epistemology. Ronald Gregor Smith offers a readable and competent treatment (although he tends towards excessive manipulation of the texts in order to clothe Hamann in the garb of existentialism). All of them undertake the task of introducing 'the Magus of the North' to the anglophone world. It would be somewhat superfluous to add to these. My purpose is to illuminate Hamann's location within the history of political thought and to indicate his importance for political philosophy today.

This application might at first glimpse surprise the reader. The bulk of extant Hamann scholarship exists in three fields of study: theology, comparative literature, and philosophy. Theological writers have sought in Hamann a particularly modern way of remaining Christian in the wake of metaphysics' demise. To these writers, Hamann presents a helpful mode of recuperating God's address to humanity and of salvaging meaning in a post-metaphysical world. Hamann's insistence on human limitations is a source of fideistic glee to such interpreters.[4] In the field of comparative literature, Hamann holds an important place in the development of the Sturm und Drang. Writers have examined the influence and meaning of his curious style and located it within the traditions of the baroque and the Renaissance – here Hamann both foreshadows the romantic stylistic extravagancies and recalls the humanistic insistence on rhetoric's philosophical importance.[5] Finally, there has been significant attention paid to Hamann's philosophical claims, and particularly to his reception of Hume and reaction to Kant.[6] Here, Hamann is located as one of Kant's earliest critics and as an important mediating voice between Hume and Kant. Writers from all of these disciplines have noted the degree to which Hamann's inquiries were very much in the spirit of practical philosophy, and all of Hamann's interpreters have been struck by the fervour of his political outbursts, but there has been no systematic study of his thought from the perspective of political philosophy.

The subject that occupied Hamann throughout his life was communication – the communication between people and the communication between God and humanity. As a young man, Hamann was a bibliophile with a great enthusiasm for the latest literature. But in his twenties he had a spiritual crisis and an encounter with the divine, not on a road to Damascus, but in an equally unlikely place for God to appear, London. Undertaking a commercial/diplomatic mission (whose exact nature remains obscure but whose result was utter failure), and having led a somewhat dissolute life, Hamann had a crisis of conscience and religious conversion experience. On his return from England he was altered; the energy that he had previously wished to devote towards philosophy and commerce was now redirected to the subject of faith. Such a radical alteration confused and embarrassed his friends and well-wishers, who attempted, on more than one occasion, to help find some useful intellectual work for him. (Among these friends, it should be noted, was Immanuel Kant.) Hamann both rejected these overtures and immersed himself with renewed vigour into the study of languages (ancient and modern) and literature, this time with a heavy leaning towards scripture. Hamann's reaction to his friends' offers, and his attempt to explain his position to them, came across as bizarre and overly proud enthusiasm. He was, indeed, a *Schwärmer*, that polar opposite of the cultivated, sociable *philosophe*. His friends' attitude appeared to him as a kind of anti-Christian proselytizing. Hamann's entire writing career can be seen as a response to the problem of making himself understood – it was an extended *apologia pro vita sua*. Hamann found himself in the position of defending his faith and this led him to wage war on the faith of his century.

In defending one type of life and attacking another he was engaged in the foundational question of political philosophy, what is the good life? More specifically, he found himself situated in a print culture that was setting itself as a new standard of justification in a world whose old standards it sought to tame. The culture of critique with its tolerance, its appeal to universal reason, its publicity, its elevation of the rationally autonomous person, and its simultaneous rational hubris and radical scepticism was making itself into a fighting creed. Hamann found himself raising troubling questions about his age's ideals – questions that have become even more pressing in the era of Enlightenment's triumph. Can the appeal to impartial reason really be sustained? What basis is there for reason's claims to authority? How do we understand human communication? In what way can the good (understood by Hamann as God's address to humanity) be articulated? Are there limits to this expression? Aspects of the Enlightenment's incipient liberalism are called into question as well. Hamann undermined the atomism at the heart of modern natural rights theories. He questioned the ideal of autonomy and wondered about the source of duty. He emphasized the priority of the passions in thought, and articulated a view of man as both passionate and dutiful. And he defended a type of religious language whose banishment has been and continues to be one of the Enlightenment's most important goals.

Hamann did not address these questions in direct treatises, but in discursive, polemical pieces aimed at his opponents. He saw himself as a Socratic gadfly in the republic of letters. Or, to switch metaphors, he saw his works as purgatives. Taking a cue from his father's occupation (a minor physician and keeper of the public baths), he intended to publish his final collection of works under the title *Saalbadereyen*, or 'Curative Baths.'[7] Throughout he was at loggerheads with the vanguard of the progressive Enlightenment. Kant was his most famous adversary, but he equally directed his attacks against materialists like La Mettrie, deists like Voltaire, atheists like Frederick the Great, and rational theologians like Moses Mendelssohn. Hamann saw himself as an opponent of a philosophical movement, and, though he expressed himself in entirely immoderate terms, often lumping together many disparate figures, he succeeded in carving out an opposition to a series of positions that were dominant in his time and remain dominant in ours.

From the perspective of intellectual history, Hamann gives us an important – and widely neglected – step in the development of Continental philosophy. He was of direct influence on Herder and Jacobi who both spurred the development of German idealism and historicism. Hegel found Hamann a fascinating (if fatally flawed) writer and devoted a lengthy review to his work, and Kierkegaard was highly influenced by him, as is clearly evident in the *Philosophical Fragments*. The list of writers who expressed a mixture of wonder, curiosity, and frustration with Hamann is surprisingly long (Herder, Jacobi, Goethe, Jean-Paul, Schelling, Schleiermacher, Hegel, Kierkegaard, Dilthey, Jünger, von Balthasar ...). My intention is not, however, to provide a *Wirkungsgeschichte*. While I will periodically make comparative claims, indicating Hamann's distance from some subsequent intellectual movements, this is not a study that will appeal primarily to the historian.

There is a great deal of writing that takes for granted the death of both religion and metaphysics. It is argued that the world is too old for such fairy tales. Or, rather, it is not argued, but assumed, for the insignificance of metaphysical and religious speech (two very different but related phenomena) is widely accepted as fact by numerous writers of radically different stripes. The attack on metaphysics is quite old – indeed, it is a central preoccupation of the Enlightenment. Leo Strauss's opinion that Plato's doctrine of the forms was mere window dressing was anticipated by an earlier thinker, Frederick the Great:

'Si le sentiment de la divinité de Jesus-Christ s'accrédita dans l'Église, il ne s'affermit que par la subtilité de quelques philosophes Grecs de la secte des péripateciens qui, en embrassant le Christianisme, l'enrichirent d'une partie de la métaphysique obscure, sous laquelle Platon avoit cru cacher quelques vérités trop dangereuses à publier.'[8] It is one of the Enlightenment's enduring legacies to reject both faith and 'obscure metaphysics' in the same breath. This post-metaphysical aspect of modernity is a central element of Enlightenment thought. For all that Kant attempted to save a chastened metaphysics from Humean doubt, we find ourselves in a world in which even Kantian transcendentalism is widely treated with suspicion, and thick ontology is treated as fanatical error. Surprisingly, given his self-consciously anti-metaphysical stance, Hamann's attack on the Enlightenment is a valuable tool in the salvation of ontological thought. To this end, those readers who cannot conceive of travelling down the road of faith with Hamann can nonetheless learn much from his denunciation of the modern condition.

Having said this, we must signal an opposition that will be important to this work. Hamann was a thinker of the first rank, but he was not a philosopher in any traditional sense. He treated philosophy generally as a competitor of faith.[9] This opposition will be resisted by those who like to see in Hamann a philosophy. But though Hamann gave a number of arguments that can be counted as philosophical (and that I intend to analyze philosophically), his general intent was to undermine philosophy's methods and claims, for philosophy and revelation do battle on the ground of ontology. Hamann's constant refrain – and it is an argument that has a long tradition – is that there is an element of mystery that cannot be grasped by unaided human cognition. What's more, the philosophical wheat in Hamann's arguments is difficult to separate from the anti-philosophical chaff – if indeed it is chaff. (Hamann would certainly have us invert the evaluation.) If his position has difficulty commanding assent in a secular, diverse world today, it should trouble us in our enlightened progress. Its philosophical claims are universal enough to give our purest reason pause; its faith claims are, at the very least, coherent enough to tell us much about faith's relation to its philosophical opposite.

The importance of Hamann's position today should be evident from the culture wars being waged between the Enlightenment and its enemies. What is most helpful in reading him is his tendency to muddy the conceptual oppositions we have come to take for granted. It is not an exaggeration to say that he launched the trend of thought that led to historicism and existentialism, yet he was a firm adherent to the universal truth of scripture. His thought was, in many respects, radically individualist (one's encounter with scripture was a personal *Höllenfahrt*, as befits a Protestant), but he defended a conception of human beings as communal and linguistically situated. He was an opponent of toleration discourse and public reason, yet he decried dogmatic orthodoxy, the persecution of religious difference, and the censorship of writing. He was anti-cosmopolitan, but he was equally anti-nationalist. He was anti-philosophic, but not necessarily irrationalist. He was a champion of aesthetic language and rule-defying creativity, yet he decried taste and the language of self-creation. Hamann, then, presents an opposition to Enlightenment that defies the simple schematisms we have been sold in recent years. For those who think that we are forced to choose between a dogmatic foundationalism[10] and some empty, 'postmodern,' über-tolerant fifth-column of jihad, Hamann is a difficult figure to place. Or, for an older crowd that prefers to group reason, empiricism, liberty, and progress against medieval darkness, dogmatism, and authoritarianism, Hamann throws a wrench into the works (he opposed dogmatism, authoritarianism, and rational progress, championing empiricism and many elements of medieval darkness!). Of course the caricatures that I have just outlined are conceptually confused, but their widespread existence is testament to the need for more attention to the nuances within the modern reaction to Enlightenment.

A caveat is required here. This book concerns a religious writer and his confrontation with a secular vocabulary. The work attempts scholarly distance from the subject matter, but nonetheless attempts to present it as a reasonable and cogent possibility for thought. It will become clear enough that I look upon Hamann's position with some ambivalence – his polemics are extreme, his generalizations are sweeping, and he often rejects out of hand aspects of political life to which we are not unreasonably attached. At the same time, I clearly think that there is much worthy of attention both in his thought and in his clash with his age. But to take a religious thinker seriously is to entertain the possibility that the idea of God is cogent. There is a certain dismissive attitude concerning the actual content of religious thought that pervades writing in political theory. This is not to say that political theory is dominated by anti-religious sentiment. Many take polite stances on various 'religious traditions'; many more feel that the political importance of religions is a central 'fact of pluralism' that needs discussion. But it is often felt, with considerable reason, that positions having their basis in any particular theological system lack the universality necessary for scholarly argument. This is one important theme treated in this work. What do these borders of communicability mean? Where do they come from, and what authority do they have? This book considers the place of faith in public reason.

I wish to emphasize at the outset that this work's sympathetic treatment of divine lunacy is not intended as a confessional act. There is a sizeable body of Hamann scholarship that is clearly of a confessional nature emerging from German schools of Protestant theology (and, indeed, Catholic theology, as von Balthasar's example indicates). Oswald Bayer, the world's most detailed Hamann exegete, is also an exponent of a school of theological thought derived directly from Hamann's view of divine condescension.[11] For all that I have benefited from the invaluable scholarship of the theologians, the theological superficiality of this work will be ample proof that I am not of their number. Nor do I share the confessional motivations of these authors. But neither do I think it possible to give serious attention to the thought of a writer without attempting to grasp it, as it were, from the inside. The fact that I feel compelled to place my lack of confessional colours on the table is indicative of the very climate of Enlightenment that Hamann challenged. Our historical condition should not be taken as a reason to ban the problem of piety from political philosophy. For the pious, there is no greater question, for the irreligious no greater muddle than the place of God in the good life. This was the central political issue of the eighteenth-century Enlightenment and remains the central cleavage around the Enlightenment project today (witness the current slate of devotional books and militantly anti-devotional books on the bestseller lists). Thought needs to take account of this problem and not flee it by according piety the silent treatment of dogmatic awe, polite tolerance, or unreflective rejection. Whether or not George W. Bush was correct to declare Christ to be history's most important political thinker, *Nolo me tangere* is not a valid principle in political philosophy.

If I have attempted, then, to understand Hamann from the inside – if I take this to be a fundamental hermeneutical requirement – I do not wish to be read as an apologist for Hamann's excesses. Indeed, I am both ambivalent about Hamann's theological assumptions and wary of adding to the laudatory tone that dominates most treatments of Hamann. I am sympathetic to his arguments about the liberal social-contract position, as well as about the nature of mind. I think there is fundamental importance in the view of existence as communicative, and I think the communitarian implications of Hamann's thought

ought to be commended to us. Finally, I wish to highlight the importance of his attack on the mores of the public realm and the difficulties it poses for us. But I am less sympathetic to Hamann's somewhat exclusionary theological certitude, and I do not think that this is something that can be received in an unproblematic manner (an issue to which we will return in the conclusion). Indeed, embedded within many of Hamann's most profound thoughts are troubling possibilities that I do not wish to sweep under the carpet (as has been the tendency in much Hamann scholarship thus far). Thus, if there is a degree of pugnacious iconoclasm in this book, my intention is to be aporetic, not apologetic.

This brings me to my final claim on the normative undertones of this work. In an essay purportedly based on Kant, John Rawls writes, 'The aim of political philosophy, when it presents itself to the public culture of a democratic society, is to articulate and to make explicit those shared notions and principles thought to be already latent in common sense.'[12] Rawls is not talking about political philosophy (perhaps he is talking about opinion polls).[13] Philosophy is to common sense what knowledge is to opinion. Political philosophy does not 'present itself to the public culture of a democratic society,' and it is rendered sterile when it merely parrots 'shared notions.' As Socrates' practice indicates, philosophy *begins* in opinion but moves steadily away from it. Rawls and his followers have found that the unpleasantness of substantive philosophical disagreement must be kept out of political thought. As I see it, it is the nature of political philosophy and the task of the philosophical historian to be unpleasant, to find those writers in our past who challenge our shared notions, particularly on the nature of the good life.[14] If I were living in a theocratic republic I would probably have chosen Voltaire as my subject matter. But as a child of the Enlightenment, I fear that we post-theistic, post-metaphysical, and now even 'post-secular' (!) persons have all too much spiritual comfort, and I consider the engagement with Enlightenment's opposite to be a central duty of political thought.

Chapter Outline

The first chapter serves as an introduction, dealing with the conceptual centre of this work, the Enlightenment. It argues for the utility of treating the term both as a referent to a historical philosophical movement and as an ongoing project of purifying reason. On a historical level, it argues that the Enlightenment must be considered as a singular movement, if only insofar as it had opponents. Hamann thought that there was something to oppose, and, for all his simplification, he found a constellation of ideas against which he situated himself.

The second chapter begins our exploration of Hamann's work by attempting to account for his obscure style. It argues that Hamann was reacting against the abstract universalism that underlies the Enlightenment's central article of faith – public reason. Public reason (both the fact of the literary community and the ideal of a realm of disinterested communication where the best argument is the only source of hierarchy) is decried as an empty idol for three reasons. First, it masks hidden power relations. Second, it fails to account for the *personal* nature of conversation. Third, it relegates the poetic to the level of ornament or rhetoric. Hamann's strange style is an attempt to subvert the Enlightenment ideal with an ironic appropriation of his opponents' terms of art in order to draw them personally into the confrontation. At the same time, he holds up the mythopoetic aspects of writing as more direct and less alienating than abstract concepts. These two elements of the personal and the poetic combine in his method of 'metaschematism' or 'transfiguration.'

The subsequent three chapters deal with Hamann's *Metakritik* of Kant's *Kritik der reinen Vernunft*. The purpose of these chapters is to indicate how Hamann's *Metakritik* entails a questioning of Kantian ethics and the ideal of autonomy. Following an exegesis of Hamann's dense text (chapter 3), we proceed, in chapter 4, to explore Hamann's attack on the Kantian a priori. Here, we see that while Hamann usefully pointed to a linguistic dimension of thought that Kant tended to ignore, he actually performed a move that paralleled the Kantian 'Copernican turn.' The fifth chapter fleshes out the different implications of their respective transcendental arguments. Here we see that the Hamannian formulation is both bolder and more timid in what it is willing to assert. The timidity derives from an insistence on humility and ignorance; the boldness, from an acceptance of revelation (and hence, of *transcendent* matters about which Kant would have us remain silent). The chapter proceeds to draw out the ethico-political significance of Hamann's linguistic opposition to the Kantian a priori. Man encounters his essential nature in communication/communion. Kantian autonomy is, from this perspective, pathological.

Chapters 6 to 8 examine Hamann's reaction to liberal social contract theory by exploring his attack on Moses Mendelssohn's *Jerusalem*. Chapter 6 considers Hamann's reaction to Mendelssohn's theory of natural rights. Hamann's *Golgotha und Scheblimini!* indicates the Hobbesian dimensions of Mendelssohn's text, but notes Mendelssohn's attempt to give cold Hobbesian atomism a warm veneer of benevolence. Our second chapter on the Hamann/Mendelssohn quarrel is devoted to the question of the externals in thought. Mendelssohn is shown to hold a surprisingly Hobbesian view of the mind's relationship to the external, historical world. Hamann is able to draw out a tension in this view and to undermine the Enlightenment ideal of pure, extra-historical thought. The final chapter illustrates the similarity of Hobbesian and Mendelssohnian views on language and contrasts these with Hamann's understanding of *logos*. Hamann challenges the Mendelssohnian/Hobbesian view of words as arbitrary signs: Hamann's view of language suggests an alternate account of politics – one that rejects the atomistic premises of social contract theory.

Chapter 9 is the most historical chapter. It examines Hamann's reactions to Frederick the Great, indicating his lines of attack in condemning enlightened despotism. If enlightened absolutists all thought of themselves as countering despotism through the rule of reason, Hamann undermines the distinction between sophist and philosopher, and thus between despotism and absolutism. Through Hamann's eyes we perceive enlightened absolutism as a kind of secular soul-craft. Hamann's objections amount to a defence of individual conscience against a systematic rationalization of life.

The tenth chapter returns to the subject of style, elucidating Hamann's aesthetics. It opposes his theological aesthetics to the taste discourse of the eighteenth century and to the aesthetic turn in political philosophy following Nietzsche. It attempts to open a third front in the eternal battle between the philosophers and the poets, and it indicates the dangers of a Hamannian position when stripped of its theological presuppositions.

We will conclude, in chapter 11, with some brief reflections on the possibilities for Hamann reception today, touching particularly on the stumbling block posed by Hamann's confessional polemics.

Acknowledgments

I owe a great deal of thanks to Ronald Beiner, Simone Chambers, Melissa Williams, and Fred Dallmayr for their careful readings, challenging comments, and kind encouragement in the writing of this book, and to David Kelly for many lively conversations on the nature of language. I am particularly indebted to Edward Andrew, whose towering erudition is matched only by his generosity of spirit. Ed is one of those rare individuals for whom teaching is truly a labour of love, and I am more grateful than I can express for having had the privilege of being his student. The other person who most deserves thanks is she without whom the book could never have been written: Sophie Bourgault. In addition to providing extremely thorough and penetrating commentary (and tempering my impulse to make arcane jokes that only I find amusing), Sophie has been a constant guide for my work. She is the reader I most aspire to impress, and she accompanies me through every torturous twist of argument. I would also like to express my gratitude to my parents, Timothy and Christine Sparling, who have been a steady source of support throughout the writing. And I would like to thank Esmée and Rose, from whom I have learned – and continue to learn – so much that is inaccessible to public reason. *Wahrlich, wahrlich, Kinder müssen wir werden, wenn wir den Geist der Wahrheit empfahen sollen.*

Thanks go to Daniel Quinlan at the University of Toronto Press and to Ian MacKenzie for his careful copy editing. The anonymous readers from UTP provided very helpful suggestions that improved the text greatly. I would like to thank *Monatshefte* for permission to reprint a portion of chapter 2, which appeared as 'Transfiguring the Enlightenment: J.G. Hamann and the Problem of Public Reason,' *Monatshefte* 98, no. 1 (2006): 12–29. Finally, I would like to express my gratitude the American Political Science Association and in particular to the 2009 Leo Strauss Award committee, Roxanne L. Euben, Cristina Beltran, and Tommie Shelby, for their generous recognition of the work in its earlier, dissertation form.

This book has been published with the help of a grant from the Canadian Federation for the Humanities and Social Sciences, through the Aid to Scholarly Publications Program, using funds provided by the Social Sciences and Humanities Research Council of Canada.

A Note on Citation

Throughout the text I have followed the reigning convention and cited Joseph Nadler's edition of the complete works (Johann Georg Hamann, *Sämtliche Werke*, six volumes edited by Joseph Nadler) with the initial **N**.

For Hamann's correspondence, I have employed the seven volumes of his *Briefwechsel*, edited by Arthur Henkel and Walther Ziesemer, and the initials for these volumes are **ZH**.

All translations, unless otherwise indicated, are mine. The quotations in the original are given in the endnotes for those who wish to avoid the infelicity of my translations.

PART ONE

Enlightenment and Hamann's Reaction

1 Introduction: The Enlightenment as a Historical Movement and Political Project

Nearly all monographs on Hamann deal with the question of his rela tionship to the Enlightenment. Isaiah Berlin begins his brief work with the boldest formulation: Hamann was 'the most passionate, consistent, extreme and implacable enemy of Enlightenment ... of his time.'[1] Oswald Bayer, the world's leading Hamannite, has written a book making the apparently opposite claim that Hamann was a 'radical enlightener.'[2] James O'Flaherty has apparently taken a conciliatory position of making Hamann part critic and part participant in the Age of Reason.[3] With such manifest disagreement, talk of Enlightenment might well be subject to the Hobbesian charge of 'insignificant speech.'

Many, indeed, have been tempted to give up entirely on the term as anything other than the designation of a particular century (or a century and a half, if one is generous). This accounts for the pluralization of Enlightenment – national Enlightenments abound, as do topical ones (there is now the Christian Enlightenment, a Conservative Enlightenment, a religious Enlightenment ...).[4] At the same time as the historians have been busy expanding the embrace of the term, political philosophers have been engaged in a vociferous debate about the merits of Enlightenment, or more often of 'the Enlightenment project.' James Schmidt, the editor of an interesting volume on the question *What Is Enlightenment*, has gone so far as to condemn these latter debates as chimerical, arguing that there is no unified historical movement called 'the Enlightenment,' and that malcontents should cease using it as a 'convenient scapegoat' for anything they dislike in the modern world.[5] Yet, if Schmidt appears to undermine the term's philosophical utility he nonetheless is not entirely unwilling to employ the term *Enlightenment* as a meaningful label for a politico-intellectual movement – one that has its programmatic formulation in Kant's notion of public reason.[6] Even Schmidt would seem tacitly to grant the existence of an Enlightenment project, despite his explicit rejection of the term's utility.

The question, what is Enlightenment? was famously posed by the editor of the *Berlinische Monatsschrift* in 1783, and it stimulated considerable interest. At the time, the parameters of the question were far from clear (Zöllner himself, who first posed it, suggested that an equivalent question is, what is truth?);[7] if we were to be so bold as to pose it again today, we would also be forced to consider the appropriate tense: what was it, or what is it? Ought we to speak of a historical or a transhistorical phenomenon? Or of no phenomenon at all?

There has been inordinate debate in the last two decades about the existence of the Enlightenment as a unified movement. The following discussion, then, cannot hope to be anything approaching a complete review of the literature on the concept, nor indeed would such a survey be particularly enthralling. Rather, I intend to do two things. First, I will offer a defence of 'the Enlightenment' as both a historical movement and a universal project that is alive and well today.[8] We can reasonably speak of it as a movement because numerous writers of the eighteenth century saw themselves as part of it. More importantly, disparate groups of people saw themselves as opponents of it. It remains a viable and contested political ideal today. Second, I will introduce Hamann's reaction to his age, making some brief remarks about his relationship to other counter-Enlightenment projects. We will see, in a preliminary way, the radical opposition that he sought to establish between the Enlightenment and its opposite.

Enlightenment as a Contested Concept

This work treats the Enlightenment as a singular movement containing a number of themes that Hamann challenged. This is not to say that the particular arguments that Hamann confronted are the final word on what the Enlightenment was, or that all eighteenth-century philosophers shared them. To treat an intellectual movement as a series of specific arguments is to set oneself up for a fall; however, to ignore unifying themes is a recipe for triviality. Consider, for instance, the celebration of progress. Analysis of particular thinkers would make us wary of generalization. Herder, in many respects a strong counter-Enlightenment figure, believed in a kind of human progress; Moses Mendelssohn, the poster boy for Berlin's enlightened community, was less optimistic, giving a cyclical view of historical development and decline. But Herder's progress was idiosyncratic and entailed the retrieval of much primitive thought that was commonly despised by the rational heroes of the age, and Mendelssohn's pessimism did not amount to a rejection of the standard coupling of reason and progress (he simply thought that nations often reverted to barbarism).[9] The utility of linking progressive thought and Enlightenment is justified and helpful, despite such differences.

Some other claims are trickier. Many would assent to the proposition that the Enlightenment was generally influenced by materialism, empiricism, and anti-metaphysical thought. Yet Kant, often portrayed as its culminating philosophical voice, rehabilitated a realm outside of experience and was opposed by the radically empiricist Hamann for this reason. Because it is so difficult to place writers neatly into boxes, the historically minded might be tempted to jettison the term, or at least let it remain entirely too ambiguous for deployment in theoretical arguments.

This would, however, be a mistake. The Enlightenment is a battleground for the soul (or perhaps the mind) of the modern world. Among historical categories, it has rightly become exceptionally political. At the most simplistic, there is a battle between those who see the Enlightenment as the source of Nazism and those who view it as the only bulwark against fanaticism and the disregard for human rights. In this debate the epistemological questions at the heart of eighteenth-century enquiry have been lent overwhelming political significance. The Enlightenment entails a unitary view of truth and nature as fundamentally knowable and controllable. It is thus the enemy of freedom and difference. Or, to mouth the opposing polemic, the counter-Enlightenment project (from Nietzsche through to postmodernism) has created a relativism that leaves no room for the rights of man, or the Kantian dignity of each human being, or some such thing. (Some take joy in the fact that Hitler thought himself Nietzschean; others like to recall Eichmann's thoughtful Kantianism. At this level, one encounters the scholarly equivalent of the drive-by shooting.) The polemic can also take a different tone based upon an opposite estimation of what the Enlightenment was. If one emphasizes anticlericalism and scepticism in the Enlightenment (perhaps making Hume's scepticism or Diderot's materialism the dominant models for the movement), one can charge the enlighteners[10] with the murder of certainty and meaning (responsible, say, for the Terror), or, alternately, one can indict the counter-enlighteners as terrorists or fascists. These are, broadly speaking, the strategies of modern Burkeans and anti-Burkeans respectively.[11]

These caricatures are nothing new. Speaking of modern indict-
ments of the Enlightenment project (both from the left and the right),
Darrin McMahon, the author of an interesting study of French anti-
Enlightenment writings, writes, 'A good number of the more violent
claims against the Enlightenment have been with us since the movement itself.'[12] When we look to Hamann, we find a similar violence in
his reaction to 'philosophy' and 'Enlightenment,' and a similar group-
ing together of disparate thinkers as the enemies of faith. It is a truism
that those who condemn the Enlightenment project often do so by
greatly simplifying the output of the eighteenth century's best writers.
We are given caricatures of Voltaire, Rousseau, Hume, or Kant. Some
of the Enlightenment's earliest critics were also guilty of this. Recall
Edmund Burke's assertion, 'We are not the converts of Rousseau; we
are not the disciples of Voltaire; Helvétius has made no progress
amongst us. Atheists are not our preachers; madmen are not our law-
givers.'[13] And Burke would not be the only one to unite probably the
two most implacable literary and philosophical enemies of the eighteenth century (Rousseau and Voltaire). Blake's indictment of the two
fellow mockers is justly famous, despite being strangely imprecise.[14]

Yet the tendency to simplify should not blind us to the significance of
these attacks. Indeed, few readers today need to be convinced of the
power of Burke's analysis; few need convincing that Blake's spear drew
blood (Voltaire and Rousseau, after all, shared a certain minimalist
deist creed). If counter-Enlightenment generalized, it did so with a purpose. For the purposes of political philosophy, we may happily ignore
some counter-Enlightenment scribblers (just as we may ignore, save for
the purposes of social history, the minor works of hopeful *philosophes* in
Robert Darnton's work), but we do well to attend to the more sophisticated generals in the army of darkness. For all the tiresome battles over
Enlightenment's responsibility for the modern world's ills, we cannot
entirely ignore the concept's significance either in our own time or
in our interpretation of history. Historically, we see that these polemical battles were part of the eighteenth century's own quest for self-
knowledge. Today, the battle over the 'Enlightenment project' is a
central preoccupation of political reflection: how many of today's normative debates do not hang on questions concerning the nature of reason, its sovereignty and universality?

Since generalizations about the Enlightenment as a singular intellectual movement are several hundred years old, it is a curious purism
that causes historically minded writers to water down the concept (or

even to remove all conceptual content from the term, reducing it to a mere historical period). Let us consider a recent book whose strategy is to expand the meaning of Enlightenment. In *Enlightenment against Empire* Sankar Muthu explores the work of Diderot, Kant, and Herder, arguing that they all share a certain 'anti-imperial' tendency (largely because they weren't racist, except for Kant, who apparently shed his racism as he became Kantian).[15] The work is generally a decent piece of scholarship, but it suffers from a contradiction based upon its rhetorical strategy. The work gets its rhetorical power from the concept of *the* Enlightenment and the widespread view that this philosophical movement was unsympathetic to diversity, reason being singular and universal. By employing the term in his title, Muthu is able to present a counter-intuitive claim that Enlightenment is actually in love with difference, or at least is not necessarily wed to the idea of subjugating foreign peoples. Readers thus feel that they have gained an important corrective. But we learn in the work that, in fact, the claim is not so much about 'Enlightenment' because there was no such intellectual movement. Following J.G.A. Pocock, James Schmidt, and others, Muthu would have us 'pluralize the Enlightenment.' But unlike Pocock (and even Schmidt), he waters it down such that it contains nearly no conceptual content whatsoever (save, it appears, the exclusion of Joseph de Maistre).[16] Thus, having excited his reader with a claim about 'Enlightenment,' he then renders 'Enlightenment' an empty concept.

Naturally, this is the only thing for him to do since he has included Herder as an Enlightenment figure. Herder's most anti-imperialist work is also a rant against his century's philosophy (he castigates variously Voltaire, Hume, Robertson, Rousseau, Helvétius, Montesquieu, Diderot, and Bayle) and against some project called 'Enlightenment.'[17] Perhaps it is because of Herder's own choice of words that Muthu appears somewhat unconvinced by his own inclusion of Herder as an Enlightenment figure: 'Rather than redescribe Herder as a kind of *Aufklärer*, however, it may be more productive, and certainly more accurate historically, to interpret his thought as part of a larger series of eighteenth-century attempts at relating human unity and human diversity.'[18] The title of his book, it appears, would be more accurately *Eighteenth-Century Attempts at Relating Human Unity and Human Diversity against (or at least not with) Empire* (although this might have marred an otherwise attractive book cover).

I have dwelt on Muthu because his is a very recent and very well-received work.[19] He represents a growing trend in Enlightenment studies to empty the term of conceptual content. Nonetheless, we can sympa-thize with Muthu's plight: if we wish to treat the term as more than a mere reference to a century, we are led to difficulties with every general claim we make. One might, until recently, have felt confident seeing revealed religion as something against which Enlightenment writers struggled. Yet S.J. Barnett has recently argued that 'Enlightenment deism' is more of a historian's myth than a historical reality. Barnett joins himself to the 'growing consensus that the characterization of the Enlightenment as the Age of Reason, in which reason was diametrically opposed to religion, cannot be sustained.'[20] To support this revision he makes several claims. First, he notes that there was a great deal of reli-gious dissent that should not be confounded with anti-clericalism or deism. He goes on to argue that there was, in general, much religious thought in the eighteenth century. This second point is particularly un-compelling, for, among those who contend that Enlightenment has a strong strain of anti-clericalism, one will rarely find any denying the importance of religious life and reflection in eighteenth-century Europe. He has taken claims about the Enlightenment to be claims about the eighteenth-century society as a whole. As such, they are rather easy to refute. His first claim involves a straw man. Barnett insists that many thinkers who had some deist tendencies saw an important social role for the church. Voltaire is the example he cites.[21] But Voltaire's view of the social significance of the church is entirely consistent with his deis-tic views, and is, indeed, a central pillar of Enlightenment social psych-ology. Of course, there is a debate to be had here about the degree to which Enlightenment thinkers tended to argue for universal emancipa-tion versus the guardianship by the rational. I suggest (and am rather unoriginal in so doing) that on balance, they tended towards the latter. The somewhat populist Hamann certainly had this impression. What is certain is that the question of how desirable or possible it would be to emancipate the bulk of humanity was very much at the centre of Enlightenment social debates. But Barnett's opponents – those who think that Enlightenment reason is 'diametrically opposed to religion' – do not exist. Who, after all, would not concede that enlightened treat-ments of religion differed considerably, dependent upon national, per-sonal, and confessional contexts? Who would contest the view that many Enlightenment writers saw religion as a useful institution for so-cial control? Those who think that Enlightenment reason is diametric-ally opposed to counter-rational revelation and enthusiasm, however, might well have a case that is not so easily dismissible.

I do not wish to indulge in a lengthy argument about method, but would merely like to suggest that a great number of quarrels have been fomented because some very good and detailed historians of ideas refuse to work with generalizations or to treat history philosophically. Few intellectual movements in the history of ideas will stand up to the scrutiny of detailed empirical research. Romantics did not carry membership cards; humanists did not all share a set of doctrinal propositions; not all so-called liberals share precisely the same views about the limits of state power. Both the Enlightenment and its enemy movement are widely diverse phenomena. (Much more divides Hamann and de Maistre than unifies them.) But to abandon general claims is to abandon the task of thinking in favour of amassing facts. This is not to say that all the generalizations made about a given intellectual movement are impervious to empirical challenge. When Horkheimer and Adorno complain about the Enlightenment's will-to-system, they are clearly mistaken about the thinkers widely considered under the banner of the term. Much more typical of eighteenth-century thought was the view, expressed so forcefully in D'Alembert's *Preliminary Discourse* to the *Encyclopédie*, that the *esprit de système* belonged to the bad old days of philosophy: 'A writer among us who praised systems would have come too late.'[22] Thus, for Horkheimer and Adorno to emphasize Kant's systematicity and its similarity to that of Leibniz or Descartes and to treat this as characteristic of Enlightenment is to gloss over a significant amount of the *philosophes'* work.[23] Now, the *Dialectic of Enlightenment* is not a study of the eighteenth century, and assessing it with a historian's eye is not terribly instructive. Nonetheless, by referring to what is commonly taken as a historically located movement, Horkheimer and Adorno do intentionally raise certain historical associations, and the utility of their assessment of Enlightenment will depend to some extent on how accurately we perceive them to have understood the movement.

To consider the Enlightenment a unified project is not to consider its thinkers to be all of one mind.[24] And, indeed, one must make the same claim for the counter-Enlightenment popularized by Isaiah Berlin. Throughout this work I will emphasize the degree to which Berlin's schematic view of these two movements equates Hamann's view to the views of those who differ from him a great deal. But if I quarrel with Berlin on content, I do not decry schematism as such. To schematize I take to be among the central duties of someone reflecting on philosophical history. And, indeed, the subject matter itself demands such treatment: attending to Hamann forces one to confront the intersection between history and idea. Certainly my arguments about Enlightenment are not theses to be proven by the exploration of Hamann. To provide such a proof would be ridiculously ambitious, unachievable through the study of one idiosyncratic, late eighteenth-century Prussian writer. Rather, they are working hypotheses. In theory, if not in life, words are tools, and this particular word will be judged on the basis of its philosophical and historical utility. Anyone who treats in the singular an intellectual movement as diffuse and varied as the Enlightenment risks falling into unsustainable generalizations. Such is the nature of the enterprise. Any study of a single figure that claims relevance for a wider movement necessarily risks synecdoche. In a wonderfully erudite and synoptic marriage of political and intellectual history of the Enlightenment, Franco Venturi made the preliminary observation that Enlightenment studies had for too long ('from Kant to Cassirer and beyond') been dominated by philosophical treatments that obscure more than they clarify. He cautioned scholars against 'distorting historical judgments by transforming them into a philosophy of history.'[25] He was correct to emphasize caution, but I intend to have my historical cake without renouncing the pleasure of its philosophical consumption.

What, then, is this movement? For many, it would appear to be simply bad philosophy. The widespread disregard for metaphysical speculation and for fundamental ontology that dominated the empirical century has led many to the conclusion that *philosophes* were not philosophers at all. Already in 1840 J.S. Mill could write, 'To insist upon the deficiencies of the Continental philosophy of the last century, or, as it is commonly termed, the French philosophy, is almost superfluous.'[26] The famous *Oxford English Dictionary* definition of *Enlightenment*, which refers to 'the spirit and aims of the French philosophers of the 18th c., or of others whom it is intended to associate with them in the implied charge of shallow and pretentious intellectualism, unreasonable contempt for tradition and authority, etc.' sums up two centuries of abuse levelled at the 'age of reason.'[27] If lexicographers are to be relied upon, the counter-Enlightenment appears to have been a successful movement. Perhaps, however, we should not begin with nineteenth-century prejudices, but rather with eighteenth-century manifestos.

Both the terms *the Enlightenment* and *les lumières* are historians' conventions. The metaphor of the 'light of reason' had an old and reputable history, counting Aquinas and Descartes among its users, so the fact that it was commonplace in the eighteenth century does not really say much. Nonetheless, the eighteenth-century designations *les gens de lettres* or *les philosophes* refer to a type of person or a group of people who make this light their principal guide. These are the citizens of the republic of letters. In this city, reason – the force of the best argument – is sovereign. Citizenship is based on one's capacity for reason. (Indeed, Bayle's metaphor of a republic requires some qualification, in that reason's sovereignty undermines all voluntarism. Strictly speaking, the city of reason is a monarchy. It is reason's unity that leads pluralists to consider all rationalism authoritarian; it is reason's supposed impersonality that leads its champions to see in its sovereignty a liberation from the capricious will of masters.) The *Encyclopédie* informs us that to be a *philosophe*, it is not enough to have read a few books, to be eccentric, or to display a bold contempt for commonly held prejudices: one must be thoroughly instructed by reason. And reason is a master who is quite particular about method. 'Le *philosophe* forme ses principes sur une infinité d'observations particulières ... L'esprit philosophique est donc un esprit d'observation & de justesse, qui rapporte tout à ses véritables principes.'[28]

The empiricist superman (or perhaps not a superman, for he does not exceed human capacities, but rather, perfects them) who emerges in the *Encyclopédie*'s definition is a sociable creature, in two senses of loving society and living for it. He is the opposite of a cloistered monk or an ascetic: 'Notre *philosophe* ne se croit pas en exil dans ce monde ... il veut jouir en sage économe des biens que la nature lui offre; il veut trouver du plaisir avec les autres: & pour en trouver, il en faut faire: ainsi il cherche à convenir à ceux avec qui le hasard ou son choix le font vivre; & il trouve en même tems ce qui lui convient: c'est un honnête homme qui veut plaire & se rendre utile.'[29] He is thus loosely Epicurean, a rational seeker of pleasure whose self-interest corresponds with the self-interests of others. He wishes above all to make himself *useful*, and we understand him thus to augment people's pleasure and decrease their pain. While he judges everything in the court of reason, his reason tells him of the significance of social mores: 'La société civile est, pour ainsi dire, une divinité pour lui sur la terre.' His is a natural aristocracy: the *peuple* obtain their morality by blindly following principles of religion, but the *philosophe* follows the guidance of his own reason. Thus, we are given the distinct impression that religion is a useful social device but one to be supplanted (or controlled) by philosophy. 'La grace détermine le chrétien à agir; la raison détermine le *philosophe*.' Worldly, anti-ecclesiastical (but not necessarily popularly irreligious), utilitarian, empiricist, dispassionate, unprejudiced, and driven by a desire to help humanity, the *philosophe* is a good candidate for political life: 'Entez un souverain sur un *philosophe* d'une telle trempe, & vous aurez un parfait souverain.' If the counter-Enlightenment can be said with some correctness to have created the Enlightenment, we might also note the degree to which the movement's champions provided their own caricatures.

Aufklärung is apparently man's emergence from his self-incurred tutelage.[30] An enlightened man is not necessarily one who follows any given epistemological route, but one who no longer relies on others for his judgments. Free from superstition,[31] he thinks for himself. And, lest we think that this ideal spells the end of coherence, we are reminded throughout that he thinks according to the impersonal standards of royal reason. Enlightenment is not necessarily egalitarian, but it demands that all authority be subject to reason's rule. Rightly has the tiny footnote from the first preface of the *Critique of Pure Reason* been treated as a manifesto: 'Unser Zeitalter ist das eigentliche Zeitalter der Kritik, der sich alles unterwerfen muß. Religion, durch ihre Heiligkeit, und Gesetzgebung durch ihre Majestät, wollen sich gemeiniglich derselben entziehen. Aber alsdenn erregen sie gerechten Verdacht wider sich, und können auf unverstellte Achtung nicht Anspruch machen, die die Vernunft nur demjenigen bewilligt, was ihre freie und öffentliche Prüfung hat aushalten können.'[32] Kant opposed himself to nothing more than the epicurean creed of the *'philosophe'* article, but in his championing of critique Kant was at one with diverse thinkers whom he otherwise opposed.

The very first person to raise this footnote to the level of a manifesto was not some historian compiling an anthology, but the *Kritik der reinen Vernunft*'s very first reader (he received an advance copy from the publisher), Johann Georg Hamann. This reading was perspicuous. Kant's famous formulation sums up a century's philosophical activity and its clear political consequences. Kant was a somewhat authoritarian man, but his intellectual project, largely shared by the bulk of the century's writers, entailed a radical revolution in thought: monarchs and priests take note! Condorcet summed up his century's philosophico-political project thus: 'Les philosophes des diverses nations embrassant, dans leurs méditations, les intérêts de l'humanité entière sans distinction de pays, de race ou de secte, formaient, malgré la différence de leurs opinions spéculatives, une phalange fortement unie contre toutes les erreurs.'[33] If Kant could defend God and Helvétius could mock him, they both were of the same non-partisan party.

If there is no room here to line up the endless eighteenth-century professions of this sort, we can draw solace from the fact that the late

Robert Wokler, a man possessed of greater historical scruple than I, shared Kant and Condorcet's views that there was an Enlightenment project: 'As I understand them, the *philosophes* of the age of Enlightenment were public moralists, the *engagés volontaires* of reason and truth, determined not only to interpret the world but to change it. They may not have had a common blueprint of reform, but they all too frequently had the same enemies and they very often made common cause. To the extent that they did so, I doubt whether they would have objected themselves to our describing it as their project.'[34] Indeed, they would not. Wokler correctly identified toleration, cosmopolitanism, and the opposition to dogma and inhumanity as Enlightenment ideals, and he defended the Enlightenment with considerable grace against the facile association with modernity's ills. (It is a lack of Enlightenment, he suggested, that gave birth to the nation state and to all ethnic bigotry. These are claims, shared by Condorcet, that require careful consideration.) The 'party of Humanity,' as Peter Gay has termed them, were indeed united at the very least in their self-estimation as champions of rational justification, empirical observation, cosmopolitanism, and tolerance. They were concerned equally with the emancipation of reason from religious control. Thus, while few writers of the Enlightenment were outright atheists, all believed that religious claims required rational justification. While they had radically different philosophical positions, they all shared the promise of cleaning out both mind and society, brushing away the cobwebs of metaphysics, mythical thought, feudal corporatism, and the authority of tradition.

Hamann and His Age

As we noted, interpreters of Hamann are somewhat mixed in their interpretations of his reaction to his age. The title of one collection, *Johann Georg Hamann und die Krise der Aufklärung*, is as striking as it is broad.[35] (Was Enlightenment itself in crisis? Does it cause a crisis? Did Hamann bring the crisis to a head? The authors within differ radically.) Rudolf Unger, in a work that is somewhat unsatisfying on a philosophical level but unsurpassed for its elegance and comprehensive scholarship, treats Hamann as a proto-Romantic irrationalist.[36] Bayer's definition of Hamann as a radical enlightener places him somewhat closer to the tradition of counter-Enlightenment that seeks a kind of greater Enlightenment.[37] Certainly Berlin's unequivocal statement of Hamann's opposition to the Enlightenment requires the following equivocation:

Hamann responded to his age with some of the tools of his age. What he shared with the Enlightenment mainstream was an empirical bent that made him extremely wary of metaphysics. For Hamann, Enlightenment sought to replace faith – it attempted to undermine the very language of divine revelation by substituting a language grounded on earth. But this was an unstable project because this earthly reason constituted another dogmatism – one that was even less justified than its religious predecessor. If all this sounds Nietzschean, it should. Hamann was among the first (perhaps the first) to indict rational autonomy as simply another dogmatism. But the move bears no resemblance to the transvaluation of values, for Hamann attempted to recapture a religious language that he felt was under attack. Employing the language of the Reformation, he decried Enlightenment as a new popery.

Hamann's counter-Enlightenment bears some relationship to the positions of Hegel, Adorno, and Foucault. He certainly articulated a kernel of the dialectic of Enlightenment: rational universalism and utilitarianism can lead to a universal domination of man. Moreover, he did so in an extremely polemical manner. And, indeed, he celebrated poetry to the extent that he might be confounded with the aesthetic modernity of Nietzsche's followers. However, as we shall see in our final chapter, Hamann's aestheticism is the antithesis of this (post)modern move. His position bears some relation to the romantic insistence on the passions and to the particularism that so excited the minds of nineteenth-century nationalists. And, indeed, we will see that Hamann's thought resonates with ideas central to communitarian critiques of Enlightenment rationalism, individualism, and cosmopolitanism. But these echoes tell only part of the story; the rest is made intelligible by his theology. The difficulties that Hamann raises are the relationship between particularism and universalism and the problem of intelligibility in the absence of conceptual abstraction. Among all the modern critics of Enlightenment, Hamann is perhaps closest to Alasdair MacIntyre, who also questions disembodied, ahistorical reason and who appears to want a kind of theologically inspired reconciliation of immanent historicism and universal truth. But Hamann's anti-scholastic tone and Reformation inheritance entail a great silence on the intellectual heritage of medieval Europe. St Thomas himself receives scant mention in his oeuvre, and the reconciliation of Athens and Jerusalem is not his project. Thomas's Aristotelianism is to be celebrated as strategy but dismissed as content: Thomas was, for Hamann, merely 'the apostle to the peripatetics,' as much to be prized for his evangelism as condemned for his scholasticism.[38] More importantly, MacIntyre's call for a return to virtue hints at a kind of works-righteousness to which Hamann would have had some Lutheran qualms.

We can follow Hamann's anti-Enlightenment by attending to his series of post-conversion intellectual encounters. We recall that the young Hamann was an enthusiastic partisan of his century's innovative thought. He was an avid reader of contemporary philosophy, he was cosmopolitan in outlook, he held the highest hopes that sweet commerce would bring peace and prosperity to the world, and he wrote somewhat elegant articles for a women's journal (along the lines of the English moral weeklies such as the *Spectator*).[39] After his failed diplomatic/commercial mission to London (where he wasted his employers' money, lost himself in debauchery, and possibly had a homosexual love affair with a lute-playing male prostitute[40] before commencing an intensive period of solitary biblical study), Hamann had a reversal of commitments. The degree to which Hamann's piety was entirely new is debatable (and debated); in any case, his enthusiastic disposition was hardly new. As Volker Hoffmann shows, Hamann's later studies continued to show the same poly-historical, scattered tendencies of his youthful forays into the library.[41] He threw himself into faith with the same fevered intensity that he had thrown himself into commerce and literary pursuits. His excess in this last regard proved somewhat problematic upon his return to Riga, where he rather discomfited those around him. He fell madly in love with the sister of his friend and protector J.C. Berens. The Berens (or Behrens), a successful family of merchants, did not think that the young, unemployed Hamann, now a full-blown *Schwärmer*, was a very good catch for Katharina, and he left their household.[42] (He wound up living in a kind of civil union with a peasant woman with whom he raised four children.)[43] This tumultuous period involved a lengthy quarrel with Berens over his newfound vocation. In the name of faith and a curiously extreme intellectual independence, Hamann sacrificed both love and worldly success.

But he did not sacrifice friendship. Indeed, Hamann took his friendships very seriously and was himself admired for his constancy.[44] It is remarkable to note how close he always remained to those with whom he had profound disagreements.[45] This capacity for friendship (remarked upon by Hegel) was not merely an aspect of his character, but was also part of his thought.[46] In its highest form, communication itself was personal. But friendship also complicated matters: 'Friendship puts barriers in the way that I do not find with strangers or enemies;

and to this [friendship] belong new rules.'[47] The intensity with which Hamann waged his war against Enlightenment was very much due to the affection he professed for his interlocutors and with the mode of communication he thought this affection demanded.[48] Indeed, he took an extremely polemical tone with those of whom he was fondest. If this heat periodically lost him the esteem of others (Goethe, who enjoyed reading his letters to Herder, thought him a bit self-important and bombastic; Hippel thought him a bit ridiculous), it equally won him the lasting affection of many of his correspondents.[49] But what is most important in this is the very personal nature of his writings. Thus, his private and public personae tend to merge. The public writings are replete with private references; the private letters are crafted for wider consumption (and, indeed, were passed around in the circles associated with Hamann's correspondents). As we shall see in the next chapter, Hamann was extremely critical of the impersonality of public reason; his was a defence of particularity in the face of abstraction.

The kernel of his opposition to his age is to be found in his lengthy commentary on the Bible written in London. This youthful text (which gives us the key to his idiosyncratic use of scripture) begins by looking rational biblical criticism in the face. What was he to do with Voltaire or Bolingbroke? How was he to deal with the strangeness of scripture? Hamann realized that if he was going to switch his allegiance from the party of humanity to the party of God, this was going to require a radically different way of thinking, and particularly of thinking about communication. From child of his times to enfant terrible, Hamann's transformation launched a lifelong opposition to his friends in which he would defend scripture by rethinking its symbolic nature; in so doing, he would rethink the nature of thought and communication, leading to a paradoxical turn against philosophy in the name of the contemplative life.

His lifelong disagreement with Kant, more central to his thought than to Kant's, is quite instructive (and we will have several occasions to revisit it), for the two authors embody two ways of meeting the challenge of rational maturity. One incident is illustrative both of their strange relationship and of Hamann's wider reaction to his age: the young Kant proposed to the newly born-again Hamann to collaborate with him on the production of a physics textbook for children. Naturally, the project failed at the outset, for the two had such radically different notions of education, reason, and the meaning of nature. (In hindsight, the very idea of such a collaboration is amusing.) Hamann's response is typical of his epistolary style: playful, amusing, proud, obscure, and always on the verge of insulting. The substance of Hamann's letter is the invitation to Kant to become as a child in order to speak to children: 'A philosophical book for children would therefore have to appear as simple-minded, foolish and tasteless as a *divine* book written for human beings. Now examine yourself to see whether you have the heart to be the author of a simple-minded, foolish and tasteless science book. If you have, then you are a philosopher for children. "Vale et sapere AUDE!"'[50]

The inversion of maturity and Enlightenment is one to which we will return. So too is the comparison of God with human authors. This is central to Hamann's theology of divine condescension. Another central Hamannian theme here is the attack on the universality of any given presentation. To communicate with children requires us to see the world with their eyes. We are forced to confront the complexity of the hermeneutic situation – a complexity that undermines the univocal pretensions of public reason. Hamann confronted Kant's attempt to popularize the latest teachings of natural science with a suggestion that the best book on physics would be the book of Genesis! 'The idea of nature according to the six days of its birth thus presents the best schema for a child that believes in the legends told by its nurse.' This is neither the message of an elitist, Masonic *Aufklärer* (with which it might be confused) nor the equivalent of our contemporary creationists, but an appeal to attend to the multilayered nature of scriptural meaning: 'A philosopher however reads the three chapters of Genesis with the sort of eyes with which that crowned star-gazer looks at heaven. It is natural therefore that nothing but eccentric concepts and anomalies should appear to him; he prefers to find fault with holy Moses rather than doubt his own educated fads and his systematic spirit.'[51]

What violence this view must have done to Kant's ideals! To teach physics one must turn to scripture? To teach the child one must become as a child? Certainly Kant agreed that one should not burden children with information beyond their capacity to understand,[52] but this was hardly because there was anything to be celebrated in the childlike manner of cognition. As for religion, Kant argued that it was an awkward subject that could not be avoided in education but must be minimized. When not perverted, religion is the rational moral law wedded to the idea of God. Religious upbringing is dangerous in that children cannot understand theological concepts. If they must get religious upbringing (which they must in the real world, lest they be led astray by the religious attitudes of others), let it be a minimal creed that links their fear of God to their conception of moral duty.[53] Let the basic metaphor of God the father suffice; there is no need for bizarre stories that will only confuse children. After all, all proper religions are at base the same: rational invocations to duty. We will explore later the contest between the Kantian religion of morality and Hamannian Christianity. For the moment I merely wish to highlight the gulf between their world views.

As for the project of popularizing natural science, Hamann clearly repudiated this goal as insufficient to the moral task of the educator. In a further letter, Hamann wrote, 'Nature is a book, a written message, a fable ... Supposing we know all the letters in it as well as is possible, and we can spell and sound out every word ... is that enough, in order to understand the book, to judge it, to make sense of it, to epitomize it? So we need more than physics in order to interpret nature. Physics is nothing but the alphabet.'[54] The project's moral purpose will be fulfilled only when physics' task is understood through the lens of biblical hermeneutics.

Kant must have received this with some exasperation – this was his second attempt to find useful work for the impetuous Hamann.[55] But Hamann's queer proposals were part of a thorough rejection of Kant's world view – a rejection that he would articulate with increasing vigour in his lifelong reaction to the project of Enlightenment. Where Kant wanted to pursue a project of natural science based on the observation of natural phenomena and the generation of physical laws (we recall the myriad interests of the pre-Critical Kant), Hamann sought to treat nature as a book of revelation and treat their project as a morally charged quest to receive revelation. The goal is not to observe matter and infer laws, but to interpret a message. Where Kant saw the pedagogical goal of propagating useful and rationally compelling information, Hamann saw the goal as the awakening of the child to a divine message. Where Kant saw the method as discipline whereby the child's passions are curbed, Hamann thought he should appeal to the passions. Where Kant championed the maturity of the philosophic reasoner, assessing arguments dispassionately, Hamann prioritized the mind's less disciplined faculties and looked upon all claims to dispassionate objectivity with suspicion. Hamann made his opposition to Kant's way of life clear: 'I look upon the best [philosophical] demonstration as a reasonable girl looks on a love-letter.'[56] 'Lying,' he told Kant, 'is the mother tongue of our reason.'[57]

Given the directness of this claim, Hamann certainly appears to deserve the charge of 'irrationalism.' Hegel, who shared many of Hamann's concerns about one-sided, objective abstraction, nonetheless objected to Hamann in the following terms (which capture the most powerful objection to all counter-enlightened thinking): 'The Enlightenment, which Hamann fights, this striving to assert thought and its freedom in all the interests of spirit, is, as with that indeed merely formal freedom of thought pursued by Kant, completely misjudged by him, and if he rightly was unsatisfied with the form to which this thought led, he nonetheless blustered, if we may dare to say, until he was blue in the face against thought and reason in general, which alone can be the true means to that conscious unfolding of truth and its growth into a Diana-tree [or tree of wisdom].'[58]

Hegel was correct in his assessment of the negative significance of Hamann's project. This meta-critical activity is at the centre of Hamann's work (and it has contemporary significance, given the centrality of neo-Kantian political theories that set out with the conviction that the Enlightenment has never successfully been undermined). But Hegel was expressing more about himself than about his subject when he assessed Hamann's positive contribution as a mere 'Poltern' against reason or, as he says in the following sentence, as a retreat into the 'intensive subjectivity' of personal piety. He dismissed Hamann's positive project because it was at odds with Hegel's own wish to set reason (although a more capacious reason) as priest, prophet, and king (indeed, as world, too). In this way, pantheist/rationalist Hegel opposed himself to Christian Hamann.

Sympathetic as he was to Hamann's attack on his age, Hegel was the absolute manifestation of what Hamann combated: philosophy overcoming religion. From Hegel's perspective, Hamann's desire not to be enchained with the concept was a flight into subjectivity.[59] Hegel did do Hamann the honour of characterizing him as a Hegel-*manqué*: 'Hamann did not take the trouble' to work out the unfolding of truth into a system of 'the state, right, ethical life, and the system of world history.'[60] This *conceptual* appropriation of the particular, the given, is precisely that to which Hamann objected. We will return to this problem repeatedly throughout our study, but let us take a moment to articulate the difference between Hamann and Hegel on the relationship between the particular and the universal.

Readers of Hamann have been mixed in their reception of his philosophical teaching on this matter. Older scholarship conceived of Hamann as somewhat confused – half Platonist, half particularist/subjectivist, Hamann is painted by Rudolf Unger as philosophically schizophrenic. Representing the more receptive mood of recent philosophy, Gwen Griffith Dickson has suggested that Hamann's central claim concerned the 'relational' nature of knowledge, something she sees as akin to a 'postmodern' view in which 'subjectivity is an essential presupposition but not the central point of the methodology.'[61] Dickson's insistence on the relational nature of Hamann's epistemology is *extremely* important, but she is sometimes unsatisfying in her elucidation of the philosophical content – in addition to calling it postmodern (and likening it to Richard Rorty's view or the views of Richard Palmer or Richard Bernstein), she also hints at similarities to Gadamer *and* Habermas.

Allow me to touch on the position I shall defend by way of Hamann's and Hegel's different treatments of history. History is particularity. Enlightenment criticism is universal. This anti-historical aspect of Enlightenment reason is one of its hallmarks and a strong basis for its anti-scriptural tenor. What relationship can some contingent historical events have to Truth with a capital *T*? The historical nature of Judeo-Christian revelation – and its eschatological insistence on seeing all time as the unfolding of God's plan (of truth) poses a problem for the rationalist separation between eternal truth and temporal fact. Hamann was, as we shall see, a firm defender of Christian eschatology, and he considered it a stumbling block to the philosophers. The extra-historical universality of abstract reason was for him a sinful concoction of a fevered philosophical imagination; becoming is the realm of human thought. But Hamann did not reject the view that another realm existed. God, after all, is not man and is not world.

The very notion of divine revelation takes as given a dualism of Platonic resonance. Hegel was most stimulated by Hamann's rejection of extra-historical Enlightenment reason, but he equally rejected the essential mystery and otherness of God necessary for the concept of revelation. This is the aspect of Hamann's thought that Hegel simply saw as intellectual laziness; historical truth must be comprehended in the concept. Hegel adopted the ideals of criticism but attempted to incorporate what is alien to criticism, the historical nature of Christian eschatology. He thus produced a wondrous half-breed of philosophical historicism – neither religious fish nor philosophical fowl, the Hegelian system co-opts Christian historical particularism into a conceptual structure that is somewhat alien to Christian thought.[62] Thus, Hegel and Hamann represent starkly contrasting ways of treating becoming as a manifestation of being. This element of Hamann's view will be explored at greater length in the body of the text. For now it is enough to note the unbridgeable gulf between Hegel's enlightened, critical impulse and the religious concept of revelation from above.

But if Hamann's thought is premised upon such a shaky concept as revelation, was Hegel not correct to describe Hamann's work as a fanatical blustering against reason? In a brief exchange in the *New York Review of Books*, O'Flaherty challenged Isaiah Berlin's treatment of Hamann as an irrationalist, drawing attention to Bayer and to O'Flaherty's own description of Hamann's thought, 'intuitive reason.' Berlin responded that 'intuitive reason' was incomprehensible, and, anyway, had originally been used by Kant as an ironic denigration of Hamann's queer manner of expression.[63] Certainly Hamann ought to be saved from the calumny of being denigrated as a capricious champion of nonsense. And, indeed, in Hamann's own terms reason itself is to be prized. Nor was he a writer who thought that reason was faith's opposite. When he wrote that 'a heart without passion, without affects, is a mind without concepts' he was clearly not denouncing concepts. 'Do not carry the denial of your reason and imagination [Phantasie] too far. Reason and imagination are gifts of God.'[64] But if reason and faith are not enemies, philosophy and faith certainly are competitors. His attacks on 'philosophers' capture both the sense of the *philosophe* as public intellectual and the philosopher as expositor of a conceptually based world picture. Because Hamann lived in Germany, where the tradition of rationalist academic philosophy had never fully died, he was well placed to oppose both the public intellectuals of French and German literary culture (Voltaire, La Mettrie, Diderot, Frederick II, Mendelssohn, Nicolai, Mendelssohn, et al.) and the academic system-builders of German universities (Wolff, Baumgarten, Tetens, Kant). Where we see a great distinction between, say, D'Alembert's or Diderot's rejection of 'esprit de système' and Kant's ornate systematicity, Hamann saw a greater affinity as a political project.

If irrationalism is defined as the insistence on the philosophical priority of non-conceptual cognition, Hamann was certainly an irrationalist, and he belongs to the camp of those who undermine ideas' universality by pointing to their fleshy origin. But this is a net that captures quite a few fish. It is the political associations raised by irrationalism that are at the heart of the debate. Was Hamann a 'reactionary'? The word itself is naturally a questionable one (it is conceptually tied to assumptions about progress, after all), but it has a certain intuitive force. Berlin placed Hamann in this camp, both denigrating him and celebrating him at the same time. (This is part of Berlin's greater project of deepening pluralism as a way of cushioning liberal modernity from the blows of its most pitiless critics.) Hamann's thought was certainly that of opposition; he clothed himself in the garb of an outsider (a standard rhetorical move, as common as it is tiresome), and he cast aspersions on the innovative nature of eighteenth-century thought. More to the point, if Enlightenment is to be seen as a kind of maturity, Hamann is a voice for 'childlike profundity.'[65] In terms of history, this amounted to a fondness for ancient ways of thinking that were widely denigrated in the eighteenth century as *childish* (merely immature and superficial rather than *childlike* and profound). Hamann's anti-progressive stance confounds our normal associations, however, for Hamann could make it the basis of radical anti-authoritarianism. In Prussia, Enlightenment was associated with absolutism; to oppose the age of Frederick was to oppose Frederick. And, indeed, Hamann declared his opposition to his regime to be the 'true key to [his] writings.'[66] Philosophy and domination were intimately linked as manifestations of human pride. Rationalism as domination through instrumental reason and rationalism as the capturing of the world in abstract concepts were equally the targets of Hamann's attack.[67]

Hamann saw the Enlightenment as the building of an altar to theory. He sought to undermine this new faith by undermining reason's confidence. Thus, his mode of expression was highly irrationalist: he took pleasure in paradox, non sequitur, baffling transition, multi-vocal assertion, associative thinking, and oblique conclusion. In content, too, he pointed towards paradoxes, calling into question the fundamental principle of logic that A = A. Hamann was irrationalist – even by Hegelian standards of reason – because he refused any cognitive reconciliation or *Aufhebung* of the paradox involved in man's thinking about God. But he was not irrationalist in that he gave arguments, albeit obliquely, for this refusal.

The most important argument made by Hamann is that reason *is* language. With this, Hamann undermined reason's universality, knocking it back down onto earth. He followed this thought with a radical historicism (concepts are historical phenomena) and subjectivism. But this is only one step of the argument, for the equation of reason and language is a double move. On the one hand, Hamann attacks pride: reason is *mere* language. On the other, he gives man a rather exalted capacity, for language is logos, the word of God. This double move of abasement and exaltation is central to Hamann's politico-theological project. It grants a view of man's relation to man and God that allows neither the rational autonomy of Kant nor the wilful über-autonomy of Nietzsche. It is a project that affirms man's dignity while condemning his continual sinfulness. It makes epistemological claims about man's subjective condition while treating truth as an extra-subjective realm.

Hamann's linguistic turn has communitarian implications. If Enlightenment rationality is universalistic (even in its twentieth-century formal-pragmatic manifestations), Hamannian language is essentially social and bounded. Enlightenment universalism hinges on a view of language as secondary to the thinking subject. The republic of letters is cosmopolitan because concepts (which are essential) can be put in any language (for languages are accidental). In this sense, while there may be a dialectic of Enlightenment, there is no particular *dialect* of Enlightenment. But for Hamann, we are not alinguistic subjects who employ the tool of language to communicate; rather, we are logos-beings. While languages are contingent, historical phenomena, language itself is not an accident appended to our substance, but is part of our essential selves. This teaching (whose Aristotelian pedigree did not escape Hamann) has profound implications for modern social-contract theories. This teaching is certainly irrationalist from one perspective, but it has a strong rational streak if we treat reason as the Greek *logos* that was co-opted and spiritualized by the early church.

There is, then, a reasonable unreason in Hamann that deserves elucidation, particularly given our Enlightenment heritage. Yet despite Bayer's desire to reconcile Hamann with modernity by crediting the 'Magus' with a more all-embracing reason, I see Hamann more as a constructor of barriers to progress. Hamann is counter-enlightened in a way that does not point forward to some greater Enlightenment, or to some radical perpetual critique. Nor does he offer a kind of conservatism (although there are important conservative elements to his thought), if for no reason other than that temporal tradition and divine eternity are at some variance. Nor yet does he offer a novel escape from the conflict of Enlightenment and its opposite. His thought serves two purposes, negative and positive. The negative purpose is to shake our faith in rational autonomy and maturity. Beyond glib Pauline polemics, Hamann gives an account of thought that opens up a non-enlightened vista. It is a distinctly communitarian and historicist teaching, but one whose anti-subjective element places moral limits on man's desire to project himself onto creation. This is the positive element of his thought: he sought, through a surprisingly modern set of arguments, to chart a path to a kind of scriptural cognition. Yet Hamann's move is not that, say, of his friend Jacobi, who thought that reason's self-destruction necessitated a wilful leap of faith. Jacobi's voluntarist fideism bears some relation to the existentialist self-creation of the twentieth century. Neither knowing nor willing, but feeling and receiving were the bases for Hamann's thought.

Attending to Hamann's counter-Enlightenment writings helps us see the contours of a religious response to the problems presented by the rule of reason. It is a response that is in some ways novel to our ears, and in others extremely old. It is a constellation of ideas that appear odd to the main partisans of both Enlightenment and its opposite, a constellation of ideas that are entirely incoherent without a God. Rights give way to duties, dignity is based on grace, difference is elevated and only reconciled with a divine mystery, history, contingency, and particularity have universal implications, willing and projecting are replaced by receiving, and, while we speak language, language in a sense speaks us. Whether this response remains open to all of us today remains a question that I do not approach.[68] What I will insist upon is that Hamann's politico-theological thought remains *irreconcilable* with the Enlightenment project. There is no coming to terms with it, no *Aufhebung*, and no polite tolerance of it: the republic of letters must stumble on it – Hamann forces the collision.

Charles Taylor has warned us repeatedly to avoid slipping into an outright condemnation or celebration of modernity; he insists on the importance of modern goods and hints at a future synthesis with the goods discarded by modernity.[69] This is an important reminder for us readers of Hamann; it is certainly advice that Hamann would not have heeded. Attention to his thought should trouble us in our hope for a greater synthesis of Enlightenment and its opposite, and my intention here is to perpetuate this trouble.

2 Transfiguring the Enlightenment: Hamann and the Problem of Public Reason

> For thou bringest certain strange things to our ears: we would know therefore what these things mean.
>
> – Acts 17:20

Johann Georg Hamann presents us with a puzzle. His writing is dense, unsystematic, and overly allusive. It demands an extensive knowledge of numerous authors, from ancient poets to the Old Testament prophets, to alchemists, theologians, and numerous obscure pamphleteers. Hamann often made allusions to minor events in his life – things that could have been known to only a small number of people. Yet he published these obscure pieces, presumably expecting a relatively wide audience. What is the meaning of this curious relationship with the public? Why did he bellow from the shadows? One might posit that he veiled his meaning in order to avoid persecution, but this seems unlikely. One of the few things that emerge clearly from his writings is his antipathy to Frederick II's regime (see chapter 9). One might also consider whether his style was simply the product of his brilliant eccentricity. He had an astounding memory and a great deal of obscure learning. In addition, he had a peculiar inability to refrain from exercising his favourite, allusive wit. Yet he also knew the reading public well, and was capable (when so disposed) of producing lucid and accessible prose. What, then, was the 'Magus of the North' up to?

This chapter will suggest that Hamann's style represents a radical challenge to a central aspect of Enlightenment: public reason. Battling on the levels of both form and content, Hamann sought to undermine the activities of criticism and philosophy. His obscure writing entails an attempt to subvert public reason with a Pauline device that he labelled 'metaschematism.' Hamann set out to alter the relationship between reader and writer, and to undermine philosophy in the name of prophetic poetry.

The three sections of this chapter explore three related charges that Hamann made against the ideal of public reason: (1) it is a mask for hierarchical relationships, (2) it holds up an undesirable ideal of impersonality, and (3) it undermines the most direct and compelling aspect of communication: figural language. The first section introduces the notion of 'public reason,' employing Kant's famous essay *What Is Enlightenment* and its ideal of enlightened literary communication. The curious mixture of egalitarianism and hierarchy that is evidenced in the piece is treated as illustrative of a widely acknowledged tension within Enlightenment itself. The second section addresses Hamann's direct attack on common sense and the ideal entity of the public, which he decried as an idol. Subverting the mores of the republic of letters, he insisted on the personal and situated nature of meaningful communication. This section concludes by suggesting that Hamann's polemic is to be understood as both an attack on the ideal of the public and an appeal to a model of literary reception that he derived from his personal biblical study. The third section touches upon the content implicit in Hamann's style, focusing on his figural, prophetic understanding of history. Hamann's notion of 'metaschematism' or 'transfiguration' lends a structure and unity to his otherwise baffling texts. Both a rhetorical device and a hermeneutic principle, 'transfiguration' locates the world and the world of texts within the mythical structure of the Bible.

Public, Private, and the *Unmündige*: The Closed and the Open in 'Public Reason'

Despite the somewhat local character of the piece, Kant's famous article in the *Berlinische Monatsschrift*, 'Was ist Aufklärung,' offers a particularly clear expression of the principle, central to Enlightenment thought, that neither force nor tradition ought to obtain in the republic of letters, but only truth (or its closest approximation), arrived at through rational, dispassionate, non-partisan discussion. Enlightenment, 'the exit of mankind from its self-incurred tutelage,' can be attained only when rational, autonomous people have the courage to debate in public.[1] Kant's article centred on the problem of maintaining order in society while introducing freedom of the press and encouraging independent reflection by individual citizens. His solution was to suggest that people have two distinct realms wherein they exercise their reason: the public and the private. In their private roles (in which they fulfil their duties), their reason is bound by their professional duties – an officer cannot debate an order he is given, but must obey. However, in his role as a *Gelehrter*, he may write a journal article condemning the military policy. Similarly, in his private capacity a pastor must teach the official symbols and dogma of his church, even if he does not believe them to be true. In his public capacity, however, he may write tracts on natural theology.[2] This distinction between the free, public use of reason, and the enchained private realm of action was, in essence, official state policy, and none too controversial.[3] Nonetheless, it illustrates how the emancipatory instincts of the Enlightenment can exist side by side with a very rigid attachment to authority. Kant's celebration of the public realm indicates the image that he had of the ideal debating public. He was not defending the scribblings of newspaper hacks – his was a defence of *critique*, the pre-eminent form of philosophical discourse. This is the realm of scholars and the learned. Those who demonstrate an incapacity (or insufficient courage) to reason on their own, free from prejudice, merit guardianship.

The conflict between the goals of political stability (and instruction) and enlightened discourse among a public of autonomous readers was often commented upon. Mendelssohn noted the possibility of cases in which philosophical truth might come into conflict with political necessity, and he concluded that enlighteners must remain silent in such instances.[4] Lessing's famous Freemasons Ernst and Falk come to wish for the triumph of reasoned debate free from prejudices of class, nation, or confession. At the same time, they concede that artificial divisions and prejudices are necessary: hence the need for a secret society in which humanity and reason are the only rule.[5]

For some interpreters, the mores of the admittedly narrow reading public held great democratic promise – the reasonable conclusion of Enlightenment was universal rational emancipation whose lack of realization is to be deplored.[6] For others, Kant's rational elitism implies control of the public by the intelligentsia (i.e., the philosophers). I do not propose to enter into the debate about the degree to which Kant was a spokesman for universal emancipation (enough has been said by his detractors and champions in that battle). Rather, I mean simply to employ Kant's article to illustrate the degree to which the two possibilities of Enlightenment can exist side by side in the same person – and represent, perhaps, a tension at the heart of the Enlightenment itself.

In Hamann's writings, we see a virulent opposition to both the closed and the open. He was a merciless critic of the hierarchy that he thought to be implicit in Enlightenment, which he must have seen as merely intensified in the Masonic ideal that placed the rational Masons in a position of fraternity while relegating the 'common man' to servitude. Thus, he provided a polemical assault on Masonic esotericism. But despite his condemnation of *arcana*, he was obscure to the point of unintelligibility, seeming to thumb his nose at the strictures of public discourse. Despite his mania for publication, he rejected the party of the liberating publicist – he opposed the 'open' by attempting to circumnavigate philosophy and subvert public reason. Thus, if thinkers such as Kant sought to construct a levee to guard the pure waters of free, rational debate, Hamann's response was not only to break the levee, but also to sully the waters.

Public reason (and I accept Kant's position as paradigmatic of the Enlightenment) is at once a tangible set of practices (newspaper writing, book publishing, public debates, discussion in academies, etc.) and a theoretical ideal (reason-giving in a semantic form and cultural medium free from coercion, authority, prejudice, and partiality). That the concrete manifestation of public reason never fully realizes the ideal is a fact that even the most enthusiastic champion of publicity would accept, but the ideal itself remains the basis of all critique and a goal for liberal-democratic institution builders today. This theoretical ideal and its empirical manifestations are not to be condemned lightly. We are aware of anti-parliamentary traditions in early twentieth-century thought that wished to undermine debate in the name of decision; we are equally aware of widespread suspicion of all media that was so central to post-war critical theory.

The Enlightenment ideal of public reason is not particular to Kant, nor is it merely of historical interest. Liberal thinkers such as John Rawls and Jürgen Habermas have rightly attempted to give a robust defence of this eighteenth-century ideal for all their awareness of the difficulty involved in its realization. Rawls's view, expressed in *Political Liberalism*, reframes Kant's strategic position on the separation of private and public. At base, Rawls insists that political arguments can proceed only on universally acceptable grounds.[7] Thus, all manner of comprehensive philosophy or religion can continue to be published and discussed so long as they not attempt to overstep their bounds. Rawls's public, political realm is akin to Kant's 'private' or professional realm. Here, Rawls wants debate, but debate that is essentially circumscribed. His rule might be rendered, 'Argue as much as you want outside of politics but obey the basic limitations required for political discourse in a free and democratic society.' Indeed, his separation between the political and non-political is actually much stricter than Kant's separation between the public and private.[8] Kant thought that open, public debate on comprehensive truth claims would eventually (if indirectly) affect state action.[9] Enlightenment was a process with a fixed goal; theory and practice were to meet. Rawls's public reason is limited to reasons given by people in their capacity as citizens, public officials, and people running for office. He attempts to limit the parameters of this debate by ruling out of 'public reason' any comprehensive truth claims. Theory and practice are thus essentially severed, since all of the important theoretical claims people make cannot inform their political deliberation, save insofar as they 'overlap.' Thus, while Rawls', use of the phrase *public reason* has an Enlightenment root in its demand for universalization, it is not really a continuation of the Enlightenment ideal, for it does not hold up any serious philosophical problems to public scrutiny, but rather attempts to carve out a space of public action where all citizens can participate without speaking past one another.[10] In this sense, unlike the Kantian ideal in which public reason ultimately results in convincing, universal propositions that find their way into legislation, Rawls's position is more akin to the Hobbesian subordination of public opinion to political necessity. Rawls hollows out political debate by insisting that there be debate only on matters where the underlying premises are basically agreed upon. In this sense, Rawls's 'political liberalism' is not merely anti-philosophic, but anti-political.

Habermas is the true inheritor of the Enlightenment teaching on public reason, since he does not attempt to circumscribe the content of debate.[11] Comprehensive critique is possible and necessary. He takes the Enlightenment suspicion of metaphysics to great lengths, rephrasing all truth as intersubjective agreement, but this simply raises the Kantian procedural ideal to even greater importance. Public reason, the refining fire for truth, becomes truth itself. Kant's ideal of public reason turned enlightened reason into a *procedure* – publishing and criticizing – which, as we have seen, trumps law-giving in its majesty and religion in its holiness.[12] The Habermasian project of articulating the necessary conditions for non-coercive, intersubjective reason-giving is a powerful attempt to define the formal qualities of public reason and to complete the anti-metaphysical task of the Enlightenment without falling into the cul-de-sacs of naive naturalism or nihilistic relativism. Where the

Enlightenment championed criticism as a means of preventing coercive dogmatism, Habermas makes criticism itself the only foundation for philosophy. Reason is itself a public procedure; reason *is* public reason.

Intersubjectivity remains a kind of subjectivity, but Habermas articulates the grounds for confidence in public critique: 'True, claims to propositional truth, normative rightness, and subjective truthfulness intersect here within a concrete, linguistically disclosed world horizon; yet, as criticizable claims they also transcend the various contexts in which they are formulated and gain acceptance. In the validity spectrum of the everyday practice of reaching understanding, there comes to light a communicative rationality opening onto several dimensions; at the same time, this communicative rationality provides a standard for evaluating systematically distorted forms of communication.'[13]

'Systematic distortions' are coercive relationships and prejudices (or 'ideology,' in Habermas's Marxian language). The universalization that is at the heart of Kantian moral reasoning and that is given a procedural skeleton in 'Was ist Aufklärung' is granted a more robust procedural description in Habermas's work. He grants normative force to the ideal of impartiality and conceptual clarity necessary for the universalization of validity claims. The ideal of impartiality is evident in the very concept of procedural universalizability; the call for conceptual clarity is manifest in Habermas's attack on the poetic turn in the likes of Derrida and Rorty: 'Reference to an object, informational content, and truth-value – conditions of validity in general – are extrinsic to poetic speech.'[14] Public reason must not degenerate into a mere exercise in poetics, nor may it indulge in monological idiosyncrasy. This model can be recognized easily in Kant's public reason, in his polemical attack on subjective feeling and expression in philosophy,[15] and even in his plea to Hamann to write 'in the language of human beings. For I, poor earthling, am not at all equipped to understand the divine language of *intuitive reason*. What can be spelled out for me with ordinary concepts in accordance with logical order I can pretty well comprehend.'[16] Habermas would have us see that this most reasonable request is an underlying purpose of any communication.

Hamann's reaction to Kant's article, expressed in a private letter, has become one of the more famous pieces of his writing, as the result, no doubt of its articulation of an attack on Kant that has become quite popular.[17] In a populist moment, Hamann railed at the separation of realms that Kant had proposed. 'Of what use,' he asked, 'are the ceremonial robes of freedom if I don slaves' rags at home?'[18] What many have seen as an attempt at liberating thought from governmental control Hamann perceived as a none-too-subtle means of solidifying the government's control of educational matters. His letter stormed at the hierarchical implications of Kant's distinction between the *Vormündige* teachers and the enslaved minors. He charged Kant with toadying to Frederick the Great in order to secure the supreme power of the pedagogue,[19] he inveighed against the injustice of the claim that 'minority' was a 'self-incurred' condition, and he concluded with a thundering re-appropriation of pedagogy: '*I too am a teacher!* And neither a mouth- nor a wage-servant of an overseer.'[20]

Kant's article must have merely solidified Hamann's long-held view about the intellectual hierarchy implicit in the city of public reason. Long before Kant employed the striking legal metaphor *Unmündigkeit* to introduce a theoretical distinction between those with and those without the courage to develop a capacity to reason, Hamann had toyed with the identity, often asserted by the learned, of children and the 'common man.'

'You know,' he wrote in the guise of an enlightened *Mitarbeiter*, ' … how happy I am to discuss such matters as concern children and the common man.'[21] But if children and the common people were somehow to be equated, Hamann felt that the enlightened evaluation of their capacities was to be questioned. He offered a typically paradiastolic reply to the charge of immaturity: 'Truly, truly, we must become children, if we are to receive the spirit of truth.'[22] Similarly, in defending the 'alberne' style of the Old Testament, he had recourse to the motto, 'Vox populi, vox DEI.'[23] Hamann embraced immaturity while rejecting tutelage.

In 1762, Hamann penned a fierce attack on the connections among Enlightenment philosophy, impiety, and despotism. Though cryptic, the piece was clearly intended as a satire of Frederick the Great and his Berlin academy. Its title page was adorned with an ironic citation of Voltaire's panegyric on Frederick: 'Socrate est sur le Trône & la verité règne.'[24] The piece proceeded, with a typically Hamannian pastiche of biblical and mythological references, to accuse the 'Salomon du nord' (one of Hamann's ironic references to Frederick) of whoring after the false (and foreign) gods of *bon sens* and *goût* and of establishing '*l'Académie de Satan*.'[25] We find in this piece a curious utterance about the state of German philosophy: 'Avançons, Monsieur, vers ce Temple de papier maché, que le *Bon Sens* & la *Raison publique* doit à notre philosophie. Le Salamalec d'un Géometre répond à toutes les enigmes du Sphinx tutélaire.'[26] The tutelary (or, indeed, *vormündige*) Sphinx is the riddle-posing Berlin Académie; the *géomètre* represents any *philosophe*, but Leibniz is the particular figure implied. In a nutshell, Hamann foresaw – and opposed himself to – Kant's famous 1784 position, later elaborated in the *Conflict of the Faculties*, that envisioned an officially sanctioned public realm of free debate led by a class of *vormündigen* philosophers. In Hamann's polemic, the doctrines of common sense and public reason are not only false idols, they also represent earthly power clothed in mystery, to which the *philosophes* must scrape and bow (offer a 'salamalec'); the form that public reason takes enslaves inquiry. Knowledge is under the control of an obscure Sphinx who keeps her realm in a state of tutelage.

If Hamann reacted violently to the hierarchy that he perceived in public reason, he was even more virulently opposed to the conclusions of Lessing's Ernst and Falk. Some of his sharpest barbs are directed at the veil that the Masonic priests attempt to draw between the abstract, philosophical truth that the initiated recognize in the divine being, and the mystical forms used in public festivals. This 'newly erected division between ex- and esotericism'[27] was not only politically harmful, establishing a new kind of papacy, but was blasphemous, through and through. Such a division entailed a conceptual purity in religion that ran counter to its true content (a topic we will discuss below) while at the same time establishing a temporal tyranny of Machiavellian dimensions.[28] Hamann's response to freemasonry was to compose a brief tract of nearly impenetrable density – a hyper-esoteric response to esotericism. He prefaced it with a quotation from Proverbs 9:17–18, in which a foolish woman who sits 'in the high places of the city' calls to a simple passer-by: '"Stolen waters are sweet, and bread eaten in secret is pleasant." / But he [the passer-by] knoweth not that the dead are there; and that her guests are in the depths of hell.'[29] The bread eaten in secret is the 'knowledge' of the Masonic priests – the Masonic lodge is pure Old Testament idolatry.

Such polemical fireworks were based on a populist posture of exclusion that Hamann cultivated deliberately. He distanced himself from all officially sponsored intellectual production: 'Beloved reader!' he cried in his *Philologische Einfälle und Zweifel*, 'I am the Magus in the North.' '[I am not any] Royal-Prussian privy-council-serving ordinary professor of philosophy [worldly wisdom] and rhetoric at the university Halle, etc.'[30] A self-described 'homme de lettres'[31] and a long-time writer for the *Königsbergsche Gelehrte und Politische Zeitungen*, Hamann nonetheless adopted the posture of an outsider to the world of the intellectuals, indulging in the most outrageous attacks on the literati. Polemic is an attempt to force the reader into a confrontation. Hamann appears to have considered himself no less successful in his writing if he irritated people – nothing, indeed, delighted him more than receiving bad reviews. His first significantly 'Hamannian' publication, the *Sokratische Denkwürdigkeiten*, received three mentions in the learned journals, two of which were generally positive and one of which condemned the piece as incomprehensible rubbish.[32] It is significant that Hamann was little impressed with the praise he received, fixating rather on the negative aspects of the reviews. He published a vigorous defence of his new style under the title of *Wolken* (a play on Aristophanes' satire of Socrates), in whose first section he reprinted the most virulent review in its entirety, with ironic (nearly sarcastic) rejoinders appended in the footnotes. With what relish must he have reprinted the reviewer's advice, 'WE advise anyone who does not want to corrupt his understanding to leave this unnatural birth of a confused head unread.'[33] When Moses Mendelssohn (the author of one of the positive reviews) sought to win Hamann's pen for the *Briefe, die neueste Literatur betreffend*, the Königsberger was clear: 'The golden age has not yet arrived in which Mardochai and the wicked Agagite will sit together and drink to one another's health.'[34] The reference to the evil 'Haman' of the book of Esther is more of a joke (consistent with the playful nature of their exchange) than a serious identification with the rabid xenophobe of the Bible, but it indicates the degree to which Hamann saw his position as irreconcilable with that of the Berlin literati.

He had made this clear in a previous letter to Mendelssohn. The two writers had chanced to meet during Hamann's brief passage through Berlin in 1756, and both young men had been intrigued by one another. But Hamann's subsequent pious turn had led him to a position, expressed with candour in a 1762 letter, that was in opposition to the literary developments in the capital: 'I loved you, dear friend, with a decided taste in the first hour of our chance meeting. I abandon the renewal of this quickly extinguished sympathy to a more tranquil epoch that will bring us *peace*. Because the character of a public and a private author collide, I cannot yet reveal myself to you. You would betray me, or, like the lion in the fable, deny your bravery at every cock's cry. Carry on, good sir! With the sickle and you, good Sir! With the sharp pruning hook – my muse with stained raiment comes from Edom and treads the winepress alone.'[35]

It is a testament to Mendelssohn's stubbornness and magnanimity that, after such an explanation, he should have persisted in trying to win Hamann to his literary cause. The allusions to Isaiah and Revelation and his references to a future harvesting and subsequent epoch of peace in which lions and lambs might lie down together suggest little hope for reconciliation in this life. Hamann adopted the voice of a prophet in the wilderness (an identification to which he would return throughout his career),[36] and he linked the solitary nature of his endeavour to that of his 'muse,' the Messiah. Despite its typically allusive style, this was a decidedly candid letter – Hamann concluded with a postscript repeating, in the clearest of terms, that the letter was a private document: this candour was not for public consumption. The public voices of Mendelssohn and Hamann must be opposed. The realm of the *Gelehrter* must not be allowed to boast a false inclusiveness.

Bon Sens, and the Impersonal Public in Public Reason

If Hamann's public persona bears some marks of the disillusioned and excluded reactionary, he was not a typical polemicist. Let us consider his reception of an anti-Enlightenment pamphlet entitled 'L'Inoculation du bon sens,' by one Nicholas Joseph Selis.[37] Hamann employed the treatise in two instances, providing an abridged (and altered) translation in his *Kreuzzüge des Philologen*, and later using it as a starting point for his anti-Frederickian *Lettre néologique & provinciale SUR L'INOCULATION DU BON SENS; – pour les fous, Pour les Anges & pour les Diables.*[38] The original pamphlet was a mildly amusing (if uninspired) rant against the mores of the salons and French philosophy in general. Selis condemned his country for having become decadent, unpatriotic, effeminate, foolish, and corrupt. 'Notre mal,' the author maintained, ' … ne vient que d'un défaut de bon sens; de sorte que si nous trouvons le moyen de le composer & de l'inoculer, nous seront [sic] bien-tôt guidés par la raison.'[39] He proceeded to suggest that tiny holes be drilled into the skulls of Frenchmen, and little grains of common sense introduced by means of a straw. This would cure them of their foolish taste for philosophy à la Helvétius.[40] Hamann must have enjoyed the image – he loved polemic, and he reviled the sort of philosophy that Helvétius represented.[41] Yet his response was not merely to ape the piece. Indeed, his translation was quite selective and altered things significantly to stress Hamannian themes. Much of the original article's emphasis on effeminacy and salon culture is missing in Hamann's 'translation,' and there are several additions of local significance indicating that the real target of Hamann's version was not France, but Prussia. But more significant than his translation is his treatment of the piece in his *Lettre néologique*: he showed himself to be ambivalent towards Selis's diagnosis. There was more to be concerned about than mere decadence, and there was something decidedly unsatisfactory about the solution of injecting 'common sense.' Indeed, Hamann made *bon sens* the target of his attack: the Enlightenment was a false religion of *bon sens*. Selis's solution, while amusing enough, was as much a product of the times as the tastes and philosophies of his homeland. Hamann, then, took Selis's text as his source, but proceeded to destroy it and to build his article from the remnants of Selis: 'La chimère en cendre; je vous chanterai maintenant la génération mythologique du Phénix.'[42]

Hamann adopted a satirical tone that betrayed both a base humour and an underlying outrage, yet he masked his intention, refusing to offer a clear position for the common reader to follow. As one baffled contemporary wrote, 'He has a dark and imprecise way of writing, by which one can only see that he wants to reprimand, but not what he believes in place of the thing reprimanded.'[43] For Hamann, the darkness of his style was a sign of intellectual modesty[44] (somewhat akin to the position of the author of Ecclesiastes). But, equally importantly, his style constituted an attack on the reading public itself. This is a theme that runs throughout Hamann's writings and has its origins in the *Sokratische Denkwürdigkeiten*, which is, among other things, an indictment of the public as an ideal.

Kant and J.C. Berens, we recall, had quite benevolently attempted to convince the young *Schwärmer* Hamann to engage in some worthwhile literary activity. Surely a young polyglot with such energy and talent could be of service to the world of letters – perhaps he might begin by translating some articles from the *Encyclopédie*?[45] Hamann's reply to their endeavours was a public indictment of the public realm, in which he allied himself to Socrates and (by typological identification) Christ. The *Sokratische Denkwürdigkeiten* begins with double dedication to 'Nobody and to two.' The two were Kant and Berens, but Hamann clothed these figures in such a way that they stood as figural representations of worldly wisdom and finance. The 'nobody' was the public itself. The public, Hamann charged, is a monstrous abstraction – an idol before which writers lie prostate. It is set as the judge over everything, but understands nothing. As an idol is to a god, so is the public to a true reader – it is but an empty form, devoid of personality. It is nobody.[46]

He presented his work as a curative to be administered to Kant and Berens through the medium of the public realm. He employed the image of Daniel, stuffing cakes into the mouth of the dragon until it burst[47] – Hamann would provide a similar sort of purgative. With a very slight metaphorical shift, he described his essay as a pill that would cure the 'two' of their vain idolatry.[48]

It is clear, then, that if Hamann opposed himself to the men of letters, he had no desire to address the crowd. 'Hamann writes as an intellectual for intellectuals,' writes Bernd Bräutigam. 'His target public are the intellectuals.'[49] This is correct in a sense – the learned nature of his writing, with its myriad allusions and veiled references, demands of the reader a facility with texts that very few attain.[50] In addition, Hamann considered the learned particularly in need of his curatives. Nonetheless, we might quibble with Bräutigam's choice of words – Hamann's target is not a *Publikum* of any sort. To accuse the public of non-existence is not to tirade against the unread masses or the superficial newspaper readers, although impatience with the latter was clearly an aspect of his anger.[51] It is rather an expression of the personal nature of communication – a phenomenon whose first and best example is divine revelation. For Hamann, God is not 'nobody,' nor does he speak to 'nobody.' There is no communication without personality, and even the most learned of 'publics' is still an empty abstraction akin to the God of the deists. He repeatedly stressed the subjective nature of literary reception – the reader and the writer are in personal communication, and the reader's ability to assimilate a text is contingent upon the state of his or her heart.[52] 'Writer and reader are two halves whose needs relate to one another, and who have, as a common goal, unification.'[53] What Hamann was doing was applying to the field of literary transmission a pietist notion of receptivity to divine grace through attunement of the heart. He cited Luke 10:26: 'In order to understand: what is written, it is indeed necessary to ask: how readest thou?'[54] For the writer, the advice was that 'the nature of the object is not alone to be consulted, but also the face of the reader.'[55]

It was for this reason that Hamann took the institution of literary criticism to task: texts, he was arguing, are not independent bearers of meaning, but instances of communication.[56] If divine revelation is the model of literary communication, the establishment of authoritative interpretation would provide a curious and troubling intermediary. 'The critic runs no danger of being taken for a Phylax [Platonic guardian], so long as he does not allow himself to remember that he can read and write. If, however, he shows but a tiny earlobe of his ability, he has begun suicide and high treason to his character. Because he allowed himself the foolish desire to enter into a competition with author and reader, he incurred the fate of the jolly hunt.'[57]

Sola scriptura, we might say. Hamann felt that a literary experience ought to involve a kind of intensive engagement of the reader with the text – like a personal engagement with the scriptures, one reads a text to receive a communication. His dedication to 'the two' (Kant and Berens) ran, 'Where an ordinary reader might see only mold, the feeling of friendship, gentlemen, may perhaps disclose to you a microscopically tiny forest in these pages.'[58] A kind of friendship is the basis of understanding.

Hamann's own experience with the Bible was his model for reading – he read intensively, and understood only when he had internalized the message and, in some literary sense, communicated with the author. His decisive moment of conversion, inspired by reflections over Cain's sin, is instructive: 'I felt my heart beating, I heard a voice from its depths sighing and lamenting, as the voice of blood, as the voice of a stricken brother who would avenge his blood ... I felt of a sudden my heart swell, it overflowed in tears and I could no longer – I could no longer conceal from my God that I was the fratricide, the fratricide of his only begotten son.'[59]

Such a personal experience is not unusual in pietist circles – nor is it, perhaps, an entirely novel notion for a Christian to think that God had afforded him a personal revelation. Nonetheless, Hamann would proceed to take the curious step of adopting this as a model for literary reception. This passage has often been misread as an example of Hamann's 'mysticism' – baffled interpreters take solace in the thought that Hamann partook in some dark occult experience in which he 'heard voices.' But we need not have recourse to such misty terminology – Hamann did not have a supernatural experience; a pious disposition awakened his mind to reception of the scripture's affective and figural meaning. This is an example of the way in which Hamann read texts, and how he wished to be read himself. This is not to say that he treated all authors with humility – on the contrary, he often read with a hostile eye. But he could not consider reading without spiritual engagement, and he had no time for readers who could. The truth was not in objective, external phenomena, or, to invoke a postmodern cliché, in the text, or yet in the reader, but in the communication.

But communication is not easy – like any intercourse, it involves a kind of courtship. In a complex and playful metaphor, Hamann alluded to the notion of the church as the bride of Christ, and played on the idea of authorship as generation: 'If the public is a peacock; so must a writer, who would please and win the favours, fall in love with the feet and the voice of the public. If he is a Magus, and calls the ancients his sister and his bride, then he changes himself into the ridiculous form of a cuckoo, such as the great ZEUS adopts when he wishes to be an Author.'[60] The public is a peacock – proud and flashy. The writer who seeks to woo lovers of the public must be a mimic of sorts (we will consider this mimicry further later in the chapter). But Hamann will take on the form of a cuckoo in order to enjoy the pretty creature. This crass humour is typical of Hamann, but there is more to the metaphor than a bawdy laughter. Zeus became a swan in order to seduce (or rape) Leda; Hamann changes himself into a cuckoo (the most absurd of birds, whose cry consists of eternal mimicry and silliness) in order to impregnate his readers. The image has a number of important dimensions. First, the symbol of the cuckoo plays on the typically Hamannian (and Pauline) trope that the wisdom of heaven is folly on earth. Second, Hamann unites authorship with creation – and both with sexual energy. Hamann could, he once said, not conceive of creative power without genitalia.[61] The burlesque image of the cuckoo mounting the peacock is both self-mockery and mockery of the reading public, for it is an absurd imitation of Christ's mystical union with his church. Finally, the violence implied in the image of Zeus and Leda is instructive – Hamann's harsh mimicry and polemic do not constitute an invitation to conversation, but an attack.

Thus, when champions of the public realm hold out the impersonal, intersubjective (or rather, extra-subjective) realm as an ideal they attempt to eliminate what Hamann took to be the concerned centre of communication. Disinterestedness, impartiality, and universalizability undermine the most important content. Hence Hamann writes to 'the two,' 'Because you are both my friends, your partisan praise and your partisan blame will be equally appreciated.'[62] He wrote to a friend, 'I shall not engage with people [Menschen] in general, this would make me unbearable. I shall always struggle with friends; it is in the *situation* and relationship with them that I should remain bearable. In the connection of these concepts there does indeed lie a *sensum hermeneuticus* or *mysticus*; but I find no *sensum communem* therein.'[63]

Indeed, the authoring of books itself is a dubious practice, given Hamann's goal. The type of communication that he thought appropriate to the most essential matters was not expressed in the medium of books, but in personal conversation. Hamann celebrated the fact that Socrates had not authored any books but rather had chosen to engage in conversations with people. [64] He cited the *Phaedrus*.[65] He might also have cited Plato's *Seventh Letter*, which goes so far as to argue that Platonic philosophy cannot be set down in a straightforward, monological fashion because of the limits of the written word.[66] Plato's ultimate hope to be able to give a rational account that avoids the contingencies of becoming is a primary target of Hamann's polemic. But insofar as Plato's Socrates recognizes the limits of language, resorts to myth and poetry, and equally insists on the personal, dialogical character of proper teaching, Hamann may well be justified in describing himself as a Socratic heir.

The 'Socratic' Hamann, then, attempted the impossible, to transform the medium of publication into one of conversation. This helps account for the obscurity of his style; insofar as he had readers, he wanted them to be forced to confront the complexity of a hermeneutic situation. To speak is not to make statements with claims to objectivity, but to reveal oneself. 'Speak, that I might see you!' is among his most famous exclamations.[67] His method emerges in his oft-quoted closing remarks to the *Metakritik über den Purismus der Vernunft*: 'I leave it to each to unfold the balled fist into a flat hand.'[68] It is the reader's job to turn the fist into an open hand proffering insight. But Hamann made no bones about his method – he was striking, and leaving it to the wounded reader, rubbing his head in consternation, to make sense of the pain. Hamann recognized that most readers would discard his work, and he expressed some concern about the loss – what a self-denial it entails, he commented in a letter, to construct so complex a work that it eludes ninety-nine per cent of readers! How blind to sacrifice the ninety-nine for the sake of that one reader who will understand. Yet, he continued, 'It strikes me, however, dear friend, that they who write for few do not act so naively as they who write for many; for it is the one way to win the many if one first has the few on one's side.'[69] Indeed, he concluded, the approbation of the engaged reader is of much greater value and of greater duration than the fleeting applause of flighty readers.[70] Invoking a famous line from Horace, he wrote that the subtle writer must truly have the courage to employ his intelligence, despite the risk of failing to communicate with the many: 'Sapere aude!'[71]

Both reader and writer, then, must dare to be wise. What is the relationship between this claim and the widespread Enlightenment notion, so clearly articulated in Kant's own *sapere aude!*, that individuals ought to judge for themselves? We have seen how Hamann's '*Anch' io*,' challenged the notion of officially sanctioned enlightenment-through-pedagogy – it remains for us to illustrate the degree to which Hamann pushed individual judgment further, perhaps, than Kant might have wished.

In Hamann's early exchange with Kant he wrote, 'He who believes the reason of another more than his own; ceases to be a man [a human being] and has the first place among the *seruum pecus* [servile herd] of imitators.'[72] How similar this sounds to Kant's 'Have the courage to use your *own* understanding!'[73] Yet these positions were quite distinct.[74] Hamann was willing to make every individual his or her own priest, but there are crucial differences between rational autonomy (reasoning on one's own) and Hamann's radical Protestant subjectivity (having one's own type of reason), just as there is a great difference between treating nature as an external phenomenon to be subjected to observation and inquiry and treating it as a message to be interpreted. Hamann's 'own reason' is not really reason in any sense that Kant would understand the word, but rather a subjectively situated form of interpretation. Hamann liked to treat reason as Luther had treated scripture and the Mosaic law: without faith, it was but a dead formalism. If faith was needed to understand scripture, it was also needed to understand the world, for the world was but a book: 'The book of creation has instances of universal concepts which GOD desired to reveal to the creature through the creature; the books of the covenant contain instances of the secret articles which GOD wanted to reveal to people through people.'[75] By treating one's experience in the world (empirical data) as an act akin to the pious reading of scripture, Hamann invested all scientific discourse with a spirit completely different from that of the naturalist. To take spirit – and divine personality – out of either nature or script is to remove the conversational aspect of existence. For Hamann, human beings are distinct from the rest of creation because God has made them in his image and given them logos, the capacity for speech and the capacity for the reception of the divine word. Human beings have a special dignity in the order of things because, for reasons that are somewhat mysterious, God has deigned to *talk* to them.

Employing one's *own* reason, for Hamann, was bringing one's own spiritual disposition into the reception of evidence. One's way of reasoning depended upon one's spiritual perspective. 'When two people are in differing positions, they must never quarrel over their sense-impressions. A guard atop a watchtower can relate a great deal to someone on the third floor. This person must not be so dumb as to deny that he [the guard] has healthy eyes, come down here: you will be convinced that you have seen nothing.'[76] Hamann was an empiricist for whom the five senses were the only bases of knowledge,[77] but he was suggesting that one ought to treat empirical evidence as a divine message. One's receptivity to the information of the world, like one's receptivity to a text, is dependent upon one's state of mind and heart.[78] When he had been graced with the right degree of attention and humility, Hamann heard a divine voice accusing him of sin; no Kant or Berens ought to tell him that he had faulty ears.

The Personal and Its Relationship to Poetry, Myth, and 'Metaschematism'

We have seen that Hamann positioned himself against both the reading public and the intellectuals by adopting the posture of a prophet that was, paradoxically, both radically anti-authoritarian and radically elitist. If his rejection of autonomy re-emphasized the hierarchy of God's relationship to man, it undermined the hierarchy implicit in the aristocracies of reason. But is there no discernable order to Hamann's writing? Was he merely pronouncing a radical antinomianism that opened the door to personal caprice or to mere dogma? Further, in his obscure writing, was Hamann simply offering a chaotic collage of images designed to baffle and infuriate the learned? His fist struck, but what was in his hand? In this section we will suggest that the jumble of references in Hamann's work has a structure that follows the logic of figural language.

In Hamann's view, when Socrates said, 'I know nothing,' he had really been condemning the form that philosophical discourse tended to take. Socrates refused to take part in a game whose rules were fixed by cheats.[79] What Hamann meant by this was that the critics and philosophers proceeded with a method that excluded spirit from inquiry. Consider his continued reflection on Socratic ignorance: 'The ignorance of Socrates was sensibility. But between sensibility and a theoretical proposition is a greater difference than between a living animal and its anatomical skeleton. The ancient and modern skeptics may wrap themselves ever so much in the lion skin of Socratic ignorance; nevertheless, they betray themselves by their voices and ears. If they know nothing, why does the world need a learned demonstration of it?'[80]

Hamann separated himself from all manner of philosophical sceptic – for him, Socratic ignorance was a sensibility (*Empfindung*). What he meant by this was a kind of sincere and humble intuitive certainty born of faith.[81] Those who attempt, through philosophical contemplation alone, to seek *proofs* of anything have a damnable pride that is akin to works-righteousness. 'Yes, you fine critics! you keep asking what truth is, and reach for the door, because you cannot wait for an answer to the question.'[82] The philosopher does not want to receive, he wants to take.[83] It is important to note that Hamann was not differentiating between different *creeds* or philosophical positions, but different attitudes towards knowledge. He did not oppose himself to reason as such, but rather to those who attempted to employ rational devices to attain *certain* conclusions on matters that were the realm of faith. As we shall see, even the Kant of the critical period, who would attempt to articulate reason's limitations, and cordon off a space in his system for God and immortality, was guilty of the philosophical sin. Hamann's response to Cartesianism and other such doctrines can be summed up thus: 'Our own existence and the existence of all things outside us must be believed, and cannot be determined in any other way.'[84] To attempt to *prove* what ought to be believed was to approach the question with an inappropriate spiritual disposition.

This focus on the spiritual disposition of the subject rather than on the objective content of the claim was central to Hamann's attack on philosophy. He cited a story from Augustine, in which a man was so convinced by a philosopher of the immortality of the soul that he killed himself.[85] The same phrase (that 'the soul is immortal'), he was arguing, can have completely different significance when it comes from a different mouth: the pious person, for instance, does not take the immortality of the soul as a factor in some calculation of his pleasure and pain. Such a person would not say, 'If my soul is immortal, I will take my chances in the next life, for my current misery is great.' The disposition of the speaker and context of the communication is as important as the idea itself. 'When the serpent says to Eve: "You will be like God"; and Jehova prophesies: "Behold! Adam has become like one of us."'[86]

This emphasis on the speaker's spirit rendered Hamann hostile to the notion of disinterested contemplation and depersonalized truth. His favourite stylistic device of mimicry can be understood from this vantage point. He often adopted the words or arguments of his opponents, but infused them with a contrary spirit: 'Like Socrates, I believe everything that the other believes – and I only set out with the intention of troubling the other in his belief.'[87] While this method periodically slips into mere parody, it is invariably intended to show the words of the snake as they can be in the mouth of Jehova.

His use of Hume is a case in point. Most scholarship on Hamann discusses the influence of Hume's famous rejection of the certainty of causality.[88] Our 'knowledge' that one event will cause another is merely a habitual mental response to repeated experiences – we do not 'know,' but 'believe.' Hamann appropriated Hume's argument, but opted to read the word *belief* as *Glaube*, in the sense of 'faith.' He did not criticize Hume's sceptical conclusions, but rather appropriated his opponent's words. In a letter to Kant, he quoted a long passage from Hume in which the Scot argued that the Christian faith professed things that ran entirely contrary to daily experience – no reasonable person, said Hume, could be a Christian without a 'continued miracle' in his own person.[89] Hamann was delighted with this phrase – it showed 'that one can, in jest, and without one's knowledge or will, preach the truth, even if one be the greatest doubter and wish to doubt, like the snake, what God says.'[90]

This helps to correct a common misinterpretation of Hamann. He is often taken to be a Humean who gave an idiosyncratic interpretation to the *Treatise*. Jacobi understood him this way and tried to follow in his footsteps, attempting to outline the significance of faith as a special faculty. He was most disconcerted when Hamann rebuked him for having misinterpreted Hume. Hamann's point was not to create another philosophical system with 'belief' as a term of art indicating a special mental capacity; he was both championing Humean scepticism in its anti-philosophical moments, and undermining it at the same time. To treat Hamann as merely drawing conclusions from Humean premises is to miss the way in which his purpose was to poke holes in general claims themselves. *What* we say is not separable from *who* we are and *to whom* we are saying it.

This brings us to Hamann's mimicry. Hamann's tendency to appropriate other writers' words was a way of altering their content. The donning of different masks was part of an evangelical tactic that Hamann believed to have found in St Paul. Hamann cited 1 Corinthians 4:6: 'And these things, brethren, I have in a figure transferred to myself and to Apollos for your sakes; that ye might learn in us not to think of men above that which is written, that no one of you be puffed up for one against another.' Paul, chiding certain schismatics, had 'in a figure' taken upon himself the view he wished to criticize in order to make his judgment of himself and his fellow evangelists more poignant. Hamann delighted in this 'umgekehrten Nachahmung,' Germanizing Paul's Greek term for *transfigure* thus: 'Metaschematismus.'[91] Hamann employed this in a more general sense of binding the ideas of his opponents to him personally – in so doing, the ideas became radically altered.[92]

'Metaschematism' entailed mimicry, irony, and reductio ad absurdum. He delighted in catching his opponents in their own logic. But it was more complex than this – 'metaschematism' often embraced his opponents' position not merely to mock or to confound, but also to complete or accomplish. Donning the mask of another's view, he would assimilate the view to his personality, altering its content. His Socratism is such a metaschematism. Several commentators have maintained (relying on the analysis of Benno Böhm) that the figure of Socrates was the 'patron saint' of the Enlightenment.[93] Hamann referred ironically to his 'Socratic century.'[94] His complex identification of himself with Socrates, and Socrates with Christ was a method of infusing the father of philosophy and idol of the Enlightenment with Christian significance. Socratic phrases, in his mouth, became charged with prophetic meaning.

What is important to note is that, when Hamann did this, he was not merely employing a rhetorical strategy. Socrates *was* a prophetic figure. To understand this is to gain an important key to Hamann's thought. 'Metaschematism' went beyond mere irony; it represented the driving force of Hamann's scriptural and natural interpretation: typology.[95] Biblical typology is a kind of mythological/literary pattern in which a significant event has an implicit prophetic meaning, and finds a kind of repetition or, rather, accomplishment in a mirror event in the future. The New Testament is replete with typological accomplishments of Old Testament events. Christ, for instance, is the fulfilment of Moses, and the hiding of the baby Moses is the prefiguration of the hiding of the Christ child in Egypt; Jesus' entry into Jerusalem is an accomplishment of Joshua's entry into Jericho, etc. Erich Auerbach, one of the most famous students of typology or 'figural interpretation,' defines it as 'the idea that earthly life is thoroughly real, with reality of the flesh into which Logos entered, but that with all its reality it is only the *umbra* or *figura* of the authentic, future, ultimate truth, the real reality that will unveil and preserve the figura. In this way the individual earthly event is not regarded as a definitive self-sufficient reality, nor as a link in a chain of development ... but viewed primarily in immediate vertical connection with a divine order that encompasses it, which on some future day will itself be concrete reality; so that the earthly event is a prophecy or *figura* of a part of a wholly divine reality that will be enacted in the future.'[96]

Hamann's radical interpretive move was to read all of history as a kind of divine revelation for which the Bible was a key, or pivot point; his typological mind saw figures or schemas everywhere. Thus, it was not merely the Old Testament that contained prefigurations of Christ, but also profane history. Indeed, Hamann's use of 'type' goes somewhat beyond classic typological thought in that he often finds analogies to biblical figures in ways that avoid the strict type(prefiguration)-antitype (realization) duality.[97] An extension of figural thought, 'metaschematism,' as Hamann understood it, was not only an evangelical but also an interpretive act in which non-scriptural phenomena (historical events, or the experiences of an individual) are lent real prophetic significance by association with biblical themes. Hamann *was* a fratricide. Socrates *was* a prefiguration of Christ.[98] We can see why the Magus was so fond of the poet Edward Young's line, 'analogy, man's surest guide below'[99] – transfiguration (metaschematism) lent a seriousness and spiritual reality to analogy. Hamann did not merely locate evidence of the divine in noteworthy figures like that of Socrates – "Perhaps all history is more mythology than this philosopher [Bolingbroke] thinks, and is, like nature, a book that is sealed, a hidden witness, a riddle which cannot be solved unless we plow with another heifer than our reason.'[100]

With what ought we to solve the riddle of nature and history? For Hamann there was an answer in mythology itself: we must understand the patterns of myth and take them seriously. Typological thought is highly historical, while at the same time playing the devil with history. Hamann's constant dispute with Enlightenment historical exegetes was that they failed to take seriously the prophetic elements of the scriptures. 'But can one know the past when one does not even understand the present? – And who will get a proper notion of the present without knowing the future?'[101] For Hamann, the history of the world was a vast book, whose introduction and conclusion are Creation and Last Judgment, and whose climax is Crucifixion. The biblical stories provide the key to making sense out of all events in nature and history – all of history is myth, including the Bible.[102] The Bible is simply *the* pre-eminent myth, the poetic/prophetic pattern to which all other myths are to be related. In a late text, *Entkleidung und Verklärung* (Divestiture and Transfiguration) he wrote, 'The spirit of observation and the spirit of prophesy are the wings of human genius. To the realm of the first belongs everything of the present; to the realm of the last, everything that is absent, the past and the future. The philosophical genius expresses its power in that it, by means of abstraction, takes pains to make the present absent; unclothes real objects to naked concepts and merely [bloß] conceivable features, to pure appearances and phenomena. The poetic genius expresses its power in that it, by means of fiction, transfigures the absent past and future into present representation.'[103]

Can Hamann have meant that the Bible was fiction? In a sense, he was accepting a view of the Bible as akin to other poetic works. He placed a great deal of importance on the notion of God's self-abasement – just as God took on human form in the figure of Christ, so was his pre-eminent text lowly and composed in terms comprehensible to limited beings.[104] The Bible was truly inspired poetry, human in the same way that Christ was human.[105] Hamann never made the case for why the Bible should be granted such pride of place among literary texts. Given his well-known love of tradition, we can conceive of reasons he might have given, but he did not himself do so. This is perhaps a spurious question; Hamann was a Christian, we might shrug – we could hardly expect him to prefer the Bhagavad-Gita. Yet the Magus's very first writings on the Bible exhibit a consciousness of this problem. Why, he asked, had God first revealed himself to a specific people; why had he chosen the Jews particularly? Hamann never offered anything but stock replies about divine mystery: 'The reasons for this choice can as little be investigated by us as the question of why it pleased him to create the world in six days, when his will might just as well have realized this work in one single instant.'[106] He clearly felt that entering into such a debate was overstepping the bounds of piety – and perhaps from within his system of thought, the question itself becomes questionable. Whatever the case, he found a very rich source of interpretation in the scriptures, and he devoted the greater part of his life to transmitting this to any who would make the effort to imbibe the strong liquors of his writing. We must delve deeper into his notion of aesthetics, however, if we are to understand the origin and significance of this method.

We have mentioned that the eschatological lens with which Hamann read all events was born of a conviction that the whole of nature was divine revelation. The character of this revelation and its exegesis was set forth in the dense *Aesthetica in nuce*. For Hamann, aesthetics was not the science of the beautiful, but the most basic (and divine) mode of communication. In brief, sensory perception (aesthetics) is the basis of all cognition and constitutes the most direct connection that we have to God. 'The senses and the passions speak and understand nothing but images. Imagery comprises the entire treasury of human knowledge and happiness.'[107] This statement about the essentially sensual and passionate nature of human cognition is followed by a brief description of Genesis in which creation is equated with revelation – the world is at once object and message, sensual pleasure and *word*: 'The first explosion of creation, and the first impression of the historian; the first manifestation and the first enjoyment of nature unite in the word: "let there be light!" with this begins the perception of the presence of things.'[108] Note that the presence of things and the *Empfindung* (the sensibility or perception that, as we noted above, was central to Hamannian faith) arise together. Creation is a kind of speaking; perception is a kind of sensuous enjoyment, or reception of this word. Human beings, Hamann states, are the crown of God's 'sensuous revelation,'[109] made in God's image.

Man is made in God's image – but what could this mean? Is God a balding biped? Hamann rejects such a naive literalism – even pagans, he says, were aware of the invisibility that is shared by the human soul and the divine essence.[110] Rather, we must understand this statement as a metaphor. 'The covering form [*Figur*] of the body, the countenance of the head, and the extremities of the arms are the visible habit [*Schema*] in which we walk; but are actually nothing but an index of the secret self within us.'[111] In a way, sensory information was metaphorical (hence poetic) – it represented our hidden, spiritual nature. We look at God's message, perceiving and interpreting it through *Empfindung*. Note Hamann's terminology – the 'figure' of the body, the visible 'schema' of the human form. Basic communication occurs through sensory perception, but it is organized in 'figures.' Hamann hints at the importance that figures or schemas will have in communication – 'me taschematism' or 'transfiguration' is a form of communication based on the prelapsarian building blocks of speech. In the garden, the message that was communicated to Adam and Eve through their senses was that of divine presence, which is to be understood through self-knowledge. God had made people in his image – all human sense-experience was but a symbol that hinted at their hidden nature, the spiritual element within them that is made in the image of God.

Hamann's prelapsarian state is not entirely idyllic. The fact that the divine essence is hidden from Adam and Eve and that their sensory perception is an imperfect means to knowledge suggests a certain distance from God. Knowledge of God is mediated, and we get the distinct impression that the naked pair are going to want to bridge this gulf. The desire to have complete knowledge of what is hidden is going to bring considerable grief. What follows is a complex reworking of the Fall in which Hamann employs the metaphor of clothing to describe the nature and origins of communication. The *Aesthetica* does not describe the sin; rather, it leaps to the result: 'The first human clothing was a rhapsody of figleaves.'[112] Hamann's use of the word *rhapsody* is multilayered – the Greek term for reciting poems is derived from the verb *rhaptein*, 'to sew or stitch together.'[113] Thus, we have a complex metaphor in which clothing is equated with communication, and the first garments that Adam and Eve don are equated with rhapsodic poetry. Things get worse, for God proceeds to make coats of skins for the ashamed pair.[114] Hamann goes even further into the development of clothing: with a humorous jab at speculative anthropology, he rejects the suggestion that the further development of garments was a product of need spawning invention. Rather, he suggests, it was the product of Adam having kept dubious company. For Adam learned this art 'through the acquaintance with the ancient poet (whose name is Abaddon in the language of Canaan, but Apollyon in Greek).'[115] Abaddon, a.k.a. Apollyon, is the king of darkness from Revelation 9:11 – typologically, the snake from the garden.

This account of the Fall (which I have simplified drastically) presents the increasing complexity of language as an artificial separation from God. As we put on more and more layers, we hide our visible figure (and, hence, muffle direct sensual experience) to an ever increasing degree. Even the most noble human language – the poetic rhapsody – is a product of sin, quite beautiful, but already at a distance from the most innocent poetry. If fig leaves obscure, how much more must furs. Hamann's most famous phrase, 'Poetry is the mother-tongue of the human race,'[116] is born of the view that poetry is a kind of expression that is closer to concrete, present sense-experience than abstract prose. 'Speaking is translation – from a tongue of angels into a human tongue, that is, thoughts in words – things in names – images in signs; that can be poetic or kyriological, historical, or symbolic or hieroglyphic – and philosophical or characteristic. This kind of translation (i.e., speech) is more than any other like the wrong side of a tapestry. *And shews the stuff, but not the workman's skill.*'[117]

Here, *in nuce*, we have Hamann's hermeneutics and theory of expression. To speak is to translate and interpret divine revelation. It is essential to human existence, but it is always a kind of distancing from the original, divine expression. It is always mediated in some way; it is essentially symbolic and metaphorical (to speak of any knowledge as immediate is to assume a human knowledge of the divine that Hamann would have rejected).[118] There are several types of speech that the passage lists, but let us merely mention the highest and lowest forms, the poetic and the philosophical. The poetic is the concrete – it expresses all manner of experience in terms that speak directly to the intuition. The philosopher, whose 'unnatural use of abstractions'[119] has dulled his senses, is the least capable of seeing the reality of revelation. In this devil's *Dichtung*, philosophy, we have the figural opposite to the divine poetry of Christ, who is the alpha and omega of literature: 'The poet at the beginning of days is the same as the thief at the end of days.'[120]

Let us take a moment to illustrate the way in which Hamann arranged profane matters according to biblical, figurative patterns. We have noted his rendering of Socrates into a Christ figure. In the *Aesthetica* we see a similar re-clothing of Homeric heroes. Addressing his readers, he said, 'The story of the beggar who appeared at the court of Ithaca you know; for has Homer not translated it into Greek and Pope into English verse?'[121] Odysseus, though the king, takes on the form of the weakest and poorest of men – a clear Christian image in Hamann's mouth (with all the implications of Odysseus' later wrath). But Hamann was suggesting that the story – essentially a Christian tale – was *translated* by Homer into Greek. Typology knows no anachronism. The *Aesthetica* suggests, 'Try to read the Iliad if you have first sifted out with abstractions the vowels α and ω and give me your opinion of the poet's meaning and euphony.'[122] What follows is the first line of the Iliad with the said letters removed. Without Christ, there is no meaning – texts become a mad gibberish.

It is in this sense that we ought to understand his passing comment to his friend Lindner, 'Every book is a bible to me.'[123] Isaiah Berlin cites this point as an example of how deeply Hamann felt one should attempt to delve into the mindset of the author one is reading.[124] This is somewhat similar to the position that we touched upon above, that the spiritual disposition of the author is an important dimension of the communication. But there was really only one author of significance, and any book worth reading was but a gloss to Him. Berlin seems to read a little too much Herder into Hamann – the Magus did not try to 'feel his way' into the spirit of pagan authors. If anything, he bulldozed over them with his one-size-fits-all Christian typological scheme. This is not to say that he was rabidly dogmatic (if anything, his view left a wide opening for radically subjective interpretations), but simply that his reading always took place at the foot of the cross.

These theological elements naturally render Hamann's work difficult to penetrate: 'A layman and an unbeliever cannot explain my writing style as anything other than nonsense, for I express myself with various tongues, and speak the language of sophists, of punsters, of Cretans and Arabs, of whites and Moors and Creoles, and I babble a mixture of critique, mythology, rebus, and principles.'[125] It is all a great jumble. But to the reader sympathetic to Christian typology, his mess of images can begin to take on a meaningful organization.

Once we understand this, we can see how Hamann differs from other writers who celebrated poetry as the original medium of human communication.[126] It was not uncommon in the eighteenth century to argue that early peoples had expressed themselves through concrete images and metaphors rather than abstract concepts and syllogisms (this, indeed, was often taken as evidence that progress had been achieved). Hamann fastened onto the more enthusiastic proponents of this view. He cited Thomas Blackwell,[127] for instance, in whose *Enquiry into the Life and Writings of Homer* (1735) we find repeated the 'ancient Opinion "That Poetry was before Prose."'[128] Blackwell took the example of the Oriental peoples as comparable to the ancients: 'They *open* their *Mouth*, and give loose to a fiery Imagination, they are poetical, and full of Metaphor.'[129] Hamann also professed fondness for Francis Bacon, who wrote a work celebrating pagan mythology, *The Wisdom of the Ancients*. Hamann quoted approvingly from the preface, 'For as hieroglyphs came before letters, so parables came before arguments.'[130] But if Hamann admired Bacon, he read ancient texts in a radically different manner.[131] This comparison is instructive.

Bacon's *De Sapientia Veterum* interprets classical texts allegorically, attributing to ancient fables insights of universal importance. However, for all that Hamann admired Bacon's work,[132] his authorship was not predominantly allegorical interpretation of the scriptures or of ancient tales (although he did not entirely shun allegory), nor is such a method of interpretation terribly fruitful when applied to the Magus himself. Northrop Frye makes a useful terminological distinction: 'Typology is not allegory: allegory is normally a story-myth that finds its "true" meaning in a conceptual or argumentative translation.'[133] The mystery of Hamann's constant juxtaposition of biblical and mythological references is not to be cleared up through conceptual translation. Much like poems, Hamann's texts cannot be rendered into plain language – they cannot be made to 'make sense' outside of the structure of prophetic thought. This is not meant to question the value of commentaries (even *systematic* commentaries) on Hamann's work. H.A. Salmony is only partially correct when he writes, 'The "darkness" of the Magus cannot be brightened up through systematization.'[134] Hamann's writings have a complex structure that requires elucidation. Indeed, despite his constant rant (typical in the eighteenth century) that his enemies were corrupted with 'esprit de système,' his historical/eschatological template offers meticulous organization to thought. If he rejected the geometrical spirit of a Leibniz, a Descartes, or a Hobbes, his thought followed strict patterns that obeyed not the laws of logic and the syllogism, but the patterns of biblical symbol and figure.[135] Thus, Hegel was perhaps incorrect to take Hamann's patchwork of oblique biblical, mythological, and personal references as examples of a clever but undisciplined wit that failed to transcend personal experience.[136]

But if there is method to his madness we must nonetheless bear in mind the fact, well established in circles of literary criticism, that commentary on a literary text is not a substitute for the text itself. There is a certain prosaic tendency among the philosophically inclined to exclaim, 'If *that*'s what the author meant, why didn't he just *say* it?' Such a question clearly misunderstands both the nature of mythopoetic communication and of criticism. Prophets and poets are not scholars and philosophers – indeed, if this chapter is at all successful, it will only be by sinning against Hamannian principles of composition. For Hamann, to push thought to the level of concepts is to remove its vitality – and, indeed, its meaning. His philosophical forays are an attempt to 'metaschematize' philosophy into philology, the love of the Word. 'Philosophers,' wrote Hamann, 'are impudent rivals.'[137]

Adorno (whose counter-Enlightenment was equally a call for greater Enlightenment) deprecated Hamann's dense writing: 'Locke's platitudes are no justification for Hamann's obscurities.' A writer has a duty to conceptual clarity, wrote Adorno: 'The thicket is no sacred grove.'[138] (*Physician heal thyself*, we might reply.) Hamann's point is that sacred groves often look like thickets from the outside. Adorno's charge against the Enlightenment is that it *reverts* to myth;[139] Hamann's charge is that it is insufficiently attentive to myth.

Hamann's style locates itself within the pattern of myth, and gives pride of place to concrete poetic language. Biblical writing puts a flavour into the mouth of the reader. The Bible does not, for instance, describe the washing of feet – it draws on the reader's experience, calling up all the myriad social and psychological elements of that daily act. It does so with a great economy of words. A visual description merely translates the event into other symbols; a conceptual explanation (i.e., 'the washing of another's feet indicates an act of humility') removes the immediacy of the aesthetic experience. The gain made in one kind of precision would be at the cost of the words' multilayered significance; the gain made in the conceptual abstraction would be at the expense of the reader's personal, imaginative experience of the event. Myth is poetic in that it makes use of a reader's intuitive knowledge of a thing (an action, a flavour, a passion, a personality, a daily occurrence) to convey a moral or spiritual insight. In this light, we may return to the above quotation from *Entkleidung und Verklärung* (note 103). Philosophy attempts to escape from more immediate, subjective experience by reducing it to 'bare concepts'; 'poetry' (the medium of myth and prophesy) seeks to 'transfigure' the future and the past, rendering them present experience for the reader. The readers of a poetic/prophetic text become located within history and prophesy – they find their place in a vast mythical tradition, or, to be more precise, within a continuum. For Hamann, fabulists such as LaFontaine or Lessing were not writing divine poetry, but (literally) uninspired allegory.[140] Voltaire may write as many miles of alexandrine verse as he wishes – it will still be prosaic in Hamannian estimation. Hamann said of the *philosophes*, 'They have made common the holy shrine of science, and translated the poetry of an original thought into the watery prose of the coffeehouse and gaming table.'[141] In his attempt to locate his writing within the framework of divine poetry, Hamann demonstrated that his celebration of biblical language was not primitivist nostalgia: the mother tongue of the human race was not a dead or foreign language – it was the living word that the properly attuned ear is as ready to hear as ever, 'yesterday and today!'[142]

Poetry, Philosophy, and Public Discourse: Aufklärung oder Verklärung

The desire of allegorical interpreters to translate myths into conceptual prose is derived from a concern that the poetic language of myth is somehow either too imprecise to be useful, or of dubious honesty. If charitable, such literally inclined people will look upon a sacred text with some delight at its charm ('how prettily these claims are ornamented'); if wary, they will see in it a kind of propaganda. In liberal concerns about the decline of communication in the public sphere, we see a similar worry about the affective aspects of poetic language.

Propaganda's aim is to muddy the intellect and raise the basest passions to a dominant position within the psyche of the dupe. This leads the enemies of domination to be wary of forms of communication that appeal to the passions, escape rigorous definition, or rely overly on metaphor. We have seen that Hamann celebrated types of discourse that champions of discursive clarity tend to associate with domination. At the same time, he was harshly critical of temporal hierarchy, whether that of Frederickian bureaucracy, the Prussian professorship, or the whim of the ineffable 'nobody' of public judgment (three social forces that were united in Hamann's imagination). He seemed to think that the language of mythology could and should live on in the modern mind, and he warned (with frantic, apocalyptic urgency) that failing to be attuned to this aspect of existence had disastrous consequences.

Despite the reactionary overtones of his position, we should be reminded that Hamann was not calling for censorship. Indeed, he viewed censorship as a rotten institution that smelled of the Inquisition.[143] He seemed, at times, to have a certain liberal faith that openness might actually increase piety: 'The looseness of the reigning mores and freethinking,' he wrote in a 1763 letter, 'must, through the freedom of the press, partly betray itself and fall on its own sword, and partly diminish the strength of ignorance, and hasten the dawn of the day that we all await.'[144] But if he delighted in the freedom to publish, he made a conscious attack on the institution of debate.[145] His texts were not to be debated – they were to be loved or hated, assimilated or thrown out with disgust. Hamann came not to send peace, but a sword.

He took pleasure in opposing philosophy to faith, delighting in the Pauline inversion of wisdom and folly: 'If, then, the divine style of writing chooses the foolish – the shallow – the ignoble in order to shame the strength and ingenuity of profane writers, then the eyes of a friend, inspired, enthusiastic, and armed with jealousy, will be needed to recognize the rays of heavenly grandeur in such a disguise.'[146] Divine writing was not argument – it was not philosophy. But it was not dogmatics either – dogmatic orthodoxy speaks the same language as philosophy (propositions). Hence his claim, 'Neither the dogmatic thoroughness of the pharisaical orthodox nor the poetic luxuriance of sadducean freethinkers will renew the sending of the Spirit, which impelled the holy people of God ... to speak and write.'[147] The divine message could make sense only to a person who approached it with passionate desire and a pious humility.[148]

If the Enlightenment project entails rendering authority legitimate by making it subject to rational public debate, Hamann indicates an instance in which this project must cross paths with the demands of faith. The language of philosophy might well clash with the language of myth. Public reason cannot accept the mythical, the partisan, or the personal. Hamann's inversion of the Enlightenment hierarchy between particular and universal, passionate and detached, concrete and abstract both makes and goes beyond the ad hominem charge that philosophers seek to dominate the unlearned. It draws clear lines of battle between the Enlightenment project and its mythopoetic 'other.' Hamann forced a confrontation between two modes of discourse indicating the degree to which the matters most essential to him could never be rendered in a public form. By transfiguring philosophical texts, Hamann was able to attack the Enlightenment without accepting its rules of engagement. In so doing, he left his readers with a maddening task of judging between the different modes of discourse. For who among us is healthy enough to be entirely devoid of *bon sens*? And so we wonder, is it Socrates the philosopher, or Socrates the philologist whom we should follow? And with what standards might we determine which Socrates is the greater cheat? *Sapere aude.*

PART TWO

The Politics of Metacritique:
Hamann contra Kant

3 Critique and Metacritique: Kant and Hamann

Among Hamann's more famous writings is his brief and dense attack upon Kant's *Critique of Pure Reason*. Hamann was probably the first serious reader of Kant's first *Critique* – he obtained an advance copy from the publisher and wrote several responses to the piece, the last and most satisfying of which is the *Metakritik über den Purismum der Vernunft*. His neologism *Metacritique* is apt: Hamann was not concerned with a detailed study of Kant's argument. On the contrary, like most of Kant's contemporaries, he felt overwhelmed by the work. Hamann's metacritique is a critique of Kant's fundamental premises. It attempts to get behind Kant, undermining the root assumptions of transcendental arguments. At the same time it is *critique* in a Kantian sense, probing the very possibilities of Kantian critique itself. But the *meta* appears to overpower the *critique* – considering the mammoth work with which it deals, the *Metakritik* is surprisingly brief. Nonetheless, its eight pages are dense enough to have recently elicited a five-hundred-page monograph from the world's leading Hamann scholar, Oswald Bayer.[1]

Hamann, who died in 1788, never saw the bulk of Kant's expressly political works, but he did live to see many of Kant's more seminal essays. He even managed to make brief, disparaging remarks about the *Grundlegung*, and throughout his writings we see manifest opposition to the central pillar of Kant's ethical thought, rational autonomy. It is thus reasonable to extend his arguments in the *Metakritik* to the basic and lasting elements of Kantian practical and political philosophy. The following three chapters take as an assumption the inseparability of Kantian moral theory from Kant's speculative philosophy, and, specifically, from his a priorism. They argue for a political interpretation of transcendental idealism as the conclusion of a century of Enlightenment and as a high articulation of the Enlightenment project. This latter was Hamann's interpretation, and we will attempt to indicate the cogency of this position.

This first chapter is preparatory: it gives a detailed exegetical summary of the *Metakritik* in order to (re)familiarize the reader with this difficult text. We will attempt to refrain from lengthy analysis of references (save in the few instances where it is inescapable), but we will nonetheless devote some considerable space to mere exegesis. While we risk tiring the reader with repetitions of things found in other expositions, it is useful, given the text's denseness and readers' legitimate unfamiliarity with it. The second chapter argues for the fairness of Hamann's charge that Kant sought to transcend the limits of language. More importantly, it argues that there is a surprising similarity between Hamann's linguistic turn and Kant's famous 'Copernican' turn. Both Hamannian logos and the Kantian a priori perform a transcendental function of making experience possible. The third chapter draws out the radical differences between Kantian reason and Hamannian language, particularly with regard to the aspects of Kant that have the greatest resonance in political thought, personality, autonomy, and human dignity. The epistemological arguments in Hamann's *Metakritik* are part of a theologically motivated attack on the autonomous person. Hamann's replacement of the a priori with the logos overcomes the individualism inherent in the Kantian conception and recasts human dignity such that it is derived from divine grace. Human duty becomes situated and contingent, but, being located in a divine order, it escapes radical subjectivity. When pure reason cedes to language, the parameters of moral reflection are radically altered.

In assessing Hamann's response to Kant, we must note that Hamann did not have the benefit of two centuries of Kant exegesis. He read the 1781 version when the ink was still wet, and was literally the first reader to see the significance of the work. It must be said that even the most avid Kantians avow that the first *Critique* is an awkwardly written work. It contains several terminological inconsistencies, and many of its arguments are far from evident. It was not the superficiality of the times that made the work so difficult for readers like Mendelssohn (who never got through it), but rather the infelicities of presentation (which Kant fully admitted). Like many readers of Kant, Hamann often felt overwhelmed and inadequate to the task of assessing the work. 'Against Kant's,' he lamented, 'my poor head is a broken pot – clay against iron.'[2] It is with unforgivable enthusiasm for 'the Magus' that Georg Baudler describes this phrase not as an admission but rather as an expression of Hamann's 'flexibility, spontaneity and many-formedness' compared to Kant's stiff, inflexible 'hardness.'[3] That Hamann saw the significance of Kant's work and that he devoted serious reflection to it is undeniable; that he mastered it is surely doubtful.[4] Hamann expressed his ambition thus: 'To find and expose the *proton pseudos* would be enough for me.'[5] But Hamann's polemic did indeed go to the heart of the *Kritik der reinen Vernunft (KrV)*, and, Hamann's fustigations against philosophy aside, it does contain some philosophical arguments that merit analytical scrutiny. Hamann may have attempted to be beyond (*meta*) critique, but we will attempt not to be, in Leacock's memorable phrase, entirely 'behind the beyond.'

In many ways, Kant's first *Critique* marks the end of the Enlightenment. It is the trumpet of last judgment on the more radically materialist, irreligious wing of the eighteenth-century movement. Yet, in a more profound way, it is also the culmination of Enlightenment – it is an honest coming to terms with the empiricist challenge to ideas and ideals, one that ultimately submits politics and religion to the rule of reason. Reason, the century's priest, prophet, and king, had undermined itself; Kant placed it back on the throne and in the temple, even as he reduced the throne and temple to a comfortable chair and lecture hall. Nonetheless, the first *Critique* poses a challenge to the schema of this book, which pits Hamann against the Enlightenment and the Enlightenment project. If the Enlightenment was predominantly empiricist in outlook, Hamann's empiricist reply to Kant's first *Critique* appears to be the revenge of the eighteenth century. In other ways, there are many aspects of Kant's argument with which we might expect Hamann to have sympathized. Hamann was, after all, rather fond of God and the immortality of the soul, and he shared the basic move described by Kant in the 1787 version, 'Ich mußte … das Wissen aufheben, um zum Glauben Platz zu bekommen.'[6] Hamann was particularly enthusiastic about the *KrV*'s 'critique of all speculative theology,' which he thought sufficiently powerful to 'stop the mouths' of Berlin's leading Enlightened theologians,[7] a point that he made in his journal review of Kant's book (an otherwise very negative review that he decided not to publish out of respect for and gratitude to Kant).[8] We will, then, have to proceed with some care here to avoid drawing overly simplistic lines of demarcation while nonetheless indicating the questions on which the two writers are fundamentally opposed. The disagreement between Hamann and Kant has a delightfully dramatic quality to it – they embody a transhistorical opposition between faith and reason – but there are many devils and angels in the details.

Metakritik über den Purismum der Vernunft: **Exegesis**

The basic argument of the *Metakritik* is quite simple. Hamann attacks Kant's a priori as a non-existent realm. (Just as the 'public' is a nobody, the a priori is an intellectual nowhere). Kant's fundamental error is to have ignored the centrality of language for cognition (and especially philosophical cognition), and to have thus mistaken abstract terms of art for reality. In the following exposition, we will proceed linearly through the text. The paragraph numbers are indicated in the left-hand margin. Throughout, I will refer to the pagination in the A edition of the *KrV* (1781), for this is the edition to which Hamann referred.

1 The *Metakritik* begins by quoting Hume's celebration of Berkeley's claim that 'all general ideas are nothing but particular ones, annexed to a certain term, which gives them a more extensive signification, and makes them recall upon occasion other individuals, which are similar to them.'[9] Right away, Hamann indicates that the question at hand in Kant's work is intimately tied to the question of abstract terms, their origin, and their signification.[10] This nominalist insistence that abstract ideas are a linguistic appending of a general 'term' to more concrete experiences is an important claim for Hamann. (It does not, however, tell the whole story. Hamann's relationship to nominalism is complex and will be dealt with elsewhere.) By citing Hume's celebration of this as one of the most important 'discoveries' in recent experience, Hamann employs an authority to signal Kant's failure to place the linguistic question at the heart of his analysis.

2 Hamann continues by calling attention to Berkeley's importance for Hume and suggesting that Kant's philosophy owes a great deal to both Berkeley and Hume. This is not merely an interpretive remark; rather, it indicates a historicist claim about the genealogy of Kant's work. Hamann will later insist that all philosophical arguments are historically situated.[11] Hamann follows this claim by indicating that Berkeley's linguistic discovery should remind us to privilege common language usage. Hamann hints that the 'sensus communis' in everyday language is what we should be studying.[12] The *surface* of language yields rich truths that are missed in the Kantian attempt to dig deep below experience.

3 The following paragraph continues in this vein, charging that Kant, like some sort of Gnostic, has sought to find 'hidden secrets' by inquiring into the human capacity for 'cognition of objects of experience

without and before all experience' and 'the possibility of a sensible intuition before all sensation [*Empfindung*] of an object.'[13] Hamann has clearly phrased this in such a way as to make it appear paradoxical at the outset. Kant's view was not that we can cognize objects without experience, but that there are a priori elements to cognition.[14] Hamann's point is that the discovery of such elements is impossible, requiring us, as it would, to escape experience. It is 'on this double im-possibility [Hamann's hyphenation] and on the mighty differentiation between analytic and synthetic judgments'[15] that Kant grounds his argument.

4 Hamann proceeds to give a three-stage history of philosophy as a process of purification. This is a play on Kant's three stages of philosophy: the dogmatic, the sceptical, and the critical.[16] (It is to be noted that Kant calls the final stage 'mature and manly' as opposed to the immature philosophies of the past. This thought, echoed in 'Was ist Aufklärung,' occupies us elsewhere.) Hamann replaces these steps with three 'purifications' – philosophy's cleansing itself first of tradition, then of experience, and, finally, of language. Hamann's three stages are not to be understood as representing different philosophical schools, or any sort of history of philosophy, nor are we to take these stages as essentially distinct for Hamann. Actually, all such purifications are part of the same philosophical project to which Hamann objects. This three-fold division is simply a play upon Kant's history of philosophy and his keenness for tripartite divisions.[17] The first stage, the elimination of 'tradition,' refers to the philosophical goal (of Platonic origin) of attaining eternal truths. In this pursuit, philosophers have always tended to treat history as contingent and uncertain; traditions come to be seen as prejudices. Individual experience also has this contingent characteristic – it too is a posteriori. Thus, Hamann characterizes the 'second stage' as motivated by this same philosophical desire to attain knowledge of being rather than becoming. The quest for an unchanging, eternal truth involves not only the elimination of history, but of all experience (Kant's a priorism is clearly in his sights here, but so are all philosophies that depend on an intellectual realm that is eternal and unchanging). Hamann charges that the first stage was a complete separation from all one's ancestry, while the second included a complete separation from all one's contemporaries. He reads into this Cartesian solipsism a kind of contempt for others and the basis for social alienation. Hamann suggests that it is akin to the alchemists' search for the

philosopher's stone. For good measure, he throws in a few polemical references to the impatience of such philosophers and their despotic tendencies (the *Herrschaft* of reason), employing Kant's famous footnote about the age of critique and its rule over religion and politics.

5 The final stage is the 'purification' of language. Ultimately, philosophers aim at a kind of universality that transcends the contingencies of language. This is especially problematic, Hamann suggests, because language is the medium of philosophy. Here we receive one of Hamann's more programmatic statements about language: it is 'the single first and last organon and criterion of reason, without any other *Creditiv* than tradition and use.'[18] The Kantian project to describe what is rationally necessary prior to experience involves a contradiction: any words used must, as words, be tainted with experience. The quest for the Kantian a priori thus ought to lead to a kind of muteness: 'The longer one reflects, the deeper and more inwardly is one struck dumb and loses all desire to speak.'[19]

6 Hamann alters a passage from Kant's transcendental logic in which Kant defined the two sources of cognition as 'receptivity to impressions' and 'spontaneity of concepts.' Hamann writes that the two sources are 'receptivity of language and spontaneity of concepts.'[20] Hamann states that these are the source of all reason and philosophy, whether dogmatism (*Rechthaberey*), scepticism (*Zweifelsucht*), or criticism (*Kunstrichterschaft*). Hamann's linguistic alteration has important theological overtones: rather than receptivity to sense impressions, we are given receptivity to a word. This alters the question at hand: we are no longer to consider Kant's epistemological question, but rather to situate experience in a communicative context. A similar transformation occurs with Kant's 'spontaneity,' which is given a new, poetic content: one is spontaneous or creative with *words*. But if there is a creative element to words, they are equally the contingent products of tradition and usage. Ultimately, they have their foundation in man's linguistic, communal nature, and they are a source of error if one attempts to take them beyond the range of normal communication, which is always interpersonal and contextual.

7 Hamann gives the example of the word *Metaphysics*, noting how this pervasive term had its origin in a historically bound act of appending a prefix to another concept. (Hamann is referring to the famous title of Aristotle's *Metaphysics*, which originally referred to the book *after* the *Physics*.) Now, coining neologisms is a creative, poetic act and is not in itself foolish, but it can be dangerous if such terms become

reified. Hamann argues that refined philosophical language is as quicksilver compared to other metals: it slips out of one's grasp because of its abstract nature. To aim at non-experiential truth with such artful creations is to attempt more than one's tools allow. An artist who attempts to make a God with his tools will succeed only in making an idol. We see now the point in his earlier polemical reference to idols: philosophy and idolatry are on similar ground.[21]

8 What follows is the text's closest philosophical treatment of Kant's work. Because it is a mixture of polemic, ironic rendering of Kantian terminology, and straightforward argument, we will need to slow down and quote at some length. 'Indeed, one should deduce from so many *analytic* judgments a gnostic hatred of Matter or also a *mystical* love of Form; nevertheless the synthesis of the predicate with the subject, in which consists the actual object of pure reason, has for its mediating concept nothing but an old, cold prejudice for mathematics before and behind it, whose apodeictic certainty rests primarily on an, as it were, kyriological characterization of the simplest, most sensible intuition and hereafter on the ease with which it can prove and represent its synthesis and the possibility of the same in obvious constructions or symbolic formulae and equations, through whose sensibility all *misunderstanding* is excluded of itself.'[22] The first two lines indicate Hamann's disagreement with Kant's separation of analytic and synthetic a priori judgments: Hamann denies the essential distinction between the two and condemns them both for empty formalism.[23] Let us take a moment to outline the Kantian arguments being targeted here.

We recall that the *Critique of Pure Reason* begins by rejecting the standard treatment of analytical judgments as a priori and synthetic judgments as a posteriori. Kant defines an analytic judgment as one in which the predicate is 'contained in' the subject through identity. The clearest such statements are perfect tautologies such as A = A. The example that Kant gives is 'all bodies are extended' – the predicate *extension* is contained in the subject, in that the statement is tautological. In addition to this logical argument, Kant gives a psychological corollary: it is impossible to consider a body without the idea of extension. The predicate and the subjects are joined by identity, and thus the predicate 'adds nothing' to the subject.[24] However, Kant was not content merely to accept tautology as the only source of knowledge, and he sought to expand the realm of the a priori. Hume had demonstrated that the statement 'every change has a cause' is on

very shaky foundations for the very reason that there is nothing necessarily – analytically, Kant would say – uniting cause and effect.
Cause and effect, then, are concepts that can make no claims to logical certainty. Kant assumed from the outset that we have a great deal
more certainty than Hume had been willing to allow. Thus, he ex-
panded the domain of the a priori. Not only are tautologies certain
(according to the principle of non-contradiction), but there are also
judgments whose certainty is assured because they are necessary for
us to experience the world as we do. These are *synthetic* a priori judgments, and they include mathematical judgments.[25] Kant's question,
how are synthetic a priori judgments possible? contains a rejection of
Hume at the outset.

With regards to mathematics, Kant was both more credulous and
less credulous than Hume. Hume claimed that algebra and arithmetic (unlike geometry) were capable of 'perfect exactness and certainty'[26] as a result of their 'demonstrative' nature.[27] Thus, while he
castigated the geometers' hubris of Platonists and Cartesians, he
seemed willing to accept that arithmetic was analytic.[28] Kant (perhaps influenced by Hume's attack on the geometers) took this a step
further, and doubted the analytical nature even of arithmetic mathematical equations. He argued, famously, that the statement '7 + 5 = 12'
is not analytic because seven and five are not 'contained within' the
concept of twelve. As Vaihinger explains, 'Equality of the objects is
not identity of the concepts.'[29] An equation of this sort involves more
than a mere tautology (which is the basis of the analytic). It does indeed rely on the principle of non-contradiction, but it involves saying
something *more* about the subject than is immediately evident in the
subject itself. No one can possibly think about a substance without
extension (or extension without substance), but if one thinks of the
concept 'twelve,' one does not need to think of 'five plus seven.' The
success of this argument is not our topic here. Scholarship on Kant
has been quite divided about his analytic-synthetic distinction, and
for my part I cannot see how Kant can base his distinction on a somewhat vague psychological observation that might well be applied to
Kant's example of the analytic. After all, if the distinction between
analytic and synthetic is meant to be a priori, the datum of what any
given mind immediately thinks when confronted by a given concept
should have nothing to do with the matter.[30] However, what is important for us here is merely to note that Kant was assuming the
rational, universal, and apodictically certain nature of mathematics

while at the same time denying its analytic simplicity. Thus, Kant was less credulous than Hume about the analytical nature of arithmetic, but entirely credulous about its a priori certainty. His question is not, what is the nature of the certainty mathematics affords? but rather, how is mathematics, which is certain, possible? How is a *synthetic* a priori possible?

The beginning of the Hamannian paragraph quoted above indicates an outright rejection of Kant's move. Hamann agrees with Kant and Hume that our knowledge of the world cannot come entirely from analytic judgments, and he mocks those who would think their way out of uncertainty with pure tautologies.[31] Kant had criticized Plato for having attempted to 'fly away' from the sensory realm;[32] Hamann goes Kant one further, condemning the rationalist's dependency on analytical judgments as indicative of 'mystical hatred of matter.' But Hamann follows this by levelling the same attack on the synthetic judgment – Kant's confidence in the synthetic a priori is simply another version of the much-maligned rationalist endeavour to attain certainty through mathematical system. Thus, Kant is charged with having an 'old, cold prejudice for mathematics.' This is not a rant against the caricature of 'stiff, cold, rationalistic' Kant that has dominated the popular imagination since the early nineteenth century (and is so evident in Heine's satirical sketch). It is a castigation both of Kant's insistence on the existence of a priori knowledge and of his fundamental assumption that mathematical proofs are certain. Despite Kant's very clear argument that mathematics and philosophy were different endeavours and that philosophy should *not* attempt to ape mathematics,[33] Hamann insists that Kant's synthetic a priori shared something of the Pythagorean or Cartesian outlook that sought a philosophy modelled on that science.

The second part of the above paragraph ('whose apodictic certainty') is Hamann's positive statement regarding the source of mathematical knowledge. Here, he does for all mathematics what the young Hume (following Berkeley) had done for geometry: he insists on its empirical roots. When he says that mathematical certainty is 'kyriological' he means that it has a concrete and sensory basis, in the same way that poetic expression is concrete and sensory. (The term *kyriological* was derived from a contemporary treatise on the history of script – we encountered the term in our discussion of the *Aesthetica in nuce*.)[34] Hamann's claim is that mathematics is based *entirely* on sense impression. Note that Hamann does not question the certainty of mathematics. Rather, he insists that mathematics owes its certainty to its origin in immediate sense impression; mathematics is an empirical science. This, naturally, strikes us as a counterintuitive observation, but it is a perfectly consistent extension of empiricism. If, after all, all of our mental activity derives from experience and mental habits acquired through experience, then we might just as well say that the capacity to do sums is merely another learned behaviour. What is striking in Hamann's claim is that he attributes the astounding certainty of mathematical systems to their *sensory* origin – that is, it is not primarily mind's capacity for abstraction, but rather the effect of the given on our senses.[35]

What follows is a sentence that might well be taken as a paraphrase of Hume: Hamann insists that the geometric notions of 'points without parts' is an ideal construction that is determined only through 'empirical symbols and pictures.' And, just as Hume had castigated philosophy for attempting to imitate the geometers in flights to pure intellect, so too does Hamann think that the certainty of closed mathematical systems can have only a troubled relation to philosophical questions – he does not question the degree to which demonstrative, mathematical proofs can evoke agreement, but he questions the degree to which the assent given to sound mathematical conclusions grants them a privileged ontological status. On the contrary, he suggests, it is the senses that are ontologically prior to our symbolic manipulations of their information, and mathematics' certainty is merely a result of our more original and trustworthy sense-impressions.[36]

Following this, Hamann condemns the philosophical tendency to think one can discuss things that are not dependent upon sense impressions. 'Metaphysics misuses all the word-signs and figures of speech of our empirical knowledge as lukewarm hieroglyphs and types of ideal relations, and with this learned misdemeanour reworks the straightforwardness [*Biderkeit*] of language into such a senseless, ruttish, unsteady, imprecise Something = X, that nothing remains but a windy sighing.'[37]

By now, we are familiar enough with Hamann's castigation of abstract ideas and celebration of everyday language (in fact, we have had cause to visit this quotation once before in chapter 2); here we see it applied to the undermining of the transcendental project. The passage he has in mind (although it might well refer to one of several passages) is from Kant's division of objects into phenomena and noumena. Repudiating dualistic views of an intellectual and a sensory knowledge, Kant argues that we must nonetheless maintain the concept of the 'thing in itself,' although we cannot know anything about it: 'All our representations are, it is true, referred by the understanding to some object; and since appearances are nothing but representations, the understanding refers them to a *something*, as the object of sensible intuition. But this something, thus conceived, is only the transcendental object; and by that is meant a something = X, of which we know, and with the present constitution of our understanding can know, nothing whatsoever, but which, as a correlate of the unity of apperception, can serve only for the unity of the manifold in sensible intuition.'[38]

This is a Kantian mouthful that has often engendered confusion. Is this curious 'transcendental object' an ontological claim about the world as opposed to its appearance in our perception? Is it merely a sceptical claim about the limits of our knowledge and our need to think about the world in a certain way? Norman Kemp Smith (who presents a very muddled Kant) argues that this passage is a vestige of pre-Critical Kantian thinking, containing a confused 'combination of subjectivism and dogmatic rationalism.'[39] What Kant meant, he suggests, is that the distinction between phenomenon and noumenon is not one between two realms, but of a relationship between aspects of cognition: 'In the higher field of Reason, as in the lower field of understanding, it is not through the given, but only through the given as interpreted by conditioning forms of an ideal nature, that the meaningful reality can disclose itself to the mind.'[40] Henry Allison argues that Kant's 'thing in itself' is to be understood as an epistemological necessity (an assumption required for experience) and not as a metaphysical proposition.[41] It is outside the range of our present inquiry to decide on a definitive interpretation of Kant's noumenon/phenomenon distinction. The root claim, however, is that there is a noumenal element necessary for experience and that it is something that cannot be known. A central point of debate in Kantian scholarship has been just what we are to understand by this transcendental object about which we can know nothing. In chapter 5 we will discuss the kinship between this 'limiting concept' (*Grenzbegriff*) and the limiting concepts that Kant identified as 'God' and as the 'I,' or the transcendental subject.[42] Hamann hints at the similarity between this view and the deist God: Kant, Hamann wrote, displayed a 'transcendental superstition for *entia rationis*.' Whatever the ontological status of the noumenon in Kant's thought, Kant's expression, a 'transcendental something = X,' strikes Hamann as the natural result of philosophical distancing from experience. With this phrase, Kant has attempted to say the unsayable, to define in words something that is never encountered in the intuition.

Hamann concludes this paragraph with a non sequitur about Kant's grounds for having faith in the certainty of mathematics, joking that if 'certainty and reliability' are the source of our respect, human reason must take a back seat to the instincts of insects, which are perfectly reliable. Mathematics, with its certainty, is often considered one of the pre-eminently human activities, a crowning capacity of a rational creature; Hamann clearly thought that the rhetorical force of Kant's recourse to pure intuition was weakened if we afforded the same certainty to grasshoppers.[43] Hamann's implied argument is that unlike insects, human beings have language, the nobility of which does not rest on logical infallibility.

9 Hamann proceeds to repeat Kant's question, how is the capacity to think possible?[44] Hamann's response, based on the 'genealogical priority of language' over any logical function, is as follows: 'Not only does the entire capacity to think depend on language ... but language is also the central point of reason's misunderstanding with itself.'[45] Hamann is suggesting that Kant's famous antinomies are good examples of the difficulties into which philosophers get themselves. He is further arguing that the antinomies (and, indeed, all metaphysical pitfalls) have their basis in the nature of language. He cites two reasons for this misunderstanding (although he suggests that there are many more of the same kind): the 'coincidence of the greatest and littlest concepts' and the 'endless figures of speech before the conclusions [*Rede- vor den Schlußfiguren*].'[46] The first reason is the problem of universals and particulars. Hamann is warning of errors that can occur when one applies general concepts to particular realities. One risks a great deal going up and down the ladder of abstraction. While I must caution the reader that this is not the pure nominalism it might appear to be (as we shall see in the following chapter), it does draw our attention to the errors possible when abstract terms are confounded with particular experiences. The second problem alludes to the metaphorical basis of language: Hamann hints that awareness of this renders the purity of philosophical discourse doubtful. Kant was aware of analogical thinking, but Hamann is pointing out not merely the ubiquity of metaphor in thought but rather that metaphor *constitutes* thought. If, for instance, Kant speaks of a predicate 'contained in' its object, or if he speaks of a 'limiting concept,' he is thinking with spatial metaphors.

Now, Kant wrote in the *Critique of Judgment* that when we attempt to represent a priori matters like the ideas as objective realities (in the intuition), we are forced to employ *symbols*. But he conceived of this as conscious metaphor, a setting of one thing for another. 'In symbolic hypotyposis,' Kant wrote, 'there is a concept which only reason can think and to which no sensible intuition can be adequate, and this concept is supplied with an intuition that judgment treats in a way merely analogous to the procedure it follows in schematizing.'[47] For Hamann, this pure concept itself was a figment of the imagination, a will-o'-the-wisp. All we have is concrete imagery and the linguistic accretions attached to it. One may draw conclusions with austere, syllogistic rigidity, but one will nonetheless not avoid the basic imagery and metaphor that makes up the building blocks of language and thought. This observation is, naturally, one that resonates in twentieth-century thought.[48] If the basis for abstract thought is metaphors drawn from concrete images and if this manifests itself primarily in culturally specific turns of phrase, then the universality and objectivity of reason is undermined. What is suggested in its place is a kind of situated, hermeneutic reason. This is reason as logos, as speech itself.

10 Hamann then formulates his counter-thesis, though it is once again expressed in ironic turns of Kantian phrases: 'Sounds and letters are, then, pure forms a priori in which nothing is met which belongs to the sensation or concept of an object, and [they are] the true, aesthetic elements of all human cognition and reason.'[49] These things, sounds, and letters, are in themselves empty of sensory content. Thus, they are completely empty like the Kantian a priori. On another level, however, they have, he says, a 'genealogical priority.' The very concept of an a priori is what Hamann rejects at the outset, choosing rather to accept this temporal priority as granting the sensory basis of language a privileged ontological status. He proceeds to suggest that the 'oldest language' was 'music,' based on the sensory rhythm of the pulse, the sound of breathing, etc. We see a repetition of the thesis, so fully articulated in the *Aesthetica in nuce*, arguing for the intellectual priority of our aesthetic (sensory) reception and his treatment of all sense impressions as *words*. We have touched on this treatment of the world as *word* in previous chapters. We will expand upon it below. Hamann castigates the Kantian view of time and space as forms a priori, implying that this is simply another way of calling them 'innate ideas,' the rejection of which

he takes as axiomatic. Rather, these are concepts that are derived in experience from the persistent impressions upon our senses of hearing and sight. His point, once again, is that space and time are not some chimerical 'pure forms of the intuition,' but rather are experienced in our direct impressions of breathing or of seeing objects. Indeed, to conceive distinctly of time without conceiving of some progression of events in the physical world appears to be impossible.[50]

11 He continues with the argument that sense reception and understanding are not to be separated – we ought not to consider sense as that through which we are given objects and understanding as that faculty through which we *think* them. Hamann expostulates against Kant's 'violent separation' of what nature put together. These are two aspects of the same thing. Now, Kant himself had insisted that these things are inseparable; we recall his quip, 'Thoughts without concepts are empty, intuitions without concepts are blind.'[51] But Kant's whole exercise was to analyse cognition in order to separate the certain aspects of the understanding from those tied to variable experience. Kant wrote, 'Only through their union can knowledge arise. But that is no reason for confounding the contribution of either with that of the other; rather it is a strong reason for carefully separating and distinguishing the one from the other.'[52] As W.M Alexander points out, Hamann's argument is not that Kant believed the rational faculty to be possible without the faculty of sense, but rather that he thought that reason was possible – indeed, necessary – prior to or without experiences.[53] The pure forms of the intuition make experiences possible. Much of Kant's argument will rest on this, with Kant holding up the a priori elements as the foundation of all cognition and the basis for all certainty. In addition to objecting to Kant's separation, Hamann charges it with having inverted the importance of each part of the understanding. Playing on Kant's references to the 'given,' Hamann suggests that Kant prefers to *take* by ordering experience along the lines of his forms and categories. Kant's famous 'Copernican turn' is thus treated as a product of pride; Hamann treats the given as literally *given*.

12 What follows is a typically Hamannian piece of manipulation in which Kant's words are twisted around to an accusation against Kant himself. Kant had spoken of Enlightenment as a cure for the darkness caused by the philosophical 'indifferentism' occasioned by the impasse in metaphysics.[54] Hamann charges Kant with abetting

the 'dominant indifferentism' of the Enlightenment itself (by which he naturally means religious indifferentism), and he ties this charge to the desire to have a pure natural language. Natural language and natural religion are one and the same for Hamann.

13 What follows is a baffling mixture of theological and mythological references: 'The evil snake in the bosom of common folk-language is the most beautiful analogy for the hypostatic union of the sensory and understandable natures, the common idiom-exchange of their powers, the synthetic secrets of both corresponding and self-negating forms a priori and a posteriori, with the transubstantiation of subjective conditions and the subsumptions in objective predicates and attributes through the *copulam* of a decree or curse [*eines Macht- oder Flickworts*].'[55]

This is a mouthful, but it indicates the crux of the issue: the metaphysician seeks to find the link between being and becoming, the eternal and the temporal, the objective and the subjective, or the one and the many. This, however, is not a problem that philosophy can resolve because it is fundamentally a question about God's relationship to his creation. That is, Hamann does not entirely abandon the distinction, but he alters it drastically by changing the question from one of being and becoming to one of God and Man. Bayer explains the references as follows: the snake is a double reference to the snake in the garden and to a fable from Aesop in which a young man attempts to save a snake from the cold by warming it under his coat. Once warm, the snake promptly bites him.[56] Hamann is indicating that in common language there is a mysterious union of eternal and temporal, but it is not something under our control. The references to 'hypostatic union' and 'transubstantiation' dress Hamann's dispute with Kant in the language of Luther's quarrel with the church. Kant is accused of seeking a magical power to decree the change through a powerful word *Machtwort* – to effect *transubstantiation* – but this is merely a curse (that is, the opposite of a blessing), for it is an attempt to usurp the divine *Logos* with the *ratio* of philosophy. As Luther wrote in his treatment of transubstantiation, 'The authority of the word of God goes beyond the capacity of our mind.'[57] Note that Hamann does not condemn the distinction between temporal and eternal; *the fundamental problem of metaphysics is not denied in this passage*, just as Luther had not denied that there is an important event that occurs in the sacrament of the Eucharist. Rather, it is the attempt to overcome these distinctions through conceptual means to which Hamann objects. There is a mystery in the divine/temporal duality – God reveals himself in time, in the world. Once again, Luther wrote, 'It is not necessary for human nature to be transubstantiated before it can be the corporeal habitation of the divine, and before the divine can be contained under the accidents of human nature.'[58] When Kant attempts to 'subsume an object under a concept'[59] he is, Hamann implies, attempting something as dubious as the scholastic attempt to explain the sacrament through terminological distinctions between substance and accident.

14 Hamann expresses a wish to be as eloquent as Demosthenes and to 'open his readers' eyes' in order that they might see 'the hosts of intuitions ascending to the firmament of pure understanding, and hosts of concepts descending into the deep abyss of the most palpable sensibility, on a ladder of which no sleeper has yet dreamt.'[60] This reference to Jacob's ladder is a castigation of Kant's attempt to reconcile the subjective with the objective. Only faith can resolve the tension between such opposites. Jacob's dream was a personal communication from God. (Hamann will later return to the theme of dreaming when he will once again accuse Kant of having sought a universal language that was merely 'dreamt in his spirit,'[61] possibly a reference to Kant's earlier mockery of mysticism, *Dreams of a Spirit Seer*.) This and the following references in this paragraph all entail an attack on philosophical hubris. Man receives; he does not take. Hamann proceeds with a densely packed series of images from the Song of Songs, Hesiod, and Genesis, ending in a polemical thrust at the 'purity' of Kant's reason: it is an unspotted virgin, but not in the sense of Mary, rather in the sense of the vulgar mythological character Baubo, who is virginal only because she masturbates.[62]

15 Hamann proceeds with what at first appears to be a positive teaching concerning language: 'Words have … an aesthetic and logical capacity.'[63] Words themselves are mere sounds and letters, yet they also convey ideas. Thus, in Kantian terms, they affect both our aesthetic and our rational capacities (capacities, recall, that Hamann thinks inseparable). This separation into aesthetic and logical is an ironic appropriation of Kant's method. Hamann attempts to find the empirical and pure content of words. This is clearly not a serious proposition, since Hamann finds the separation itself artificial, but it is intended to set up an argument of Kantian appearance that leads to an absurd conclusion. The distinction he draws is as follows: the empirical content of a word, its physical sound or spelling, is an

entirely arbitrary thing, meaningless in itself without reference to some object. Meaning, he insists, is derived from *use*. Words are *pure* insofar as their meaning is entirely unconnected with the sense impression of the object.

16 Having set up this implausible distinction, he proceeds to roll out an absurd set of questions that parallel aspects of an argument made by Kant. We will order these questions by letter and refer to them in our subsequent explanation. (a) Referring to the letters and sounds of the word *Vernunft*,[64] Hamann asks whether one can, from the mere intuition of the physical word (the sounds and letters) intuit the word's conceptual meaning. And can one take the concept alone and divine from it the sense-impression given by the specific word? Naturally this is completely absurd, but Hamann indicates that the *Critique* is ambiguous on this question.

17 (b) He proceeds to ask whether one can deduce the form (the letters and syllables) from the content, and notes that the *Critique*'s response is 'no.' (c) But the *Critique*, he claims, argues that one can 'deduce the form of the empirical intuition in the word from the concept, and determine by means of this form' how the syllables and letters must be ordered and observed.[65] This would be possible only if there were a universal philosophical language that escaped the contingencies of real human languages.

This odd joke requires explanation; certainly it is not evident that Kant's argument can be turned to this application. Hamann's intent is to ridicule Kant's separation of the pure from the empirical by translating it into the problem of signification and sign. But let us examine the argument in Kant that is parodied here: Hamann is still referring to Kant's distinction between noumenon and phenomenon.[66] Here, Kant discusses our capacity for experience, and he divides experience into its a priori and empirical aspects. He poses the question of how we ought to conceive of these a priori, noumenal concepts. His discussion leads him to the conclusion that these are noumena in a 'negative' sense, by which he means that we ought not to treat them as objects, but rather as the conditions of possible experience.[67] These noumena cannot be known as objects (and thus can't support speculative ontological claims), but they are certain, and their a priori certainty both determines experience and provides a kind of stability to our limited knowledge. The questions that Hamann poses about the conceptual and empirical content of the word *reason* are akin to questions that Kant considers with regard to concepts and objects. Kant's position appears equivocal with regards to the question (a) of whether one can separate out the concept itself from experience of objects. Kant clearly thinks that one can, but at the same time he thinks that objects themselves don't define the concepts. (b) He is equally clear that concepts alone do not give us knowledge of objects.[68] But there is a relationship between concept and objects. (c) 'In the absence of ... an object, [the concept] has no meaning and is completely lacking in content, though it may still contain the logical function which is required for making a concept out of any data that may be presented.'[69] The mind, then, contains this perfect capacity for ordering experience; it projects this onto experience, making experience make sense. The form determines the ordering of the given. Kant attempts to avoid the pitfalls of 'dogmatism' by treating the a priori concept as unknowable in an objective sense, but as certain and necessary for experience. Defining it as a formal necessity for human thought, Kant thinks he has avoided the hubris of previous speculative philosophers while at the same time avoiding the morass of scepticism. Hamann's response is that even talking about such forms betrays the experiential – because linguistic – nature of the concepts themselves. If Kant thinks he can speak about a 'pure intuition,' or even more problematically, about 'ideas' of pure reason, he is doing the very thing that he himself thought was illicit, attempting to speak outside of experience. But words do not have this purity; they cannot express non-experiential or pre-experiential things. To do so would require a language that is itself unconditioned by experience – a universal, intellectual language.[70]

18 The possibility of 'the form of an empirical intuition without object or sign thereof,' something that exists purely in the mind, is thus, according to Hamann, the fundamental error, the 'proton pseudos,' of critical idealism.[71] Kant's desire for a priori purity is the root of this error; there is no standpoint outside of experience. The great danger is explained with the following joke: 'Analysis is nothing more than a cutting of one's cloth to suit fashion, as synthesis is the artificial seam of a guild's leather worker.'[72] There is probably a double entendre with the last part of the line – Kant's father was a saddler. But the point of the charge is that Kant's analytic divides up experience in an illegitimate manner, privileging certain aspects of it as eternal. Hamann thinks this is merely a fashion – a taste for abstract universals – that is at work. But the danger is in the synthesis, for one then

reconstructs one's account of experience according to one's own design. This becomes a kind of blindness to experience, for one's philosophical terms of art come to appear as reality to the philosophical synthesizer.

Hamann concludes with his oft-quoted line about leaving the reader to take his clenched fist and open it into a flat hand. The line gives an oblique indication of his method: he has metaschematized Kant's work, applying it to the 'sacrament' of language.[73] That is to say, his argument about language is not a reductio ad absurdam of some points Kant made (Kant's argument can clearly not be stretched to include this silly statement about deriving the form of the empirical intuition of the word from its concept); rather it is a transposition of Kantian arguments onto the question of language, the foundation of all communication and hence of all philosophy.[74] If the 'critical' Kant seeks to examine the very possibility of philosophy itself, the 'meta-critical' Hamann seeks to go even further below, into the realm of language. And, as in all his writings, his religious motive is clear – language is to be understood as a *sacrament*. We are not simply dealing with a radically empirical phenomenologist, but with someone who interprets language in the sense of John 1:1.[75]

4 Varieties of Copernican Turn

Both Kant and Hamann shared a sceptic's desire to look into the foundations of philosophical claims. Kant did so in a way that saved philosophy and metaphysics (although of a more modest kind); Hamann did so in a way that returned philosophy to its role as handmaid to theology. In so doing, he condemned philosophical terminology, privileging ordinary language. Hamann can be considered a theologian insofar as his thought deals with God's Logos; as far as dogma is concerned, we have seen that he was entirely unprepared to take faith as a matter of dogmatic statements, which run the same risks as philosophical ones. From our exegesis in chapter 3, we see that Hamann's linguistic objection to Kant is well captured in the manner of W.M. Alexander: 'Language is a tool which affects Kant's experiments.'[1] Or, to put it in clichéd terms, Hamann accuses Kant of trying to lift himself up with his bootstraps. However, this statement, if accepted, would tend to undermine any philosophy at all. If we can't reasonably speak of anything universal and necessary, what sort of philosophy are we likely to have? We are reminded of Wittgensteinian hyperbole, 'Have the philosophers up to now always spoken nonsense?'[2]

This chapter asks two questions: (1) Is Hamann justified in his charge that Kant was unaware of the degree to which language intruded into the philosophical task? (2) What is the relationship between Hamann's language principle and Kant's transcendentalism? For the first question, we will respond in the affirmative; for the second we will indicate that both principles have a surprisingly similar structure. Hamann's 'metaschematism' of Kant's *Critique* is born of a similar 'Copernican' turn.

Did Hamann Miss His Mark?

First let us ask whether Hamann was correct to charge Kant with linguistic hubris. Josef Simon has sought to counter Hamann's charge, maintaining that 'Kant is not of the opinion that he ... can "speak *above* language."'[3] For Simon, Kant saw the limits of language in the same way that he saw the limits of philosophy: the thing in itself could not be known.[4] Thus, much of Hamann's charge appears to lose its strength in this observation. Kant did not believe that to name something was to know it, after all, and his repeated reference to a 'something = X' indicates his unwillingness to take expression in places it can't go. This is not an unreasonable Kantian reply, and we will discuss momentarily the similarities between the Hamann's hidden God and the Kantian thing-in-itself.

Yet Simon goes even further, drawing our attention to Kant's later writings, suggesting that Kant knew of the inescapable sense-based nature of language. He points to the *Critique of Judgment*, section 51, in which Kant, dividing the 'beautiful arts,' has recourse to comparing them with language. Here, Kant suggests that 'speaking' has three dimensions: words, gestures, and tones. These correspond to its mixed function of expressing both concepts and sensations, or, more precisely, 'thoughts, intuitions, and sensations.'[5] But is Simon correct to draw the conclusion he does from this? After all, in this passage, Kant is describing the aim of *speaking*, which involves 'die vollständige Mitteilung des Sprechenden.' He is not describing the nature, say, of written philosophical expression. Indeed, the passage in question does not appear to indicate, as Simon says, the 'unaufhebbare Sinnlichkeit in der Sprache,' but quite the opposite, that the word divorced of gestures and tones contains the purely conceptual element of language. The later Kant clearly saw that a significant element of communication was non-conceptual (aesthetic ideas, for instance), but not that thought is dependent upon language and must thus always be impure.

In the *KrV*, Kant discusses philosophical terms thus: 'Despite the great wealth of our languages, the thinker often finds himself at a loss for the expression which exactly fits his concept, and for want of which he is unable to be really intelligible to others or even to himself. To coin new words ... seldom succeeds; and before we have recourse to this desperate expedient it is advisable to look about in a dead and learned language, to see whether the concept and its appropriate expression are not already there provided.'[6] Here, Kant (who is about to defend his idiosyncratic use of the Platonic term *idea*) is quite clear that philosophers *seek* precise terms for concepts that they already possess. This is a fairly clear indication that Kant, at least at the writing of the first *Critique*, saw words and concepts as separate things, and saw it as the philosopher's task to append the most precise word he can as a label for a clear concept.

This is clearly where Kant and Hamann disagree. According to Hamann, we possess no wordless concepts, for reasoning *is* the use of language. The quotation from the *KrV* is somewhat ambiguous. Kant does not say merely that the lack of the mot juste makes it difficult for one to communicate the concept to others, but also to *oneself* ('so gar sich selbst'). Here, then, appears to be a kind of inner colloquy where the left side of the brain doesn't know what the right side is doing.[7] We get the image of someone stumbling around in the dark trying to get a sense of an object upon which he keeps stubbing his toe. The concept exists in the philosopher's mind, but he can't quite name it. It is a queer image, and Hamann, for whom reason is language, would have nothing of it.

But perhaps we ought not to draw strong conclusions from Kant's passing comment on neologisms. Simon is more convincing in his appeal to the late Kant's periodic statements that philosophy must be *communicated* in order to avoid a kind of empty, enthusiastic quietism. Yet here, too, we have to cavil at the emphasis that Simon places on these passages. He cites, for instance, the *Kritik der Urteilskraft*, section 40, where Kant insists on the priority of the *sensus communis* as an idea necessary for the communicability of a judgment (of taste).[8] This appeal to the Shaftesburian concept might be seen as a move towards Hamann's position that all thought is social and linguistic. Now, setting aside the question of whether Kant's insistence on communicability of taste judgments can be translated to his speculative or moral philosophy, we must note that the position taken in the *Critique of Judgment* is equally subject to Hamann's charge that philosophy finally seeks to purge itself of language entirely. Consider the paragraph from Kant: 'We must [here] take *sensus communis* to mean the idea of a sense shared [by all of us], i.e., a power to judge that in reflecting takes account (a priori), in our thoughts, of everyone else's way of presenting [something], in order *as it were* to compare our own judgment with human reason in general and thus escape the illusion that arises from the ease of mistaking subjective private conditions for objective ones, an illusion that would have a prejudicial influence on the judgment.'[9]

As Simon notes, Kant is not saying that thought itself is 'intersubject-ive,' but rather that communicability is the check on philosophical *Schwärmerei*. We might go further: Kant is emphasizing an a priori ground for agreement. It is precisely because thought is *not* dependent upon language that it is communicable. The process of abstracting from one's position and considering a matter from the position of another, or, indeed, from the position of *all* others assumes the existence of an a priori truth in which all subjects participate. This generalized, abstract-ed other is precisely 'nobody the notorious' whom we encountered in the *Sokratische Denkwürdigkeiten*. This process by which Kant believes we attain *Aufklärung* is precisely that argued for in his famous appeals to public reason. Philosophy might need to express itself in language, but the very act of communication assumes a universal human reason transcending the contingencies of human expression. This comes across clearly in his essay, 'What Is Orientation in Thinking.' Kant recognizes that communication – public reason, the source of Enlightenment – strengthens thought. Thought is, in a sense, dependent upon externals. Nonetheless he maintains the old Hobbesian chestnut, 'Whereas a higher authority may deprive us of freedom of *speech* or of *writing*, it cannot deprive us of freedom of *thought*.'[10] That said, Kant continues, without free public expression thought languishes, so in a sense gov-ernments *can* stifle thought by stifling expression. Communication is necessary for reflection, and without the ability to reason publicly we would be incapable of thinking fruitfully, but thought is nonetheless a thing independent of the language in which it is expressed.

The A Priori and Language

But if we have suggested that Kant, indeed, behaved as if language were something to be transcended, we must return to our question: is it as absurd as Hamann suggests to attempt to philosophize? Kant cer-tainly did not think that words themselves were a priori, but why should we not attempt to employ words as markers for things that make up (or make possible) our experience? Kant himself was quite insistent upon the claim that we can't know things outside of our ex-perience.[11] His point was that we cannot make strong ontological claims because we can't know fundamental reality, but that we need to inquire into the source of our experience. What, if we're going to avoid the troubling path of the sceptics, grounds our experience? Kant thought that we need to make the claim that there is something being looked at.

This assumption of a real, objective world does not give us insight into the world in itself, but is necessary for experience. Nor is it intuitively clear that time spent in considering the meaning of abstract concepts is lost. Fortunately, despite his polemics and his tendency to sound emptily dismissive, Hamann is not saying this. What he is saying is that thought is always distanced from its source; it is always mediated, and its medium is language. When he complains of the 'violent separation' of reason and sense, it is not to condemn all reflection or all abstraction per se, but particular uses of abstraction that he thinks unjustifiable. In a later chapter we will devote some attention to the type of abstraction that Hamann thought legitimate.

But Hamann's attack on Kant does, on first reading, seem a somewhat superficial rejection of speculative thought in general. In a sense, Hamann appears to be making the type of error often attributed to naive empiricists who think that temporal priority somehow trumps philosophical priority. Thus Hamann's anti-metaphysical rants have all the appearance of the Enlightenment tendency to undermine metaphysics in the name of observation and generalization. The scientific method, when it does not overstep its bounds, makes no metaphysical claims. But Hamann was not a natural scientist who wanted merely to get on with the project of charting the universe; he was principally concerned with the very problems that animate metaphysical inquiry. Hamann, too, sought to point to truths that underlie experience. Like Kant, he saw that these were the matters of utmost concern to us.

Despite their radical opposition, the authors have a remarkable similarity that is often overlooked in accounts of their disagreement. We should not find it entirely surprising that Hamann, when considering his two main opponents in the 1780s – Kant and Mendelssohn – concluded, 'Kant is closer to me than Mendelssohn.'[12] Underneath all Hamann's polemic is a structure of thought very much resembling Kant's 'Copernican' turn. Kant translated questions about the world into questions about our capacities. He did not ask, how is the world constructed? but rather, what is it about cognition that enables us to experience the world in the way we do? Kantian transcendentalism differs from traditional ontological questioning by changing the perspective to one that is anthropocentric and, in a limited sense, subjective: no longer are we to ask, what is? but rather, how is the world possible for us? Hamann, too, takes this subjective turn, but simply takes it a step further. If the first *Critique* looks to the necessary conditions of all cognition, Hamann converts Kant's problem to one that is psychological and empirical. When Hamann poses the question, how is the capacity to think possible? he looks to our experience of thinking and can find no thought that is not at the same time a symbolic structure. For Kant (to employ an old cliché), the a priori is like a pair of coloured glasses that we can't remove and through which we necessarily see the world as coloured; for Hamann, language serves this function. But because he is considering the question from a psychological (a posteriori) standpoint, Hamann, unlike Kant, does not think that there is any universal certainty or necessity in these matters. In this – as far as philosophical epistemology goes – he remains firmly rooted in the sceptical tradition that Kant felt he had overcome. Thus, in the passages where Kant attacks the pretensions of speculative theology Hamann cheers loudly, but the 'magus' nonetheless performs the same move on the aspects of cognition that Kant seeks to save from the sceptic's blade.[13]

The battle between Hamann and Kant is between two metaphilosophical assumptions about what parts of subjective human cognition to privilege. Kantian a priorism seeks something firm and unchanging, philosophically prior to psychology (the observational science of inner experience) by attempting to identify the necessary conditions for experience. Kant claims that the forms of time and space and the categories of the understanding are necessary for experience and therefore *pure*. As we have seen, Hamann argues that the forms of time and space are merely abstractions – time, for instance, is a concept that is derived from the original sense-impressions of heartbeats and breath.[14] Recall, Hamann considers these direct sense-impressions to be *words*: the first language was the pulse, or, as he says in another essay, in the early world, 'Every appearance of nature was a word.'[15] Thus there is no possibility of an 'immediate' knowledge of things, for Hamann understands human cognition as something requiring mediation. These original, sensory 'words' are less mediated than our more abstract terminology. His treatment of the world as a text, the living logos, is not a mere rhetorical flourish, but something he takes quite seriously (I would say 'literally,' but my use of that much-abused word would require substantial clarification). The formula from the *Aesthetica in nuce*, 'To speak is to translate – out of a language of angels into a human language,' indicates the linguistic – and thus necessarily mediated – nature of experience.[16]

There is much to be said about Hamann's use of the medieval trope of the world as divine language, but for the moment I wish only to illustrate the functional similarity between Hamannian language and the Kantian a priori. Kant's 'Copernican turn' managed to reconcile Protagoras and Plato by indicating that man is the measure of all things *that man experiences*. The *noumenon* is to be understood negatively, an inescapable corollary of phenomenal thought.[17] Hamann performs a similar move – anthropomorphism is not absurd in discourse about God because God speaks to man in a language that man can understand, first in the language of the senses, then in the figural language of scripture.[18] What human beings can cognize is determined by their limited capacities. At base, just as Kant can point to formal structures that make experience possible, so too can Hamann, with less precision but equal plausibility, point to the structure of logos as the foundation of all thought.[19]

Consider, for instance, the manner in which Hamann justifies the anthropomorphic elements in scripture with this anthropocentric epistemology: 'Because the tools of language are, at least, a gift of the alma mater nature, … and because … the creator of these artificial tools also wanted, and needed to, install their use, then the origin of human language is indeed divine. But if a higher being, or an angel, as with Bileam's [Balaam's] donkey, wants to work through our tongues, then all such effects, like the talking animals in Aesop's fables, must express themselves in a manner analogical to human nature, and in this relation can neither the origin of language nor yet its progress be and appear to be anything but human.'[20]

In this passage (occurring in the context of Hamann's *Streit* with Herder over the origin of languages) Hamann reconciles the divine and the human by insisting on the necessity of divine condescension for human comprehension. Again, 'Everything divine is also human, for man can neither work nor suffer save according to the analogy of his nature … This *communicatio* of divine and human *idiomatum* is a fundamental law and the main key to all our cognition and the entire visible economy.'[21] There is a communicative structure of human experience that conditions all of our cognition.

What Hamann was doing was akin to what a great deal of post-Kantian philosophy has attempted. Radicalizing the Kantian transcendental method, one locates thought in the world.[22] Kant himself was wary of emphasizing the subjectivist implications of his thought because he sought to rest philosophy on firm foundations. Once one makes the Hamannian charge that Kant has merely taken some elements artificially severed from experience, rendered them abstract, and then hypostatized this abstraction, one undermines the foundational solidity of knowledge that Kant so desperately sought. (The social and political implications of this move will be addressed in the next chapter.) What appears on one level to be an ad hominem refutation of the Kantian system emerges, on another level, as an extension of the transcendental method. Hamann begins from a shared world of experience and, through highlighting one aspect of experience – our receptivity to language – leads to a set of remarkable conclusions that can be seen as themselves conditions for experience. Hamann's view renders the anthropomorphism that is so central to mythical thought a perfectly rational basis for reflection on nature. The Hamannian 'Copernican' turn paradoxically leads back to Ptolemy!

It is for this reason that Hamann grew so irate at his friend Herder's attempt to locate the 'origin' of language. The very question of the origin of language, this question that sparked such speculative anthropological writing as that of Rousseau and Condillac, was, in Hamann's view, artificial since creation itself *was* language (or so we logos-beings must experience it), and the entirety of human cognition is based on the capacity for communion. To conceive of a human being without language was, for Hamann, the equivalent of conceiving of a human being without the capacity to eat or drink.[23]

Hamann inverts Kant's purism, offering a purism of his own: sensory and emotional reception has not merely epistemological priority, but greater ontological significance.[24] Now, if Hamann is correct in his ad hominem, if Kant is indeed arbitrarily focusing on certain elements of experience, we might equally turn this polemic on Hamann himself. But here the champion of faith needs not answer, since he does not take his theological premises as propositions capable of being refuted or accepted philosophically. 'The ground of religion lies in our entire existence and outside of the sphere of our powers of knowledge, which taken altogether make up the most contingent and abstract *modum* of our existence.'[25] Hamann's argument is not to be taken as establishing through transcendental argument the a priori necessity of the idea of God: Hamann certainly did not believe that he had proven the existence of God. As far as argument goes, Hamann offers a claim about the linguistic structure to human cognition. The subsequent claim that *all* sensory experience is to be interpreted as we interpret language is not one that can be established by argument: Hamann's insistence on faith is, in this respect, clearly extra- if not anti-philosophical.[26]

Let us recall Hamann's discussion of the 'genealogical priority' of the musical sound of breathing and the pulse (*Metakritik*, paragraph 10) or his emphasis in the *Aesthetica* on the passionate and sensory nature of poetic language. Logos underlies existence: 'The first appearance and the first enjoyment of nature are united in the words, Let there be light! With this began the sensation [*Empfindung*] of the presence of things.'[27] Creation is an 'address to the creature through the creature.'[28] 'All that man in the beginning heard, saw with his eyes, contemplated, and touched with his hands was a living word: for God was the word.'[29] Human language itself is a poor imitation of this word (and, as we've seen, it gets poorer the more it distances itself from its sensory origins), but it is the image of it. This underlying treatment of existence as communication assumes a linguistic structure to experience. Thus, while there is no a priori in the sense of something that can be known outside of experience, we can treat existence itself as obeying certain principles – a grammar, if you will – of communication. The fundamental basis of human cognition is our receptivity to communication – we are capable of experiencing the world only as we do in a social and communicative horizon. Our ability to think is thus dependent on the mystery of language.

But if these two meta-theoretical positions (Kantian a priorism and Hamann's language principle) rest on a similar 'Copernican' move, there are clearly radical differences entailed in transcendental philosophy and philological faith. In the following chapter, we will turn, somewhat pragmatically, to the implications for practical philosophy of these different Copernican turns. The significance of Hamann's confrontation with Kant goes well beyond the speculative boundaries of epistemological questions. Hamann's personification of nature, his re-enchantment of the world, and his treatment of the entirety of existence as a *communicative* act utterly transform our understanding of self, community, and duty. The following chapter attempts to flesh out these differences by comparing Hamann and Kant on concepts central to Kantian moral philosophy.

5 The Ideas of God and the Person

For the purposes of political thought, Kant is most stimulating for his positive doctrines. The *KrV* is largely a negative book – one intent on limiting and separating the faculties such that they do not overstep their bounds. However, the purpose of this procedure is to overcome the sceptical objections to the most concerned matters of metaphysical inquiry: 'God, freedom, and immortality.'[1] These are what Kant terms 'Ideas,' and they are of supreme *practical* importance. In political philosophy, freedom and its related concepts of personality and autonomy are perhaps the most persistent Kantian ideas, the stock and trade of many who don't feel compelled to honour their philosophical basis in the first *Critique*. Kant's politics – and the political implications of Hamann's meta-critique – hang on these transcendental ideas, these 'concepts of reason' 'transcending the possibility of experience.'[2]

The purpose of this chapter is to illustrate the different implications of the Hamannian logos and the Kantian a priori by comparing the two writers' respective treatments of these concepts central to Kantian practical philosophy. My aim is to show the stark contrast between these two views and their social implications. We will begin with the most obvious point of difference between the two authors: their respective views of God. We will then proceed to other contentious 'ideas,' particularly human personality. Kant will be accused of excessive boldness and excessive reticence toward essential matters like the nature of the soul. Kant is excessively reticent in denying speculative reason any knowledge of the soul; he is bold in granting a priori certainty to the moral laws and the dignity of the person.

The Divine Idea

What should already be clear from our exegesis of the *Metakritik* is the degree to which Hamann thought Kant's view to be impious dogmatism. This is a curious position, given that radical freethinkers have always tended to portray Kant as a religious throwback. Nonetheless, the briefest consideration of Kant's idea of God should indicate the basis for Hamann's antipathy. The *KrV* provides a thorough critique of theodicy that, we have noted, Hamann appreciated. However, it does not do so with fideistic intent, but rather in order to free up the space for the God of practical reason.[3] God as an idea is a concept that is self-sufficient but is wholly noumenal; it cannot be represented as an object (to attempt to do so is the fundamental error of rational theologians). Transcendental ideas, for Kant, can determine transcendental *ideals*, regulative, practical principles.[4] God, 'the ideal of the supreme being,' is 'nothing but a regulative principle of reason, which directs us to look upon all connection in the world *as if* it originated from an all-sufficient necessary cause.'[5] If one wishes to insist upon a personal God, Kant is somewhat tolerant, but we ought not to forget that this is a *mere* metaphor: 'We may freely, without laying ourselves open to censure, admit into this idea certain anthropomorphisms which are helpful to the principle in its regulative capacity. For it is always an idea only, which does not relate directly to a being distinct from the world ... What this primordial ground of the unity of the world may be in itself, we should not profess to have thereby decided, but only how we should use it, or rather its idea, in relation to the systematic employment of reason in respect of things in this world.'[6] God is a useful idea for moral beings. He is a hypothesis that follows from the moral law. His actual existence may not be considered, being outside the possibility of thought; he is a postulate of morality. Indeed, we cannot imagine God as having willed the moral law; rather, the moral law is reason itself, and the idea of God follows from it, lending it a majesty and authority.[7]

We need not enter into detailed exegesis of Hamann to see how difficult it is to reconcile this God with the God of Christianity. Like Socrates in the *Euthyphro*, Kant strips away God's will, being a mere contingency compared to universal reason itself. The Christian God also loses his historical existence, his personal concern, his forgiveness, and all the other determinative aspects upon which the New Testament insists. The result is a rational principle of morality even emptier than the God of Voltairean deists, who at least is the objective cause of the universe.[8] The degree to which Kant's God was offensive to Hamann ought to be self-evident. An ideal is a creation of the mind, not a palpable presence.[9] 'Kant makes God into an ideal,' he wrote to Jacobi, 'without realizing that it is rather his pure reason that is one.'[10]

The Soul and the Person

If Kant's God was an abstract nobody, his moral theory upon which this God rested was thoroughly un-Hamannian, given Kant's Pelagian insistence on self-justification through the good will. Upon reading the *Groundwork of the Metaphysics of Morals*, Hamann was, as expected, irate. He wrote to Herder, 'Instead of pure reason, the talk here is of another idol and phantom of the brain: the good will. That Kant is one of our sharpest minds must be admitted even by his enemy, but sadly! his cleverness is his evil daemon, just as with Lessing; for a new Scholasticism and a new Popery are the two Midas-ears of our ruling *Seculi*.'[11] Let us, then, consider the practical differences between Hamannian logos and Kantian a priori by exploring their different conceptions of the person, its autonomy and its dignity.

The nub of Hamann's disagreement with Kant is the relationship between the universal and the particular, the unconditioned and the conditioned. For Kant, the myriad particular experiences of a given person or of different people are more than simply arbitrary points, but are granted a universal justification a priori in the (subjective) forms of time and space and the categories of the understanding. We have seen that Hamann considers Kant's a priori to emerge from language, something necessarily a posteriori. He holds fast to the Berkeleyan-Humean view of abstract terms having their basis in simple sense impressions – thus Kant's universals are mere inductions. But for Hamann, the myriad impressions experienced by the subject are not essentially disconnected – these impressions are themselves a type of word, thus implying, as we have seen, that experience itself has a structure akin to the structure of language. Human experience (even the simplest of simple impressions) is necessarily mediated; the word is the basis for coherent experience. But who is the one hearing the word? How does the Hamannian subject differ from the Kantian?

Hume had left the problem of a subject in a rather difficult place. The 'self,' he contended, was not some substance of which we had certain experience (as in Descartes), but was rather an inference from our myriad experiences. The 'self' is but a 'bundle or collection of different perceptions,'[12] or a 'succession of perceptions.'[13] There is no impression, Hume was convinced, from which we can extract the idea of a 'self.' Hume destroyed all notions unconnected to impressions and all necessary links between particular impressions, and thus the self as an abstract, distinct entity disappeared with them. Yet this point is somewhat perplexing, as he continued to employ metaphors such as the following: 'The mind is a kind of theatre, where several perceptions successively make their appearance.'[14] And despite attempting to avoid the repercussions of the metaphor by insisting that we do not have 'the most distant notion of the place where these scenes are represented,' he nonetheless gave the impression of some incomprehensible entity bearing witness to representations. Yet this is a notion that he regarded as untenable, arguing that 'the identity which we ascribe to the mind of man is only a fictitious one.'[15] The greatest ambiguity attends Hume's discussion of personal identity. He eventually suggested that there is a single memory that possesses the power of creating – or, rather, discovering – the notion of personal identity. But then is the 'self' simply a synonym for 'memory'? Hume canvasses the question of whether identity is a fictitious invention or a discovery, noting that we do not possess a distinct memory of certain days but that we assert with confidence that *we* existed on those days. Thus, identity appears to 'extend ... beyond our memory.'[16] If there was a self to be discovered, Hume recognized that he would have to do more than merely identify it as memory. But if the self is merely a fiction 'created' by the mind, he would have to explain who is doing the creating, if anyone at all. Ultimately, he suggested that the question of identity (both personal identity and the identity of 'connected objects') was 'merely verbal' rather than philosophical (an interesting statement, given Hamann's later assertion that all philosophy can be reduced to 'grammar'). This is the type of perplexity that led Hume to heavy backgammon playing.[17]

Kant was not content with the place in which the subject had been left by empirical psychology such as that given by Hume, or with the rational psychology such as that provided by Descartes (or Leibniz, or Mendelssohn). Kant's famous but illusive response to the problem of the self was to term it 'transcendental apperception,' arguing (to simplify drastically) that we cannot have experience without an experiencer. Kant approached the problem of how it is that the manifold of impressions can somehow be synthesized into a unified experience (instead of being a mere random series of events). After discussing ways in which this manifold is synthesized by sense and imagination, Kant indicates the underlying, 'transcendental' ground of this action: the unity of self-consciousness or 'transcendental apperception.' Apperception is transcendental because it is prior to experience and necessary for experience. Unified experience exists – Kant assumes this point.[18] Experience is composed of myriad sense impressions – this Humean contention is never seriously questioned by Kant either. It follows that there could be no unified experience without something that unifies the various impressions: 'All necessity, without exception, is grounded in a transcendental condition. There must, therefore, be a transcendental ground of the unity of consciousness in the synthesis of the manifold of all our intuitions, and consequently also of the concepts of objects in general, and so of all objects of experience, a ground without which it would be impossible to think any object for our intuitions.'[19] We are not to understand this 'self-consciousness' in the sense in which we normally use the word – as an actual awareness of our inner experience. Such an inner sense would be empirical and changeable. The 'I' of apperception is a priori: 'This pure original unchangeable consciousness I shall name *transcendental* apperception.'[20] This is not thought of as unitary through any empirical evidence: it is necessarily unitary and prior to experience. No coherent representations could exist without a subject, for 'the abiding and unchanging "I" (pure apperception) forms the correlate of all our representations.'[21]

Without the 'I' there would be no representations. Thus, by transcendental argument, it is a priori. In addition to being a priori, the 'I' is empty of content (it is merely a formal necessity, after all). Thus, we cannot say anything definite about the 'I' because it is pure logical unity. It accompanies, precedes, and makes possible all thought. Empiricist attempts to derive a substantive account of the self or soul from experiences are bound to fail, for we do not experience the self, but rather, the 'I' makes experience possible. Kant thinks equally little of rational accounts of the soul as an immaterial, simple substance: there is a logical flaw in philosophical attempts to derive substantiality from the premise of the unity of apperception. In his 'paralogisms of pure reason' he indicates that all these attempts to make concrete claims about the self overstep the bounds of our knowledge.[22] The 'I,' which is merely the logical subject of any judgment, can be represented only as a 'transcendental subject of thoughts = x.'[23] The basic error of rationalist metaphysics is to confuse the formal, logical identity of the subject in 'I think' with the numerical identity of some discernable object known as the 'soul' or 'the self.'[24]

But if Kant denies that we can make the leap from transcendental apperception to the ontological doctrine of personality – if the 'person' is not something proven by speculative reason – he insists with equal force that the 'person' has an importance in speculative philosophy and is an essential concept for practical philosophy. For speculative philosophy, the notion of the soul is a 'regulative idea.'[25] What Kant means by this is that certain ideas (such as the soul, the cosmos, and God) are not knowable in any sense because they refer to things outside of our experience, but they useful for 'directing the understanding to a particular end.'[26] 'In conformity with these ideas as principles we shall, *first*, in psychology, under the guidance of inner experience, connect all the appearances, all the actions and receptivity of our mind, *as if* the mind were a simple substance which persists with personal identity (in this life at least), while its states, to which those of the body belong only as outer conditions, are in continual change.'[27]

As we have seen with the idea of God, such ideas are not merely helpful speculatively (so long as one does not treat these ideas as objects in themselves), but they are essential practically.[28] The thing of which we have been denied speculative knowledge is granted practical significance. The significance of the person is spelled out more clearly in the *Kritik der praktischen Vernunft (KpV)*, where Kant explains that the *noumenal* self, the rational, free person, is the bearer of autonomy and the end of moral action. Personality, defined as 'the freedom and independence from the mechanism of the entirety of nature,'[29] is the noumenal, rational aspect of the self that bears the responsibility of acting morally. The 'person,' as a rational being, ought to be treated as an end in itself.[30]

Kant, then, denies our knowledge of the self, rendering it, as Hamann so derisively put it, 'an unsteady, ruttish something = x,' yet at the same time he raises this non-object, this mere logical necessity, to the level of the absolute end in our moral considerations. The 'I' is a formal necessity, and it cannot be known, but, as a 'person,' it is an idea deserving the utmost respect. Rational and autonomous, a person must never be treated as a means only, but also as an end in itself. Epistemological limits are overcome by practical necessities.[31] Kant does not reconcile the distinction between the unconditioned, universal and the conditioned, particular; rather, he treats them as two different aspects of the same thing, aspects that ought not to be confounded. The separation of noumena and phenomena, then, not only allows one to escape a tricky set of antinomies, but also to separate moral from speculative thought.

Hamann did not approve of Kant's move in its moral or its speculative manifestation. He disapproved of Kant's reduction of the self to an empty, unknowable formalism, and he rejected the practical concept of person as exceeding our bounds. Kant was, in his speculative moment, too humble, and, in his moral and political moments, entirely too bold. He was too humble in denying the possibility of self-knowledge, and too bold in granting quasi-divine dignity to human reason. Let us begin by considering Hamann's response to the speculative question. If, as Hamann wrote, '*sensus* ist das *Principium* alles *intellectus*,'[32] what can be said about the location in which the *sensus* is organized and cognized? What could he offer to replace Kant's something = X?

At the centre of the Hamannian subject is an individual soul that shares in the divine nature: 'He [God] created man in his image, in the image of God did he create him – we are of his race.'[33] And lest we think that this divinity on which man's inner self is patterned is a pure abstraction, we ought to recall Hamann's strong vindication of anthropomorphism.[34] Kantian persons are terribly impersonal; Hamannian souls are conceived entirely in terms borrowed from their changing, corporeal world. Hamann considers self-knowledge the supreme spiritual task and both a 'hellish journey' and a source of revelation precisely because we contain both the divine nature *and* the sinful, fallen nature of man inside us.[35] What is ruled out by Kant on epistemological grounds – self-knowledge – is the most important moral duty, both to ourselves and others. 'Self-knowledge and self-love are the true measure of our knowledge and love of human beings.'[36] Charity – love of one's neighbour – is based on the recognition of a fundamental likeness among all people.

As radically different as this is from Kant, it does appear to be a move towards universality through abstraction. If charity and the love of neighbour are founded on a fundamental identification between people as possessors of the divine spark, how can we understand Hamann's particularism? Further, if human cognition rests entirely upon the communicative nature of existence, is there not an original order hovering behind all human thought? Indeed there is: Hamann replaced the forms or ideas of the philosophers with something called 'language.' But the theological underpinnings of logos alter its content. I will be suggesting that there is a difference between the questions, what is it? and, who am I? just as there is a difference between the treatment of the universal as a regulative and practical idea and the acceptance of God as an ever-present interlocutor and commander.

But for all this, it remains unclear how we are to bridge Hamann's spiritual view of the soul and God – the divine pattern within and its source – with his empiricist premises. If there is nothing inside – if he wished to take the Lockean route and deny innate ideas – how could he insist on essential personality? If he were a thorough empiricist, should he not be as perplexed as Hume? More to the point here, how does the Christian soul differ from Kant's inscrutable transcendental subject? Hamann wrote, 'Granted then also that man came into the world as an empty sack: so does this very lack make him more capable of an enjoyment of nature through experiences and of community with his kind through tradition. Our reason, at the very least, emerges from this two-fold education of sensory revelations and human witnesses, which are communicated through similar means, namely markers [Merkmale], and according to similar laws.'[37] The Lockean blank slate or 'empty sack' is filled with experience, but we get a sense that the sack is not entirely empty in that it is both capable of desire and 'enjoyment' (*Genuß*), as well as reception of language.[38] The world is a series of markers by which God communicates with us (filling our empty sack of a self) in the same way that human witnesses communicate tradition, language, and, ultimately, scripture. But the laws of communication and the fact of our capacity to receive are pre-established by God: we can be filled because God has given us this hunger. What exists 'prior' is the desire for communication, the passionate hunger for communion. When Hamann stresses *Genuß* and *Empfindung*, when he writes that 'looks and kisses of love, this eloquent passion, serve as a universal dictionary,'[39] he indicates the degree to which he understands existence as communication and communication as passion. Kisses are words; the world is a dictionary.

But this might still be taken as akin to the Kantian model muddied with the language of passion and the personification of nature. Hamann's soul, after all, appears to perform the function of Kant's transcendental apperception. Can it therefore be conceived of as a formal principle entirely devoid of changing, worldly elements? Hamann's response is clearly, *no*. There can be nothing conceived outside of experience, and thus the mind ought not to strive to conceive in this way: it is experience for which we thirst. Logical formalities 'necessary for experience' are simply abstract descriptions *of* experience. The philosophical priority that Kant ascribes to the transcendental realm is simply misconceived – what Kant is really doing, the *Metakritik* argues, is describing experience in terms whose abstractness gives them a deceptive air of virginity. Hamann wrote of the soul, 'Just as man was made in the image of God, so too does the body appear to be a figure or picture of the soul.'[40] The body is a sign referring to something unseen and essentially invisible. The imagination somehow makes sense of experience because experience is communicated through the 'angelic language' of sense.[41] Analogy is 'man's surest guide below' because concrete, sensory experience is to be taken as akin to a metaphor.[42]

But if the physical body is analogous to the soul, what *is* the soul? This appears to be the Kantian thing-in-itself radicalized. We continue to have an unclear indication of what it is that the first person pronoun *I* represents and Hamann indicates that this 'I' can be referred to only obliquely. Yet here we see that the term *represents* is problematic. As Charles Taylor notes, the medieval view of the world as divine language is opposed to the understanding of language as a representative placing of 'word x' for 'object y.' In this medieval view, 'there can be no more fundamentally designative relation, precisely because everything is a sign ... For words can only have designative meaning if there is something else, other than words or signs, which they designate.'[43] Ultimately, what this view of language does is to undermine language's distinctiveness, for everything becomes a reference. Taylor indicates that this view was cogent for medieval Christians because they were essentially Neoplatonists, treating the ultimate referent as something unseen – the Ideas, Forms, or God.[44] Now Hamann often indulged in anti-Platonic polemic – when he was wrangling with Herder over the origin of language, he charged his friend with Platonism, equating this with Swedenborg and mysticism,[45] and, more to the point for this chapter, he accused Kant of Platonic 'idealism' and 'enthusiasm.'[46] Nonetheless, Hamann shows himself to be very much in this tradition of Christian Neoplatonism when he writes, 'Every appearance in Nature was a Word – the sign, sensory picture, and pledge of a new, secret, unspeakable but thus more profound unification, communication and community of divine ideas and energies. Everything that man heard in the beginning, saw with his eyes, beheld and felt with his hands, was a living Word; for God was the Word.'[47] Plato would have had little time for this personification of being and the good, just as Hamann's prime target was the crystalline perfection of the philosopher's truth, but they both held the view that experience participated in some wider meaning that was invisible to the senses.[48]

Hamann's linguistic determinism, his appeal to everyday language, and his insistence on the untranslatable, unique nature of human languages are in tension with his theological assumption of a unifying meaning understood through the metaphor of the divine Logos. The abstract exists for us only in the concrete. Hamann did not undermine this opposition between the universal/divine and the temporal/human, nor did he attempt to overcome it like Kant by treating ontology and morality as separate realms; he embraced it as Christianity's supreme paradox. This occupied him throughout his life, and he came to think that the paradox itself was essential. He termed it the 'coincidence of opposites,' writing that the 'principium coincidentiae oppositorum is worth more in my eyes than all Kantian critique.'[49] The divine entry into history is an example of the paradox; so too is God's taking of human form.

We employ words; language has an abstract nature. The divine Logos is general, eternal; experience is particular and temporal. Human words have both elements, the universal and the particular. The Enlightenment seeks to purify words of their particularisms such that one is left with pure universalism. This, Hamann was arguing, goes precisely in the wrong direction. Just as we can know God only from behind, so can we only approach the universal with the particular. The Enlightenment's purifications are self-defeating: in principle, they lead to a purity beyond expression (the 'third purification' discussed in our exegetical third chapter). Rather than trying to raise ourselves to more and more abstract concepts, we ought to prize the concreteness of poetic expression. The mundane, understood as divine poetry, is transfigured. Recall his claim that the 'communicatio of divine and human idiomatum is a basic law and the main key of all our knowledge.'[50] The divine condescension – the use of human idiom – is the reason that we can make sense of religious speech. The notion of divine condescension maintains eternal truth external to the receiving person: what is beyond human understanding is expressed in analogies drawn from human experience. 'For this reason has Protagoras already called man mensuram omnium rerum,' wrote Hamann.[51] (Naturally, it is not for this reason in the least that Protagoras thus expressed himself!)

The universal – the realm we associate with undetermined Platonic ideas – is thus not eliminated in Hamann's thought, but is transformed. The anti-ontological extreme of some linguistic philosophy tends to treat the realm of being as a fiction cobbled together with language (one might think of Rorty's invocation of 'jargon' as an example of this view). For Hamann, Plato's dualism does not disappear, but the higher realm remains inaccessible to conceptual assault. Nothing absolute is accessible to thought without mediation, communication. 'Original being is truth; revealed is grace.'[52] On the speculative level, Kant had denied any access at all to such knowledge; on the practical level he had proposed airtight definitions. The second reached too far for Hamann, while the first did not reach far enough.[53] When Hamann spoke of the 'heaven and hell within' and of the quest for self-knowledge as a pious *Höllenfahrt* he clearly thought that there was a soul to explore. The soul is both a mystery and an essential fact.[54]

One might be tempted to reject this mystery as a mere escape from philosophical difficulties. Like a dramatist who brings in a God to pull his characters out of a lion's pit, Hamann, we might complain, offers a facile exit from trouble. This misses the importance of the problem, however. Mystery is conceptually coupled with revelation. Kant's thing-in-itself is by definition absolutely unknowable – the very notion of thinking it in objective terms is the source of error. For Hamann, this is an unacceptably strict separation. Hamann's position is much closer to the Platonic view that the ideas 'participate' in the world of becoming.[55] If we are to *interpret* history, nature, and human actions we must assume the existence of meaning external to these actions. But Hamann rejects the possibility of a dialectical ascent from the sensory realm just as he rejects the view that being is a realm of ideas. Indeed, it is Kant's 'Platonic' error to have made God, the soul, and the world into mere ideas.[56] Philosophic speculation and religious reception must conflict. To invoke mystery is not to abandon the duty of thinking, but rather to challenge thought's possibilities. Whether or not mystery is a cogent idea is one of the most important problems for thought.

The Soul in Community: Dignity, Autonomy

For Hamann, then, the metaphorical, sensory basis of cognition cannot be overcome. 'Because the mystery of the marriage between so opposed natures as the outer and the inner man [Mensch], or body and soul, is so great, earthly signs are required to reach a graspable concept of our human essence's fullness and unity.'[57] We look for clues in the phenomenal realm, which is the only realm to which we have access. This entails thought that draws analogies from sensory experience.

The necessity to look outside of oneself, to the empirical world has important moral implications. With regards to self-knowledge, we cannot remain with solipsistic introspection: 'In every neighbour my self is visible as in a mirror ... God and my neighbour belong therefore to my self-knowledge, to my self-love.'[58] If both Hamann and Kant reject the speculative overreaching of reason in theological and psychological realms, Hamann accuses Kant of having abandoned the all-consuming problem of self-knowledge on the one hand while at the same time extending his moral claims to extreme ends with his 'newest critique and politics.'[59] As he put it in a letter to Jacobi, 'To err is human – but our *infallible* philosophers aspire to a more than human authority, and thus fall into transcendental ignorance and folly.'[60]

Kant's noumenal self is, as we noted above, entirely free: it is un-determined by the changing world of phenomena, but can act purely on the basis of reason. The most essential fact about human beings is our capacity to act as free, rational, autonomous agents. 'A *person* is a subject whose actions can be *imputed* to him. *Moral* personality is there-fore nothing other than the freedom of a rational being under moral laws (whereas psychological personality is merely the ability to be con-scious of one's identity in different conditions of one's existence).'[61] Moral personality, defined in terms of rational capacity, is the core of man's humanity, and is what grants him the dignity to be treated as an end in himself. The famous formulation in the *Groundwork* bears re-peating: 'Act in such a way that you always treat humanity, whether in your own person or in the person of any other, never simply as a means, but always at the same time as an end.'[62] The rationality of one's *person* – one's capacity for rational self-legislation and obedience to the moral law – is essentially worthy of respect.

That rational autonomy could be rendered perfectly compatible with authoritarian politics is clear in Kant's *Rechtslehre*, and Hamann hit on a significant point when he exclaimed, 'What use are the ceremonial robes of freedom when I am in a slave's rags at home[?]'[63] (Keen readers of Kant will note, in our chapters on Mendelssohn, the degree to which much of Hamann's response to Mendelssohn's *Jerusalem* applies equal-ly well to Kant's *Doctrine of Right*, particularly to Kant's separation of justice and virtue). But the idea itself of an autonomous person with inherent dignity due to his or her (or *its*) rational nature was itself prob-lematic for Hamann.

There is a basic similarity in Kant and Hamann's mutual attribution to man of holy and sinful elements. Kant wrote, 'Man is indeed unholy enough, but the humanity in his person must be holy to him.'[64] Yet there is a radical difference between claiming the divinity of the person on the basis of its rational autonomy and claiming that there is an in-comprehensible gift of divinity in the human soul. Kant exhibits much greater moral rigour than Hamann, but for Hamann this self-divinization of our rational capacities – the essential dignity of the moral person – was the product of a damnable pride. Our dignity is not dependent on any qualities we might possess. 'Now, this [human] dignity, like all honours, presumes no inner worthiness or merit for our nature, but is, like this last, an immediate gift of grace from the great all-giver.'[65]

Dignity, then, is essentially a question of divine grace, something conferred on us by an external power, not something essential to us through an intellectual capacity. Just as Hamann was unwilling to ac-cept the separation of pure intuition and pure reason from their empir-ical base, so too did he reject this postulate of essentially dignified moral personality. Heteronomous psychological personality (to use Kant's terms) was the only personality that Hamann recognized. 'Pure reason and good will still remain for me mere words whose concept I am in no condition to attain with my senses, and for philosophy I have no *fidem implicitam*. I must therefore await the revelation of these mysteries with patience.'[66] Since the separate noumenal realm is a mere product of ana-lytical artifice, the ideals of personality, autonomy, and the pure moral law can have just as little purchase.

Hamann's attack on our essential dignity has a certain bleakness, lacking the certitude of the Kantian person's moral claim. But the Kantian person is tied to a particular mental faculty and is thus on shakier ground that it might at first appear. Kant insists that the prin-ciple of the moral law is within, but it can be lost through vicious actions. Someone indulging his carnal appetites 'surrenders his person ality,' a drunk is 'not to be treated as a human being,' and the teller of a lie 'throws away and, as it were, annihilates his dignity as a human be-ing.' He has 'less worth than if he were a mere thing.'[67] Since Hamann conceives of man as essentially sinful but granted dignity by a divinely conferred grace, he affords little room for such rigorous withdrawal of human status from sinners.

Hamann underlines the significance of human sinfulness and one's capacity to say with David, 'I am a worm, and no man.'[68] He follows this humble lamentation with a truncated account of liberty that sounds very much like Kantian autonomy. Man, he says, is at liberty to sin (otherwise there would be no knowledge of good and evil). 'Freedom is the maximum and minimum of all our natural powers, and both the basic impetus and the final end of their entire direction, development, and return. Thus, neither instinct nor *sensus communis* determine humans; neither do natural right nor the right of nations determine the prince.'[69] People are free to act in a despotic manner; this is an ambivalent capacity: 'Are reason and freedom not the most noble gifts of humanity and both at the same time the sources of all moral evil?'[70] If Hamann can sound Kantian with the quip 'Everyone is his own lawgiver,' he is quick to add, 'but he is at the same time the first-born and neighbour of his subjects.'[71] Paradoxically, human freedom entails dependency and even subjection. Kant's call to rational autonomy is the radical antithesis of this freedom, which is extra-rational and heteronomous. Consider Hamann's reaction to Jacobi's stormy and stressful character *Woldemar*: 'The ideal of his autonomy is perhaps too superior for my weakened nervous system that finds more certainty and peace in a happy dependency. This favourite hero [of yours] appears to me almost to belong to that class of beings that would like to join an unlimited independence or raw nature to the delights of social life.'[72] The proud autonomy of the Jacobian or Rousseauan hero is incompatible with the receptive and dependent conception of man as a communicative being. Human freedom exists, but it is realized only in social and communicative context. 'Without the complete law of freedom man would be incapable of any imitation, on which depends both all education and invention; for man is by nature the greatest pantomime of all the animals.'[73]

For all his apparent autonomy, man is entirely dependent for his reason and morality on tradition and revelation. This is due to the heteronomous, sensual origin of his cognition: 'The *stamina* and *menstrua* of our reason are thus correctly understood as revelation and traditions that we take as our property, transform in our fluids and forces, and through which we grow to our telos [Bestimmung], the critical and architectonic dignity of a political animal, partly to reveal and partly to pass on.'[74] Human beings are essentially imitative, our knowledge is supplied by our traditions, and our purpose is found in community. We receive and pass on. I have translated *Bestimmung* as 'telos' to give the intended Aristotelian flavour to this passage. Hamann, indeed, cites from the *Politics* 1.2 on the question of man's linguistic/political nature (1253a 9–18).[75] We are constituted by our linguistic community and we find our purpose within this community. Both in terms of teleology and of one's dependency on externals, Hamann indicates a certain limited affinity with the Aristotelian tradition.

Naturally, however, his real source is biblical: man is a servant, a neighbour, and a king of the earth.[76] He cites Corinthians 3:9, 'For we are labourers together with God: ye are God's husbandry, ye are God's building.' Hamann and Kant both think that man partakes of divine nature, but Hamann indicates that there is an essential distinction between the 'self-idolatry' (*Selbstabgötterey*)[77] or the self-deification of the 'I' ('*ihr Ich, durch die Abstraktion zur allgemeinen Vernunft vergöttert*')[78] and the claim that God made man in his image. The latter is conferred, the former self-designated. Kantian persons have absolute dignity; Hamannian people gain their dignity from external sources. Kantian persons have an absolute, abstract duty to all other persons based on an imperative that derives its force from a concept of a supreme being. Hamannian people have duties to particular people and attain their essential nature in their communities.[79]

One scholar of Kant, defending Kant's 'teleological' treatment of persons as ends in themselves, suggests that this can be understood in the language of Martin Buber: 'Every rational being is always a "Thou" never an "It."'[80] On the contrary, however, every rational being is, for speculative reason, a 'transcendental subject = x,' not a 'thou'; for practical reason it is a 'person,' a pure concept. It may be that Buber slips into the type of abstraction that is amenable to Kant (I leave the question aside), but Kant is clear that abstract personality, the bearer of dignity, is an entirely a priori practical principle. Indeed, to be motivated by love or fear for anyone in particular is characterized by Kant as 'pathological,' not moral.[81] Hamann writes, 'He who would see men walk as if they are trees and wants to see shadows of the mountains as people trusts the eye of a rogue or has no desire to open a healthy eye properly.'[82] Hamann's allusions (from Mark 8:24 and Judges 9:36) are playful,[83] but his meaning is the following: to communicate with someone is to ask *who* he or she is (*Rede, daß ich dich sehe*), in particular. Respect for persons in the abstract not only rests on a dubious epistemological basis, but also runs counter to Hamann's moral intuitions. 'Sociability is the true *principium* of reason and language.'[84] The Hamannian self is not conceivable in static, objective terms. It is something that exists and grows in conversation. Knowledge of this dynamic being is perpetually out of our grasp, yet passionate attention to others can help us approach the elusive goal. This attention to the changing, historical, phenomenal world is thus both an epistemological and moral imperative.

The relationship between the divine and the human, the undetermined and the determined, the free and the foreordained is for Hamann one of mystery, which is naturally unsatisfying to philosophy. Hamann nowhere resolves these paradoxes, but rather embraces them. Human beings are essentially sinful, yet made in the divine image. Hamann harps on the first in response to the Enlightenment's celebration of humanity and its natural goodness; he harps on the second in response to the objectification of human beings. But what is important is his complete inversion of the Kantian view that the free and divine is ideal or rational. Hamann, it is true, conceives of a kind of supersensible meaning, but he sees this meaning as something embodied in nature. The word of God is embodied in experienced nature and in scripture, which itself is composed of human words and historical events. All of this is phenomenal. If there is a mystery in the transition from the human to the divine, the divine is not to be conceived as disembodied reason. Hamann thus overturns a long tradition in Christian thought – a tradition that is secularized in Kant – of perceiving the body as sinful. Evil is a product of the intellect, not the body.[85] 'How revolting man would probably be if his body did not keep him within limits!'[86]

This insistence on the centrality of the body naturally entails a reassessment of the passions (a subject we will discuss in the concluding chapter), human needs, and the externals. The self-love and emotional commitments that Kant decries as pathological are treated by Hamann as the basis of morality. Self-love is an essential part of the divine command to love one's neighbour as oneself. Kant interprets the Christian law thus: 'Perform your duty for no motive other than unconditioned esteem for duty itself, *i.e.*, love God (the Legislator of all duties) above all else; and … Love every one as yourself, *i.e.*, further his welfare from good-will that is immediate and not derived from motives of self-advantage.'[87]

Hamann's treatment of the same issue is as follows: 'Just as all of our cognitive capacities have as object self-knowledge, so do our inclinations and desires have self-love [as their object]. The first is our wisdom, the last our virtue.'[88] But self-knowledge is possible only through knowing others, as is self-love through the love of others. 'What a law, what a delightful lawgiver, who order us to love him with our whole heart and to love our neighbour as ourselves. This is the true and only self-love of man.'[89] For Kant, no external can alter the nature of virtue and the moral person; for Hamann our essential nature and our virtues reside in these relations that Kant would have seen as contingent. 'If I want to fathom my own self, it is not merely a question of what man is, but also, what is his condition? Are you free or a slave? Are you a minor, an orphan, a widow?'[90]

Hamann's thought retains the individualism that accompanies Protestant inwardness while at the same time conceiving of that individual soul inseparably from the socio-linguistic world that constitutes it. Human language determines our patterns of cognition. The linguistic source of cognition grants priority to communal existence. To paraphrase Aristotle, the linguistic community precedes the individual and the household. This dialogical principle is granted an ontological foundation in the concept of a divine Logos, of which human language is a somewhat foggy mirror.

Kantian morality follows the basic premise of the *Critique of Pure Reason*, separating the external, experiential from the rationally pure realm of the a priori. In so doing, it claims the right (and indeed the duty) to legislate for all. For Hamann, this cordoning-off of an a priori realm was an arbitrary act with no epistemological justification. Its effect was to render an abstract self its own deity and to suppress all the considerations in which real, fleshly people find meaning. History, naturally, is swept away, as are all determinate relationships and all contingencies. This rendered Kant's critical philosophy the crowning achievement of a century's battle against the particular. Hamann's thought – and indeed all eschatological thought – rests on the importance of truth's historical embodiment; figural thought takes the determinate relationships between people as the whole content of cognition. The existence of external meaning – what, for philosophy, is the realm of ontology – hangs for Hamann on the twin concepts of mystery and revelation.

Conclusion

The materialist Enlightenment stripped away human dignity in the quest for utility, thereby creating a man who is both the technical master of the earth and the slave of technique. Diderot was both perfectly consistent with his materialism and more prescient than he knew when he speculated jokingly about the possibility of breeding half-man-half-goat creatures.[91] Genetic engineering for the purpose of alleviating man's estate might well prove this to be more than an idle whimsy. But for Kant, who solidified a Rousseauan respect for natural man into a granite foundation of rational dignity, such treatment of persons was the very opposite of Enlightened. Enlightenment and dignity would be saved together with the help of a purified reason. Kant's autonomous person took up the flag for an Enlightenment that had lost its moral purchase. For Hamann, however, this 'person' was a troubling creature resting on a non-existent foundation and claiming an altogether un-measured place in his own salvation. Hamann would have appreciated Iris Murdoch's quip, 'Kant's man had already received a glorious incar-nation nearly a century earlier in the work of Milton: his proper name is Lucifer.'[92] For Hamann, the problem was not to legislate for a city of devils; the dangers of moral persons were great enough.

The battle against Kant's a priori was thus the most important battle in Hamann's counter-Enlightenment, for Kant's work represented the most sustained defence of self-sufficient, extra-historical, and extra-linguistic reason. With Hamann, timeless reason is dethroned, and we are cast back into a world of lived experience and textual tradition: Christian humanism replaces the Cartesian turn against tradition. If the universal and the particular are somehow reconciled through scripture and a typological 'reading' of the world, then interpretation (of scrip-ture and experience) – hermeneutics – takes on the mantle that Enlight-enment reason had attempted to wrest from the shoulders of the priests. If the Enlightenment equated faith with priest-craft, secularizing rad-ical Protestant anti-clericalism into reaction against the notion of divine authority, Hamann sought to rehabilitate the book as a divine creation, and interpretation as the essential task of the moral thinker. Since the Enlightenment had sought to interpret the book as merely a human expression and since it had been reluctant to discard hierarchy, the nat-ural conclusion was to presume the sovereignty of reason, which, in practice, becomes the sovereignty of the rational. Appeals to interpreta-tion became somewhat arbitrary enthronements of cultural tradition. Hamann's treatment of reason-worship as idolatry and his shift to the text are the bases for his 'aestheticism' and his interpretative turn, but while he celebrates specificity, he avoids the romantic celebration of the *Volk* and its possible descent into antinomian, dandyish, or fascist aes-theticism. How he does this will be the subject of chapter 10.

PART THREE

Language and the City in Modern Natural Law: Hamann's Controversy with Moses Mendelssohn

6 *Leviathan* and *Jerusalem*: Rights and 'the Laws of Wisdom and Goodness'

On the surface of things, it's hard to see quite what all the fuss was about in the debate between Johann Georg Hamann and Moses Mendelssohn over the role of the state in the religious lives of its citizens. Both believed that the state ought not to force faith upon its citizens and both abhorred intolerance. In addition, both found serious weaknesses in the Hobbesian doctrine of natural rights. It is not surprising, then, that Hamann's early reception of Mendelssohn's *Jerusalem oder über religiöse Macht und Judentum* (1783) was, if not fully laudatory, not entirely negative: 'The more I read it, the less I understand it … He appears to me, however, to be fully justified in remaining a Jew himself, and in retaining his brothers in the faith of their fathers.'[1] Hamann considered himself a friend of Mendelssohn, the famous Berlin enlightener. In an earlier literary incident, when Christian polemicists had attempted to draw Mendelssohn into a public confessional dispute, and had called upon him either to refute Christianity or convert, Hamann had condemned the affair as absurd and contrary to the spirit of faith – faith was not a matter of debatable propositions to be refuted or accepted.[2] In a letter to the instigator of this squabble, he had added, 'This man [Mendelssohn] is really a light and salt of his race, and would have lost all of his merit and worth if he had become as one of us.'[3]

What a distance was this from the virulent polemic of Hamann's *Golgotha und Scheblimini*,[4] in which Hamann condemned Mendelssohn's *Jerusalem* as an overly speculative babble of words in the 'spirit and essence of pagan, naturalistic, atheistic fanaticism.'[5] In a torrent of apocalyptic symbolism, Hamann blamed the underlying theoretical position of his erstwhile friend for rendering politics tyrannical and religion idolatrous. The more Hamann read the work, the more he perceived in it the spirit of his century.

There are numerous levels to Hamann's attack on *Jerusalem – Golgotha und Scheblimini* contains many of the essential elements of his mature thought. Indeed, Hegel considered it to be the most important work in Hamann's oeuvre.[6] The work is certainly of great interest to political theorists, for we see in it Hamann's reaction to the modern tradition of natural rights, and particularly to its Hobbesian source.

Jerusalem contains a thorough reworking of Hobbesian natural rights discourse. But Mendelssohn himself was anything but an avowed Hobbesian. While clearly indebted to the philosopher of Malmesbury, he sought to reformulate a theory of social contract from natural rights precisely in order to turn Hobbes on his head: might, Mendelssohn insisted, was entirely distinct from right, society was not a product of fear, but of benevolence, and, most importantly, the Erastian conclusions of *Leviathan* were completely inadmissible. Such a despotic peace as Hobbes's theory entails, Mendelssohn wrote, was like the 'dreadful calm which, as Montesquieu says, prevails during the evening in a fortress which is to be taken by storm during the night.'[7] How, then, could Hamann make the charge that Mendelssohn is 'in agreement with Hobbes, [and] sets the highest happiness in outer rest and security'?[8]

In the following three chapters we will attempt to make sense of this charge that Mendelssohn was a crypto-Hobbist. This three-way conversation among Hamann, Mendelssohn, and Hobbes will enable us to outline Hamann's powerful attack on the social contract tradition and to articulate Hamann's alternate conception of human community. This first chapter considers Mendelssohn's defence of natural rights. It begins by setting out Mendelssohn's treatment of Hobbes, and his reformulation of natural rights doctrine. It then illustrates how Hamann objected to Mendelssohn's attempt to wed modern natural rights to a language of benevolence. Emphasizing the difficulty in separating subjective rights from the cold logic of *Leviathan*, Hamann's polemical tract charged Mendelssohn with holding a lightly veiled Hobbesianism that weakened the demands of the divine law. We will proceed, in chapter 7, to consider the epistemological basis of Enlightenment natural religion. Chapter 8 will explore the relationship between language and society in natural rights theory.

Leviathan and *Jerusalem*

In *Jerusalem*, Mendelssohn attempted to do two things: first, he sought to provide a theory of the state based upon natural rights, delineating the boundaries of temporal and ecclesiastical power in order to justify near-universal toleration[9] and to argue for the civic emancipation of the Jews. This he did by providing a sharp distinction between the state's power (the power to coerce people with regard to external actions) and ecclesiastical power (the power to teach and console people with regard to internal convictions). Second, he attempted to show that his enlightened, rationalist 'natural religion' was not at all at odds with his continued adherence to Judaism. In so doing, he defined the essence of Judaism in such a way that it did not depend on any extra-rational revelation in the Christian sense (Jewish revelation was merely a revelation of ceremonial law, not of metaphysical truths). Thus, he defended himself from the attacks of enlightened freethinkers who had charged that he could not reconcile his religious convictions with his philosophical position: on the contrary, he argued, Judaism was essentially rational (unlike Christianity, he implied).

Now, Hamann's primary objection was to the theological content of these claims, which he thought offensive both to Judaism and to Christianity. Essentially, by making the core of Judaism eternal, natural religion, unaffected by specific, historical events, Mendelssohn had implicitly rejected the central tenets of Hamann's historical theology of salvation wherein the eternal could be manifested *only* in temporal events. (We will explore this concern in greater detail in the next chapter.) But as we shall see, there is more to their debate than this battle over *Heilsgeschichte*, despite the centrality of that concern.

Jerusalem begins by outlining the weakness of Hobbes's system and reformulating the doctrine of natural rights and a state of nature. Mendelssohn's central objection to Hobbes was that Hobbes had given excessive weight to the need for fear to establish moral relations among people. Mendelssohn had two objections to this. First, he questioned whether this provided an adequate basis for a commonwealth: 'If there is, in the state of nature, no binding obligation other than that based upon fear and powerlessness, contracts will remain valid only as long as they are supported by fear and powerlessness. Thus, men, by their contracts, will not have come any step closer to their security.'[10] This was somewhat weak, in that Hobbes had been quite clear on this point – the *Leviathan* was to create a permanent source of fear for men, a 'visible Power to keep them in awe, and tye them by feare of punishment to the performance of their Covenants.'[11] However, as we shall see below, Mendelssohn's objection here has a more significant basis than this rather tepid passing-over of Hobbes's unambiguous statement.

His second objection was that Hobbes *himself* had seen that the state of nature was not a state of licence. Hobbes, we recall, had been somewhat equivocal on the source of moral obligation in the state of nature, writing of natural laws, 'These dictates of Reason, men use to call by the name of Lawes; but improperly: for they are but Conclusions, or Theoremes concerning what conduceth to the conservation and defence of themselves; wheras Law, properly is the word of him, that by right hath command over others. But yet if we consider the same Theoremes, as delivered in the word of God, that by right commandeth all things; then are they properly called Lawes.'[12] It was to this latter definition that Mendelssohn (without explicit citation) drew his readers' attention, arguing that Hobbes knew of a moral obligation anterior to contractual existence: 'And so we would once again have a *solemn* law of nature, even though Hobbes does not want to admit it.'[13] For Mendelssohn, then, Hobbes had known all along that the state of nature was not a state of licence, and that obligation was not grounded on fear.

Without entering into a discussion of this rather sticky issue in Hobbes interpretation, let us merely note that Mendelssohn was, in fact, articulating a rudimentary form of the (in)famous 'Warrender thesis' concerning moral obligation in Hobbes's state of nature.[14] But Hobbes's law of nature is *solemn* only because it involves the fear of divine retribution: God's will is right because of God's might, and fear is the basis of obligation. And even if we note that God's punishment seems to dissolve in Hobbes to a mere natural consequence of imprudent actions,[15] we are still left with a moral law that is law only insofar as it can punish: fear of consequences remains one's motivation for acting justly.

Mendelssohn followed Leibniz in objecting to this: Hobbes had erred in defining freedom in such a limited way as to make it compatible with necessity. Leibniz had argued that Hobbes misunderstood necessity, turning it into an ironclad, materialist determinism that destroyed piety and morality.[16] Similarly, for Mendelssohn, freedom of conscience is the basis of all moral action – the moment coercion is required (or necessity is posited), the moral worth of an action is lost. His view may be summarized thus: individual human beings seek felicity, the pursuit of which God approves. Felicity is attained through the exercise of duties towards men and God. 'Now, two things belong to the true fulfillment of our duties: *action* and *conviction*. Action accomplishes what duty demands, and conviction causes that action to proceed from the proper source, that is, from pure motives.'[17] Education and government are the two institutions that help men to learn and to fulfil their duties. One's duties to man entail benevolence, which 'in reality, makes us happier than *selfishness*,'[18] but these duties can be fulfilled in two ways: through conviction or through coercion. Civic education attempts to form men's characters such that they do their duty willingly, and hence attain the felicity that the willing fulfilment of duty purchases. But, if civic education fails, then 'coercive laws, punishments of crime, and rewards of merit' are necessary for the maintenance of society: 'If the *inner felicity of society* cannot be entirely preserved, let at least *outward peace and security* be obtained, if need be, through *coercion*.'[19] Ecclesiastical authority differs from civil government in that it concerns man's relationship with God. In this relationship, mere actions without convictions are worthless – God, after all, is in no need of our worship.[20] Hence, religious institutions can have only a moral authority – only the authority to teach and convince, not to compel, for compulsion detracts from the purity of the action, thus robbing the worshipper of the chance to merit felicity.[21]

Mendelssohn provided an account of 'the origin of the rights of coercion and the validity of contracts among men.'[22] He began by defining a right as 'the *authority* [*Befugnis*] (the moral capacity) to make use of a thing as a means for promoting one's felicity.'[23] For him, as for other repudiators of Hobbes, natural rights entailed corresponding, negative duty on the part of others – rights were 'moral capacities.'[24] He proceeded to define the rights of nature, employing a very Lockean scheme concerning the natural origin of possessions. In the state of nature, man possesses his own physical capacities (the equivalent of the Lockean *person*), the products of his industry, and those natural goods that he has rendered inseparable from these products.[25] Thus, contra Hobbes, Mendelssohn established a *natural property* prior to any contracts. But unlike Locke, Mendelssohn did not intend to make the preservation of one's property the central end of civil government. Following Samuel Pufendorf, Christian Wolff, and Hugo Grotius (and, very distantly, Cicero),[26] Mendelssohn adopted the theory of *perfect* and *imperfect* rights, the theoretical function of which, for him, was to marry possessive rights to a notion of moral obligation. In the state of nature, a man has a *perfect right* to all of his natural property – he may protect himself against injury or theft, and he has a *perfect duty* not to injure others. However, there exists on the part of others an *imperfect right* (a right that can be petitioned, but not enforced) to another's goods (among which are included his capacities). Now, a man has an *imperfect* duty to give his surplus goods (those unnecessary for his self-preservation) to others. The moral basis for this duty is the above-mentioned link that

Mendelssohn drew between felicity and benevolence: man's aim in life is happiness, and he cannot be happy without helping others. But a needy person's imperfect rights cannot be enforced – they merely lay an obligation upon the wealthy person's conscience. The wealthy person retains the 'right of independence' to make decisions in cases of 'collision,' when imperfect, positive rights of a needy person run counter to the perfect, negative rights of the owner. Society arises when individuals seek to change their 'fluctuating rights and duties into something definite,' and make promises to one another.[27] The state comes into being when men 'renounce [their] right of independence by means of a *social contract* and ... transform these imperfect duties into perfect ones by the enactment of *positive laws*.'[28] They transfer rights to the 'moral person' of the state.

By adopting this distinction between *perfect* and *imperfect rights*, Mendelssohn was attempting to maintain a duty to charity in rights discourse without compromising property rights. It is interesting to note that, in this respect, he came quite close to Pufendorf without actually following him to the same results. He followed Pufendorf in arguing that an *imperfect* right could be claimed but never guaranteed by force. Pufendorf had argued that it was necessary both for the cultivation of a strong work ethic and for the sake of morality that charity remain at the discretion of the possessor. Nonetheless, Pufendorf argued that in a case of absolute, faultless necessity on the part of a needy person, there was a theoretical window open for an imperfect right of the needy to become a perfect right without the consent of the possessor: 'Though what is due on the basis of humanity may absolutely not be taken by force in normal circumstances, still extreme necessity has the effect of providing a right to such things no less than the things which are due on the basis of perfect obligation.'[29]

Mendelssohn did not go so far as to allow such a thing. In this respect, despite his stress on benevolence, he closed a window that even the most possessive Pufendorf had left open. But he was much closer to Pufendorf on the moral significance of maintaining the distinction between the perfection and imperfection of rights – the property holder must have the moral freedom to make the decision regarding charity. Pufendorf had put many barriers in the way of a needy person's perfect right to charity because he believed that such a right would undermine moral freedom. If one were to assume that a needy person had a perfect right to the property of the wealthy person, the latter would no longer be able to gain the moral merit points for his generosity.[30] This was also essential to Mendelssohn's view, and it provides us with an important reminder that his view ought not to be misconstrued as making the redistribution of property the central goal of the state. While Mendelssohn wrote that social contract granted the state the capacity to render imperfect duties perfect through positive laws, thereby appearing to undermine the Lockean sanctity of property, it is somewhat misleading to say, with one interpreter, that Mendelssohn's state 'regulates beneficence' or that Mendelssohn considers man in the state of nature to be 'plagued by natural liberty.'[31] While men might grant their governments (through the social contract) the right to convert imperfect rights into perfect rights (and hence to demand taxes or service), Mendelssohn was not advocating what would, in our modern vernacular, be called 'big government.' The right to decide how much of one's property one gives or keeps, he wrote, 'constitutes man's *natural liberty*, which makes up a great portion of his felicity.'[32] Charity has its basis in self-interest, for benevolence is necessary for individual happiness. Hence, some portion of one's additional revenues *should*, for one's own happiness, be set aside for charity, but the right of the needy cannot rise to the position of a perfect right that can be enforced. Rather, it was essential for Mendelssohn that the wealthy be free to buy felicity with sacrifice: 'It is, for example, not advisable for the state to assume all the duties of love for our fellow man down to the *distribution of alms*, and to transform them into public institutions. Man is conscious of his own worth when he performs charitable acts, when he vividly perceives how he alleviates the distress of his fellow man by his gift.'[33]

Now, we might be tempted to twist this view to give it a Hobbesian ring, and, indeed, it does accord somewhat with the psychology of *Leviathan*. Generosity, Hobbes had said, was a sign of power, and power determined worth.[34] However, Hobbes had maintained that worth was assessed by others; Mendelssohn appears to champion self-esteem. More importantly, this view was in stark contrast with that of Hobbes because it insisted that one must be free from compulsion for an action to have any moral worth. By claiming that natural rights entailed corresponding natural duties on the part of others, he denied the Hobbesian position that two people might both have a right to the same thing.[35] By subordinating the *imperfect* right of the needy to the *perfect* right of the possessor, he argued that natural property arrangements were actually on a more objective moral basis than Hobbes had been willing to allow. Thus, where Hobbes had suggested essential tensions between people striving for eminence and had provided an ingenious account of how these antagonisms could be transformed into a unity, Mendelssohn, in a most Lockean manner, rendered the state of nature a state in which property relations were morally clear. Every perfect right corresponds to a perfect duty on the part of others.

This was the basis of his disagreement with Hobbes: Hobbes did not think that natural rights entailed natural duties on the part of others. It was, indeed, his different conceptions of rights that caused Mendelssohn to articulate a somewhat misleading interpretation of Hobbes: 'According to his [Hobbes's] system, all *right* is grounded in *power*, and all *obligation* in *fear*.'[36] That Hobbesian obligation is ground-ed in fear will not come as a surprise to readers of *Leviathan*, but the argument that Hobbesian right is grounded in power is clearly inaccur-ate. For Hobbes, we recall, people in the state of nature are impotent, but they all have a right to all things. My right to X does not entail any-one else's duty to respect my right. The subjective rights of people con-flict, and the peaceful *enjoyment* of any rights becomes dependent upon the establishment of a common power that guarantees the mutual obli-gations to respect one another's limited rights. In other words, it is *only under the sword of the sovereign* that my right to X entails a corresponding duty on the part of other subjects to respect my right. In a natural condi-tion, no such duty can exist.

For Mendelssohn, this natural conflict was far too morally troubling; he could not conceive of a right that did not entail a corresponding duty on the part of others. The idea of perfect rights coming into conflict struck him as contrary to the very concept of rights. The 'collisions' that Mendelssohn located in the state of nature were merely the basis of a moral question in the possessor as to how much he should give to his needy neighbour. There was no collision between perfect rights. If a possessor in the state of nature might be faced with certain moral diffi-culties, the nature of *rights* and of *what is right* was ultimately unprob-lematic and objective. 'The laws of wisdom and goodness,' he wrote, 'cannot contradict each other … Wisdom combined with goodness is called *justice*.'[37] And if the natural, pre-civil condition might have some inconveniences (which Mendelssohn did not enumerate, but which readers of Locke and Pufendorf might easily supply), the state of affairs was conceptually clear: 'Omission of compulsory duties is an offense, an injustice; omission of duties of conscience, however, is merely *unfair-ness*.'[38] Justice is not fairness, but is rather the keeping of contracts. Civil society is useful not because it establishes moral boundaries, but be-cause it allows people to plan for the future by setting promises upon a firm basis of positive law backed by coercion. It was not established for the redistribution of property, but for the guaranteeing of promises and for the betterment of man's moral condition, for the state also has an educative function, and Mendelssohn argued that the best form of government would be the one in which the education of the populace had proceeded so far that its laws had become superfluous: such a people would do its duty without coercion.[39] But the state is not instituted to alter the pre-civic moral relationship in any significant way – it guarantees perfect rights, helping preserve the moral freedom to perform imperfect duties. It is, in short, liberal.

Hamann and Natural Rights

Hamann had a basic distaste for the modern language of natural rights and for speculative metaphysics, both of which smacked somewhat of pride to his zealously Lutheran palate. Even more troubling to him was the notion of a 'social contract,' which struck him as a profane antitype of the divine covenant.[40] Nonetheless, he began by attempting to refute Mendelssohn on the basis of the argument's internal contradictions.

We have seen that Mendelssohn took the position that a right was a 'moral capacity' to use something for one's own happiness. It entails the duty on the part of others to respect it. For Hamann, there was a fundamental error in relating every right to a duty: if the terms simply collapse into one another – if every perfect right corresponds to a perfect duty – why bother with subjective rights at all? Why not stick to a language of morality? In a dense passage, he drew on Mendelssohn's discussion of 'moral capacities': 'The capacity is called moral if it is consistent with the laws of wisdom and goodness: so also should wisdom and goodness united be called morality.[41] If, however, one calls their unity Justice,[42] then one should, just as fitly, call a capacity that is consistent with the laws of wisdom and goodness "just."'

Here, drawing on different phrases in *Jerusalem*, Hamann completed Mendelssohn's terminological calculus. He hinted at a curious weakness in the 'laws of wisdom and goodness' in that they merely support *perfect* rights and duties. Mendelssohn had indicated that the duties of conscience (charity) were quite distinct from the demands of justice. But if justice and morality are synonyms, what becomes of charity's moral weight? Hamann continued, 'If, further, power and right are, already in the state of nature, heterogeneous concepts, then capacities, means, and goods appear to be far too closely related to the concept of power not to emerge as a unit.' Here, Hamann called into question the claim that Mendelssohn's moral capacity, or right (the 'authority … to make use of a thing as a means for promoting one's felicity') is not related to one's power, or physical capacity. Given Mendelssohn's Lockean theory of natural appropriation, one's right to a thing is clearly dependent upon one's power to appropriate it. In turn, one's power appears to be very much affected by one's rights. 'But whence came the laws of wisdom and goodness? If there are such laws, why does one need to study the light and right of nature? Would not these laws in themselves be the best natural right?'[43] If the purpose of speculation on people's rights in the state of nature is to allow us to deduce moral laws, then it is an unsatisfying theory that merely points to undefined 'laws of wisdom and goodness.' What's more, they are somewhat unsatisfactory moral laws if they merely enshrine the power relations that determined the acquisition of perfect rights.

Hamann objected to the moral clarity that Mendelssohn established in the state of nature, and he drove a Hobbesian wedge between rights and duties: 'If I have a right to use a thing as a means to happiness, then every man in the state of nature has the same right; just as the soldier, during war, has the authority [*Befugnis*] to kill the enemy, and the enemy to kill him. Or are the laws of wisdom and goodness as manifold as my and every other "I"? or does the metaphysical law of royal love of self and selfishness [*selbst- und Eigenliebe*] also belong to the right of nature?'[44]

Hamann refused to accept Mendelssohn's rosy picture of the state of nature, emphasizing conflict instead. And, in the absence of any clear, internal knowledge of a moral law, Hamann conceived of a most Hobbesian scenario in which two parties had rights to the same things. Mendelssohn had provided a footnote on the soldier's predicament, but had said that the soldier has the right to kill as an employee of the state, not as a man, and that it was his state that acted on the basis of its perfect natural right – or that violated its perfect natural duty, for 'obviously, only one of the warring states has right on its side.'[45] Now, this naturally raises a difficulty beyond merely the question of who shall be judge. For if individual self-interest is at the base of one's natural rights, can one ever have anything less than a perfect right of self-defence? But if one cannot (as in Hobbes's view), then does not each human being become the author (or at least the possessor) of his own moral law – do not the 'laws of wisdom and goodness' lose their universality, or, as Hamann put it, become as numerous as every individual rights-bearer?

But if Hamann hinted that Mendelssohn's view that natural rights entail natural duties on the part of others muddied what Hobbes had made quite clear, he nonetheless suggested that *Jerusalem* was essentially Hobbesian in that it did not safeguard moral freedom as Mendelssohn wished. *Jerusalem* asserted that perfect rights (and duties) are compulsory, and 'compulsory rights may be *exacted* by force.'[46] This, indeed, is their defining feature. But if one is bound naturally to a perfect, negative duty not to infringe upon others' property, and this duty is backed up by coercion, it is difficult to see how this escapes the Hobbesian reconciliation of liberty and necessity, right and might. Hamann wrote, 'If all the conditions to which a right pertains are given to the rights-havers, the duty-bearer is completely robbed of his knowledge and conscience [*Wissen und Gewissen*] and of all his moral capacities.' He without property has no moral freedom. Hamann asked, 'Will freedom there [in the state of nature] not be, as here, a victim of moral necessity and of the dreadful "must" according to the laws of wisdom and goodness in which, thus, there already lies a right of compulsion[?]'[47] Through Hamannian lenses, Mendelssohn's moral necessity (unlike its Leibnizian forefather) begins to look very much like Hobbesian physical necessity. Thus, Hamann wrote, 'The place of the moral capacity is usurped, in the case of perfect rights, by physical violence, and with perfect duties, by physical necessity, with violently extorted actions. With such a perfection, the whole speculative right of nature is rent, and spills over into the highest wrong.'[48]

In brief, then, Hamann was arguing that Mendelssohn had attempted to reinvest the concept of rights with more moral content than Hobbesian theory had suggested (with its emphasis on the need for the sword to establish mine and thine) but that the attempt was unsuccessful. Hamann forced the Mendelssohnian theory back into a Hobbesian mould, insisting that this is the necessary corollary of relying upon the concept of perfect natural rights that can be defended by force: 'Compulsory duties, whose perfection consists of the fact that they can be extorted by force, appear to border on the obligation of fear.'[49]

Divine Law, Property, and Justice

Modern natural rights are properties; within the limits of positive law, they may be used in any way their possessor wishes. This is in sharp contrast with the medieval views of natural law (which both constrains and exhorts certain actions).[50] In a sense, Hamann was defending some version of the latter, but with important Lutheran caveats about the limits of reason and the nature of law. Thus, while he was impatient with scholastic systems or their modern, philosophical incarnations, he was not entirely ironic when he praised Leibniz, the originator of the phrase, the 'law of wisdom and goodness': 'Is it wisdom and goodness to give and leave to each his due? Granted in the singular case in which there is no other right to property but the wisdom and goodness of the giver. This case, however, is the only one of its kind. How fitting is it to use a class word for a single thing that does not classify with anything, and cannot be brought under one rubric with anything?[51] Leibniz was right, then, for that one case, about which one can speak only in a theodicy.'[52]

If there is such a law, it must be understood through faith: Leibniz had been right, insofar as he had realized that to discuss this matter was to discuss God. If there are such laws, they have nothing to do with giving to each his due, nor with a distinction between charity and justice. Hamann complained, 'The never-conflicting laws of wisdom and goodness, contrary to the knowledge and will of the theorist, are broken in two in his hands, and require a new connection through justice.'[53] But Mendelssohnian justice, favouring perfect rights, the realm of coercion and the propertied, seems a far cry from divine law. 'How can Justice,' Hamann asked, 'present her own unchangeable unity as two that are so different from each other as they are from her?'[54] To attempt to elucidate natural justice on the basis of natural rights and corresponding natural duties was, for Hamann, to provide an extremely truncated version of justice, one that is at a distance from traditional Judeo-Christian views: 'Due to these cases of collision between positive and negative authority, between self-use [*Selbstgebrauch*] and painful dependency on the benevolence of wiser self-users in the condition of natural independence, there emerges out of the brain of the theorist, like a machine-Pallas, the law of justice! – What an outlay of mystical laws in order to bring out a puny law of justice that is hardly worth one's breath, and fits neither the state of society nor the matter of Judaism!'[55] Mendelssohn, Hamann was arguing, had robbed the concept at both ends: it undermined charity (by limiting the demands of divine law), while, at the same time, imposing surprising constraints upon liberty.

Let us begin with the first charge. For Hamann, Mendelssohn's imperfect duty to be benevolent sounded quite empty: 'For duties and Conscience appear to be, for the rights-haver, dispensable concepts, unknown quantities and *qualitates occultae*.'[56] With the essential freedom to

decide for himself how much he ought to give to the poor, every propri-
etor becomes the final judge of his own moral duty. Mendelssohn had
written, 'In the state of nature, to me, and to me alone, appertains the
right to decide *whether, to what extent, when, for whose benefit*, and under
what conditions I am obliged to exercise beneficence.'[57] Mendelssohn
never suggested any external standard to which an individual might
appeal in making this determination – he merely linked felicity to benevolence, suggesting that there was a correlation between the two.
Hamann's objection was not merely that Mendelssohn's imperfect
rights were too weak – he was not re-articulating the old argument that
absolute necessity rendered imperfect rights perfect. Rather, he was lamenting the way in which the language of rights diluted universal
moral imperatives. Mendelssohn's insistence upon the moral autonomy of the giver struck Hamann as a theory worthy of despots. In a
polemical outburst he asked, 'But if the "I," even in the state of nature,
is so unjust and vain, and if every man has the same right to Me! and
Me alone! – then let us be happy about the We of God's grace, and thankful for the crumbs that are left over for us *unmündigen* orphans from their
hunt- and lapdogs, greyhounds and bulldogs.'[58] The dogs are a none-too-
oblique reference to Frederick II's famous hounds (and to his courtiers).
Hamann interpreted the moral autonomy of the giver as grounds for refusing to give to those in need. With each setting his own moral standard,
there was effectively no absolute moral basis for charity.

   This reference to Frederick II was a double barb, for in addition to
pointing out the way in which this moral autonomy diluted the obligation to be charitable, it also pointed to the types of social organization
that resulted from such a view. Hamann clearly thought that the 'Mir,
und Mir allein' had a Hobbesian ring, and he drew the conclusion that
a social contract between such morally autonomous individuals was a
recipe for Leviathan. The following Hamannian outburst might appear
at first, then, to be a liberal response to Mendelssohn's (and Hobbes's)
theory of state: 'But is it wisdom and goodness to clip and mangle even
more with laws our – I don't know if perfect or imperfect? – right to the
means to happiness and the meagre capacities of our property [*habselig-
keit*]?'[59] Mendelssohn's positive law, we are told, is neither wise nor
good because it entails the complete subjection of our persons. But this
presents us with a strange picture. Hamann appears to have been
attacking Mendelssohn from both the left and the right, charging that
Jerusalem not only undermined charity by making it subject to the
moral autonomy (i.e., the selfish whim) of the giver, but that it also

compromised freedom by rendering property (including one's physical capacities) subject to the state's control.

What, then, was Hamann's position on property? He wrote,

> But if there is a social contract, then there is also a natural one that is more real and older and on whose conditions the social must be grounded. Through this, all natural property becomes conventional,[60] and man in the state of nature is dependent on its laws; that is, he has a positive duty to live up to these laws that he has to thank for the whole of nature and especially the preservation of his being and the use of all the means and goods necessary for this. Man, as a duty-bearer of nature, has, according to this, least of all an absolute right or a loathsome monopoly over his capacities, nor over the products of them, nor over the unfruitful mule of his industry and sad bastards [*Wechselbälge*] of his usurping brutality over the creature made subject to his vanity, not willingly.[61]

The thought-experiment of the state of nature and the social contract, he was arguing, is a poor imitation of the older, 'natural' contract, God's covenant with man, the true source of moral obligation.[62] There is no absolute right even to our person: everything that man is and has is a gift of God and entails a moral duty. Readers familiar with Locke's prohibition against suicide (based upon God's ownership of our lives) might be tempted to see a resemblance here, but Hamann was going much further than asserting that we cannot alienate our lives. We cannot alienate anything, since everything is a divine possession and a divine gift. The convention of private property is merely a device by which we are called upon to exercise our duties – we are stewards, not owners. Hamann's reference to the 'unfruitful mule of man's industry' is a reference to Mendelssohn's definition of justice, which Hamann portrayed as a sterile offspring of two different animals, perfect rights (mastery) and perfect duties (subjection). The last phrase is taken from Romans 8:20, in which passage the creature is distinguished from the spirit: 'For the creature was made subject to vanity, not willingly.' The reference involves a double charge, pointing both to the inherent limitations of the fallen man, but also to the dangerous implications of failing to base justice on a divine pattern. To treat perfect rights as if they have an absolute moral basis is to render egoism morally salutary. A justice that merely enshrines property relations – one that, in the most mundane sense of the terms, gives to each his own – merely renders domination more rigid.

Hamann, then, indicated both the Hobbesian basis of Mendelssohn's view, and its anti-Hobbesian gloss. He condemned Mendelssohn's theory of property and distinction between perfect and imperfect rights, arguing that this undermined charity, and he employed a Hobbesian razor to cut the connection between rights and duties, revealing Mendelssohn as a radical advocate of possessive rights. Mendelssohn's freedom of conscience came to be reformulated, in Hamann's writing, as a vain reliance on one's *own* judgment, and an undermining of universal, divine justice. For Hamann, Mendelssohn had pulled the ethical rug out from under man's feet, and left him with the bare grounds of power, fear, and contracts, while, at the same time, attempting to associate these property relations with the language of benevolence and the solemn law of nature, the *law of wisdom and goodness*. Hamann hinted at an alternative way of seeing man's relation to ownership in the world, one of extreme subjection to God, in which man's sole possession is duty.[63]

Conclusion: Rights, Community, and *Leviathan*

Hamann called *Jerusalem* 'epikurischtoisch,'[64] and with this designation we might well sum up his attack. Mendelssohn himself had ended the first section of *Jerusalem* with the story of a sneering Epicurean who is brought to shame by Stoics. Thus, Mendelssohn clothed himself as a champion of the stoa, taming the Epicurean beast whose scales are pride. The Stoic element was clear enough: universal reason and its moral claims were certainly aspects of that school's doctrine. Yet for all this apparent moral clarity, Hamann charged, Mendelssohn was Epicurean (read Hobbesian) at base. The Berlin philosopher sought the source of morality and the state in a pre-civic condition of radical atomism. In one sense, Hamann was much closer to Hobbes than Mendelssohn, because he thought that property was merely the product of positive law. He refused to see any 'law of wisdom and goodness' that existed in a pre-civic condition (if such a state was even a useful analytical tool), or, indeed, in any product of fallen mankind. For Hamann, Mendelssohn was a Hobbes with a moralistic gloss.[65]

There is no space to enter into a full discussion of what Hamann would propose as an alternative account of the relationship between right and wealth. We can only quote several suggestive passages: 'According to another dogmatic [that of Christian faith], taking little and giving double are neither convictions nor actions *deterioris conditionis*.'[66] The 'royal law to love one's neighbour as oneself' places a duty that runs counter to the 'exclusive self-love' that Hamann perceived to be at the root of social contract theory.[67] Since Hamann spent a great deal of energy late in his life complaining about the reduction of his salary, perhaps he is not the clearest embodiment of his vaunted Christian principle. Nonetheless, the thrust of his position is clear enough: Hamann was concerned that Enlightenment champions of natural rights undermined a religious world view in which human life is entirely conceived in terms of duty and subjection to divine will.

Mendelssohn would have agreed with Hamann's assessment that political association was less than ideal. Given that Mendelssohn sought moral freedom in the absence of coercion and that he saw the political realm as that in which the threat of coercion is the rule, we can infer that the world of *perfect* rights was less than perfect for the Berlin philosopher. Hamann was, then, incorrect to say that Mendelssohn set the 'highest happiness in outer rest and security.'[68] Mendelssohn's account of the origin of the state indicates, albeit obliquely, that political life is corrupt. But it is not essentially so. The educational role of religion is to move the state closer to an ideal where duty and inclination are one – an ideal that had its original (but unrepeatable) model in the ancient so-called Mosaic constitution. Yet, by basing his entire moral philosophy on subjective rights, Mendelssohn undermined moral universalism and enshrined an order in which coercion is an inescapable fact. Hamann pushed this tension to its limit, refusing to accept the attempt to reconcile in theory the kingdoms of this world with that of the other. He forced Mendelssohn to confront the brutal clarity of Hobbesian positivism. For all its polemical excess, Hamann's attack on Mendelssohn serves as a reminder that liberals who seek to unite rights and the good often manage merely to dilute the good.

7 Faith, Inside and Out: Convictions versus Actions, Eternity versus History

Hamann's accusation that Mendelssohn was a Hobbist appears most bizarre when we consider *Jerusalem*'s argument about the correct relationship between church and state. If there was one thing that Mendelssohn clearly opposed it was the Erastianism of *Leviathan*. Church and state were essentially distinct; people must be free to worship in any manner they think acceptable to God. A comprehensive toleration based on the separation of political and ecclesiastical realms was Mendelssohn's project.

But this argument for the separation of realms had several pillars that would have been perfectly acceptable to the philosopher of Malmesbury. First, Mendelssohn separated internal conviction from external action. Second, he separated eternal truth from temporal truth. These separations are related to one another. Faith, for Mendelssohn, requires sincere internal conviction about eternal matters. Both the realm of 'eternal truth' and the mental faculty that seeks this truth are predicated on an epistemological assumption of a pure realm of reason uncorrupted with externals such as contingent historical events or laws, which appeal to the passions through threat. This chapter looks at Hamann's reaction to these two related separations and at his view of Mendelssohn's concept of tolerance.

Having explored the *Metakritik*, we are sufficiently well acquainted with Hamann to see how he could have found troubling the purity of both the eternal truths of reason and the inner convictions necessary for salvation. *Golgotha und Scheblimini* was intended as a companion piece to the *Metakritik*, and readers will be correct to spot a continuity between the texts. We will begin by outlining Mendelssohn's distinction between the internal and the external and that between the eternal and the historical. We will note, in passing, the accuracy of Hamann's charge: Mendelssohn shared a great deal with Hobbes. The second section explores Hamann's objections to Mendelssohn's parallel divisions between eternity and history and between inner conviction and outer action. With his eschatological view of history, Hamann could not accept the distinction between history and eternity. Nor could he accept the rational purity of Mendelssohnian religious conviction. What's more, he charged Mendelssohn with an internal contradiction: on *Jerusalem*'s conception of human understanding, there is no basis for Mendelssohn's ideal, the purity of inner convictions. The third section turns to the problem of tolerance. Mendelssohn's separations of inner conviction and outer action, eternal truth and historical truth provided for a strict division between ecclesiastical and temporal institutions: Hamann too thought that there was a distinction between the divine and the temporal, but he condemned the assumptions necessary for Mendelssohn's separation of realms. As we shall see, Mendelssohn's liberal ideal of state-neutrality toward religion is predicated on a set of claims about reason's universal and extra-temporal status. Once one accepts Hamann's claim that cognition is passionate and temporal, one loses a strong argument for liberal toleration and finds oneself reduced to a liberalism of fear. Hamann offers, in return, an illiberalism of good hope, which rightly makes the timorous among us uneasy.

The Externals

As we noted in the previous chapter, Mendelssohn's separation of ecclesiastical and civil powers rested upon a sharp distinction between conviction and action. He argued that people are motivated by two types of reasons: 'reasons that motivate the will' (*Bewegungsgründe* – or the grounds of action/movement), and 'reasons that persuade by their truth' (*Wahrheitsgründe*).[1] Both governments and churches have the aim of educating people such that their convictions correspond with their actions. In the secular realm, he suggested that the best form of government is that in which the people's education has progressed so far that their inner convictions correspond with their duties – they pursue the common good without requiring coercion or bribes, but rather from a sincere conviction that this is how they ought to behave.[2] This ideal condition, however, does not always obtain. Thus, Mendelssohn argued, we require the state to give external motivations (the carrots and sticks involved in positive law). The state, then, is a moral institution insofar as it educates its members towards virtue, but its positive law is essentially based in utility: we need to guarantee contracts with strict laws in order to make the misguided among us into reliable compatriots. Thus, while both religion and the state seek to instil virtue in people, the state has the added recourse of punishment when education fails. Religion has no such recourse. The need to guarantee promises in the state is born of temporal *needs* (if the law is not followed, the social order will fall apart). God, however, has no needs – if people do not believe as they ought, it is their loss, not his. Thus, it is absurd to grant the same powers to civic and ecclesiastical institutions: 'The relations between man and man require actions as such; the relations between God and man require them only insofar as they lead to convictions. An action beneficial to the public does not cease to be beneficial, even if it is brought about by coercion, whereas a religious action is religious only to the degree to which it is performed voluntarily and with proper intent.'[3] If I pay my taxes grudgingly, I still benefit my neighbour; if I pray grudgingly, I accomplish nothing but an empty mummery.

Religion, then, requires sincere conviction. However, Mendelssohn does not merely champion subjective sincerity but also objective truth. The sincere conviction must be attained through personal rational inquiry divorced from corrupting emotional elements. We will look at this in depth below, but for now let us merely note the radically rationalist account of faith that Mendelssohn gives: 'I recognize no eternal truths other than those that are not merely comprehensible to human reason but can also be demonstrated and verified by human powers.'[4]

This rationalism went a great way towards radical deism. But Mendelssohn stopped there, retaining his commitment to his religion. Thus, he had to defend himself against two related charges from deists: (1) How could he both deny the church the power of coercion and remain committed to the religion whose lawgiver punished blasphemy with stoning? (2) How could he reconcile his rationalism with the miraculous events of the scriptures? Was he denying revelation? Mendelssohn answered the second challenge by separating Judaism into two parts: a rational, natural religion that is universal to the human race, and the revealed *law* that is particular to the Jews. The law gave a particular people a particular avenue to universal, eternal truth. This revelation was not the revelation of religious doctrine – Moses gave laws, not articles of belief. Hence, Mendelssohn could argue, 'Judaism knows of no revealed religion in the sense in which Christians understand the term.'[5] His reply to the first challenge followed from this. Early Judaism was a theocracy. Originally, Moses had exercised coercion not in his role as a religious leader, but rather as the civil authority: he had not attempted to create *belief* through coercion, but merely the necessary obedience to civil law. This unique 'Mosaic constitution' was corrupted with the creation of a secular king (1 Samuel 8:5–22), and, ultimately, with the destruction of the temple and the dispersion of the Jews. The ancient theocratic state (in which ecclesiastical and civil institutions had been united) disappeared. With the end of the pure theocratic state, the unique instance of religious law equalling civil law ceased, and the ecclesiastical authority of the rabbis became purely that of comforting and educating Jews through continued ceremonial practices, commentary on the law, and the study of the nation's history. The covenant had not ceased, and Jews were still bound by their personal laws, but these in no way conflicted with their civic duties.

Mendelssohn thus separated eternal truths and temporal truths. Eternal truth consists of the 'immutable' truths of reason (a priori, logical, mathematical truth), and the 'contingent' truth (the laws of the natural sciences, discerned through the senses). All humankind has access to these truths because all people have access to creation. Temporal or historical truths, on the other hand, have a different epistemological status: only the witnesses to a historical event can attest to it. Thus, to believe a historical truth is merely to believe the witness(es). All that is required for salvation and happiness is contained in the eternal truths (and it is thus universally available). Revelation to the Jews was not a revelation of doctrine, but of law – this was a set of prescriptions specific to the nation. It was attended with miracles, indeed, but these were not proofs of doctrine. Rather, it was people's anterior knowledge of doctrine that enabled them to recognize divine revelation for what it was. After all, Mendelssohn asked ingeniously, even if an event were attended with miraculous earthquakes and trumpets from the heavens, who would be able to understand such signs as the work of God? 'Surely not the unthinking, brutelike man, whose own reflections had not yet led him to the existence of an invisible being that governs the visible.'[6] To understand revelation, one requires an anterior knowledge of God. Universal reason (when it is not perverted by sceptical philosophy or deceptive priest-craft) allows all people to come to a basic knowledge of the necessary, natural religious doctrine. Miracles do not affect doctrine but merely attend God's issuing of commandments. The Jews had received, by divine revelation, a set of laws specific to their nation. 'All these are historical truths which, by their very nature, rest on historical evidence, *must* be verified by authority, and *can* be confirmed by miracles.'[7]

Alexander Altmann notes the Leibnizian ring to all this, citing the distinction made in the *Essais de théodicée* between *vérités de raison* and *vérités de faits*. But, Altmann argues, Mendelssohn diverged from Leibniz in denying that miracles could buttress eternal truths.[8] Mendelssohn was quite clear: a miracle that ran contrary to the truths of reason was to be rejected as false – he even invoked the rather harsh penalties prescribed by the Bible for false prophets and witches as evidence of this point.[9] If Leibniz was an influence, Hobbes too clearly supported this position.[10] *Leviathan* suggested a similar distinction between the universally accessible, rational, natural religion and the specific historical claims of churches. Monotheism is a conclusion to which men naturally incline, for 'it is impossible to make any profound enquiry into naturall causes, without being enclined thereby to believe there is one God Eternall.'[11] A specific people might receive revelation from God, but this does not touch on the essence of divinity. The Jews, as God's chosen people, had been set aside to be governed 'not onely by naturall Reason, but by Positive Lawes, which [God] gave them by the mouths of his holy Prophets.'[12] Concerning such events – as, indeed, concerning any historical facts – we have nothing to rely upon but those who relate the events to us. There is, after all, a radical difference between science and knowledge of fact. In the case of miraculous events, we rely upon the authority of our ecclesiastical institutions: 'When wee Believe that the Scriptures are the word of God, having no immediate revelation from God himselfe, our Beleefe, Faith, and Trust is in the Church; whose word we take, and acquiesce therein.'[13] In this sense, believing in the church or scripture differs not at all from believing a historian's account. How similar this was to Mendelssohn's view that, 'without authority, the truth of history vanishes along with the event itself.'[14]

Like Hobbes, then, Mendelssohn thought that essential doctrine was rational, and that God had provided a special law for his chosen people. He also shared Hobbes's view when he claimed that 'fear and hope act upon men's *appetitive urge*, rational arguments on their *cognitive faculty*.'[15] To confound these faculties, he claimed, is both immoral and illogical. From these premises, Mendelssohn drew the conclusion that religious institutions ought not to have any powers of coercion. Nor ought membership in a religious group to confer any worldly benefit or carry any negative material consequences. Indeed, not only may religious institutions neither wield nor be supported by the power of the sword, but they may not even have the power of excommunication, for this inevitably has worldly consequences for the person thus expelled.[16] Nor ought the church to hold property.[17] 'The only rights possessed by the church are to admonish, to instruct, to fortify, and to comfort; and the duties of the citizens toward the church are an *attentive ear* and a *willing heart*.'[18]

Religion is the subject for rational argument. Mendelssohn had sought to avoid public assessment of Christianity for reasons both prudential and benevolent. What good would it serve to enter into such miserable confessional squabbles? Yet, in his definition of religion's basis, and in his description of Judaism, he intimated the superiority of Judaism over Christianity – as Ze'ev Levy notes, 'Mendelssohn makes us understand though, very discretely, that the religious concepts of Judaism fit the first two strata [of religion] – eternal and historical truths attained by reason – far better than Christianity which is based on irrational elements, belief in unconvincing miracles, etc.'[19] Mendelssohn's religion was essentially rational, and based on *conviction* (*Gesinnung*): 'Let him who has reason examine, and live according to his conviction.'[20] Some difference in convictions was justified, however – Mendelssohn defended pluralism. He even went so far as to give a providential interpretation to his tolerance: 'Let us not feign agreement where diversity is evidently the plan and purpose of Providence ... Let everyone be permitted to speak as he thinks, to invoke God after his own manner or that of his fathers, and to seek eternal salvation where he thinks he may find it, as long as he does not disturb public felicity and acts honestly towards the civil laws.'[21] But if there were good reasons to avoid the rancour of confessional squabbles, this did not mean that religion was above debate – on the contrary, it was rational, universal, and a subject upon which people must be permitted to say what they think. What is essential is that people, as autonomous, reasoning beings, be free to attain a *sincere* conviction – that is, to be convinced.

Mendelssohn's distinction between internal conviction and external action did a lot of work in his theory. In an apparent paradox it both differentiated absolutely between civic and ecclesiastical authority and defended the theocracy of the ancient Israelites. Mendelssohn argued that the Mosaic constitution had been a unique event in the history of humankind[22] in which the divine law had been civil law. But this uniqueness did not mean that the ancient theocracy had had priests with the authority to enjoin belief. *Belief could not be enjoined.* 'Under this constitution these crimes [blasphemy, the breaking of the Sabbath, etc.] could and, indeed, had to be punished civilly, not as erroneous opinion, not as *unbelief*, but as *misdeeds*, as sacrilegious crimes aimed at abolishing or weakening the authority of the lawgiver and thereby undermining the state itself.'[23] Not internal convictions, but external actions were punished.

Hobbes had also been quite clear on this point: 'Faith hath no relation to, nor dependence at all upon Compulsion, or Commandement; but onely upon certainty, or probability of Arguments drawn from Reason, or from something men beleeve already. Therefore the Ministers of Christ in this world, have no Power by that title, to Punish any man for not Beleeving, or for Contradicting what they say; they have I say no Power by that title of Christs Ministers, to Punish such: but if they have Soveraign Civill Power, by politick institution, then they may indeed lawfully Punish any Contradiction to their laws whatsoever.'[24] The clergy are to teach and to comfort; their 'precepts [are] not laws.' They attempt to convince men, 'not by Coercion, and Punishing; but by Perswasion,'[25] for inner convictions cannot be commanded, only external actions can. Thus, if Moses commanded that certain rites be followed, these laws were not an example of ecclesiastical power overstepping its bounds, but merely of civil power enjoining certain actions.

For both Hobbes and Mendelssohn, law was a civil matter that could compel external actions, while religion was to bring people to internal convictions by way of persuasion. It is only at this point that they diverged. Mendelssohn argued that the unique instance of these powers being united had passed, and that civic and ecclesiastical authorities were to understand the essential distinction between their roles, and not infringe upon one another. Nonetheless, he insisted (contra Spinoza) that God's covenant with his people had not ended; Mendelssohn urged his co-religionists to hold fast to the Jewish personal laws, even at the expense of full civic membership.[26] This would have been anathema to the more pliant Hobbes, who famously argued that the civil sovereign must have authority over the doctrines spread by their ecclesiastical authorities. Mendelssohn took more seriously the importance for individuals to worship as they thought appropriate. Hobbes consoled dissenters with the assurance that 'Profession with the tongue is but an externall thing, and no more then any other gesture whereby we signifie our obedience.'[27] Mendelssohn agreed but nonetheless objected to being forced to worship hypocritically. He insisted upon the liberty for churches to teach as they saw fit. 'Adapt yourselves,' he counselled his fellow Jews, 'to the morals and the constitution of the land to which you have been removed; but hold fast to the religion of your fathers too.'[28]

Hobbes naturally would have disagreed with this injunction, but their disagreement was merely a result of the two writers' different estimations of the degree to which doctrinal unity was necessary for

Table 1
Mendelssohn's eternal truth and temporal truth

Eternal truth (logic and observational science)	Temporal truth (historical event)
Universally accessible through reason	Requiring authority
Doctrine necessary for salvation	Law necessary for a particular people
Education through *Wahrheitsgründe* (Both state and church engage in this)	Threat (hope and fear) *Bewegungsgründe* (Only the state can legitimately do this)
Cognitive faculty	Will, passions
Conviction	Action
Necessary for happiness, conscience	Necessary for justice

peace. Mendelssohn said as much, implying that if Hobbes had lived in a more reasonable and less uncertain age he would have allowed more liberty for diversity of religious doctrines.[29]

In brief, then, Mendelssohn's divisions can be mapped as in table 1.

Hamann on History and Eternity, External and Internal

Mendelssohnian tolerance and Hobbesian Erastianism both relied on a distinction between internal conviction and external action and between eternal truth and historical facts. Hamann's objections to both the ideal of rational religious conviction and the separation of eternal from historical truths were of a piece: both Mendelssohnian claims rested on a kind of rational purism. Mendelssohn's ideal, while not entailing the kind of pure a priori that we encounter in Kant, was nonetheless subject to a charge quite similar to the one laid against Kant in the *Metakritik*. Let us begin with Hamann's objection to Mendelssohn's view of history.

Hamann's objections were inseparable from his Christian eschatology: temporal truths *were* universal truths. Thus, it was wrong to see Old Testament events as merely historical facts: 'No, the entire mythology of the Hebraic establishment was nothing but a type of a transcendent history, the horoscope of a heavenly hero, through the appearance of whom everything is already completed and still to come, as is written in their laws and prophets.'[30] As we have already seen (in chapter 2), Hamann's insistence upon the transcendent nature of historical events was central to his theology. It is neither philosophically nor theologically justified to create categorical separations between eternity and history: 'These temporal and eternal historical truths of the king of the Jews, the angel of their covenant, the firstborn and head of his community, are the A and Ω, the foundation and summit of our faith's wings.'[31]

Consider the following Hamannian remark (which includes a dense Hamannian reworking of Mendelssohn's phrases): 'The characteristic difference between Judaism and Christianity does not concern, then, either mediated or unmediated revelation, in the sense in which this is taken by Jews and Naturalists[32] – or eternal truths and doctrines – or ceremonial and moral laws: rather, it concerns solely temporal, historical truths that occur once and never occur again – things that have, through a connection between cause and effect, become true at one point in time and space and that, therefore, can be conceived as true only in respect to that point in time and space,[33] and must be confirmed by authority.'[34] The confessional aspect of Hamann's response is clearly evident here. All history – and particularly the history of God's chosen people – must be understood as prophetic. For Hamann, this entailed seeing Old Testament historical events as typological prefigurations of New Testament events. As he wrote elsewhere, 'Moses, the greatest prophet and the national lawgiver, was only the smallest and most fleeting shadow of his office, which he himself recognized as the mere prefiguring of another prophet whose appearance he promised his brothers and their descendants with the express order and command that they obey that one.'[35] That said, even if we set aside the clear confessional differences to which such a claim gives rise, we can see how Hamann's defence of prophetic history might equally be employed by many religious traditions. *Heilsgeschichte* of any sort contains eternal truths emerging immanently in the historical world. Mendelssohn's enlightened reduction of history to contingent events undermines all prophetic interpretation.[36]

Mendelssohn's rationalist interpretation of the Pentateuch, Hamann was suggesting, failed to see the typological significance of the Sinaitic revelation and thus turned Moses into 'the pope of the profane nation.'[37] The Hobbesian/Mendelssohnian treatment of the ancient theocracy as a civic state was thus for him profanation. The meaning of the Old Testament's historical events was spiritual. Hamann suggested that not even Moses himself had fully understood the nature of the covenant, whose ultimate meaning would become clear only in the incarnation and crucifixion of Christ: 'Just as Moses himself did not know that his countenance had a shining clarity that gave fright to the people, so too was the law-giving of this divine minister a mere veil and curtain of the old covenant-religion that to this very day remains unexposed, swaddled, and sealed.'[38] But authority was required for the transmission of these events: 'Jewish authority alone gives [the historical events in the Old Testament] the required authenticity.' The scriptures themselves are authoritative, coming from the divine author of the world:[39] 'Christianity knows and recognizes no chains of faith other than the firm, prophetic Word in the very oldest document of the human race and in the holy scriptures of true Judaism.'[40] This teaching is entirely reliant on scriptural authority.

This accounts for Hamann's juxtaposition of two lines out of Mendelssohn: 'Authority can, indeed, humble, but not teach; it can strike down reason, but not bind it. Nevertheless, without authority, the truth of history vanishes along with the event itself.'[41] Quite right, Hamann was arguing. The authority of scripture should humble; it does not teach in a rational manner, but is itself an authority upon which the believer relies: 'For this reason is the revealed religion of Christianity rightly called belief, trust, confidence, reliance, and child-like assurance in the divine pledge and promise.'[42]

If Mendelssohn's understanding of history entailed an attack on *Heilsgeschichte*, his rational religion was naturally antithetical to the faith that Hamann celebrated: *Gesinnung* is a far cry from *Empfindung*. While Mendelssohn wisely refused to enter into a rancorous debate over the merits of different religions, we have seen that he did not offer a view of faith fundamentally different from that of his opponents who sought a public debate: religion was philosophy in another form. Hamann was unequivocal in his opposition to such a view: 'Christianity ... does not believe in doctrines of philosophy, which are nothing but an alphabetic scribbling [*schreiberei*] of human speculation,[43] and subject to the changing moon and fashion!'[44] Faith was not based upon propositions that one weighed and accepted or rejected. (Ironically, as we noted in the previous chapter, Hamann's insistence that faith was not a matter for philosophical propositions had been the basis of his earlier defence of Mendelssohn against Lavater.)

The confessional dimensions of Hamann's attack are significant – they indicate how the Hobbesian/Mendelssohnian treatment of biblical events undermines immanent historical revelation that is difficult to divorce from traditional readings of the Bible. But what is even more important for our purposes is what this separation says about the place of externals in thought. Mendelssohn had been so keen to keep the rational mind free from bribery or coercion that he had insisted on the necessity of keeping all our reflection on religious dogma free from hope and fear. The church, we recall, did not even have the power to excommunicate, for such an act would always harm someone's material condition and was thus an inappropriate appeal to the will instead of the intellect. That the mind might have some compartment that examines *Wahrheitsgründe* entirely dispassionately was, for Hamann, a doubtful proposition.

What's more, Hamann thought that the distinction between the cognitive faculties and the will was not consistently maintained in Mendelssohn's own work. Hamann reopened Mendelssohn's question, 'Are there, according to the law of reason, rights over persons and things that are connected with doctrinal opinions, and are acquired by giving assent to them?'[45] His answer was not to enter into a discussion of the 'law of reason' or of rights, but rather to show Mendelssohn's inconsistency in this separation of inner convictions and outer actions. Mendelssohn's defence of the ceremonial law had been based on the connection between actions and truth – God had given the Jews a set of ceremonies that gave them a unique path to the universally accessible truths of reason.[46] Laws and doctrines, Mendelssohn argued, are related like body and soul.[47] In a manner that Mendelssohn never fully articulated, these ceremonial actions led to certain reflections. In addition, Mendelssohn, in his discussion of the origin of language (which we shall discuss in the following chapter), had suggested that the various developments in script affected the development of thought. Hamann wrote, 'If one cannot deny the connection between the physical and the moral, and the various modifications of writing and forms of expression have also variously affected the progress and improvement of concepts, opinions, and knowledge, then I do not know whence come the difficulties in positing a connection between moral capacities [i.e., rights] and doctrines.'[48] Cognition was, by Mendelssohn's own admission, a function of the fleeting, external world. To cordon off a realm for independent, individual moral judgment was to attempt to step out of the physical, historical world. The liberty that Kant would later envision for the noumenal realm of practical reason was there in embryonic form in the Mendelssohnian ideal of an internal realm of conviction free from power relations. It was a realm whose existence Hamann found epistemologically indefensible and one that Mendelssohn was somewhat inconsistent in defending.

The relationship between law and conviction is somewhat more complex in both Hobbes's and Mendelssohn's arguments than the clear division might indicate. Hobbes insisted, 'Faith is a gift of God, which Man can neither give, nor take away by promise of rewards, or menaces of torture,'[49] but this was probably more of a bone thrown to tender Protestant consciences in order that they might feel less apostate when they mouth words offensive to their hearts. After all, Hobbes was quite clear that 'it is annexed to the Soveraignty, to be Judge of what Opinions and Doctrines are averse, and what conducing to Peace; and consequently, on what occasions, how farre, and what, men are to be trusted withall, in speaking to Multitudes of people; and who shall examine the Doctrines of all bookes before they be published.'[50] Despite his apparently unambiguous statements about the state's power to coerce belief, he was quite clear that the state could (and should) regulate public speech.

Mendelssohn, for whom the distinction between conviction and action served as the basis for keeping the state out of doctrinal matters, nonetheless ran up against the problem of pernicious religious doctrines. 'Neither state nor church is authorized to judge in religious matters,' he wrote. The judge of doctrinal disputes is 'he to whom God has given the ability to convince others.'[51] But this proto-Habermasian insistence on the power of the best arguments sounds odd when uttered in the same breath as the following: 'The state, to be sure, is to see to it from afar that no doctrines are propagated which are inconsistent with the public welfare.'[52] One can, it seems, throw Hobbes out with a pitchfork, but he sneaks back in. Specifically, Mendelssohn argued that atheism was to be suppressed, for it is a pernicious doctrine, destructive of all morality: 'Without God, providence, and a future life, love of our fellow man is but an innate weakness, and benevolence is little more than a foppery into which we seek to lure one another so that the simpleton will toil while the clever man enjoys himself and has a good laugh at the other's expense.'[53]

Now, Mendelssohn never explained why atheism led naturally to such Thrasymachean extremes, and we would be accusing him of a grave contradiction if we suggested that his argument was based on the popular eighteenth-century view that fear of divine punishment made people keep their oaths. Indeed, he insisted that hope and fear cannot be at the root of rational religion. Puzzling as this is, however, it is no more puzzling than the tension between his insistence that there can be no coercion where doctrine is concerned and the view that pernicious doctrines must be destroyed and salutary ones taught.[54]

The separation of conviction from action had been necessary for Mendelssohn's defence of toleration. The old chestnut that convictions are not subject to the will is, indeed, a mainstay of toleration argument. For Hamann, this division was untenable and ran counter to all traditional Judeo-Christian thought. 'Actions without convictions and convictions without actions are a halving of whole, living duties into two, dead halves. If the reasons that motivate the will [*Bewegungsgründe*] may no longer be the reasons that persuade by the truth [*Wahrheitsgründe*],[55] and reasons that persuade by the truth are no longer worthy as reasons that motivate the will; if the essence depends on necessary understanding, and the reality on arbitrary will: then all divine and human unity ends, in convictions and actions. The state becomes a body without spirit or life – a carrion for eagles![56] The church a ghost, without flesh and bone – a scarecrow for sparrows!'[57]

Hamann is somewhat shrill here, and we who inhabit secular states are bound to find this apocalyptic tone unnerving. Indeed, the virulence of the statement appears to be a basis for a kind of intolerant fanaticism. As we will see, this is not the case – Hamann was a champion of tolerance – but it does raise significant problems in a religiously pluralistic society. What it would mean concretely to infuse the state body with spirit is a troubling question. In practice, as we will see, Hamann appeared to champion no more than an established church. But for the moment let us merely note that Hamann's shrillness here is born largely of his ire at a doctrine that would render meaningless the love and fear of God. Now, Hamann was being somewhat unfair; Mendelssohn, we recall, had insisted that duty ultimately required both honest convictions and correct actions. But in separating the passions of hope and fear from the intellect he had undermined the most *concerned* aspect of religion. What for Mendelssohn was a means of protecting religious thought from political control was, for Hamann, a reduction of religion to philosophical propositions. And while religion becomes thus emptied of care, political life becomes emptied of its spiritual significance.

Liberal Peace and Illiberal Tension: Tolerance versus Tolerance

The intemperate nature of Hamann's claim should not blind us to its importance. Mendelssohn had offered a separation between the right and the good that would later become essential for Kantian political philosophy (both in its original and its twentieth-century varieties).[58] That Mendelssohn's politics privileged subjective rights over the good was the subject of our last chapter. That his defence of toleration required a separation of conviction and action and of eternal and historical truth was the subject of this one. Mendelssohn's conviction exists in a realm apart from experience; neither temporal facts nor passions may intrude. Without the premise that individual convictions are free, Mendelssohn would not have been able to declare religious coercion illogical. However, his psychology and his counsel regarding the suppression of atheism indicated that he did think that the altering of convictions could be a matter of policy (that is, educational policy).

This privatization of faith is not to be rejected lightly. Hobbes had insisted upon the privacy of conviction in the hopes of attaining peace in an environment when claims of holiness had fomented rebellion. Hamann expressed himself intemperately when he exclaimed, 'What is it to me and you, the peace the world gives?'[59] This intemperance is a direct inversion of the Hobbesian emphasis (which Hamann imputed to Mendelssohn) on outer peace and security as the highest ends of the state.

By insulating universal doctrine from history and passion, from historical facts and laws, Mendelssohn managed to reconcile Rome and Jerusalem, rendering unto Caesar control over rights and retaining for the church what is, politically, *adiaphora*. Hamann insisted that there could be no easy reconciliation: 'The obligation to give unto each his due, to Caesar his tribute penny, and to God the glory of his name: this is in his [Mendelssohn's] eyes "a manifest opposition and collision of duties."[60] But was it Jesuitical prudence to call the hypocrite and tempter by his right name? ... That just answer, full of wisdom and goodness, that Caesar should be given his tribute-penny and God should be given his glory, was, then, no Pharisaic counsel to serve two masters and to carry the tree on both shoulders.'[61] One ought not to understand Christ's words as a compromise, or as a basis for liberalism. We do not have mixed obligations: rather, the injunction to give unto Caesar was a condemnation of the state. Church and state must necessarily be in tension because God and man are in tension.

But how are we to understand Hamann's response to Mendelssohn's call for the separation of church and state? Are we to understand, with Ze'ev Levy, that, for Hamann, 'religious coercion is permissible even if he does not say so explicitly'?[62] I do not think that this can be inferred from the text. Quite the contrary, the tension between state and church is essential:

Dogmatics and ecclesiastical right belong solely to the public institutions of education and administration, and are, as such, subject to executive arbitrariness, and now a crude, now a refined outer training, according to the elements and grades of the ruling aesthetic. These visible, public, common institutions are neither religion nor wisdom that descendeth from above; rather, they are earthly, sensual, and devilish according to the influence of French cardinals or Ciceroni, poetic confessors or prosaic belly-priests [*Bauchpfaffen*], and according to the varying system of statistical balance and overbalance, or armed tolerance and neutrality – both ecclesiastical and educational institutions, like creatures and miscarriages of the state and of reason, have as infamously sold themselves to the state and reason as they have betrayed those two; philosophy and politics have, to all their common deceits and brutality, found the need for the sword of superstition and the shield of unbelief, and have, as much through their love as through their hatred, abused dogmatics more wickedly than Amnon did the sister of his brother Absalom.[63]

There is no escaping the corruption of earthly institutions – they change form on the basis of the dictates of fashion, but are essentially in tension with faith. Mendelssohn had suggested that churches are 'public educational institutions for the formation of man that concern man's relations with God.'[64] Hamann returned that, though they can be better or worse, depending upon their leadership, they are essentially human institutions and cannot hope to bridge the 'infinite *misrelation* between man and God.'[65] State tolerance was but an armed neutrality; intolerance in the name of religion was an even greater abuse. The two sides are illustrated by Amnon's mad love of Tamar (that drove him to rape), and his ensuing hatred of her (that caused him to cast her out of his chambers).[66] Like superstition and doubt, intolerance and indifferentism are two sides of the same coin.

Hamann was able to reconcile his insistence on the connection between faith and politics with his view that the state should not coerce belief by positing an essential tension between the city of man and the holy city. Thus, he was able to make a totalizing religious claim without demanding the enforcement of confessional uniformity. 'HE [God] and the Son are one single essence that forbids, in political as in metaphysical realms, the slightest separation or plurality[67] and no man hath seen God; only the only begotten Son which is in the bosom of the Father, has given an exegesis [*hat exegesiert*] of his fullness of grace and truth.'[68] Religious truth was not accessible to some extra-historical reason, but was given only via historical fact. Hamann claimed no knowledge of eternal truth outside of historical revelation. What relationship does this eternal truth have to politics? 'A kingdom that is not of this world can thus make no other demand of ecclesiastical right than, with real need, to be tolerated [*geduldet*] and suffered; because no public institutions of mere human authority can stand up next to a divine lawgiving.'[69]

Faith was as much the recipient as the giver of tolerance. As for the Enlightenment's discourse of tolerance, Hamann had some reservations. In an earlier work, Hamann wrote, 'Tolerance is, of course, the most sublime Christian virtue; how much more, then, does it surprise me to see how it has pleased our century to fall so mortally in love with this, the most beautiful, heavenly daughter of the three Pauline graces.'[70] Evert Schoonhoven reminds us that the Pauline graces are faith, hope, and charity (1 Corinthians 13:13), and we note that Paul underlines charity as the most important.[71] If, then, Hamann's Christian tolerance is born of charity, what is the virtue that is loved by the enlighteners?

Opponents of Enlightenment toleration discourse have often made the charge that the champions of the doctrine are 'indifferentist.' Hamann went further, charging the champions of toleration with outright hostility to Christianity and, indeed, to religious enthusiasm of any sort. (This certainly was the case with Voltaire or Frederick, for which reason Hamann saw them as particularly objectionable.) In *Golgotha und Scheblimini*, Hamann levelled the charge of indifferentism at Mendelssohn. Indeed, as we have seen, he even went so far as to accuse Mendelssohn of atheism. This was most unfortunate, as the charges were manifestly incorrect: Mendelssohn was not indifferentist (although, we must note, in thinking that the essential truths of religion were accessible to all reasonable creatures, regardless of their confessional particularities, he certainly left some grounds for such an interpretation), and he was certainly not an atheist. Indeed, Hamann ought to have appreciated at least the spirit of Mendelssohn's defence of tradition. Hamann later repented of the charge of atheism, fearing that he had gone too far. It was especially absurd because Mendelssohn was also attacked, this time by a militant atheist, for religious fanaticism. Mendelssohn does not appear to have lost his humour, however: he is reported to have said that he felt like a man 'whose wife accused him of impotence and whose maid charged him with having made her pregnant.'[72] Yet Hamann, reporting Mendelssohn's joke to Herder, added the additional punchline that both the wife and the maid were right.[73]

Christian charity has often been employed as a justification for persecution (tough love, as it were).[74] Hamann does, however, provide some theological defence for accepting difference – we need not attribute his lack of persecuting zeal to a lack of charity. It is very important that we resist the simplistic suggestion that one is either a liberal pluralist or a defender of bloody persecution. Hamann wrote, 'For, with regards to the unrecognized philosophical and political sin of Gallionism, there is yet more to be said ... indeed these tares and the best and most noble wheat of tolerance and providence of the great householder remain commended until the time of the harvest.'[75] 'Gallionism' is indifferentism.[76] But, as Hamann wrote, 'there is more to be said' about tolerance than this. Hamann invoked the parable of the tares and the wheat (Matthew 13:24–30) to suggest a Christian meaning of tolerance: God's tolerance of man until the time of the final harvest. To speak of God's tolerance is also to speak of his providence – salvation comes despite sin. This parable also indicates a Christian's duty not to play God: one must not attempt to root out the tares, for one would also destroy the wheat. Hamann clearly did not think that inquisitions were a doctrinally acceptable extension of Christian charity; on the contrary, tolerance was a divine command.

The separation between internal conviction and external action was a powerful means of making the crime of unbelief logically impossible. If thought is by nature free, then law can reasonably affect actions only. This separation paved the way for the liberal separation of church and state and the privatization of faith. Hamann thought, however, that this separation was an epistemological error. It was simply untenable to claim that we have dispassionate knowledge of eternal matters – all our truths are grounded in history and our passions. For Hamann, a faith that requires conviction made in the absence of all temporal corruptions is a figment of the brain. What's more, it is morally problematic since it severs politics from any considerations greater than 'outer peace and security.' If the greatest good, the 'eternal truth,' is essentially extra-historical – if it is solely the possession of the inner realm – then it becomes disconnected from the historical and political world in which we live.[77] Since Hamann thought the split between internal and external to be artificial, he drew the conclusion that this theoretical separation entailed the elevation of the *Leviathan* over the good.

The disturbing elements of this should not escape us. If Hamann is correct epistemologically, there is an error at the heart of Enlightenment toleration theory. We are thus forced to abandon the chimera of neutrality and confront the clash between competing goods. Toleration requires a thicker justification. But if Hamann thought Christian charity itself could provide that justification – if he was clear that there was no contradiction between an established church and a policy of universal toleration – he was equally intemperate in dismissing the dangers of such a spiritually infused politics as he advocated. The peace the world gives is a powerful good, and we do well to note the intemperance of those who grant higher importance to the state of one's soul.

8 Language and Society

If Mendelssohn was going to insist on the necessity of maintaining Jewish personal laws, he needed to give a rational justification for their continued relevance. What use were these curious practices if the truths necessary for salvation were attainable with reason alone? How could an independent, rational agent submit himself to external rules and the authority of rabbis? Mendelssohn's answer to these questions was an ingenious reconciliation of Enlightenment rationalism and a theoretical defence of tradition.

Mendelssohn's defence of tradition is brilliantly paradoxical, making use of tools normally employed by those seeking to undermine tradition. What is most striking is that Mendelssohn, who offered the most unambiguously optimistic view of the human capacity to attain all that is necessary to salvation by means of reason alone, also articulated a scepticism about the written word and about language in general that would appear to run counter to this optimism. This sceptical component appears at first glance to derive from sources similar to Hamann's rejection of dogmatism. But despite the two writers' shared disapproval of the reduction of religious claims to linguistic formulae, Mendelssohn's view of language is radically different from Hamann's. Both Mendelssohn's attack on enforced credos and his defence of traditional Jewish ceremonies were predicated on a radical Hobbesian nominalism. This view of language makes several assumptions about the relationship between individuals and their communities that Hamann contested. Hamann's insistence on the primacy of logos entailed an attack on the atomism of social contract theory.

Mendelssohn on the Limits of Language

Jerusalem entered into a discussion of the origin and nature of language for two reasons. First, Mendelssohn wished to highlight the rationality of the apparently arbitrary Jewish ceremonial law. By indicating the limits of the written word, he was able to open up a space for ceremonial practice. Second, he wished to bolster the traditional claim of toleration advocates that belief *cannot* be enforced. He achieved both of these ends by establishing the limits of language.

Mendelssohn, we recall, distinguished between truths that can be known by reason alone and divine laws whose revelation is historical, and whose acceptance is based on faith in the authorities that report the event. His distinction between conviction and action becomes a distinction here between religious doctrine and religious law.[1] But, as we will see in greater detail, Mendelssohn somewhat muddied his essential distinction between laws (which motivate the will) and arguments (which convince the intellect) by suggesting that the Jewish ceremonial law is somehow connected to the truth, both being based upon universal truths and having the function of turning the mind of the faithful towards the universal truths. The law has a certain advantage over arguments; arguments can be abridged, while the laws remain irreducible. True, Mendelssohn conceded, at the centre of the law is the golden rule, 'Love thy neighbour as thyself,' but this sort of maxim is not really an abridgement of the law – the law's significance is its complexity and particularity.[2] No brief list of maxims or principles can fully articulate the law (a point that buttressed his arguments against the utility of official professions of faith). Indeed, not even the scriptures can serve as a full treatment of the law. The law is dynamic and complex – thus, it is necessary for the faithful to do more than merely assent to certain abstract principles. Their lives must be led in constant intercourse with the revealed law. Thus ceremonies and the ecclesiastical institution of the rabbis serve the same purpose of keeping the law alive. The first render law a 'living script, rousing heart and mind'; the second provide the oral tradition that renders the written law meaningful, and without which the law becomes a 'dead letter.'[3]

This argument must have been among those that led Hamann to his initial, sympathetic reading: he must have felt that he had encountered a kindred spirit. Obsessed with the reduction of religious debate to impersonal propositions, Hamann constantly returned to the insistence upon the communicative nature of faith and the divine Logos. When Mendelssohn indulged in a polemical excursus decrying his overly literary age ('In a word, we are literati, men of letters'), Hamann can only have heard a baffling echo of his own expostulations against the Republic of Letters. (Perhaps, indeed, it is not surprising that the most favourable reviewer of the *Sokratische Denkwürdigkeiten* had been Mendelssohn.) But for all this apparent sympathy, there are essential differences between the two writers' positions – differences that Hamann came to see as irreconcilable.

Before we delve into the theory of language that Mendelssohn provided in support of this thesis on the continued relevance of post-biblical Jewish practice, we should take a moment to note a curious tension within his argument. On the one hand, he was championing a view of autonomous reason that was accessible at all times and all places by rational beings. On the other, he wanted to insist upon the relevance of historical traditions. By differentiating between the revealed law and rationally attainable truth, he both celebrated and undermined rational autonomy. Everyone had the ability to reason on conceptual matters and to attain the essential doctrines of the universal religion of mankind, but Jewish law was not conceptual in this way, nor was it subject to individual judgment. Thus, he insisted on intellectual humility before the divine law: 'Who can say: I have entered into God's sanctuary, gauged the whole system of his designs, and am able to determine its measure, goal, and boundaries? I may surmise, but not pass judgment nor act according to my surmise.'[4] Judaism, then, is essentially bound to tradition, and rational autonomy has rather strict limits.

Mendelssohn wanted to defend the ceremonial law and the continued existence of tradition by arguing that the law was supremely complex and could not be reduced to some simple text, but needed to be kept alive constantly through individual practice and the instruction of religious teachers. Like Luther, he thought that the written law was a 'dead letter' without the proper spiritual preparation. But for Luther, the written law was completed by Christ and the gospel, while for Mendelssohn, the law was completed by the ongoing tradition and teaching. There is an important difference here, because, while Luther had insisted that the Gospels were not to be treated in the same way as the Old Testament, he had nonetheless made the key to the law another book, *not a human institution*. It became perfectly reasonable for Protestantism (despite Luther's objections) to take a radical turn inwards, and, in its more extreme variants, to oppose itself to any ecclesiastical authority. Mendelssohn's attack on the dead letter had precisely the opposite intention: the law was not complete in any written form – one could not turn to the pages of a John or a Paul for the definitive formulation of faith that gave law living spirit. Thus ceremonies and ecclesiastical authorities were indispensable. This had to do with the limits of writing and, indeed, of language.

Books, Mendelssohn argued, were a mixed blessing. They had greatly increased learning, but they had also caused people to neglect wisdom and conversation.[5] The origin of this decline is not merely the technology of writing (although Mendelssohn had something to say on this), but the nature of language itself. *Jerusalem* gives a truncated but important account of the origin of language. It begins thus: 'Scarcely does a man cease to be satisfied with the first impressions of the external senses … scarcely does he feel the urge implanted in his soul to form concepts out of these external impressions, when he becomes aware of the necessity to attach them to perceptible signs, not only in order to communicate them to others, but also to hold fast to them himself, and to be able to consider them again as often as necessary.'[6] The soul begins to separate out general characteristics of its impressions. In order to be able to think, the soul 'attaches, either by a natural or an arbitrary association of ideas, the abstracted characteristic [of an impression] to a perceptible sign which, as often as its impression is renewed, at once recalls and illuminates this characteristic, pure and unalloyed.'[7] The development of human reason depends on the development of distinct conceptual labels. 'The designation of concepts is, therefore, doubly necessary; first, for ourselves, as a vessel, so to speak, in which to preserve them, and keep them near at hand for use; and, next, to enable us to communicate our thoughts to others.'[8] Signs are primarily private possessions and secondarily means of communication. We can recognize here the outlines of Hobbes's nominalism. Hobbes, too, thought that we have need of markers for things in order both to communicate and, more originally, to retain ideas for ourselves: 'The first use of names, is to serve for *Markes*, or *Notes* of remembrance.'[9]

Mendelssohn argued that people employ many things as markers or signs of abstract ideas. Sounds are ideal for transmitting an idea from one person to another, but their use assumes that the concept we wish to transmit is already in the mind of the other person, and that the sign will cause our listener to draw forth the idea. But sounds cannot have been the first markers – primitive people did not simply separate a concept, designate a sound for it, and then employ that sound to draw forth the concept at will. Rather, Mendelssohn speculated, people originally must have employed the thing itself as a constant reminder of the general characteristic.[10] The thing was the sign. Later, they made images of the things, such as statues (a process whose conclusion is the use of hieroglyphs), and proceeded, by way of sounds, to developing alphabetical writing.[11]

This use of signs to designate ideas is essential for the development of the sciences but has some deleterious social consequences.[12] The moment one designates a religious idea with a sign, unenlightened people begin to invest magical significance in the sign, rather than to understand its original, abstract signification. The sign begins to be taken for the thing itself (i.e., God).[13] Thus, the origin of idolatry is in the misinterpretation of signs: hieroglyphs, plastic forms, written words, and other signs begin to be treated as gods, in a misunderstanding that is often helped along by duplicitous priests.[14] Because of this tendency, the world finds itself in a constant state of corruption. Periodically philosophers appear and attempt to explain the simple, rational signification of religious symbols, but they are usually thwarted.[15] Here, Mendelssohn, who had originally argued that the truths about religion were clear and simple enough to be discerned by all men, argued that the common man tended to seek fantastic explanations rather than to be satisfied with the simple, rational truth: 'What is comprehensible to him is soon looked upon as tedious and contemptible, and he constantly searches for new, mysterious, inexplicable things, which he takes to heart with redoubled pleasure.'[16] The Torah solves this problem – this universal tendency to turn signs into idols – by prescribing ceremonial laws that render everyday practice into a constant reminder of the divine truth. Instead of proclaiming an article of belief (that, as a bundle of conceptual signs, would be prone to corruption), the law prescribed practices that 'were to serve in place of signs.'[17] The perpetual enactment of ceremony in addition to the wise counsel of elders, was the means by which the original purity of religion and morality was to be preserved from corruption and idolatry. Against the standard Enlightenment practice of decrying tradition as the source of prejudice, Mendelssohn defended tradition as a bulwark against prejudice.

For Mendelssohn, then, doctrine was universal, objective, and discoverable by reason: 'All human knowledge can be reduced to a few, fundamental concepts, which are laid down as the bases.'[18] Mosaic law, on the other hand, was extremely complex, and as inscrutable as the divine mind. The ceremonial law had the function of preserving, through constant enactment, the purest doctrines: in place of written words, which could be misunderstood and abused, it instituted a perpetual education in the form of ceremonial actions and attendance to the instruction of elders. Conceptual clarity was ever elusive and doctrines were ever in danger of being corrupted. 'The great maxim of this constitution seems to have been: *men must be impelled to perform actions and only induced to engage in reflection.*'[19]

The illusive nature of conceptual clarity is somewhat troubling. If Mendelssohn displayed on one hand a Hobbesian optimism for the universal capacity to progress rationally, he also articulated a surprisingly pessimistic view about the possibilities of communication. Mendelssohn not only argued that signs could become idolatrous – he also contested the possibility of shared belief and complete terminological clarity. Hobbes had argued that beliefs could not be coerced, only actions could. Mendelssohn took Hobbes one step further – not only could we not crawl into the heads of other people in order to make sure that their credo was sincere, but we could not even be certain that our own professions of faith are correct, consistent, and honest. He wrote, 'I may feel sure of something right now, but a moment later, some slight doubt of its certainty may sneak or steal its way into a corner of my soul and lurk there ... Many things for which I would suffer martyrdom today may appear problematic to me tomorrow. If, in addition, I must also put these internal perceptions into words and signs, or swear to words and signs which other men lay before me, the uncertainty will be still greater. *My neighbor and I cannot possibly connect the very same words with the very same internal sensations, for we cannot compare them, liken them to one another and correct them without again resorting to words.*'[20]

Reason may be public, but language is essentially private. Hence, it is impossible to have complete doctrinal unity because we, in our little shells, can never be certain that the words we use evoke the same concepts in our listeners. Mendelssohn would have liked Pope's quip, ''Tis with our judgments as our watches, none / Go just alike, yet each believes his own.'[21] Yet he might even have quibbled with Pope's suggestion that 'each believes his own': each thoughtful person, knowing that his opinions have often changed in the past, doubts his own enough to be reluctant to make doctrinal oaths.

Mendelssohn insisted that this was not an argument for scepticism, although his claim to that effect was somewhat ambiguous: 'I am perhaps one of those who are the farthest removed from that disease of the soul, and who most ardently wish to be able to cure their fellow men of it. But precisely because I have so often performed this cure on myself, and tried it on others, I have become aware of how difficult it is, and what little hope one has of success.'[22] Mendelssohn was not a sceptic, but he was sceptical about his ability to refrain from doubting! This is a most curious position for him to have taken, considering his repeated assertion that eternal truths 'are legible and comprehensible to all men.'[23]

The positions might be reconciled by appealing to his argument about man's natural monotheism – recall, he had suggested that miracles were intelligible to people only because there existed within them the tendency to see a single cause of the universe, even if this concept did not find adequate expression. Perhaps it will not be inelegant to quote Pope again: 'Yet if we look more closely, we shall find / Most have the seeds of judgment in their mind.'[24]

Hamann on the Priority of Language

We are, according to Mendelssohn's image, isolated individuals – words (and all signs) constitute markers of our (more or less distinct) concepts. To think is to append labels or signs to concepts within our heads. When we speak, we assemble a little bundle of signs that refer to our concepts, which, in turn, refer to the world. In a speech situation, we can't really know whether we have got the message our interlocutor has sent us because we can't get into his head. If we are not careful, we even become tangled in our own chains of thought. That said, there is a natural rational capacity in all people that leads them to conceive of one creator. This they do even in their most pre-linguistic state, 'stammeringly.' Hamann saw the naivety of Mendelssohn's faith in reason and his doctrinal scepticism as inseparable: 'Lust for the doubting of truth and the credulousness of self-deception are thus just as inseparable symptoms as the chill and heat of a fever.'[25] For Hamann, Mendelssohn's doubts are born of an insufficient faith in the possibilities of communication, while his certainty is born of a misguided confidence in the truth of concepts. In what follows, we will flesh out this charge.

 Golgotha und Scheblimini calls into question the picture of human beings as isolated atoms. Language is not a bundle of signs that an isolated individual attaches to some abstracted characteristic he wishes to separate out from his impression of external phenomena. Rather, it is the constitutive basis of existence. God spoke the world into being; the world is a divine message. Man, too, speaks, and, being made in the image of God, his words are both creative and revelatory, a view that we have already encountered in the memorable phrase from the *Aesthetica*, 'Speak, that I might see you!'[26] Human existence is *essentially* linguistic and communal. To be a human being is to communicate. For Mendelssohn and Hobbes, language is artifice – it is a human construction that enables us both to reason and to bridge the gap between ourselves and other human beings. Hence, for Hobbes, the giving (and keeping) of our word forms the basis of society, and the precise use of a publicly settled language establishes the foundation for science and for peaceful coexistence. Mendelssohn takes this notion of our original isolation a step further, maintaining that, where the divine law is concerned, even language fails to bridge the gap between us – we require common ceremonial *practices* in place of signs. For Hamann, this is a fundamental misunderstanding of language and communication. Mendelssohn and Hobbes are both too optimistic and too pessimistic about the possibilities of language.

The optimism, or 'feverish heat,' is easily explained. Mendelssohn's claim that the existence of a deity was a conceptual proposition to which all men had access was the type of philosophical pride that Hamann combated throughout his writing life. Hamann denied that faith was a matter of conceptual propositions. He also denied the possibility of having some sort of inexpressible but vivid and meaningful concept of monotheism. We recall the *Metakritik*'s insistence that 'the entire capacity to think rests on language.'[27] In addition, language is essentially contextual and bounded – essentially a posteriori, 'without any other credentials than tradition and use.'[28] Thus, for Mendelssohn to suggest that there were universally accessible, truth-bearing concepts that rational creatures could attain *prior* to their linguistic life was to speak in riddles: there were no words that bore meaning independent of context. To think that there were was, for Hamann, a 'mystical' error.[29]

Mendelssohn's Enlightened optimism about reason struck Hamann as misplaced. Invoking Mendelssohn's description of the process by which the human mind progresses scientifically, Hamann wrote, 'With such a crab-wandering of the understanding, without flight of inventiveness, the immeasurable is just as easily conceivable as the measurable,[30] and the reverse – it is with just such ease that, through an immediate indication of the thing, German literature cannot merely be surveyed, but improved by an imperator from Peking, as by a deaf-born Johann Ballhorn!'[31]

Mendelssohn's suggestion that conceptual progress can lead to a measuring of the immeasurable heavens is mocked here by Hamann, who hints that the method seeks to measure the Godhead. To treat a sign as an 'immediate indication' of a thing (a phrase Mendelssohn had used when speaking of symbols)[32] is to treat the manipulation of signs as somehow leading to an absolute knowledge of the world. It posits an objective reality to which an arbitrary language refers, and suggests that the purification of language might produce clear conceptual knowledge of that reality. This rationalism is perfectly in keeping with Hobbes's optimism about the progress of science through the precise use of words. Hamann suggests, with an apparent non sequitur, that, under such a theory, a Chinese emperor might consider himself as good a judge of German literature as any German. The joke is a pointed reference to Frederick II. Frederick, a notorious Francophile, had famously written a scathing evaluation of German literature, holding up French models as examples that German writers should follow. The references to deafness are sarcastic allusions to a passage in *Jerusalem* where Mendelssohn attempted to defend an aspect of his speculative genealogy of script by noting that deaf people can have access to concepts and signs without needing the intermediary of sounds. As for the reference to Johann Ballhorn, it is more obscure to us than it would have been to Hamann's readers. It refers to a sixteenth-century printer whose name had become proverbial (*ballhornieren* had become a verb). He had edited and printed an extant book, placing on the cover page 'verbessert von Johann Ballhorn.' As the new edition was full of new errors, 'to ballhorn' came to be a term for making 'improvements' that were actually detractions. Frederick's ballhorning was an example of the 'deafness' to the nuances of different languages that Hamann thought was the result of this language-as-label theory.

Frederick and his enlightened ilk were 'deaf' because they did not attend to the nuances of languages, but rather, were attracted by the promise of conceptual clarity. The Hobbesian solution to the problem of knowledge is to refine one's terms – epistemological problems are overcome through 'perspicuous words.' Well used – with precise definitions and consistency – words are a source of knowledge; ill used, they are a source of absurdity and confusion. But for Hamann, words are multilayered, and their meaning is always affected by their context. To attempt to define one's way out of the complexities of everyday usage was to attain an abstract clarity at the expense of experiential complexity. There was an error in thinking that such terminological precision says something essential about the world. What actually happens is that one builds more and more elaborate structures that are more and more divorced from experience. One does not talk one's way out of the cave, but rather digs deeper. Hamann both condemned the ideal of conceptual precision in Mendelssohn and indicated its Hobbesian dimension: 'In a valley of vision full of imprecise and precarious concepts, the glorying of greater Enlightenment is not good! – better development! – more correct distinction! – and sublimated linguistic use of healthy commonsense! – against the times and the system of a Hobbes.'[33] Hamann wished to make the situation explicit: Mendelssohn, who decried Hobbes's age and system, ought to recognize his own Hobbesianism.

In a letter to Jacobi, in which Hamann sought to explain both his *Golgotha* and his thoughts on Kant's first *Critique*, he wrote, 'With me, indeed, the question is not, what is reason? but rather, what is language? and here I suspect the basis of all paralogisms and antinomies that one lays upon reason. It is because of this that one takes words for concepts, and concepts for the things themselves. In words and concepts no evidence is possible – evidence appertains only to matter and things. No enjoyment can be pondered-up – and all things – including the *Ens Entium* [the being of beings] – exist for the sake of enjoyment, and not for speculation.'[34] Hamann was arguing that 'speculation,' the philosophical refinement and manipulation of concepts, was an activity that distanced one from experience. It was misguided to think that one's concepts pointed directly to reality – to do this was, to use a twentieth-century cliché, to confound the map with the territory. It might well be useful in some circumstances to manipulate abstract concepts, but one must not think that one's concepts are in any way more real than immediate sensory experience, or any more meaningful than one's everyday language.

We are by now comfortable with Hamann's objection to philosophical hubris: his attack on Mendelssohn's rational optimism should come as no surprise. But Hamann was equally critical of Mendelssohn's scepticism. The inescapable boundedness of humankind to particular language and history is also the basis for Hamann's objections to Mendelssohn's limited faith in the capacity of language to cross the divide between separate minds. *Jerusalem* paints the picture of an objective world external to the perceiving subject who, in turn, attempts to abstract from the constant flow of his internal impressions by separating out some element of his impressions and forging a concept. To this, he fixes a sign (arbitrary in itself, but often, in practice, related to the object in the world he wishes to designate). But communication, we noted, is never satisfactory because we always remain uncertain of our interlocutors' ideas. Even our own ideas are difficult to pin down. Thus, not only is the world a scary place, full of incomprehensible beings, but one can barely comprehend oneself. For Hamann, these doubts were misplaced: just as one can't think without language, so too is it an error to doubt in this manner. 'Zweifelsucht' is the result of applying inappropriate standards of truth to speech. We have cause to repeat Hamann's objections to the 'third purification' that we encountered in the *Metakritik.* 'The longer one reflects, the more deeply and inwardly one is struck dumb, and one loses all desire to speak.'[35]

Jerusalem's emphasis on the lack of certainty in one's use of language is actually, in Hamann's view, based on a dogmatic *purism.* As we have seen, Mendelssohn treated reason as universal and public, but language as private. Our personal mental discourse and our discourse with others are on the shakiest ground; while Mendelssohn treated religious doctrine as the subject for enlightened debate, he also found himself reduced to a kind of religious quietism. Mendelssohn's traditionalist solution – that Judaism avoided the linguistic trap by having actions as living signs – appeared to the Magus to be a cheap conjuring trick akin to popery. 'Christianity,' Hamann snorted, does not believe in 'lasting actions and ceremonies to which one ascribes a secret power and inexplicable magic!'[36]

Hamann was certainly correct to note a severe problem in Mendelssohn's claim. If actions are 'living signs,' it is hard to see how they overcome the problem posed by subjectivism. After all, how can we be certain that the performance of ceremonies conjures up the same conceptual content in all performers' minds? The problem of radical subjectivity remains. Certainly Protestant complaints about the Catholic liturgy are replete with condemnation of idolatrous ceremony. But more important than this criticism is Hamann's rejection of the radical individualism in Hobbes and Mendelssohn.

For both Hobbes and Mendelssohn, social unity is the product of artifice. For Hobbes, this artifice is linguistic; for Mendelssohn's religious community it is ceremonial. Hamann turned this thought on its head. He articulated a kind of linguistic realism in which everyday language is taken to be fundamental, natural, phenomenally prior to any process of conceptual clarification. Consider his cento on Mendelssohn's social contract:

All social contracts are grounded, according to the law of nature, on the moral capacity to say Yes! or No! and on the moral necessity to realize that said word. The moral capacity to say Yes! or No! is grounded on the natural use of human reason and language; the moral necessity to fulfil one's given word depends on the fact that the explanation of our inner will cannot be expressed, revealed, or perceived in any way other than orally, in writing, or in action, and our words, as the natural signs of our convictions [*Gesinnungen*] must be valid. Reason and language are, then, the inner and outer bonds of all sociability, and if one separates or severs that which nature, through her establishment, put together, then one annihilates faith and fidelity, and renders lies and betrayal, slander and vice confirmed and stamped means to happiness.[37]

We are not isolated individuals constructing unity through the giving of our word; words are not artificial chains that bind our thoughts or our relationships. Rather, they are an essential part of ourselves. There is a clear allusion to Matthew 5:37: 'But let your communication be, Yea, yea; Nay, nay: for whatsoever is more than these cometh of evil.' There is, of course, an element of populist anti-intellectualism in this. But the claim has a greater significance: the separation of thought from language and the treatment of language as artifice takes away from the revelatory function of language. It places a thick wall between ourselves and others. It is not that artificial linguistic acts make society possible, but society and language are inseparable and equally essential to human beings: 'Sociability is the true principle of reason and language, through which our sentiments [*Empfindungen*] and representations are modified.'[38]

Hamann is not undermining Hobbesian justice, the keeping of one's word. Fidelity to one's contractual obligations is important. But the capacity to make contracts follows from and is made possible by the communicative context in which human beings exist. Language, to use a Kantian phrase, is the necessary condition for contracts. Language is not something that we can think up on our own; we could neither understand others nor express ourselves if we had not previously learned the grammar and usage of a particular language. Now, clearly neither Hobbes nor Mendelssohn would have had trouble with this claim, but Hamann's point is that this says something essential about mind and language. This necessary 'genealogical priority' (as the *Metakritik* had it) makes language more than simply a tool that a rational individual employs to reckon or to exchange information. It becomes an organic part of ourselves.

Hamann, we know, takes this further: existence is essentially communicative. God spoke the world into existence. He speaks to man in human idiom; people, built in the image of God, share in the creative and revelatory nature of language. Human sociability is based on our essentially linguistic/divine nature. Since Mendelssohn had praised the Stoics, Hamann cited Cicero here: 'The bond or cement that holds men together is reason [RATIO] and discourse [ORATIO].'[39] But

Hamann did not mean this in a Hobbesian sense – recall that 'reason and language' are 'the *inner and outer* bond of all sociability.'[40] Let us consider the following quotation (noting the admixture of biblical language and Mendelssohnian natural rights):

> He spake, and it was done! 'and whatsoever man called every living creature, that was the name thereof.'[41] According to this model and likeness of determination, every word of a man should be and remain the thing itself. On this, the stamp and the title's similarity with the pattern of our race and the guide of our youth[42] – on this right of nature to use words as the truest, noblest, and most powerful means towards revelation and transmission of our most inner declaration of will [*Willenserklärung*], the validity of all contracts is grounded, and this mighty fortress[43] of the hidden truth is superior to all political arithmetic, machinery,[44] school-foxiness, and charlatanism. The misuse of language and its natural signs is, then, the grossest perjury, and makes the violator of this first law of reason and its justice into the wickedest misanthrope.[45]

Hamann would not have us treat words as artifice chaining naturally separate individuals together, but rather he would have us see ourselves as *essentially* social and linguistic. The foundation of all human cognition is communion, both the transmission and reception of revelation.

It is in this sense that we should understand his repeated charge that philosophers are 'babblers': while the populist claim grows tiresome to read, it is not glib, but is rather a theoretically justified commitment to ordinary language. Thus, he objected to Jacobi's attempt to render *Glauben* a philosophical term of art: 'I still know neither what Hume nor what we two understand by *belief* – and the more we would speak or write about it, the less we will succeed in grasping firmly this quicksilver.'[46] Language must be treated, not as a tool, but as an organic part of ourselves. There is an essentially subjective element to language; it cannot be radically individualist since language itself presupposes a social context.

Ian Hacking has offered an illuminating essay outlining the intellectual kinship between the later Wittgenstein's rejection of the private language argument and Hamann.[47] Much like Wittgenstein, Hamann claimed to transform philosophical questions into questions of 'grammar.'[48] Also akin to Wittgenstein, he insisted on the centrality of context and use for meaning. We have seen in our discussion of the *Metakritik* that Hamann performed a 'Copernican' move similar to Kant's, but he substituted language for the a priori. At the base of this thought is a religious motivation beyond philosophical defence to treat the world as meaningful, a subject for interpretation and a context of communion. The philosophical aspect of the argument is its insistence on the priority of linguistic community. Hamann argued that a scrupulous empiricism unveiled the priority of existence over thinking[49] and the manner in which individual human being is affective, needy, and essentially communicative/relational. The will to abstraction entails a desire to attain objectivity by setting these particular relations at a distance. Of course, we *do* use abstract language – indeed, every noun might be considered abstract when compared to the atomic sensation of a thing. Hamann's somewhat intemperate dismissal of abstraction in the above quotation is tempered by his suggestion in the *Aesthetica* that there are natural and unnatural forms of abstraction. The point of his rejection of abstraction – and it is a fundamentally political point – is that we must overcome the view of language as the artificial instrument of individual minds, a view he thought the corollary of radical political objectification. The abstract nature of 'public reason' is a product of private language. The attempt to cobble together a community of strangers is necessary only when the ground of unity has been denied.

To repeat, while Hamann objected to the view that philosophy could build a ladder to heaven, he indicated that rigorous doubt was equally due to excessive reliance on precisely defined terminological abstractions (hence his claim that dogmatism and doubt were two sides of the same coin).[50] What Hamann was criticizing was the tendency in eighteenth-century philosophy to think in solipsistic terms. If other people are strangers to us, they are no more strange than we are to ourselves. 'Just as the image of my face reflects back in water, so is my "I" thrown back at me in every fellow man [*Nebenmensch*]. In order that this "I" be to me as my own, providence has sought to join so many advantages and amenities to the society of men.'[51] Thus, Hamann considered doubt of God and doubt of social unity to have a similar source. It is possible to doubt God, just as it is possible to doubt one's spiritual affinity with one's neighbour: in this sense, error and vice are kin. This doubt constitutes an attempt to separate oneself from the world of experience and communication, to separate oneself from one's society.

Solipsism, on this linguistic/theological reading, is not merely error – it is sin rendered philosophical. Once one jettisons the individualistic premises of Hobbesian, Lockean, Rousseauan, or Mendelssohnian linguistic theory, one no longer needs to *account for* social unity. Society no longer becomes a creation, but is a natural phenomenon based on the fundamental identity of human beings. Once one divests oneself of the view that thought and language are separate phenomena, one ceases to take communication to be a secondary moment, but rather sees human existence as essentially communicative. Hamann may use Cicero's metaphor of language as social cement, but the metaphor is somewhat in tension with his view. Hobbes binds thoughts and people with words; Mendelssohn employs words for political community and actions for religious community. Both treat individuals as essentially separate, connected by artifice. In the social contract tradition, society is a wall made up of individual stones held together with the mortar of words. Hamann quoted from Nehemiah 4:3: 'An Ammonite would say, "let them just build it; Even that which they build, if a fox go up, he shall even break down their stone wall."'[52] For Hamann, Jerusalem was not built with stones and mortar.

Appendix: Hamann and Judaism

It is clear from our discussion that the contest between Hamann and Mendelssohn did have a confessional dimension. But, as we noted at the outset, Hamann was not primarily opposed to Mendelssohn's Judaism. Of course, Hamann was too committed a Christian to be able to reconcile his religious views entirely with those of any other religious tradition, but what he found most troubling in Mendelssohn was his rational theology. Shortly after Mendelssohn's death, Hamann wrote to Jacobi (who had waged a polemical battle against Mendelssohn), 'I have nothing to do with either the living or the dead [i.e., Mendelssohn] Jew or rabbi, I want neither to convert him nor to condemn him; rather, the Berliners are my opponents and the philistines against whom I will rage.'[53] It is this that preoccupied Hamann – if he held the typically Christian view that Judaism was understandable only as a prelude to Christ, he was uninterested in anti-Jewish polemic: 'The Jew,' he wrote, 'remains ever the actual, original nobleman of the entire human race.' Mendelssohn's philosophy was most problematic because it 'speaks half Ashdodic, and not pure Jewish.'[54]

The reaction to Judaism that emerges in Hamann's *Golgotha und Scheblimini* is somewhat ambiguous, however. Isaiah Berlin is quite simplistic when he argues Hamann simply bore some residual 'anti-Semitism' that was part of the Zeitgeist.[55] Both to charge and to excuse him for a repellent, unreflective prejudice is to ignore the significance of

'Judaism' as a category in his thought. Steeped in Pauline language, Hamann constantly argued that the Greek and the Jew – standing for reason and law, respectively – stumbled on Christianity. For Hamann, the Jews are the chosen people, but they are also the stiff-necked. Hamann speaks of Jews in unmeasured tone, both positively and nega- tively. There is little doubt, however, that anti-Semitism (as we would term it) influenced the rhetorical thrust of some of his writing, espe- cially where Mendelssohn was concerned. Extremely attuned to the subtleties of language, he employed the capital of communal prejudice and New Testament anti-Judaism in seeking rhetorical effect. Phrases such as the following were clearly intended to make use of popular feeling: 'Exclusive self-love and envy are the inheritance and trade of a Jewish naturalism.'[56] One cannot but feel a distinct revulsion when con- fronted with such a rhetorical strategy; Hamann never chose a word carelessly, and if he was always immoderate in his tone he knew pre- cisely what he was doing. Indeed, considering his professed friendship with Mendelssohn (which, from his correspondence, does not appear to have been feigned), one can only wonder at Hamann's complete in- sensitivity to the delicate position of a Jew in Prussia (or in any German state). Perhaps this is the sort of thing that Leo Strauss had in mind when he accused Hamann (with Luther and Heidegger) of 'high-class intelligence and low-class character.'[57] But, if we should be wary of whitewashing Hamann, we should be equally wary of misunderstand- ing him. Mendelssohn had made the essence of Jewish religious doc- trine rational, 'natural religion,' and the essence of God's revelation, law. Hamann's project was based in a Lutheran disapprobation of rea- son and law without the cross. If his rhetoric periodically made use of populist bigotry, it did not rest upon it, but rather upon Pauline asser- tions (made most clearly in the book of Romans) that the law is fulfilled only through Christ. Nonetheless, Hamann was supremely aware of language and a master at deploying words' multifaceted powers – in- deed, Hamann's writings depend very heavily on associative thought. Given this awareness, his repeated equation of 'Jews' and 'naturalists,' despite deriving from Mendelssohn's equation of Jewish doctrine and natural religion, was clearly a means of exploiting anti-Semitic feelings in his readers, and it is a tactic deserving severe opprobrium.[58]

In defence of Hamann, Alexander quotes from him, 'Has Jesus ceased to be King of the Jews? Has the inscription on the Cross been changed? Do we not therefore persecute Him in His people?'[59] This would seem to be contradicted by a passage from a late letter, quoted by Levy: 'Why should the civil repression [*Verstossung*] of the Jews or Negroes concern us? Their time is not yet come.'[60] However, Levy's quotation is problematic. The Henkel edition of Hamann's letters has *Verfassung*, not *Verstossung*.[61] This would make Hamann indifferent to their *constitution*, rather than to their persecution. Indeed, the tenor of the letter is that one should not concern oneself overly with different confessions. However this might lessen the cruelty of the statement, the quotation does indicate that, if he was more positive in his estimation of 'the original noblemen of the entire human race'[62] than many of his contemporaries, he was certainly no Lessing, nor did he demonstrate much concern for the civic emancipation of the Jews.[63] (And he did not display much concern for the plight of serfs, or yet, as the above quotation indicates, for that of African slaves).[64]

If Hamann's views on Judaism are ambiguous, what is perfectly clear is that Hamann was not a religious pluralist. While he did not think that pagans were damned, for instance, it was because he thought that he could discern Christian figures in pagan texts. God gave the revelation of nature to all mankind, but there was a key that, for unfathomable reasons, was given to a particular people. We must, then, avoid falling into the trap of Hamann's apologists who insist that *Golgotha und Scheblimini*'s defence of a more spiritual Judaism against the Enlightened, reform-minded position of Mendelssohn is a sign of Hamann's capacity to embrace radically different faiths. Ecumenical counter-Enlightenment thinkers will find many helpful resources in Hamann, but they will never be able to embrace him wholly, for the Christocentrism of his thought is simply inescapable. Hamann did defend Judaism to Lavater thus: 'What Moses saw in the burning bush that burnt without being consumed, that is for us Judaism and Christianity, and the founder of both is not the God of the dead, but of the living.'[65] Religious differences should not be a basis for rancour or disputation: 'In another philosophy, in another religion, is another language unavoidable, other representations, other names for the same objects, that each designates from the perspective of his necessity or spontaneity.'[66] Nonetheless, he also suggested clearly that Judaism entailed a lack of proper faith, and that, just as Moses had been denied entry into the Promised Land, so was Judaism outside of the Christian promised land because of its failure to attend to the figural, Christological meaning of its law.[67] Hamann nowhere gives a clear doctrine of salvation, and he is extremely wary of presuming to know who is damned and who is saved. But it would be misleading to ignore the exclusionary, confessional dimension of Hamann's thought in order to render him more palatable.

But we should be wary of the Manichean tendency to condemn all non-pluralists as dogmatists. Hamann's strong belief in the centrality of Christ did not entail intolerance (tolerance, we have seen, was a high religious duty). On the level of doctrine, Hamann was wary of banishing to hell those with whom he disagreed. 'We can do more harm with truths than with errors,' he wrote. 'That is why many an orthodox soul can ride to the devil, in spite of the truth, and many a heretic gets to heaven, despite excommunication by the ruling church or the public.'[68] This sort of assertion, and his repeated statement that Jews ought to retain their faith appears to clash with the exclusive truth he saw in Christ. For those sympathetic to Hamann's thought, yet of a more ecumenical disposition, it is a lamentable fact that he did not think of fleshing out a means of reconciling, or of conversing between competing theological positions. As I will indicate in chapter 11, even if Hamann was far from intolerant, his theological exclusivity presents a major stumbling block to his reception in a pluralistic world.

PART FOUR

Practical Reflections of an Impractical Man:
Hamann contra Frederick II

9 The Language of Enlightenment and the Practice of Despotism: J.G. Hamann's Polemics against Frederick the Great

Any study of politics in Hamann's thought must necessarily take account of his direct forays into the political life of his state. Hamann penned a series of remarkably sharp attacks on his monarch. It is perhaps surprising (although it ought not to be) to see a thinker with such a conservative frame of mind express himself in so radically anti-authoritarian a manner. Looking at Hamann's anti-Frederickian salvoes helps free us of habitual connotations opposing radicalism and conservatism.

Hamann's charge that Enlightenment philosophers veiled their desire for personal power in the garb of impersonal reason was the opening volley in a battle that continues today. It is a charge, however, that is not entirely radical. That theorists wish to dominate in practice was as much a claim in counter-enlightened tirades as it was part of the *philosophes'* own self-image. Voltaire sought to be a teacher of princes and *peuples*; Bentham had dreams of grandeur; Kant wrote panegyrics to Frederick II; Diderot and D'Alembert wished to teach Catherine II and Frederick II.[1] The philosophers of the eighteenth century were quite removed from the view that philosophy was principally a contemplative activity. Burke, no fan of rationalist hubris, was nonetheless expressing what for most eighteenth-century thinkers would have been a redundancy when he described himself as a 'philosopher in action.'[2] No less than Frederick the Great had seen himself in similar terms.

For Hamann, the unity of enlightened theory and *despotic* practice was to be expected, and Frederick the Great – the embodiment of reason mixed with power – was the dominant symbol of the century's ills. The unbeliever of *Sans-Souci* (Frederick's palace in Potsdam) represented the true political face of the *philosophes*. Frederick's enlightened credentials were certainly sound. He surrounded himself with French literati (Voltaire, Maupertuis, Helvétius, La Mettrie, D'Alembert), he patronized an influential academy, he controlled the universities, he prided himself on his tolerance (or religious indifference), and he gave himself airs as a freethinking *philosophe* and cultural critic, writing articles, dialogues, and poems celebrating Lockean empiricism, the progress of education, the arts, and the sciences. He championed industry and trade, called for humanity and toleration, legal reform, and the slow emancipation from 'prejudice' (which he equated with an emancipation from Christianity). Hamann was quite capable of working himself into semi-satirical, semi-prophetic outrage: Berlin was Sodom, Babel, a 'French Bedlam.'[3] At one point he even went so far as to declare 'my hatred for Babel [Berlin] ... that is the true key to my writings.'[4]

This chapter attempts to piece together Hamann's specific objections to enlightened despotism by studying his polemics against Frederick the Great. Frederick was a political constant throughout Hamann's life: Hamann was ten years old at the accession of Frederick II, and he lived to see only one year of Frederick William II's reign. In addition, Hamann worked for the Prussian bureaucracy, and in Frederick's Prussia that meant that every decision affecting his career was decided at the top – Frederick was a notorious micro-manager, and this, combined with a top-heavy administrative structure, led to the situation where the most minor administrative decisions were taken at Potsdam.[5] To seek a post, file a complaint, or even ask permission for a vacation or for travel inside or outside of the country (which Hamann sought late in his life) one needed to write directly to the king. Thus, Hamann's perception that Enlightenment and absolutism were kin was not merely born of an abstract conceptual connection between the two, but of a very immediate sentiment of vulnerability to royal whim and the dictates of royal reason. Indeed, as we shall see, Hamann's polemics against Frederick are based on not only intellectual and religious objections, but also on personal grievances.

Given this personal dimension, Hamann's attacks might seem like the incidental ravings of a disgruntled employee. One might be tempted to think that putting a coherent face on Hamann's anti-Frederickian writings will involve separating the wheat from the chaff. But if we recall the degree to which Hamann saw the universal in the personal – the degree to which he assimilated his personal experiences to biblical patterns – we see that his complaints to Frederick, like his complaint to Kant and Berens, had, in his view, universal significance. There is a degree to which any successful interpretation of Hamann must endeavour to find sympathy with his most important claim: we must not insist on the separation of objective, timeless argument and subjective, historically bounded experience. That is to say, we may not separate theory from biography.

This chapter begins with a discussion of 'enlightened despotism,' noting the degree to which the term fits poorly with the most widespread political self-understanding of the *philosophes*. Despotism is arbitrary government; the enlightened absolutists sought to undermine despotism through rational reforms. The second section provides an exposition of Frederick the Great's claim to be an enlightened monarch, followed, in the third, by a description of Hamann's relationship to his country and his king. Having set the stage, we will proceed to draw out the more sustained aspects of Hamann's anti-Frederickian utterances. While this is some of the less philosophically compelling material in Hamann's oeuvre, we will see that, at base, his argument about Frederickian absolutism is at one with his argument against the universality of reason. His historically and communally located reason enabled him to condemn both the natural philosophy of the Enlightenment and the rationalization of the Prussian administration. In Frederick's program, Hamann perceived a project to undermine traditional moral claims and craft a kind of new man, a utilitarian self-seeker, a *homo economicus* whose virtue is a product of his love of wealth and praise. In Hamann's reactions to Kant we perceived his objections to rational deontology; here we will see clearly his rejection of Enlightenment utilitarianism. Frederick's policy emerges, through Hamannian lenses, to be a kind of intrusive soul-craft, a deliberate assault on the ideals of faith. For Hamann, the classical link between regime-form and individual soul was very real, and the Frederickian attempt to reform his state was a direct attack on the souls of believers. For all the quixotic fury of Hamann's positive political views, his polemics against his king contain a consistent, defensive project: the souls of believers must be shielded from the reforming impulse of Enlightenment reason.

Enlightened Despotism

Condemnation of despotism is not new. Despotism – derived from the Greek word for mastery – was traditionally understood to mean the rule of an owner over his slaves. The classic text on despotism is one that never used the term. Aristotle's *Politics* defined the tyrant as the single man who ruled despotically – ruling in his own interests, the tyrant treated the populace as a master treats his slaves, a manner of rule that was defensible only for slavish barbarians.[6] Another aspect of the Aristotelian definition of tyranny was rule in the absence of law. Montesquieu, who gave the term *despotism* its strongest theoretical expression, defined this form of government as rule according to the caprice of the single ruler, with the absence of fixed laws.[7] What was clear in Montesquieu's presentation was that an enlightened despot was a contradiction in terms. If this emerges clearly from his *Spirit of the Laws*, it is even more poignantly illustrated in the *Persian Letters*, where we follow the wealthy Persian master Usbek in his Parisian adventures. It becomes clear that despite Usbek's most enlightened and humane reflections on the manners and government of the French, his behaviour with regard to his seraglio back home is monstrous and unjust. It is the nature of despotism that is at fault, and no amount of personal Enlightenment will cure the ills of a corrupt system of government.[8]

Montesquieu was not alone in his condemnation of absolutism unadulterated with law: no Enlightenment writer championed the absence of law. When Enlightenment writers celebrated absolute rule, they generally did so with a view to establishing legal reforms that would make the state more equitable and its workings more predictable. The eighteenth century did not see the widespread use of the term *enlightened despotism*; rather, the term *despotisme légal* was the expression employed by several physiocrats. For most writers of the eighteenth century, this phrase would have been considered insignificant speech, and La Mercier de la Rivière, the physiocrat widely credited with its invention, was aware that he was swimming against the current.[9]

Whence came the view, then, that despotism and Enlightenment could go hand in hand? In brief, we might respond that philosophers have often been tempted by the idea of enacting sweeping reforms by instructing absolute monarchs: Plato with Dionysius, Aristotle with Alexander, Seneca with Nero, Machiavelli with Lorenzo, Hobbes with Charles II, etc. Hobbes might well serve as one of the earliest champions of enlightened despotism if only because he both championed the public proclamation of a clear, *rational* doctrine, and denied that despotism was essentially different from monarchy.[10] It was not, after all, law that ruled; rather, the sovereign ruled with law. Universal reason and despotic practice were, in his view, perfectly reconcilable. But few members of the Enlightenment fully embraced Hobbes's cold legal positivism. Voltaire (correctly) treated the term *despotism* as an innovation, and he claimed that it merely denoted 'the abuse of monarchy, a corruption of a fine system of government.'[11] However, Voltaire did with cynicism what Hobbes had done with logic, asserting that despotism was an empty term since such a regime was an impossibility: no country could be completely without law. Indeed, neither Voltaire nor his favourite monarch believed that kings ought to behave in a lawless manner, or that kings were above law. Voltaire held a somewhat Lockean view of natural law as rational self-interest that demanded reciprocity and the keeping of contracts prior to the existence of sovereign power.[12] Frederick expressed a similar view when he suggested that people had originally formed political communities for the common defence of their property and lives, and had elected a sovereign power to see to their defence and the upholding of their laws, which essentially entailed reciprocity and the preservation of property.

Enlightened despotism, then, appears to be a historian's term, and one of dubious theoretical utility.[13] For this reason, many have chosen to employ *enlightened absolutism* in its stead.[14] This is an important revision and does express more precisely what philosophical kings (and queen) sought. Yet even here, the historical reality of the 'enlightened absolutist' is equally open to revision. As Walter Hubatsch notes, Frederick the Great was not the sole controller of a vast state machine; rather, the state was an intricate (and, in Hubatsch's view, *organic*) web of relationships that were not open to the arbitrary whim of the monarch. Frederick's legal ties to the Holy Roman Empire were not negligible, nor, given the difficulties of ruling such a geographically dispersed state, was control truly as centralized as the stereotypical view would have it. Frederick was often forced to negotiate between the interests of the estates, the existing laws, and the independent spirit of his ablest administrators.[15] Significant as this point is, it should not blind us to the theoretical justification for centralization that emerged from Frederick's pen or the pens of his philosophical admirers. Absolute rule, whether based upon divine right or upon Enlightenment rationality, has always been more honoured in the breach than in the observance, yet this does not undermine its theoretical significance.

Enlightened absolutism represents accurately a regime widely championed in the eighteenth century: reason, law, and utility should rule, and prejudice, tradition, and caprice should be banished. Enlightenment and liberalism are (contra Peter Gay) not synonymous, but it is true that all Enlightenment writers sought to avoid dreaded arbitrariness.

Frederick and the Politics of Enlightenment:
Manufacturing Prussians

When Frederick ascended to the throne, there were great hopes among enlightened writers, and most notably Voltaire. However, those who hoped for a ruler who differed dramatically from his militaristic father were to be disappointed. Frederick had long begun to imitate the autocratic administrative style of his father (and, unlike his father, he intended to *use* his army). But, as Voltaire had made clear, there was no essential antipathy between absolute monarchy and Enlightenment, and it was with a clear Enlightenment conscience that Frederick, *le prince éclairé*, sought to take even more direct control of his state (to the point where his interventions were often perceived as a source of inefficiency by his officials).[16] Voltaire had idolized the young prince and had gone so far as to edit and have published Frederick's youthful essay, the *Anti-Machiavel*. Voltaire was a little disturbed by the fact that the king's first royal action was to break all the laws of nations and conquer a wealthy territory. Given the *Anti-Machiavel*'s outright condemnation of avaricious conquest, the theft of Silesia created somewhat of an 'optics problem.'[17] Nonetheless, Voltaire found it relatively easy to overcome these scruples, and he spent a great deal of time vying for the position of top *philosophe* to the Prussian king.

Frederick's mature theoretical reflections on regime forms are encapsulated in his 1781 *Essai sur les formes de gouvernement*.[18] Beginning with the origin of political life, he argued that wandering tribes had originally grouped together for common defence and had established government to defend the state and to uphold the law that protected their lives and property. He proceeded to examine the different forms of government, noting the tendency to corruption and revolution in aristocracies and democracies. Finally, he turned to monarchy, a form that he championed but one that was subject to much abuse. He condemned the Turkish regime as 'despotic'; unbound by law, the sovereign 'peut commettre impunément les cruautés les plus révoltantes.'[19] The key is that the prince must know that he 'represents' the nation, has his right from them, and is thus obliged to work for their well-being. Frederick saw the magistrate as a 'sentinelle permanente' who watches over the well-being of his subjects and the defence of their laws and borders. The greatest danger for a monarchy is when the monarch fails to be attentive to every detail of the state. Rather breezily, he enumerated the ways in which a monarch's laziness, ignorance, or dissipation can harm the state or even cause revolutions. Indeed, he thought that a monarch's downfall was a fair recompense for inattention to duty. A monarch must never forget that he is 'the first servant of the state.'[20]

This is, no doubt, windy stuff. Even Kant, who often praised his king to the skies, treated it with a grain of salt.[21] But Kant nonetheless emphasized the significance of the principle: monarchy is a trust, and there is a higher law. For Frederick, this was not the law of God, but rather a 'pacte social' that had preceded and occasioned the creation of kings.[22] This appears to be a defence of natural rights – for instance, Frederick wrote that religious tolerance was a duty of princes because the initial social contract that had established political power had never given the sovereign rights over people's thoughts.[23] Nonetheless, it is clear in both the *Essai* and his other writings that the justification for tolerance is not primarily a matter of right, but of utility. This is, indeed, the rhetorical thrust of the essay: the king's duty is to see to welfare. Frederick did not enter into a consideration, for instance, of the rights of serfs. He found the practice of serfdom blameworthy, but he thought its elimination would be harmful to the state's economy.[24] Frederick never worked out the relationship between the view of the sovereign as an upholder of people's rights and the view of his duties to see to their happiness, but the bulk of his justifications for rule fall on the utilitarian side of the question.

A good king reigned as a result of his superior merit; utility was the test of his worthiness. Like the champions of early-modern divine right, Frederick did not sanction rebellion, but nonetheless held out the loss of a state as a punishment for negligent kings.[25] Frederick credited his merit partly to his stoic attention to duty (he liked to model himself on Marcus Aurelius), but equally to his superior intelligence. Frederick also believed that every aspect of life in the state, save for the religious convictions of its subjects, called for his eternal management. It is interesting that a text that betrays the influence of Machiavelli's *Discourses on Livy* (which Voltaire had introduced to the young Frederick)[26] shows no interest in mixed regimes; despite indicating the degree to which the health of monarchic government hangs on the *virtù* of the monarch, Frederick treated absolute monarchy as the best form of government, so long as the prince was aware of his duties. As he wrote in his *Testament politique* of 1752, 'Il faut qu'un gouvernement bien conduit ait un système aussi lié que peut l'être un système de philosophie … Or, un système ne peut émaner que d'une tête; donc il faut qu'il parte de celle du souverain.'[27]

We noted that Frederick exempted religion from a prince's control. To the degree that this was truly his view, it was a policy born of a mixture of prudence and indifference. As he wrote in his 1752 *Testament politique*, 'Toutes les religions, quand on les examine, sont fondées sur un système fabuleux, plus ou moins absurde.'[28] In practice, however, he also thought that people's religious convictions were very much his concern, and he made this abundantly clear in the same text, when he spoke of his policies concerning the various sects. He was not joking when he wrote, 'Je suis en quelque façon le pape des luthériens et des réformés le chef de l'église.'[29] He was responsible for all places, he kept an eye on religious education, and he did his best to see that religion served the purposes of the state. It was the policy of the state (and had been for several generations of Prussian princes) to tolerate groups persecuted in other states as long as their presence served the financial interests of the Crown – this was neither separation of church and state, nor disinterest in the confessional make-up of the country. Berlin's Jewish, Catholic, and Calvinist populations, all selected for their affluence, were all given strict guidelines to their actions, movements, expenditures, and cultural reproduction. Toleration for Frederick, as for his father before him, was a policy justified by *raison d'état*; wealthy refugees were welcome, so long as they invested their wealth in Frederick's industrial production. Poor people were welcome in sparsely populated regions, for Frederick, good as he was at killing off his young men in an attempt to keep his stolen territory, was desperate to build his population base – and religious toleration was attractive to many.[30] (What was not tolerated was for these immigrants to leave: this was a hanging offence.)[31] So keen was he to attract peasants that he even went so far as to suggest building a mosque to attract Turks.[32] Yet if Frederick is widely thought to have cornered the market on toleration, this is more a result of successful public relations than of fact. In some matters he was more tolerant than other princes – he built, for instance, a Catholic church in the capital of a Protestant state. His treatment of the Jews, however, was less tolerant than that of his virulently racist father. Frederick II exchanged Christian anti-Semitism for Voltairian anti-Semitism. Unlike the late Luther, or the medieval bigots, Frederick did not denigrate the Jews as the killers of Christ, but rather as the foolish little tribe whose absurd metaphysics had corrupted the world. He naturally thought it a harmless prank to make Moses Mendelssohn appear before him on the Sabbath or to force him to buy overproduced porcelain monkeys from his heavily subsidized porcelain works.[33] If the theory shifted, the practice remained the same: like any medieval German prince, Frederick periodically blackmailed Berlin's

Jewish population whenever he needed cash, and he justified his toleration of Jews on the basis of the trade that they brought from Poland.[34]

Frederick was equally vaunted for his toleration of political opinion. 'Argue as much as you want, but obey!' was how Kant famously characterized Frederick's policy. Generations of enthusiasts have thought this to be an accurate depiction of events, but it requires qualification. Certainly Voltaire had cause to disagree with this statement: he incurred the wrath of the king, being confined without charge for having published a satire of Frederick's favourite, Maupertuis. Lessing wrote that freedom in Prussia consisted only of the 'liberty to bring as many idiocies against religion to the market as one wants … Let once someone in Berlin write as freely about other things … you'll soon see which is the most slavish land in Europe today.'[35]

Opinion was controlled not only through censorship. Frederick retained tight control over education, sharing the Enlightenment mania for writing on the tabula rasa of the human mind. 'Enfin,' he wrote, 'je suis persuadé qu'on fait des hommes ce que l'on veut.'[36] But education was reserved for burghers and nobility, and Frederick had too much need for cannon fodder, agricultural labour, and a contented nobility to do much about the education or status of the peasants (serfdom was, however, abolished on royal domains). In addition, Frederick's wealth was never enough to sustain serious educational projects – at any given time, the military consumed at least three-quarters of all state revenues, and if one considers his other needs (and costly schemes), one can see why the universities were so starved for resources (most professors worked for years without having a stable chair; many supplemented their income with tutoring). Frederick often employed amputee soldiers as schoolteachers; at other times, he insisted that teachers also be engaged in the breeding of silkworms to aid the development of his luxury industry.[37]

Considering the apparent distance between Frederick's educational ideals and his practice, Fritz Hartung writes that there was a tension in Frederick between enlightened theory and reason of state.[38] Certainly Hartung is correct that Frederick could not merely wave his hand and enact reforms. Nor was all his virtuous posturing and cant about humanity entirely in keeping with his bellicose foreign policy. However, one might overstate the degree to which the Enlightenment was entirely blinded by lofty ideals. The Enlightenment desire to increase the *happiness* of subjects entails a kind of utilitarian, instrumental reason that is not in keeping with the view of the *philosophes* as dreamers. In order to emphasize his thesis of a tension between *raison d'état* and Enlightenment, Hartung rejects Dilthey's enthusiastic claim that Frederick sought to enlighten the masses. But keeping the peasants in the dark was a perfectly respectable policy among most *philosophes*.[39] Or rather, the distinction between esoteric and exoteric teaching was particularly popular in the eighteenth century. Frederick both condemned prejudices and saw their utility. Hence the double movement: 'S'il [un prince] veut à l'édifice de la superstition, il faut qu'il y aille à la sape; mais il risquerait trop s'il entreprenait de l'abattre ouvertement.'[40] Frederick wrote on the one hand that an educated populace was easier to govern,[41] yet he also expressed the view that people should learn only what is necessary to make them remain content with their place (both hierarchic and geographic): 'It is not good to make the peasants too smart!'[42] 'Que gagnerait-on à détromper un homme que les illusions rendent heureux?'[43] Frederick sought to undermine all but the useful aspects of religion: it was to become a school of virtue, ultimately divested of its 'fables absurdes qui servent de pâture à l'imbécillité publique.'[44]

Education does not end in school, and Frederick exerted a great influence on Prussian arts and letters. He financed a number of artistic endeavours, including the creation of a French theatre and a massive opera house in Berlin (with parking spaces for a thousand carriages).[45] While he was more strapped for cash than any of his rival monarchs, Frederick nonetheless did manage to spend a good amount of money on patronage. While this is not the place to enter into a discussion of Frederick's aesthetics (or of the relationship between aesthetics and politics), it is worthwhile to note the significant effect of Frederick's treatise 'De la littérature allemande.' The work, which condemned German literature for failing to live up to French standards, is not significant merely because it raised the ire of German writers, but also because of its universalist tone. There was one single model for good poetry, and it was rational and French. He even went so far as to suggest (only half in jest) that the German language required reform if it were to have greater euphony. Why not add the vowel *a* to the ends of words? Hamann's letters are full of vitriol about this profound treatise.

More to the point, Frederick attempted to mould elite opinion through the Berlin Academy. Paying top thaler for French talent, he funded an institution that produced a great deal of enlightened writing (and gave him a venue for the anonymous publication of his own reflections). This 'Academy of Satan' was one of Hamann's favourite targets.[46] It must be said that since a great deal of the talent for the academy was foreign, and since it published its memoirs in French, Frederick was not entirely successful in developing an indigenous body of talent through patronage.[47] But he was able to direct the literary efforts of his country through prestigious essay competitions.

Frederick believed that religion, art, education, and public expression ought to be under the control of the prince, but the most important area of monarchical control (aside from the military) was the country's industry. Frederick was flabbergasted by Rousseau's bizarre objections to the arts and sciences, and he wrote a panegyric to their utility. The arts, sciences, commerce, and industry were the great benefits to humanity. In this, Frederick was perfectly at one with leading philosophical opinion. His economic views were thoroughly mercantilist.[48] Frederick thought that the wealth of the nation would be augmented by the development of local industry (especially the production of luxury items for export), and he placed large barriers on imports, while investing heavily in the merchant networks that made exports possible. He constantly engaged in different manufacturing schemes. One of Hamann's brief anti-Frederickian writings was occasioned by a scheme to breed a caterpillar to create a dye that would compete with the product of the South American insect, the Kermes.[49] Some of these schemes worked; others faltered. Silk manufacture and export did raise revenues that were used for the army, but this luxury industry required constant subsidization. Frederick even placed numerous tariff barriers between different regions of the country.[50] The purpose of all of this activity was to finance his massive army. Now, if Frederick celebrated sweet commerce, all this heavy-handed 'political arithmetic' was somewhat out of step with the anti-interventionist views of the more progressive enlighteners. Nonetheless, he was convinced that the wealth of his citizens and strength of his army depended on the establishment of industry, and his emphasis on the increase of trade was in line with mainstream views.[51] If he failed to create a commercial empire, this was not through a lack of desire, but through a lack of means: Frederick knew that Prussia had not the naval power to enter into the colonial world trade of the French, the Dutch, the Spanish and the English.[52] Frederick certainly was within the mainstream of enlightened thought when he wrote, 'C'est cependant ce désir [the desire for wealth] qui lie les nations et les particuliers par un ordre admirable de la providence.'[53] He was very keen to cultivate this desire in his subjects.

Hamann's Relationship with Royal Power

For Hamann, the separation of theory and practice, contemplation and action, was unthinkable. Thus, it should come as no surprise to us that his antipathy to the king was born as much of a reaction to Frederick's reign as a distaste for Frederick's thought. In his professional capacity, his literary life and his *Bürgerlich* existence, Hamann was in constant contact with Frederick. He came to look upon him as a kind of nemesis, suggesting that their fates were intertwined. Late in the life of the king, Hamann (hearing of the king's recovery from a grave illness) wrote to Jacobi, 'Our Solomon should get better – all the better for me. I don't know myself how to explain the link or pre-established harmony between this wind and my muse.'[54] More precisely, Hamann thought 'that the *Solomon of the North* has become a rival of the Magus of the North.'[55] If Voltaire had a list of nicknames for Frederick (Marc-Aurèle, César, Alcibiade, Antonin, Trajan, Salomon du nord),[56] so, too, did Hamann: Hausvater, Obil der Litterature Tudesque,[57] Père Abbé de Sans Souci, Salomon du nord (employed with irony), Saul, Sauvage du Nord, Baal, Ölgötze,[58] Midas, Herod, Old Barbarian, old *philosophe*, our Virtuos Parisien und Eunuch, Nimrod, Absalom (this last is a reference to Frederick's famous attempt to flee the wrath of his father). There was a spiritual battle being fought between the ruler and his servant (the servant, however, appears to be the only one aware that the battle was being fought). As Joseph Nadler notes, Frederick was, for Hamann, 'the embodiment of reason crowned with power.'[59] For Hamann, enlightened despotism was not a contradiction in terms; rather, despotism was the logical conclusion of enlightened universalism.

Hamann's treatment of nuts-and-bolts political matters was an odd mixture of attention and indifference. He was quite well read in matters of political economy, taking an interest in the works of Galiani and Necker and periodically expressing himself on Frederick's mercantilist policies, but he never offered any clear views of how a state should be organized or how misery might be reduced. His clearest and most direct political project can be found in his youthful, pre-conversion essay on the virtues of trade. There, Hamann had aped the widespread enthusiasm for commerce as the great source of progress, peace, and well-being of states.[60] But his ensuing conversion would leave no trace of this liberal/bourgeois article of faith, as we will see below. Rather, Hamann would actively adopt the habits of heroic indolence against the virtues of commerce and industry. (He may, it is true, be said to have lived a bourgeois life at home, although his refusal to marry the mother of his children raises a number of questions on this front.) Indeed, the only trace of this commercial creed that lived on was his periodic attack on Frederick's mercantilist barriers to the movement of goods. However, this was not born of a coherent celebration of free trade, but rather of a periodic anger that Frederick's central planning deprived the city of meat that was readily available right next door in Poland.[61]

It is surprising that a thoughtful and exceedingly literate member of the Prussian bureaucracy, convinced of the disastrous course of his state's politics and mores, should never attempt to articulate a more precise political program. Hamann levelled vitriol at the regime for its bleeding of its subjects, but there was no precise political project suggested in these attacks. Frederick II was charged with excessive consumption, a charge that, while perhaps having the appearance of plausibility to one in impoverished circumstances, does lose some bite when Frederick's court is compared with the courts of his European rivals. Frederick was attacked for having rendered Berlin licentious: this was perhaps a fair assessment.[62] Yet we get no glimpse of a Hamannian program. Besides, the Magus of the North was, himself, not entirely without licentious tastes or above socially unorthodox behaviour (he never regularized his 'marriage of conscience').[63] Nor, indeed, do Hamann's attacks make any effort to address the structural or political causes of the considerable misery that Frederick's bellicose reign occasioned. He opened his mouth and out shot lightning bolts of condemnation (and humour); he did not provide thorough analysis. Nonetheless, we can ascertain a coherent antipathy to the theory and practice of enlightened absolutism.

However, in order to understand Hamann's antipathy to the regime, we first require a clear picture of the political and administrative situation in the latter half of the eighteenth century. In order to avoid confounding Hamann with German nationalists, it is important to note the peculiar situation of East Prussia. Outside of the Holy Roman Empire, East Prussia had previously been a duchy under Polish control; in the seventeenth century it had become the possession of Brandenburg, and in 1701 Frederick I (the father of Frederick William I) had crowned himself king in Königsberg (something he could not have done in Berlin, where he was a mere elector). Frederick William I (the father of Frederick II) had secured the possession through an active campaign of immigration. However, the eighteenth century did not witness an uninterrupted rule from Berlin. During the Seven Years' War, the province was occupied by Russia, and the population accommodated itself to the shift in power with an ease that disturbed Frederick.[64] Institutions continued just as before, people fraternized with Russian officers, and the Empress Elizabeth became the titular head of government to whom subjects owed obedience. We can, for instance, read in Kant's correspondence a letter to the empress asking to be granted a newly vacant chair at the university.[65] Some even speculate that Hamann's famous business trip to London was an attempt to speak to the Russian ambassador about Baltic commercial rights in the case of a successful Russian conquest of East Prussia.

Much has been made of Hamann's tirades against the French and against Frederick's Gallic tastes – for this, Hamann has sometimes been taken as an apostle of German nationalism. Antoinette Fink-Langlois writes that Hamann, in *Le kermes du nord*, sought 'on the social as on the national level to fight the inferiority complex of the Germans.'[66] Thus she makes him into a German patriot. This is a misrepresentation of Hamann's intention. Hamann was not Fichte and Frederick was not Napoleon. It is true that Hamann objected to Frederick's desire to reform German letters on a French model, but this was based more on his attachment to particularity and on the degree to which he saw thought and language as inseparable, organic, and resistant to rational control. It was Frederick's rationalist universalism to which he objected, not his French manners (if he associated the French language with philosophical hubris, this was the result of the intellectual dominance of French philosophy). Hamann had learned French as a boy and it had been his favourite language; he had grown to dislike it through association with the encyclopaedists, the *Regie* (of which we will speak below), Voltaire, etc., but this was not born of opposition to foreigners or of patriotic fervour. 'My patriotism,' he wrote, 'is composed of just as much love as hatred of my fatherland.'[67] Certainly, he felt a certain cultural affinity with German speakers, but he never felt much attachment to the Holy Roman Empire. Indeed, he even saw Berlin as a distant and foreign place: 'I have never loved my fatherland out of inclination, but more and more out of compassion.'[68] He felt no real loyalty to the regime, but rather thought it a foreign imposition. He wrote to Jacobi, 'It was no such shame to the duchy to be dependent on Poland as it is a misfortune for the kingdom to be dependent on the politics of the Chaldeans in the German Roman Empire.'[69]

Hamann's feelings about Frederick were naturally influenced by his professional position. After Hamann's father had died and Hamann had frittered away the bulk of his inheritance, he sought some sort of bureaucratic post. With the help of Kant he managed to secure himself the position of translator in 1767; a decade later he took up the post of *Packhofverwalter* (manager of the warehouse) for the provincial excise administration. His long career with the bureaucracy was one of constant financial worry. Attempting to provide for a wife, four children, and one invalid brother on the meagre salary of a lower customs official was not easy. A particular thorn in his side was the existence of the *Regie*. In 1766, unsatisfied with the revenues from his excise duties, Frederick was convinced by Helvétius to reform his tax system by adopting a French system of tax farming. Employing 2000 people, the *Regie* had 200 Frenchmen occupying the top posts.[70] These Frenchmen, a number of whom were adventurers, amassed sizeable fortunes. Aside from his natural desire to augment the state's treasury, Frederick had several reasons for bringing in the *Regie*. First, he had a congenital distrust of his officials, and he felt that this system would bypass the standard channels of administration. This was a typical absolutist manoeuvre. Second, he thought that foreigners would have less sympathy for those who bore the tax burden, and thus would be more ruthless. Third, he thought that the foreign tax farmers would be the targets of resentment, and not the regime.[71] This Machiavellian ploy was not in the least successful. Frederick might have gratified the people had he had Helvétius chopped in two in the public square, but as it was, many *Bürger* associated Frederick himself with the Frenchmen. Certainly Hamann was prone to comparing his poverty to the enormous wealth (no doubt exaggerated in his imagination) of the French economists and *philosophe*-adventurers who gave the orders. (There is a certain irony in Hamann's tirades against the *Regie*, given that his first post of translator existed only because the French officials didn't speak German.)

The most outrageous abuse for Hamann was the removal of the *Fooigelder*, a kind of tip that was customarily paid to administrators in port cities (for Hamann it amounted to five thaler a month, or one-fifth of his monthly income). The *Fooi* money, which paid for Hamann's winter firewood, was simply taken by the administration (with no explanation) and added to general revenues. Hamann considered this to be outright theft, and he railed against the policy in his writings, in his correspondence, and in official complaints.[72] His most audacious outburst was a letter he wrote directly to the king outlining his complaints about the *Regie* and their 'autorité arbitraire'; he called on the 'Salomon du nord' to render a verdict worthy of his namesake, and he concluded with a most Hamannian wish (complete with biblical citations): 'Le BON DIEU, qui est GRAND et FORT, sans être [sic] connu (Job XXXVI.26), convertira enfin le coeur du PERE envers les enfans du Royaume, et le coeur des enfans envers le PERE de la PATRIE, avant que le jour grand et terrible de l'Eternel vienne et frappe la terre à la façon de l'interdit (Mal. IV.5,6.).'[73] We know that Hamann thought this was a vain wish; he considered Frederick to be the head thief, and he held no serious hope of receiving redress. We do not know what the king thought of this letter because he never replied. (Hamann complained to Herder, 'Neither voice nor answer nor attention from Baal.')[74] Probably the minister simply threw the letter in with other salary complaints; several months later an order came down from the king indicating that anyone who was unhappy with his salary would be replaced with an invalid.[75] Hamann's fury at the king burst out in the most disparate of places. In the midst of a critique of Herder's essay on the origin of languages, Hamann complained of the regime's excesses and exclaimed, 'Arithmetique politique rends moi mes 5 ecus!'[76] In his attack on Mendelssohn's *Jerusalem* he included a brief reference to despotic Leviathans that eat up the 'Pfuy! Pfuy! [*Fooi*] of poor sinners.'[77] (Hamann had to explain this reference to his friends.)

Hamann attacked Frederick throughout his works, but nowhere was his polemic more pointed than in his French writings, where Frederick and his *philosophes* are the clear targets. These writings (the *Essais à la mosaique*, the *Lettre perdue d'un sauvage du nord à un financier de Pe-Kim*, *Le kermes du nord*, and the biting *Au Salomon du nord*) are among his more difficult to decipher, being puzzles based on the various writings of Frederick, his 'eunuch' Voltaire, his administrators, and his academicians. Here, Hamann's intention was not public ridicule – as satires, these works are manifest failures – but personal rebuke.[78] He thought that he could succeed in 'speaking truth to power,' and he made this clear: 'Il faut bien observer l'élite des lecteurs, pour les quels [sic] notre ouvrage a été composé. Ce n'est pas la Legion, mais la Dixme, savoir les *Philosophes machines*.'[79] (We will return to the attack on La Mettrie's materialism implied in this reference to *L'homme machine*). These were jeremiads à clef, and only those intimate with the literary and administrative goings-on in Berlin and Potsdam would have been able to follow the references. It must be said that Frederick never took any notice of Hamann. As one of the king's intimates wrote to Hamann, 'Et votre lettre perdue et votre Ecce: je les ai etudiés et j'y trouve de l'esprit, de la finesse et de bonnes verités. N'ayez pas peur, que celles-cy bien que dites avec liberté vous causent de l'embarras. Le Salomon du Nord ne lit rien qui exige quelque contention de l'esprit et d'autres ne sentiront pas ce que vous dites.'[80] However, if Frederick was uninterested in reading demanding works (or obscurely allusive jeremiads), Hamann was at one point informed that his 'satires' (presumably his playfully allusive letters of complaint) had displeased the administration.[81] This did not prevent him from continuing to fill his works with derisive references to the king.

Theory and Practice

Kant famously called the 'age of Enlightenment' the 'age of Frederick,' and he indicated thereby that Frederick's toleration of religious debate and exultation of reason had liberated his educated subjects, allowing them to grow up.[82] The key to Hamann's treatment of Frederick as an enlightened despot is in his reaction to Kant's claim. We need not enter into the details of this, for we treat it extensively elsewhere, but we must repeat the kernel of Hamann's accusation: those who claim universal reason as the ultimate judge are simply giving a thin veneer to their will to power. We have seen Hamann's charge that Kant had been so nice to 'Absalom' (Frederick) only because he aspired to the position of a guardian, or master over the unripe masses.[83] Hamann considered himself to be among those unscholarly people excluded by the likes of Kant from the role of educator, and he evoked both a Pauline inversion of wisdom and folly and the Christian trope of the 'children of God,' indicating that Kant's 'immaturity' was precisely the state of grace.[84] Hamann also expressed a sincere resentment that his own children might have their education determined by the principles of the Enlightenment.[85] (He made particular mention of his three daughters, making a cutting jab at Kant's sexism.)[86] Hamann was reacting both to the vogue for education as a tool for social engineering and to the official sanctioning and patronage of popular philosophy in Prussia.

Kant's marriage of Enlightenment with authoritarianism was not novel, though his formulation of 'self-incurred tutelage' was cleverly paradoxical. Hamann was indignant with Kant's formula blaming 'immaturity' on the laziness of the immature. He, in turn, accused the followers of Kant's doctrine of obedience of a greater laziness: they were too 'lazy' to do anything but follow orders and do the state's dirty business (*Schaarwerk*). His inversion was as follows: 'True Enlightenment consists of an emergence of immature man from the highest self-incurred guardianship [*Vormundschaft* – the opposite of *Unmündigkeit*, immaturity]. The fear of the Lord is the beginning of wisdom[87] – and this wisdom makes us too fearful to lie and too lazy to invent – thus, ever the more courageous against these guardians [*Vormünder*], who at most can kill the body and suck out the contents of our purse [den Beutel] – thus, ever the more merciful towards our immature brothers and the more fruitful in good works of immortality.'[88] The powerful ought to exit from their Godless mastery, and enter into the service of God, which is a Christian's freedom. The ruled who have faith know that the worst their rulers can do is to kill or rob them. Hamann, whose reflections on rebellion consisted of the advice that 'everyone should do his job with satisfaction out of love of public order and general peace,'[89] nonetheless was offering a theory of passive obedience. We will return to this tension between the city and God below.

Hamann's accusation that Kant wanted to dress philosophers in the golden (or purple?) robes of guardians is clearly more than ad hominem;[90] it fits perfectly well with his insistence on the embodiment of language and thought, and on the historically conditioned nature of ideas. If reason, as a mere creature of human language, was subject to the vicissitudes of history, the divine Logos had universal significance and provided the fixed point around which all Hamann's thought revolved.[91] Hegel was partially correct when he treated Hamann's attack on Frederick in a Hegelian manner. Hamann, Hegel wrote, rightly condemned 'the false premise [of] the absolutism of the contingent particular will.' In its place, Hamann offered the 'in-and-for-itself general divine will.'[92] When Hamann opposed Frederick, he pointed to a higher authority.

The universality of reason is what enabled Enlightened absolutists to think that despotism could be avoided through subjection to reason itself. Hamann, who undermined reason's purity, perceived contingent will in philosophers' universal claims. Traditionally, sophistry has been separated from philosophy: sophists merely seek victory, exercising skill in verbal manipulation, whereas philosophers are possessed of a longing for the truth, regardless of victory in debate. Hamann charged Kant not merely with epistemological hubris, but also with the desire for victory and control. Thus he conflated the two categories whose distinctness had made philosophy possible. A *roi-philosophe* did not surprise him, since he saw in the *philosophes* a theologico-political project. His entire response to the Enlightenment can be found in his explosion, 'MENE MENE TEKEL, den Sophisten!'[93]

In his *Metakritik*, Hamann played on Kant's praise of critique, calling reason 'that general philosopher's stone so necessary for Catholicism and despotism that will quickly cast down religion in its holiness and law-giving in its majesty.'[94] (All outrage aside, Hamann was happy enough to let his son receive free admission to Kant's lectures.) But Hamann did not need Kant's *Critique* to tell him that the rational sought to mould people's minds. The mania for education (which is attributed periodically to the malleability of the human mind inherent in Lockean 'blank-slate' psychology) was widespread among enlighteners, and, as we have seen, was shared by Frederick himself. Kant's separation of the public from the private realm struck Hamann as a perfect expression of Frederick's aims both to subject religion to *critique* and yet to use it for social control.

Hamann summed up the situation pithily: 'State and church are Moses and Aaron; Philosophy is their sister, Miriam.'[95] (Miriam is the prophetess who got too big for her britches and attacked Moses in Numbers 12:1.) If faith was the most important aspect of human life, surely it ought to be at the centre of communal life. This is what lent urgency to his anti-Frederickian tirades. Hamann thought that both Rousseau's injunction in *Emile* that youth should not learn about religion until maturity and the utilitarian view (shared by Frederick) that youth ought to learn a 'Katechismus der Sittenlehre' were incorrect. While he agreed with Rousseau that youth ought not engage in dogmatic memory-work, he argued that they should be brought up to love God 'aus innerm Triebe.'[96] In the same breath as he condemned fashionable educational systems,[97] Hamann wrote, 'Every school is a mountain of God ... Every father of the fatherland and every citizen must be concerned with education.' A church was not an instrument of social utility, and Hamann condemned those who saw education in these terms. He referred to Helvétius' famous treatise on education (*De L'Homme*) as 'Hundezucht,' or 'dog-training.'[98] He wrote, in a clear attack on Prussian practice, 'Not only the rank service of Mammon or the slavish service of weapons, your artificial industry and nobility, but also the chimeras of beautiful nature, of good taste, and of common sense [*der gesunden Vernunft*] have introduced prejudices that have partly extinguished and partly choked in birth the life-spirit of the human race and the welfare of civic society.'[99] (We will return to this attack on Mammon below.)

Frederick disapproved of Christian otherworldliness and fanaticism, and he wrote an article (which he had read at the academy and then published anonymously in the *Histoire de l'Académie Royale*)[100] suggesting that Christianity needed replacing with a more reliable and less fabulous principle of education. Frederick's *Essai sur l'amour propre envisagé comme principe de morale* argued that morality was based in self-interest – our desire for self-preservation and for social approbation. The essay reduced most virtuous acts to acts of prudence or pride, but it also suggested that happiness is a 'tranquillité de l'âme' that arises when we are able to applaud our own actions.[101] It is not clear how Frederick connected this inner voice of self-criticism to the external considerations of praise and profit that dominate his account. Nonetheless, he called for the teaching of virtue – and thus of a far-sighted amour propre – to children in the form of new, secular catechisms. These would urge the children to act selflessly out of a desire for praise, to avoid temptation in order to preserve their reputation, to avoid crime in order to avoid punishment, etc. The piece elicited a brief response from a Berlin theologian, who thought Christianity might still have some social utility.

In a newspaper article purporting to be about the response, Hamann wrote a fiery attack on the *Essai* itself. Hamann began by citing Juvenal's second satire: 'I could wish to fly beyond Sarmatia and the frozen Sea, when I hear Lectures of Morality from those who pretend to the virtues of the Curian Family, yet live like the votaries of Bacchus.'[102] He made it clear that the *Anti-Machiavel* was his target, writing *in French*: 'la virtù chez Machiavel, c'est la perfidie.' He continued in German: 'Our head is not so happily organized nor our imagination so Herculean ... that we can see through all the labyrinths, contradictions, ambiguities, misunderstandings, ideas, prejudices, cleverness, doubts, objections, obscurities, riddles, secrets, etc., of self-love [*Selbstliebe*] to the – if not metaphysical – yet political holiness of virtue. So we also have expressed with feeling our thankful wonderment for the thought-provoking essay of the wise legislator ... happy is the people whose prince is a philosophe and an adept who knows how to transform their honey, wool, and fruit with a generous sic vos non vobis into the blind, general happiness of the state and a golden or silken age!'[103] Hamann concluded with a citation from Persius' third satire: 'Great father of the gods! Be it thy pleasure to inflict no other punishment on the monsters of tyranny, after their nature has been stirred by fierce passion, that has the taint of fiery poison – let them look upon virtue – .'[104] Hamann breaks off, but Persius concludes, ' – and pine that they have lost her forever!'

The king, then, was a victim of his own destructive morality of self-love. The Platonic tenor of the Persius citation indicates that Hamann thought the king suffered from a tyrannical soul. In the *Aesthetica in nuce* he wrote, 'If the stomach is your god, then the very hairs on your head stand under its guardianship [*Vormundschaft*]. Every creature will alternately be your victim and your idol.'[105] The incapacity to see any good outside of the immediate, temporal self-interest (narrowly understood in terms of physical gratification and reception of praise) makes Frederick idolize worldly well-being, but the same utilitarian logic makes him sacrifice people in his armies and factories. The people produce the silk, the fruit, and the honey for 'themselves,' that is to say for 'the general interest,' but it is not for themselves (*Silvos non vobis* – you [work], but not for yourselves), in that the product of their work goes towards a 'general happiness' from which they are, to employ a term that is only slightly anachronistic, alienated.

Hamann saw Frederick as a leader who was making the rule of the belly into the principle of virtue. Enlightenment reason, which prided itself on its rejection of prejudices, was itself based on its own prejudice, Hamann claimed: 'He [the *philosophe*] drives out the prejudice of antiquity [by which Hamann means Christianity] and habit through the prejudice of selfishness, novelty, and one's own invention.'[106] The result of this elimination of ancient 'prejudices' is a new consequentialist ethic that justifies all the excesses of absolutism through its promise of 'bonheur,' temporal betterment. Neither the means – the transformation of citizens into Epicureans[107] – nor the end – temporal happiness – seemed appropriate to Hamann. Hamann decried the 'great political tailor-secret of making and transfiguring men, were it also through a turning of a measly Christianity to the inner lining of the purple self-love, according to the golden natural law of economy, in order ... to be like Zeus.'[108] Making new men through the elevation and fine-tuning of their self-love under the guise of Christianity was the project he discerned in Frederick's rule. The Enlightenment sought to erect 'instead of temples, schools that resemble the birthplace of the exalted!'[109] He railed, 'Dead and unfruitful prosperity, hypocritical Pharisees of our century! Your moral and civil prejudices and the high taste or toys of your profits is nothing but caviar of the leviathan who rules high in the waves of the air (Eph. II.2).'[110]

Hamann added salt to his attack by enumerating the ways his sovereign impoverished his nation and indulged in luxury. He referred to an 'Epicurean herd' and made reference to Matthew 8:32, which describes a herd of devil-possessed swine.[111] He complained that Prussia was a state in which despots wouldn't even spend to make a burning fiery furnace for their Magi, but rather chose to let them freeze to death for lack of firewood, according to their 'political arithmetic' (*politischen Rechenkunst*).[112] He accused Frederick of taking bread from the children of the state and casting it to his greyhounds.[113]

It was, however, no one particular economic policy that most offended Hamann, but rather the inversion of the Christian virtues: 'According to the current plan of the world, the art of making gold remains, with reason, the highest project and highest good of our clever politicians.'[114] Hamann clearly felt that a lack of sophistication in matters of money was part of a Christian injunction to consider the lilies.[115] He wrote with some sympathy of Socrates' wife, Xanthippe: 'For a woman who must care for the household of a philosopher ... time is too precious to think up plays on words or for flowery speech.'[116] In this text (the *Sokratische Denkwürdigkeiten*) Socrates does not represent philosophy, we recall, but Christianity (Hamann playfully converted the patron saint of philosophers into a Christ figure). On the surface, Hamann rejected the view of those who castigated Xanthippe (who represents the household, or economy), yet he aired their view in a footnote with a rhyming couplet declaring her to be a whore. Here he demonstrated a Christian ambivalence to matters of economy, on the one hand celebrating the nobility of Christian imprudence while at the same time indicating its impracticality and the degree to which it offends against he most elementary common sense.[117]

Indeed, Frederick had too much *bon sens* for this sort of thing, declaring that 'la religion chrétienne est très-nuisible à la société civile ... Le mépris outré des richesses, que la religion chrétienne ordonne à ses sectateurs, détruit entièrement le commerce qui est l'ame de la société.'[118] Now, considering Hamann's perpetual wailing for his lost five thaler per month, we might question the degree of his 'mépris outré des richesses.' Nonetheless, the opposition is clear: the Christian is both the long-suffering slave and nature's leisured gentleman. 'Ayez pitié de moi,' Hamann wrote proudly, 'il n'y a point en moi de prudence humaine.'[119]

For Hamann, this human prudence and *bon sens* was part of a philosophical project to elevate the earthly at the expense of the spiritual. Hamann, always galloping, never walking, made a connection that is as tiresome for glib simplification as it is useful for its insight: 'C'est le sel du *bon sens* dont ... les *Hobbes*, les *Machiavells*, les *Humes* ... ont assaisonné leurs fables des abeilles.'[120] What unites these writers with Mandeville is their common tendency to ignore otherworldly concerns and to proceed in transforming vices into social utility. It is true that Hume did not share the radically pessimistic view of human nature that exists in Hobbes, Machiavelli, and Mandeville, but he too proceeded from individualist, sceptical premises. If Hume opposed Hobbes and Mandeville, placing more emphasis on benevolence, this was merely because his psychology treated social approbation as one of the things most desired by men. With Machiavelli, they all share the view that virtue is not good in itself, but is something praised or blamed for its consequences. Hamann summed up his view of the king thus: 'Despite his good will to be an anti- he became through fate and misunderstanding a meta-Machiavelli.'[121] Of course, in this view Hamann was not alone: everyone found amusing the contradiction between the enlightened *Anti-Machiavel* and the actions of the conqueror of Silesia.[122] But not everyone equated Enlightenment and Machiavellianism.

Frederick had a curious mixture of Stoicism and Epicureanism. Voltaire noted this in his scurrilous *Mémoires*, speaking of the king's famous frugality in the same breath as he discussed the notorious royal sensuality. Frederick certainly had affinities with Stoics. He thought of taking his own life in moments of great trouble,[123] and he certainly believed in the virtues of self-discipline. Yet he never grasped the more subtle teaching of his hero Marcus Aurelius, for he followed much more the Machiavellian mania for control of the external world. Indeed, his reflections late in life on fortune indicate not resigned equanimity, but constant battle with the uncontrollable. The late Frederick wrote poems on the wiles of fortune, and even the young prince, who treated Machiavelli's discussion of fortune as a bunch of twaddle deriving from Machiavelli's ignorance of secondary causes, nonetheless proceeded in the same breath to express the Machiavellian conclusion, 'Tant que nous ne serons que des hommes, c'est-à-dire des êtres très-bornés, nous ne serons jamais supérieurs à ce qu'on appelle les coups de la fortune.' That said, 'nous devons ravir ce que nous pouvons au hasard.'[124]

Au Salomon de Prusse began with an epigraph drawn from a poem by Frederick II to his cook. Hamann took the lines out of context, restructuring them to read as follows:

Les mets exquis amoçant les prussiens
Les ont changé en Epicuriens
L'illusion, le prestige et la faim
Nous rendroient tous peut-etre Antropophages [sic].

[The exquisite dishes enticing the Prussians / have changed them into Epicureans / Illusion, prestige and hunger/ would turn us perhaps into cannibals.] [125]

Frederick's verse was an easy target. The poem, which heaped humorous praise on the cook Noël, made a joke that if Noël chose to cook a mummy, his great skill would render even an embalmed corpse palatable. Taking the lines out of context, Hamann was able to draw a connection between the philosophy of selfishness and the hunger of the Prussian subjects (which Hamann attributed, among other things, to Frederick's central planning and ban on the purchase of Polish meat). The 'illusion' with which Noël makes unpalatable meat appear delicious is given, in Hamann's treatment, a vague connection with 'prestige': we get the unmistakable picture of the selfish seeker of glory, status, and physical satiety eating his neighbour. The prince's worship of the belly – his utilitarianism – had rendered his subjects objects to be exploited. In proposing to teach this doctrine, Frederick was creating a nation of anthropophages.

Materialism was the most extreme form of the objectification of people for which Hamann blamed the Enlightenment. He wrote, 'The concept of spirit consists, through our newest philosophical revelation, in a spoonful of brains, that every *homunculus* carries a strong and beautiful spirit under his golden, hairy scalp or his silver bald head, and through the monopoly of his brains makes the world of spirit, that is already shy of the light, into contraband in order to be able blatantly to grow with the powers of the current corporeal world.'[126] Frederick, with his tendency to promote deism and his treatment of Christianity as a mere philosophical sect, has made Christianity 'contraband' and has negated the spirit so as to better employ the sword. Hamann thought that the elimination of the other world was a ploy to render fear of the secular sword more effective. This was not entirely fanciful; this is, after all, the clearest educational goal of *Leviathan*.[127] Hamann thought that La Mettrie (whose name he once punned, poorly, with 'La Materie'[128]) and Frederick's materialism, by eliminating all otherworldly concerns, reduced people in society to mere gears and levers. The *bon sens* of the *philosophes* 'aspire à la monarchie universelle par la rigidité de leurs ressorts *trempés* & par la conséquence du mechanisme [sic] systématique.'[129]

If Hamann objected to the educational program entailed in the Frederickian theory of religion, he was equally dismayed by the patronage that Frederick gave to *philosophes* in his Berlin Academy. It no doubt bothered him that someone like La Mettrie received a sizable pension (and later a voluble eulogy) from the king.[130] In addition to thinking that this was a luxury paid for with the bread of the poor (including Hamann's five thaler!), he believed that the academy was the base or 'temple' from which Frederick launched his 'hypocritical philosophical reformation.'[131] The academy's essay competitions, where the questions were often devised by the king, and where one philosophical opinion was 'crowned' with victory struck Hamann as a mere means for the powerful to control thought. He treated the king's patronage of philosophy as a mere purchasing of minds: 'If I were a salaried Accedemico … it would be easy for me to compare the physiognomy of human tongues with the voices of animals.'[132] The specific occasion for this comment was the success of Herder's treatise on the origin of language in which Hamann's one-time disciple had treated man as if he had a beastly origin. Without entering into Hamann's attack on his friend's prize-winning treatise, it is enough to note his objection to the entire competition, which had channelled the literary energies of the country in a direction he found impious.[133] Hamann thought that salaried accademicos follow the will of their paymasters.[134]

When Hamann spoke of 'meiner orbilischen Regierung' he was treating Frederick as a nasty schoolmaster (after Horace's grammar teacher Orbilius who whipped the poet for grammatical errors).[135] He reacted to Frederick's derision of German literature and language with dismay. He wrote to Herder, 'I have read the Orbil of the Littérature Tudesque twice in the original and as many times in translation. What you say about the *despotism* of taste is really his intention to bring in the French. Everything must have one form, must fit one shoe, factory and servitude of vanity … The philosophical anti-Christendom has taken the place of the popish one, and philosophy is the Koran of the lying prophet and his Islamicism.'[136] There is quite a bit packed into this attack. We cannot enter into a discussion of taste here, but we should note that his objection is born, once again, of his dual belief in the world as Logos and his treatment of thought *as* language. To attack the form was to attack the content. And, since Hamann understood reason, in its healthy manifestation, as the product of tradition,[137] the desire to reform the language from above struck him as a 'mute abomination and soul-murder.'[138] This view caused him to see the desire to reform his own language and its poetry as part of a rationalist imperialism of the soul. Aesthetic domination was symptomatic of a greater project of social control.

Hamann, then, much to the confusion of his philosophical opponents, insisted on the unity between form and content. 'Without language we would have no reason, without reason no religion, and without these three essential components of our nature neither spirit nor unity of society.'[139]

He insisted on the unity of *Grammatik*, *Dogmatik*, and *Politik*,[140] and he turned an attack on the reform of language into an attack on all manner of official education and reform: 'All our reformers of justice, of the merciful profit-making, of faith in commerce and exchange, are nothing but ignorant, presumptuous meddlers in ABC and one-plus-one.'[141]

Let us consider the 'reformers of justice.' One of Frederick's more enlightened actions was the codification of laws under his famous minister Cocceji. The purpose of such codification was anti-despotic through-and-through. Frederick was an early proponent of the *Rechtsstaat*, and he sought to reduce arbitrary judgments. That said, the independent administration of justice was more theory than practice under his rule. The most famous example of Frederick's thinking on this point is the case of the miller Arnold – Frederick, having been led to believe that an unjust verdict had been rendered in the favour of some nobles, flew into a rage and imprisoned the judges for nine months. He turned out to have been entirely incorrect about the basic facts of the case.[142] In order to make his point that his was a state where the law reigned, he acted in a most arbitrary, lawless manner. Nonetheless, Frederick considered himself a great champion of the rule of law, and he was a great codifier of laws. Hamann, as we shall see, reacted with the fundamentally conservative response that the organic unity of society is thus broken by the imposition of rules drawn from abstract speculation.

The *philosophes*, waging war against arbitrary measures, sought a standard above civil government but independent of religious tradition. Either secular natural law or utility (and they were not always conceptually distinct) served as this standard. The great appeal of absolute monarchs was the possibility that they would enshrine reasonable tenets in positive law. Naturally, such appeals to reason undermined traditional privileges and practices, and the application of natural law promised to undercut the intermediary powers of the estates. Frederick's desire to codify the laws was interpreted by his enemies as another attempt to attain a greater centralization of power. In the 'Matinées Royales,' a scurrilous text purporting to be written by Frederick but clearly a satire, 'Frederick' confesses that his codification of law was born of a desire to 'sap the foundation of this growing power [aristocratic judges independent of royal control].'[143] The satire treats codification as an avowedly despotic act, undermining all intermediary powers and taking control of the law.

Hamann's objection was not based on the liberal desire to see power check power, but rather on an organic view of society and a Lutheran

wariness of legalism. It is true that he expressed a provincial conservatism when he complained of the state's reforming of matters such as
marriage,[144] but the bulk of his complaint was against the reduction of
the social bond to rules. Frederick's legal reforms had resulted in 'a
state where the Codex is a Golden Colossus' (a footnote points to
Nebuchadnezzar's golden idol).[145] 'Glossateurs laborieux mais stu-
pides! Qui ruminez comme les Dieux d'Egypte, la *lettre* des loix, ne sa-
vez-vous pas, que la lettre tuë [sic] & ne profite de rien? L'étude de
L'Esprit des lois vous sera plus glorieux.'[146] This is naturally not a comment on Montesquieu, but an application of 2 Corinthians 3:6 to political codification: 'The letter killeth, but the spirit giveth life.'[147]

The legal reforms were a sore point for Hamann not merely because
of his perception that they promoted the dead letter of the law at the
expense of the living community and its religious traditions. He also
felt that Frederick's code put the most intimate aspects of communal
life to the service of utility. Hamann saw the sexual union of a man and
a woman as an earthly analogy of the mystical union between the soul
and Christ. The state's regulation of this struck him as evil: 'Because the
condition of marriage is the most precious ground and cornerstone of
all society: so does the misanthropic spirit of our century reveal itself
most strongly in the laws of marriage.'[148] Law ought not to control love;
marriage is not a contract.

If the state was sticking its cold hands into the marriage bed, it was
equally becoming licentious.[149] Hamann attributed to the king the following statement: 'que l'on prie Dieu dans mon Royaume comme l'on
veut et que l'on f – comme l'on peut.'[150] The link between Frederick's
vaunted religious tolerance, which Hamann referred to as indifferentism unbecoming of Christian tolerance (the latter being an act of charity, or love),[151] and the notoriety of Frederick's sexual mores was too
tempting, and Hamann periodically cast aspersions on 'the sophists of
Sodom-Samaria,' joking that a prince who always sought to increase his
population and who needed constantly to replenish the ranks of his
'Schlachtheerden' (slaughter-herd) might better employ his member in
a more fruitful union. And, naturally, he did not let pass the opportunity
to make crude jokes about Frederick's favourite instrument, the flute.[152]

But Hamann did not attack toleration merely because it appeared to
go hand in hand with licentiousness (he wasn't really a prude); rather,
he feared that champions of toleration sought to make inroads into the
content of religion itself. For Frederick (ever the student of Voltaire) all
religions, though socially useful for the mob, are nonetheless inherently

fanatical, and, as we have noted, he sought to undermine the 'fabulous' in the search for the overlapping consensus of deism. Hamann also thought that Frederick's tolerance was a hypocritical mask that hid the underlying violence of his regime. When Frederick's court preacher Eberhard wrote a defence of enlightened toleration, Hamann wondered aloud how all this praise for humanity could fit so easily with patriotic duty to kill foreigners in pursuit of the nation's interests.[153]

What Is To Be Done?

Having passed through this torrent of censure, we might wish to pause and wipe our brows. Hamann, the *petit philosophe de grand souci,* covered the *grand philosophe de Sans-Souci*[154] with enough biblical epithets for twenty tyrants. Frederick was condemned for his codification of laws, his mercantilist projects, his hypocritical Anti-Machiavellianism, his sexual manners, his luxurious excesses, and his aesthetic criticism. He was charged with seeking universal domination through the employment of (ir)religion and education to change men into selfish materialists ruled by their vanity and their stomachs. His antipathy to the particularities of the German language was seen as an attack on the very souls of his subjects. His tolerance was decried as indifferentism whose purpose was the weakening of faith, a project that Hamann thought was intended to make men more fearful of the sword. Frederick worshiped Mammon, whereas Hamann celebrated the imprudence of Christian poverty. Frederick's common sense rendered nature dumb and turned people into mere items. Breaking the organic unity of society into atoms, Frederick was accused of wanting to rebuild the social bonds on the basis of law and contract. He would place cold law between warm bodies. And all of this was tied to the philosophical hubris of wanting to describe the world in abstract terms.

Now, this is quite a mouthful, and none of these claims can be given adequate treatment in the short space we have here. It will have to suffice to have shown the general direction of his polemic and to have hinted at its consistency (we will make no excuses for its excesses): Frederick carried the sword for militant Enlightenment anti-Christianity. He sought to reform his subjects from the top down, rendering them useful utilitarians.

But what was Hamann's position on the best regime? What was the alternative to despotism? Was Hamann, as Urs Strässle contends, a champion of theocracy?[155] Or, on the contrary, was he egalitarian, in keeping with the priesthood of believers? Oswald Bayer writes that Hamann's insistence on Genesis 1:25–6 ('And God said, Let us make man in our image, after our likeness: and let them have dominion over … every creeping thing that creepeth upon the earth') indicates a basis for attacking enlightened absolutism in the name of a 'political freedom.'[156] Bayer is probably the most prolific contemporary writer on Hamann, but it is difficult to follow him here as he leaves rather vague just what this political freedom entails. One suspects Bayer of fishing for affinities between his favourite author and liberal democracy. While one can certainly see that there is an egalitarian aspect to the equality of souls, Bayer will have to do more than point to man's creation in God's image to indicate Hamann's connection with liberalism.

We have seen that Hamann celebrated Aristotle's argument that man, as a linguistic creature, had the 'masterly dignity of a political animal,'[157] and he suggested that there had been a time in the garden when 'no creature was burdened against her will with the vanity and servitude of a transitory system.'[158] He called his readers' attention to the fundamental similarity between 'Fritz in a purple cradle and Fritz in swaddling clothes,'[159] a king of the earth and a beggar. However, despite these egalitarian passages, Hamann offered little critical reflection on the various hierarchies that defined his society (he has nothing to say about the emancipation of Jews, serfs, or women, for instance). Isaiah Berlin, noting Hamann's lack of a doctrine of political resistance, terms his theory 'quietist,' a view that he shares with Jean Blum.[160] But this is awkward; at the very least, calling his apocalyptic tirades 'quiet' occasions a raised eyebrow.

Yet it is true that for all his apocalyptic attacks – and there were many instances when he seemed to lose his humour and expressed rather violent sentiments[161] – he did not counsel rebellion or regime change. He wrote to Jacobi, 'I hold all regime forms to be indifferent, and I am certain that all products and monstrosities of society and nature are products of a higher will, to which we must pray and which we are obliged through conscience, necessity, and prudence not to judge.'[162] Thus, 'let the republican love his free fatherland, and let the subject of the monarch bear his burden without kicking against the pricks.'[163] We recall his argument that Christian duty was to suffer injustice. Equally, he did not think that it was the Christian's duty to punish impiety. His argument for toleration was equally his argument against rebellion: 'If the householder has patience and lenience with the tares, then let every one care for his own field and garden.'[164]

Yet we can see from the same letter that this indifference to forms of government and renunciation of rebellion is not a renunciation of judging kings, in spite of what may be implied by the providential statement above. He wrote, 'All monarchs are, in my eyes, shadow images of the golden time when there will be one herder and one flock.'[165] This image reminds us that for all of Hamann's anti-Platonic insistence on the transient, immanent nature of all language, there is an underlying Platonism in his Christianity. The cave communicates with the outside world, but it is, as it were, a passage that goes only in one direction. Rather than attempt an ascent, Hamann insists on waiting for the sunlight to make its way down. But this does not imply that one is to withdraw into an apolitical contemplation; Christianity is a political project. In a piece on ecclesiastical history, Frederick had described Christianity as a 'sect' and 'le héro de cette secte,' as 'Un Juif … dont la naissance est douteuse.'[166] Hamann replied, 'If, then, the path of Christianity must still be called a sect, then this sect deserves to be seen chiefly as a political one. The hero of this sect will soon be known according to his doubtful [*Zweideutig* – a play on *douteuse*][167] birth, as a king. He himself calls the content of his theism a Kingdom of Heaven, and he lays before his heathen judge, who executed the shameful sentence of death upon him, the good avowal that his kingdom is not of this world; – for what earthly monarchy or republic boast of such an extension and permanence, of such absolute freedom and despotic obedience, of such simple and, at the same time, fruitful basic law [*Grundgesetz*]?[168] The Christian faith is political, but Frederick is incapable of understanding the 'higher order of political science [*Staatsweisheit*].'[169]

The divine model is ultimately *despotic* and yet free. It is despotic because man is entirely subject to the unlimited will of God; it is free in the Lutheran sense, because God's love is infinite and the believer is free from temporal concerns. Only with God could the paradox of freedom in submission be sustained. Yet this doctrine, which in Luther had begun as an anti-civic creed and had terminated in support of the sword, remains in Hamann a basis for the calling of kings to account. Unlike the enlightened absolutists, who called for kings to bind themselves with laws, Hamann called for kings to make themselves into servants of God. Voltaire had treated Frederick as a god on earth; Hamann mocked this, addressing Frederick with irony bordering on sarcasm: 'You have made yourself in the image of that *King of the Jews* who is the King of Kings and who, nonetheless, was placed in the ranks of criminals and brigands and "PENDARDS." You have abased yourself in finding yourself in the figure of a miserable Prussian. You will succeed in the end in becoming our FATHER, who will know how to give his children good things, just like our Father who is in heaven.'[170] Hamann's outright scorn is strangely balanced by the sincere (if odd) hope that the king will embrace faith. The image of the divine model against which all temporal rulers are judged helps make sense of Hamann's more direct political project: in his anti-Frederickian tirades he sought to catch the king's conscience.[171]

Now, we may lament that Hamann did not attempt to address the question of how government should be organized. His mode of expression (and his entire tenor of mind) was far too oracular for the slow, systematic study of political institutions, and his biblical imagination was not made for considering the very real problem of reconciling freedom and subjection on earth. But before we condemn him for shallow simplicity we ought to note that Pope's view that one should seek good administration regardless of governmental form was relatively widespread.[172] Many *philosophes* simply insisted on fixed law. D'Alembert wrote to Frederick that regime forms were unimportant: it was law that counted.[173] D'Holbach said much the same thing: what was important was to avoid despotism, defined as rule by caprice with the absence of law.[174] But the real political problem for Hamann was not whether states can be organized such that the laws rule: as we have seen, he gave a Pauline challenge to the 'dead letter' of law. Just as Hamann denied the difference between philosophy and sophistry, so too did he deny that law could be truly independent of will. All law was insufficient; indeed, all law was corrupting if not imbued with the proper spirit. The central political problem – and the political problem that animated the scriptures – is whether rulers can be made to love God. To those who cannot, Hamann had this advice (which he wrote in capital letters): 'THEN CEASE TO BE KING!'[175]

This is not a call for theocracy. Hamann's 'theocratic' passages are plays upon Voltaire's hyperbolic praise of the king. As Elfriede Büchsel points out, this is Hamannian 'irony': 'With Hamann, the thought of the imitatio dei through the ruler is not meant to be ideological-programmatic, but rather critical, in the sense of that 'Socratic irony' that actually came more from St Paul than from Socrates himself.'[176] Indeed, Hamann wrote that all champions of theocracy end up abusing religion.[177] The relationship between church and state is a particularly tricky one to navigate. We have seen Hamann's claim that secular power invariably rapes or shuns the church, but we have equally seen his claim that to separate politics and religion is to make two empty halves.

What are we to do with this contradiction? And what are we to do with his apparent naivety in thinking his bizarre jeremiads might catch the king's conscience? The answer to both these questions is that Hamann saw in the king's predicament (and, implicitly, in the predicament of any type of sovereign) the extreme version of the human predicament: infinitely distant from the desired state, people were called to seek it. Hamann's politics were certainly quixotic, but he knew it. He wrote, 'Pour gouverner des sujets, il faut ou les *contraindre* ou les *tromper*. On ne réussit jamais dans cette double charge, sans haïr souverainement les hommes avec toute la mechanceté [sic] d'un *Tyran* et d'un *Sophiste*, mais sous le masque d'une morale et d'une humanité hypocrites. Le maître, qui *aime* ses sujets, sera toujours ou leur *dupe*, comme LE GRAND DIEU, ou leur *victime*, comme SON FILS BIEN-AIMÉ. Il faut donc tourner le dos *au grand Dieu* et à *Son Fils, le bien-aimé*, pour être *bientôt riche*.'[178]

Against the cant of the *Anti-Machiavel*, Hamann claimed that the Florentine was perfectly correct: Christian compassion and charity don't get one very far in political life. But, naturally, he inverted Machiavelli's normative assessment of this fact, celebrating the king who made himself a servant and ruled by being crucified. Hamann forced the confrontation between the kingdom of heaven and those on earth. 'The fairy tale of the kingdom of heaven is thus, in comparison with all other universal monarchies and their pragmatic histories, a tiny mustard seed.'[179]

Hamann's theological politics, then, are essentially in opposition to temporal power. We are tempted to say of him, as Sheldon Wolin has said of Luther, 'His thought represented a striking combination of revolt and passivity.'[180] But as much as Hamann shared Luther's view that the sum of a Christian's rights was to suffer at the cross, he equally thought that the kingdom of heaven was a pattern against which to judge the kingdoms of this world. If we return to Hamann's response to Kant (where he spoke of Christians being 'more courageous against these guardians [*Vormünder*], who at most can kill the body and suck out the contents of our purse')[181] we note an implicit theory of passive obedience. But if rebellion is not an option, neither is silence. Faced with an Antichrist, one ought to do as Hamann urged Frederick's court preacher: preach 'blood and fire, like the prophet Elias.'[182] Frederick had claimed to be the 'first servant of the state,' but Hamann was challenging him to make himself truly into a servant. But Hamann was perfectly aware that this was an unattainable ideal: the political life was about *Staatsräson*, not 'Staatsweisheit höherer Ordnung.'

The absolutist *philosophes*, thinking that despotism could be averted by the enactment of needed reforms and laws, sought to convert kings to their philosophical programs. Hamann, who championed love against law, and faith against utility also appealed to the monarch's conscience. His appeal was simply more demanding and less practical (indeed, it was supremely demanding and supremely impractical). We are tempted to ask, what good can this serve us in the field of political science? Yet this is precisely where Hamann was making his attack. Enlightened absolutism was such a powerful ideological notion (and remains such a tempting dream for social scientists) precisely because of its tendency to undermine questions of character and the state of the individual soul for questions of organization. The modern problem of organizing atomistic, self-interested human beings into peaceful groups was solved by emphasizing rather than decrying the atomistic, self-interested aspects of human nature. It was the rare observer who saw that this was not merely a question of organizing existing material, but of preparing the rough stones into smooth blocks: enlightened reform entailed social pedagogy. Frederick's view that 'we make men as we wish' was not accompanied by a view that we can effect radical moral improvement, but that we can effect an organizational improvement by teaching people to be what they are in their worse moments.

PART FIVE

Aesthetics:
Hamann's Anti-Artistic Aestheticism

10 Aesthetic, All Too Aesthetic: Hamann on the Battle between Poetry and Philosophy

We have seen in this study that Hamann described poetry as the mother tongue of the human race, that he deprecated philosophy in the name of poetic wisdom, and that he celebrated the senses and the sentiments over reason's abstract concepts. It is not difficult to see why Rudolf Unger spoke of his influence on the spirit of romanticism.[1] We might even be tempted to see Nietzschean aesthetic morality here; or at the very least, we might be inclined to read in this a thorough overturning of Plato on the poets. Isaiah Berlin helps us along in this view, insisting that Hamann is 'a true forerunner' of Nietzsche.[2] But this position is imprecise. Hamann's celebration of the Christian Logos over the philosophical logos is extremely anti-Platonic, yet it is also a powerful defence of the plebeian Platonism that Nietzsche attacked in the Christian religion. Indeed, to see Hamann's anti-Enlightenment as part of the (post)modern aestheticization of morality is to miss the degree to which his attack touches the aestheticizers of both the eighteenth and the twentieth centuries.

Hans Graubner sums up Hamann's position succinctly: Hamann's 'theological aesthetics ... originates from connecting the epistemological empiricism with the experience of God's address to man.'[3] It is this theological element of Hamann's aesthetic turn that constitutes a powerful condemnation of the *Temple du goût* in his century and in ours. If Hamann believed that we think poetically, his biblical imagination resisted the turn to the aesthetics of will and self-creation that characterized the romantic and postmodern reactions. The age-old war between the poets and the philosophers is more complex than it appears: Hamann, the Christian 'philologist,' represents a third front. In his view, the inadequacy of theory is surmounted through a hermeneutic stance that takes aesthetic or sensory form. But, as we shall indicate in our conclusion, the attempt to separate Hamannian arguments from his intellectual context (the Bible) runs great risks.

This chapter, then, explores Hamann's opposition to the discourse of taste and indicates his place in the battle between philosophy and poetry, between Plato and Nietzsche. We begin in ontology, indicating the degree to which Hamann, for all his anti-Platonic insistence on the temporal, the sensory, and the poetic, never entirely abandoned the duality of being/becoming, but transformed it utterly by ascribing a greater permanence to poetic expression than to philosophical expression. Thus, he is both with the poets against Plato and with Platonism against Nietzsche. The implications of this are drawn out in the following sections. The second section touches on the relationship between the passions and reason. We will see that while Hamann opposed the Platonic subjugation of eros to reason, he nonetheless did not announce the modern inversion whereby the soul is controlled by its desires. The third section explores his use of the concept of genius and corrects the misinterpretation of Hamann that places him in a tradition leading to the Nietzschean ideal of artistic self-creation. The fourth section turns from the creation to the reception of the aesthetic phenomenon, exploring Hamann's myriad castigations of Enlightenment taste discourse and illustrating his rejection of detached aesthetic criticism and the ideal of taste. We will also explain the theological significance of Hamann's championing of ugliness. The following section is a brief excursus on the aesthetic in the thought of Heidegger, with whom Hamann shared a great deal but whose view of art and revelation entails a fundamental break with Hamann's position. We will conclude with some general reflections on the importance of Hamann's aesthetic turn and the challenges it poses in the secular world.

Being and Becoming: Hamann's Ambiguous Relationship to Platonism

Hamann decried taste discourse, asserting the foundational character of affective and metaphorical speech. This appears to invert the Platonic relationship between poetry and reason. How does this relate to the Nietzschean and 'postmodern' turns towards aesthetics? In many respects, Hamann's objections to the Enlightenment project foreshadow much twentieth-century thought. He decried the alienation occasioned by scientific terminology in the same way that many decry the positivist objectification of the world; he undermined philosophical foundations by pointing to the contingency of language and the centrality of the body; he insisted that life is prior to thought; and he trumpeted the merits of poetry at the expense of philosophy. One is tempted to see an affinity between Hamann and writers as diverse as Nietzsche, Heidegger, Adorno, Foucault, and Rorty, who all, in varying ways, decried a techno-logical/scientific project and who turned to the aesthetic realm as an alternative route.

Let us examine a characteristic passage in Hamann that both gives rise to and undermines this impression:

> Just as all types of unreason assume from the beginning the existence of reason and its misuse, so must all religions have a relationship with the faith in one single, self-standing, and living truth that, like our existence, must be older than our reason and thus cannot be perceived through the genesis of the latter [our reason], but rather through an unmediated revelation of the former [the living truth]. Because our reason creates its concepts out of the mere outward relations of visible, sensory, unsteady things in order to shape them according to the form of their inner nature and to apply them for its pleasure and use, so does the basis of religion lie in our entire existence and outside of the sphere of our cognitive powers, which, taken altogether, make up the most contingent and abstract *modum* of our existence. From this comes that mythical and poetic vein of all religions, their folly and scandalous form in the eyes of a heterogeneous, incompetent, ice-cold, dog-thin philosophy that shamelessly imputes to its educational technique the higher destiny of our mastery over the earth.

As a footnote, Hamann writes,

> Le *premier art* de l'homme a été *l'education* [sic] *du chien* et le *fruit de cet art* la conquête et la possession possible de la terre. Buffon Tom VI. P.313. Compare with this Helvetius' posthumous work on the training of dogs [*De l'homme, de ses facultés intellectuelles, et de son éducation*].[4]

The footnote indicates Hamann's claim that the Enlightenment is about the technical domination of nature, which entails the domination of man. Juxtaposing Buffon's claim about the art of dog-rearing with Helvétius' work on education is his manner of claiming that social science objectifies man in the same manner as the arts employed to subject nature to control. Enlightenment reason is born of a desire to capture and control the elements of experience. The same will to dominate is the motivation for our conceptual abstractions: Enlightenment reason is a manner of subjecting life to control for the alleviation of man's estate. But as Helvétius' example indicates, the educational goals of the Enlightenment entail the turn from the domination of nature to the domination of man. The poetic offers something that is missed by those who place excessive weight on their capacity to reason. Reason, in fact, is just one 'mode' of existence; it cannot be foundational. Existence is prior to reasoning, and the poetic and mythic entail another 'mode' of existence, one whose greater attunement to the immediate, dynamic data of the senses and the passions grants it a superior status. There are numerous aspects of this that appear to resonate in post-Nietzschean philosophy. Yet consider the passage's striking Platonic overtones. Hamann does not merely argue that 'our reason' is a mask, as suspect and a posteriori as other cognition – he *decries* it for its instability and contingency. There is an eternal form that is beyond reason's reach. Nor does Hamann lay stress on the creative powers of man. Poetry and myth do not create truth; they attempt to articulate a revealed (extra-rational) truth. Reason – normally considered the realm of the permanent – is given a back seat here to a prior revelation that has greater permanence.

Writers such as Ronald Gregor Smith have termed Hamann 'existentialist,' and there is certainly some continuity with Hamann's insistence on the priority of our involved existence in the world. Hamann's view, however, is somewhat difficult to term 'existentialist' in the clear sense given by Sartre; the catchphrase 'existence precedes essence' is not in the least true for Hamann. 'Existence precedes rational analysis' is Hamann's argument, but this is a position shared by all empiricists.[5] There is something eternal that is quite separate from human cognition and from human action. 'Poetry' somehow has a better grasp of the eternal and a better capacity to transmit it. Nor is this a call for Jacobi's 'leap of faith,' as we have noted elsewhere, for Hamann did not think that this poetry was irrational. Again, he insisted that reason *was* language: 'Reason is invisible without language; however, it is indeed the only expression of the soul and the heart for the revelation and communication of our most inner selves [*unsers Innersten*].'[6] Language and reason do not determine truth, they are mere appendages: 'Our reason must wait and hope – must want to be the servant and not the lawgiver of nature.'[7] Poetry is a different form of logos, one that is less alienated from sense experience and the passions. But the point that requires emphasis here is that essences and the realm of 'being' are assumed throughout. The soul and the divine 'living truth' are eternal. It is our conception of them that resides in the realm of becoming (and our conceptual apparatus is, of course, subject to misuse).[8]

Hamann, then, accepted the Platonic view that there is a realm more permanent and stable than the realm of becoming in which we sensory creatures live. His anti-Platonism consists of his insistence that human thought is unable to ascend by means of dialectic, but must, rather, accept a passive role, receiving a symbolically mediated message. Piety, for Hamann, is attunement to the symbols in which this eternal truth is expressed. It is a receptive, hermeneutic attitude towards experience that allows one to grasp an eternal meaning contained in it.[9]

Naturally, much in Hamann's thought is a direct reaction to Platonic tendencies in philosophy. Platonism raises the good (which is rational) above the will of the gods (see, for instance, *Euthyphro*), Hamann, who subscribed to a kind of divine positivism, saw this as replacing divine will with that of proud man (for reason is simply one human faculty among many). Plato often deprecated the world of appearances, pointing to a world of mind that was eternal; Hamann saw mind as embodied and thus as subject to change as any other phenomena. Plato sought to chasten the poets and rationalize the mythical; Hamann championed poetic excess and the anthropomorphism that had so vexed Plato in the stories of the gods. The defence of the immortality of the soul in the *Phaedo* requires recourse to the realm of pure ideas that runs counter to Hamann's extremely concerned quest for self-knowledge in relationship with others. Plato's equation of the realm of Being with the realm of the intellect is, for Hamann, the primal philosophical sin.

That said, we may wish to nuance our interpretation of Plato. There is much more to the 'participation' of the forms in the world of becoming than is grasped by the claim of a naive dualism. Indeed, Hamann attended to the Platonic subtlety on this point, as is evident from his celebration of Socrates. 'Analogy was the soul of his conclusions,' Hamann wrote of Socrates.[10] Certainly one need not delve too far into the Platonic oeuvre to see a justification for such a Hamannian claim. The *Phaedo*'s allegory, the *Republic*'s metaphor of the sun and the cave, the *Timaeus*'s fanciful cosmology: Socrates' constant recourse to myth suggests that metaphysical explanations defy straightforward, univocal expression. Now, as we noted in chapter 2, Plato himself gave some explanation for his lack of univocality (in the *7th Letter* and the *Phaedrus*), and we have seen that Hamann's insistence on both the personal nature of communication and the need for analogy bears some relationship to these arguments.

There is no space here to enter into the tricky problem of Plato's theory of knowledge, his argument for the 'participation' of the forms in the world of sense, or precisely what it means for Plato to 'give an account' of something. Certainly it is not entirely satisfying to run together philosophy and poetry in Plato's oeuvre: this was a distinction upon which Plato laid great weight. Let it suffice for us to reject the interpretation of Plato as a naive dualist who thought the philosopher could close his eyes and have direct access to the realm of being. Hamann, attributing his own view to Socrates, certainly thought some mediation was involved between the divine and the human realms. He wrote, 'Human life appears to consist of a series of symbolic actions through which our soul is able to reveal its invisible nature, and brings out and communicates an intuitive knowledge [*Erkänntnis*] of its effective existence outside of itself. The mere body of an action can never reveal to us its worth; rather, the representation of its grounds for action and their results are the natural mediating concepts out of which are created our conclusions and their corresponding approbation or disapprobation.'[11] Behind interactions lies a moral meaning, an *invisible nature*.[12] As creatures with and in logos, human beings are constantly revealing their essential natures through symbolic mediation. Though the moral and figural significance of actions is invisible, it cannot be perceived in any way other than through the senses. O'Flaherty quotes from an important letter to Jacobi, 'The truth must be dug up out of the earth and not created out of the air out of terms-of-art – but rather out of earthy and subterranean objects first brought into the light through comparisons and parables of the highest ideas and transcendent intuitions that cannot be *directi* but rather *reflexi radii*.'[13]

Hamann was radicalizing a problem that is raised by the Platonic position on the relationship between being and becoming: how does one express the permanent in transitory language? It was the Platonic insistence on the *rational* nature of the forms that Hamann decried. Indeed, Hamann's personification of the realm of being entirely corrupts the Platonic view. For Hamann, anything absolute was divine and thus ungraspable without divine condescension.[14] God expressed himself in terms that appealed to human passions, in analogical/sensory – aesthetic – terms. Thus, piety – and with it morality – are somehow aesthetic, but are equally foundational. Piety attends to a universal, unchanging realm of being that is the subject of one's most concerned inquiry, for self-knowledge and knowledge of God are akin, and they are both equally elusive. This relationship between man and soul, or, to speak philosophically, existence and essence, finds expression in the paradox that we touched on in chapter 5, the 'coincidence of opposites.' The unchanging, eternal form reveals itself in changeable symbols, in the world of becoming; the universal cannot be known but reveals itself through particulars. Neither side can be dealt with in isolation.

Hamann's aesthetics, then, entail an attention to universals that exist only in particular, sensual form. This is not about art, but about the symbolic nature of experience. While Hamann inverts Plato's hierarchies between reason and the passions and between reason and poetry, he equally retains a kind of permanence that is non-conceptual, but is rather manifested for humans in particulars. What gives us access to the invisible if not reason? Hamann's answer is God's grace and his Word, communicated to our senses and passions. What, then, is the relationship between passions and the divine, the senses and the super-sensible? Let us enter into this problem by turning to the relationship between eros and logos.

Passions, Sexuality, and the Body

Plato and Nietzsche form nice antipodes on the question of the passions' place in cognition. For Plato, the appetitive part of the soul must be subjected to the rule of reason, and our erotic desires must be turned towards the object of philosophy. Nietzsche, for whom the realm of being is a monstrous birth of human resentment at the changing world, celebrates in art an affirmation and elevation of the erotic to an ideal level. 'The demand for art and beauty is an indirect demand for the ecstasies of sexuality communicated to the brain.'[15] Thus the one sought to turn eros, the other sought to elevate it. That is to say, Nietzsche turned the artistic transfiguration of subjective desires to his ideal, while Plato sought to turn the subjective desires to the objective good. If Hamann anticipated Nietzsche's view that the passions and particular sensory stimulation dominate human experience, he was not elevating pure subjective desire.

Hamann's sexual imagery has often been a source of interpretive error. Isaiah Berlin argues for the romantic resonance of Hamann's insistence on the centrality of pudenda and his celebration of man's passionate erotic energy. Berlin tells us that Hamann champions the creative and passionate in man and hates 'man-made laws.' Hamann, Berlin adds, shares Blake's view that 'Jesus & his Apostles & Disciples were all Artists,' he prefigures D.H. Lawrence, and he 'identifies reason with repression.'[16] Ultimately, Hamann saw 'the need for total self-expression as the object of the natural human craving for freedom.'[17] Berlin is extremely misleading here; we have seen that Hamann saw reason as man's means of self-revelation, that his attack on law was modelled on Christ's 'attack' on Mosaic law, and that the comparison of Christ to artists was not meant as a celebration of art, but of Christ. As for man's freedom, Berlin has not attempted to understand this in the Lutheran sense.

There is an element of truth in Berlin's interpretation of Hamann: the 'Magus' certainly decried as perverse monastic asceticism. But he decried libertinage as well – they were, for him, two sides of the same coin.[18] Passages like the following (emerging from the mouth of the Sybille) appear to bear out Berlin's reading: 'Hypocritical Pharisees of our century! Your moral and bourgeois [bürgerliche] prejudices and the taste or trifle of your profits is nothing but caviar of the Leviathan … and the blushing of your virgins, your beautiful spirits! is Gallican make-up, powder and rouge; but no nobly born purple of a healthy, heaven-given, and animated flesh and blood.'[19] However, we should be careful here. We, so deafened by a century of reproach against prudery and repression, tend to read into this an attempt to overturn sexual mores. But we forget that Hamann was not allying himself with Diderot, the vanguard of the anti-repressive Enlightenment; on the contrary, he was returning to the full-blooded sensuality of baroque pietism. Sexual union was an image of the mystical marriage of Christ with the soul.[20] His constant emphasis on the genitals of God is an attempt to thrust anthropomorphism into the faces of his deistic opponents. For Hamann, if you don't picture God with genitals, you might as well be an atheist.

Hamann was arguing that the bourgeois prejudice that places law over love fails to do justice to the passionate and spiritual core that makes marriage worthwhile. Marriage becomes a transaction; fake shame is a currency. But Hamann equally celebrated the virtue of pudeur, following the above quotation with the following claim: 'Without the sacrifice of innocence, the jewel and sanctuary of chastity remains unknown, and the entrance into this heavenly virtue impenetrable.'[21] There are numerous levels to this sexual metaphor. It is a reference to the relationship between love and law that we have often noted. But it is also a reference to the Fall, in which knowledge, sin, and virtue were born. It is an attack on puritanical, rule-bound asceticism, but equally on libertinism. The point to be noted is that, contra Berlin, the virtue of chastity is not done away with, even though it comes to be through its opposite in the institution of marriage, to which this article is a paean. One wonders what D.H. Lawrence would have made of this very Lutheran teaching about the marriage bed as the fount of chastity.[22]

Hamann's discussion of the sexual drive is quite important, for it indicates an aspect of *Genuß* that is central to his understanding of sensuous cognition.[23] Now, we can know one another in a biblical sense, but such knowledge is rarely viewed as the height of contemplative or pious existence. To be sure, Hamann was not making a claim for the epiphanic nature of orgasms when he protested that one ought not dare to enter into the 'metaphysics of the beautiful arts without being initiated into the orgies and the Eleusinian mysteries.'[24] Rather, he was making a claim about the relationship between eros and logos. If eros for Plato was something to be bridled and turned towards the ends of philosophy, one dominant tendency in the post-enlightened world has been to turn philosophy to the service of eros. Hamann placed the body at the centre of cognition, but he did not think that the soul needed to serve the desires. It is in the *Aesthetica* itself that he decried those who make the stomach into their king as both slavish and despotic at once.[25] Hamann was not railing against 'repression,' but against the incapacity of his contemporaries to read a divine message in eros. Materialists like LaMettrie or Diderot made the passions into a blind force and saw reason as a means of gratifying them best; Hamann shared their inversion of the ancient hierarchy between reason and the passions, but he nonetheless wished to realign the passions. If the Platonic position is to turn the erotic towards philosophy (to subject it to the rule of reason), Hamann (with what Nietzsche would call his plebeian Platonism) sought to indicate in the erotic the form of something divine.[26]

Anders Nygren offered an influential (and extremely Lutheran) account of the relationship between different types of love, eros and agape.[27] Eros, in its higher, Platonic form, is the desire to bring oneself into contact with what is in itself good or beautiful in order to possess or partake in that goodness. Agape, by contrast, describes God's love of humankind, and, by extension, the love that Christians are commanded to extend to their enemies – it is a disinterested love, spontaneous, overflowing, creative, and indifferent to the quality of the love object. The opposition that Nygren is highlighting is that between a theology of glory, which he identifies with Platonism, and one of the cross. The first grants the individual great place in her own salvation; the second emphasizes the individual's powerlessness. The first is anthropocentric; the second is theocentric. The first is concerned with the intrinsic goodness of the love object, a goodness that the self seeks to possess; the second is completely selfless and entails a complete regard for the other. Hamann's view of love shares much of Nygren's agape, but it is not entirely selfless. Nygren is clearly Hamannian (or rather, Lutheran) in his emphasis on human weakness. But Hamann was not one to renounce the interested, possessive love that is the basis of eros. Indeed, Nygren's denunciation of the egocentric, desiring aspects of human striving has a somewhat anti-Hamannian purity to it.[28]

Eva Kocziszky argues that Hamann was far too committed to the fullness of human experience to cordon off a disinterested love. 'Eros and Agape can as little be separated as body and spirit.'[29] Or, as Dickson puts it with regard to a passage in the *Essay of a Sibyl on Marriage*, by speaking ambiguously of the 'god of love' with both pagan and Christian references, Hamann is 'specifically integrating the two notions of love … introducing the overtly erotic and sexual aspect governed by eros into the concept of the Christian God of love.'[30] Platonic eros is clearly far too abstract and sublime for Hamann – recall, we live in particularity and ought not to seek to hold anything pure and universal. There are universal meanings to transient actions, but it would be meaningless for Hamann to turn from the love of a good person to love of goodness itself.[31] Hamann is equally with Nygren against the theology of glory implicit in the Platonic view that the lovers of wisdom are capable of ascending under their own power (or at least under the compulsion of earthly philosophers). Yet, like Plato, Hamann conceived of love as eros, as a lack, a desire to be filled. Humans share both in the divine nature (hence their capacity for what Nygren terms agape), and the human (hence their need for grace, their capacity to receive, their particularism).[32] Hamann perceived in sexual love between man and woman the image of this God–man relationship.[33] This is not to say that he thought a man had the same authority over a woman as God over man(!);[34] indeed, he indicates that both 'male' and 'female' aspects of overflowing creativity and receptivity exist in both partners. Just as Aristophanes in the *Symposium* considered our original nature to be androgynous and eros to be a desire for reunification, so too did Hamann point to the myth of Eve's creation, when God split a single being into two. Hamann's essay on marriage plays upon Genesis 2:21: 'And he took one of his ribs, and closed up the flesh instead thereof,' or as the German reads, 'he closed up the place with flesh.'[35] This follows a passage in which the Sibyl cries with delight upon seeing a 'rib,' that it is 'bone of my bone, flesh of my flesh.'[36] If the rib functions as a phallic symbol, it equally genders female in its incarnation as Eve. Similarly, it is Adam who has a space that seeks to be filled.

There is much to be said about Hamann's understanding of eroticism, but the essential point is that the erotic relationship between husband and wife and the erotic desire that colours friendship are means with which we recognize ourselves and God's grace. Eros is not a one-way street, but a series of reciprocal relationships in which we learn to know ourselves and the divine through sincere and faithful communion. Just as language is a sacrament, so too is marriage. Through these relational experiences, we are given an image of our relationship to God. Thus, onanism (and radically individualistic philosophy) and sexual objectification (and materialist philosophy) fail to do justice to the experience of eros.

If the relationship between the soul and Christ is an erotic one and if Hamannian eros is essentially reciprocal (not one-way desire), the analogy appears to strain. What, after all, is Christ's erotic motivation? The ascription to God of the weaknesses necessary for eros appears somewhat odd. Platonic eros was not essentially reciprocal in that the object of love, being perfect, can't possibly love because it can't need. Reasonable as this is, it is the same Platonic consideration that did away with all anthropomorphism. Hamann wrote, 'Who could have believed it if God had not told us himself that the first world wounded him, grieved him at his heart; who could have believed it, that he finds his glory in our obedience and the enjoyment of his majesty in our society and our interests.'[37] It seems odd to ascribe eros to God: how could a God be anything less than perfect? Hamann, however, never allows us to forget that God's condescendence entailed this adoption of human form, and the suffering God is the heart of Christian imagery.[38] The purity of Nygren's selfless agape is, for Hamann, literally as inconceivable as the abstract universality of Plato's love object, the good. Defending Socrates' physical attraction to his students, Hamann claimed, 'One can feel no living friendship without sensuality, and a metaphysical love sins perhaps more against the nervous fluids than an animal love sins against flesh and blood.'[39] When Nygren wrote, 'Between Vulgar Eros and Christian Agape there is no relation at all,' he was engaging in the kind of separation that Hamann decried.[40] For human beings, love is always both spiritual and material. To deny the spiritual aspect is the materialist error; to deny the physical is to attempt to flee the realm of particulars in which we live.[41]

The materialist inversion of the classical teaching concerning reason's relation to the passions is somewhat bizarre on etymological grounds. Hamann correctly indicated the *passivity* of the passions. To have passions is to suffer (*Leidenschaft*). Hamann employed the typical trope of gendering this role of suffering and receiving 'feminine' (consonant with the image of the soul as the bride of Christ): 'truly *actio* and action lose all manly dignity through womanly and childlike passion or *Leidenschaft* [Hamann uses both the Latin and German words]. But why is it in the most varied instances true: when I am weak, then am I strong?'[42] Passion is a need. One great error is to deliver oneself to false needs, as does the 'Epicurean'; another great error is to deny one's neediness in the manner of a Stoic (or, as Hamann has it elsewhere, to castrate oneself as did Origen).[43] Hamann's position stands in contrast both to libertinism (where thoughts are to the passions but scouts and spies), and to Kantian Stoicism (where the passions are bestial hindrances to freedom, or rational self-control). In another place, the paradox and inversion are completed, and the passions become 'masculine' and active: 'If the passions are members of dishonour, do they then cease to be weapons of manhood?'[44] As tiresome as it is to read these sexist clichés about female passivity and male action, it is important to note Hamann's inversion of strength and weakness. To recognize human need is to place the emphasis on receptivity and weakness, but such recognition, such humility, is the source of strength. This paradox has its epistemological manifestation in Hamann's celebration of Socratic ignorance as the highest knowledge.

Hamann opposed the elevation of reason above body, and he insisted on the sacramental nature of our passions and sensual experiences. Thus, both prudery and libertinism were suspect to him. But, contra Berlin, he did not see reason as essentially repressive, nor was he making an idol of sexual energy.[45] Rather, he was suggesting that there is an analogy between human sexuality and the divine–human relationship. Nietzsche, for whom Christianity was essentially an ascetic, life-denying flight from particulars, would have found Hamann somewhat unsettling had he read him with attention.[46] Hamann disagreed with Nietzsche's view that 'Christianity gave Eros poison to drink: he did not die of it, but degenerated – into vice.'[47] Hamann thought that it was precisely in Christianity that eros and virtue became compatible. Human love is transformed when it is seen in the image of divine love. 'The secrets of our nature, in which are grounded all taste and enjoyment of the beautiful, true, and good, are related, like that tree of God in the middle of the garden, to knowledge and life. Both are causes and also effects of love. Their glow is fiery and a flame of the Lord; for God is the love and life is the light of humans.'[48]

Creativity and Genius

If Hamann is anti-Nietzschean in his view of eros, how does his celebration of poetry accord with the Sturm und Drang or the later Nietzschean divinization of the aesthetic? The first thing that needs to be insisted upon is Hamann's great distance from the romantic cult of creativity. Hamann, transforming the Humean insistence on the centrality of sense impressions and imagination in cognition into a defence of 'poetic reason,' was certainly influential in the development of romantic idealism.[49] Yet Hamann was not offering a paean to creativity, as his discussion of genius indicates. As Jochen Schmidt correctly writes, 'One of the central determinants of the later [Sturm und Drang] genius concept, that of autonomy, as it is expressed most decisively in Goethe's Prometheus-Hymn, is missing in Hamann's religious horizon. It must be missing, for the religious man does not feel himself to be independent, but, on the contrary, is conscious of his dependency on a higher being.'[50] The poetic reception of revelation is not the same thing as a towering self-creation. Hamann wrote, 'The imagination, were she a sun-horse having the wings of the dawn ... cannot be a creator of belief.'[51] The Hamannian *Glaube*, that inner sensation that both gives knowledge and reminds us of our ignorance, is a product of grace, *not of imaginative creativity*. Insofar as any poet's work is revelatory it is due to the poet's conscious or unconscious relation to Christocentric prophecy.[52]

Whence comes the widespread interpretation, then, that Hamann was the apostle of artistic creativity? The response is that Hamann himself gave this impression by his dual insistence on the centrality of the passions to cognition and on the repeated sexual metaphors of man as an author or begetter. If Hamann's rhetoric was often misunderstood, it was because his readers misplaced the emphasis: man was made in God's image, but this was not to be understood as the self-deification of creative man. Ernst Jünger made a great deal out of Hamann's aesthetics. Yet there would have been nothing more foreign to Hamann's mind than Jünger's Nietzschean utterance, 'Now that the gods have abandoned us, we must fall back on their origin: art.'[53] This is the complete inversion of Hamann's driving thought: on the contrary, Hamann was insisting, we have abandoned God for art.

Consider the issue of artistic genius. Hamann is often said to be counter-enlightened in his celebration of genius and creativity. Lewis White Beck writes, '[Hamann's] apotheosis of the artist as genius and creator fructified the dissatisfactions of poets and dramatists frustrated by Gottschedian rules and Lessing's bourgeois stiff-upper-lip to bring about the attitudes and works of the *Sturm und Drang* ... The artist is the reformer of society by rebelling against it; the robber becomes the hero, the morally equivocal Werther the man who brings others to know themselves. Art takes its place along with – in fact superior to – history and nature; the theological *logos* becomes *poesis* [sic].'[54] This last phrase, while not entirely incorrect, is particularly misleading, for Hamann's purpose was not to turn the logos into poetry, but to justify the poetic nature of the divine word. Beck might be correct that Hamann's writings helped push the stressful, storming artist-geniuses on their way, but this view confounds Hamann's purpose with his effect.[55] It also overstates the degree to which the Enlightenment sought to shackle geniuses in rules.

Quite to the contrary, the Enlightenment invented the notion of the artistic genius as human exemplar. Shaftesbury melded the notion of a great artist/critic and a supreme moral exemplar into the idea of the 'virtuoso.' Hamann had taken an interest in Shaftesbury in his youth, even translating some of his writings, but he grew suspicious of this gentlemanly aesthetic ethics. He mocked the 'few nobles,' the 'virtuosos of the current aeon, upon whom the lord has caused a deep sleep to fall!'[56]

The use of the term *genius* was widespread. Diderot spoke of the 'man of genius' and 'the genius' in the same breath, indicating that this referred to some intangible, prophet-like quality that was more than taste, imagination, observation, or wit.[57] Now, the term *genius* (*génie*, *Genie*) had a number of meanings. It referred to a special ability, to a divine voice (as in the ancient notion of a daemon or tutelary spirit), and, increasingly, to a person himself. Hamann used the term in all three senses as a creative power (or talent), a divine voice within, and a type of person. Throughout, he stressed the originality of genius and its freedom from rules. But there was nothing in the least original or surprising in Hamann's use. If the eighteenth century loved to tease out the laws of the natural world, it was equally enamoured with those artistic individuals who could please through lawlessness, or even become the source of aesthetic law.[58] Addison merely gave utterance to a platitude when he spoke of 'something nobly wild and extravagant in these great natural geniuses' that defies rules and conventions (Homer and Shakespeare are given as examples).[59] 'The philosophes,' as Peter Gay notes, 'freely repeated hoary Platonic platitudes about the frenzied poet and uncritically accepted the old saying that every genius has his touch of madness.'[60] Now, when we come upon a commonplace repeated in Hamann, we cannot take it at face value. Let us consider several of Hamann's most famous utterances on individual genius: 'What for a Homer replaces ignorance of the rules of art which an Aristotle devised after him, and what for a Shakespeare replaces the ignorance or transgression of those critical laws? Genius is the unanimous answer. Indeed, Socrates could very well afford to be ignorant; he had a tutelary genius, on whose science he could rely, which he loved and feared as his god, whose peace was more important to him than all the reason of the Egyptians and Greeks.'[61] Genius is the universal answer for the success of Homer and Shakespeare, but Hamann plays with this concept, relating it to Socrates' faith in a divine, inner voice. The explanation of genius is what Hamann proposes to refine and confound. He continues on this question, substituting *genius* for the tutelary *daemon* of Socrates:

> Whether this daimon of Socrates was only a ruling passion, by whatever name it is called by our teachers of ethics, or whether it was an invention of his political cunning; whether an angel or familiar spirit, a distinctive idea of his imagination, or a surreptitious and arbitrarily assumed concept of a mathematical ignorance; whether this daimon was not more like a thermometer or the machine to which the Bradleys and Leeuwenhoeks owe their revelations; whether one can compare it most readily with the prophetic feeling of a sober and blind man or with the gift of foretelling the revolutions of the beclouded sky by means of corns and scars of badly healed wounds: so much has been written about this by so many sophists with such conclusiveness that one must be astonished that Socrates, in spite of his celebrated self-knowledge, could also be so ignorant in this matter that he could not answer Simias about it. No cultivated reader of our day lacks talented friends who will spare me the effort of going into more detail about Socrates' tutelary spirit.[62]

We are given a list of possible meanings for Socrates' genius, and Hamann makes it clear that this is a commonly discussed question. Hamann is deriding the discourse of genius and calling attention to Socratic genius as the product of faith.

We recall that the *Sokratische Denkwürdigkeiten* makes the philosophical hero into a Christ figure. As a quality, then, the rule-defying genius is not the capacity to create great art, but is the experience of grace that completes the law (see Romans). Elsewhere Hamann followed an oblique reference to Christ's healing on the Sabbath (John 5:2–17) with the conclusion, 'So must a genius condescend to shake rules.'[63] In the *Aesthetica*, the term is employed in the sense of a person himself (a genius): 'The birth of a genius will, as usual, be accompanied by the martyrdom of innocent children.'[64] The play here is clear enough: Christ is the 'genius.' 'In this divine quality of ignorance, in this human quality of genius appears to be hidden the wisdom of the contradiction on which the adept are wrecked and over which an ontologist bares his teeth.'[65] The paradox that we have noted before of humanity's dual divine/lowly nature is here employed to describe 'Socrates'' ignorance, which is the also a kind of certainty.[66] Genius as it is employed by his contemporaries is a mockery of this divinely conferred capacity: 'des *Philosophes serpens*, qui sont les plus fins Sophistes entre tout le betail & entre toutes les bêtes des champs, parcequ'il [sic] marchent au rocher du *Génie* sur le ventre & mangent la poussiere [sic] par *Gout* [sic].'[67]

Hamann, then, employed the discourse of genius in order to oppose the overemphasis on aesthetic rules (by which the scriptures could be harshly judged), but his use of the concept was not a celebration of the Promethean poet's artistic autonomy, but a typically ironic transfiguration (or metaschematism) of an Enlightenment commonplace into a Christian image. For Hamann, genius overcomes and completes the letter of the law with its spirit.[68]

Imagination cannot *create* faith, the passions are strong through passivity, and expression is an attempt to reveal what is hidden from ourselves. This is why Hamann referred to reason and language as a 'wax nose':[69] our expression is always distanced from the reality we wish to reveal. We are constantly putting on masks because we cannot get to the soul itself. 'That is the nature of passion, that it cannot hang on the thing itself, but only on its picture – and is this not the nature of reason, to hang on concepts?'[70] We have seen throughout this study that Hamann's indictment of reason's purity was based upon the insistence that mind's access to reality is linguistically and imaginatively mediated. Concepts have no greater claim to objectivity than images: indeed, they *are* images, but bizarre images in that they attempt to deny their sensory origin. His attack on philosophy was, as we have noted, to point to its subjectivity and to claim for 'poetry' a greater access to eternal truth.

This is the origin of the view that Hamann prefigured Nietzsche. But Hamann's poetic is not so subjective – its perspectivism is bounded by a universal that Nietzsche would have decried as a mere consolation for the feeble. But let us cast aside the aspersions of Christians and anti-Christians and clarify the differences in Nietzsche's and Hamann's views. Nietzsche shared Hamann's view that humans can find meaning only in things akin to them. But whereas Hamann employed this to justify the anthropomorphism of Christianity that has always struck philosophers as bizarre, Nietzsche thought that great artists could take control of this element self-consciously. When Nietzsche wrote that 'only as an aesthetic phenomenon is existence and the world eternally justified,'[71] he was turning the world into an art work, and interpretation into making. The passivity of Hamannian passions is turned into the activity of Nietzschean will. The aestheticists, Hamann charges, are incapable of understanding the Christian message because they do not have the requisite humility: 'The chamberlains of beautiful art ... cannot believe in the resurrection of the flesh because they transfigure their own worthless body themselves, here, already, through beautiful arts.'[72] Poetic self-justification is life-denying: 'Narcissus ... loves his image more than his life.'[73]

Poetic Reception: Hamann on Enlightenment Taste

If Hamann objected to the ideal of artistic self-transfiguration, how did he see artistic reception? Did he have a theory of taste? Hamann lived in 'the century of taste.'[74] Shaftesbury, Hutcheson, Burke, Hume, Voltaire, Buffon, Diderot, Montesquieu, Lessing, Mendelssohn, Baumgarten, Kant ... rare was the philosopher of note who had nothing to say about matters of taste. It is perhaps, then, not surprising that the early Hamann was equally caught up in the enthusiasm (translating Shaftesbury's essays), or that the post-conversion Hamann showed himself to be sceptical of this intellectual current (the *Encyclopédie* article that he refused to translate was Diderot's article on *Le Beau*).[75] Since the aesthetic, in Hamann's thought, is all-embracing (the opposite of aesthetic is anaesthetic), we can see how, in one sense, taste is everything – man was made for *Genuß*, and Hamann often spoke of the 'orthodox taste,' or his 'taste for symbols.' At the same time, he condemned the language of taste in the strongest terms.

For Hamann, taste and criticism, the preoccupations of the age, were problematic in themselves because they tended to entail a certain distancing from the object under consideration.[76] Marking something out as a subject for disinterested study is a way of alienating oneself from the concerned nature of one's reading: '*Nil admirari* always remains the foundation of a philosophical judgment.'[77] Certainly, the alienation that renders possible objective scholarship undermines concerned engagement with the topic. We are reminded of a professor of Bible studies who is 'religiously unmusical,' a member of a department of literature who writes learned treatises on a poet whom he can't abide, or a philosophy professor who treats reflection merely as puzzle-solving for wages. Aesthetic objects (and, for Hamann, all objects of experience are the source of *aisthesis*) are not meant for disinterested speculation. As we have noted, Hamann did not live to see Kant's *Critique of Judgment*, but we can be quite certain that Kant's view of the disinterested nature of taste judgment would have struck him as a typically Kantian figment of the brain. 'All aesthetic thaumaturgy will not replace an immediate feeling, and nothing but the journey to hell of self-knowledge will pave our way to justification.'[78] Criticism demands distance; self-knowledge seeks immediacy.[79]

If the discourse of taste is alienated, it is also totalizing. As a radically subjective category, taste might be considered to elude general theory. Yet the very tone of criticism is always universalistic. This is the paradox of taste that animated so many of its theorists (Hume and Kant, most notably). Hamann was obsessed with his individuality, and he reacted with tiresome outbursts at any suggestion that art should follow formal rules. Indeed, his rants against the 'ruling style' remind us of people who cultivate the sentiment of persecution by ranting against some abstract public entity (the 'mainstream media,' the 'literati,' the 'politically correct,' etc.). But there is a less juvenile purpose to Hamann's reaction, for the notion that there is such a thing as 'good taste' was, he thought, at one with the desire to reinforce domination. Expression is self-revelation, and stylistic strictures are hindrances to such expression.

But if there is an undeniably strong expressivist dimension to Hamann's thought, it is tempered by his grounding in scripture. He decried the universalism of taste, but not in the name of aesthetic pluralism or radical individualism. Rather, he was defending a particular mode of expression that he thought to be under attack. If systematic philosophy struck him as a threat to revelation, so too did eighteenth-century criticism appear to be an attack on religious thought. The difficulty in both cases is similar: faith speaks a language that appears both unreasonable and tasteless. If Hamann perceived in speculative philosophy an attack on the sensual, image-rich, and figural language of scripture, he perceived in the reigning tastes an attack on the scriptures' style. The more one delved into Greek and Roman authors and the more one elevated an ancient ideal of purity and symmetry, the more one tended to undermine people's admiration for the poetry of the Old Testament, the bizarre excess of the prophets, and the inelegant Greek of the New Testament.[80] At the very outset of his biblical study, Hamann posed himself the following question: how can one possibly admire this strange text? His response was a characteristic inversion: 'If God has the intention of revealing himself to humans and to the entire human race, then we see the clear folly of those who wish to make a limited taste and their own judgment into a touchstone of the divine word. We are not discussing a revelation that would be found worthy by a Voltaire, a Bollingbroke, a Shaftesbury; that would satisfy their prejudices, their wit, their moral and political whimsies.'[81] The revealed truth is universal, and the taste of these critics is a mere product of the times.

Yet clearly the style of the Old Testament is not timeless. Hamann grants the text's peculiarities: 'These books were meant to be received by the Jews; it was necessary, then, that they concern many particular circumstances of this people.'[82] The modern reader of the Bible will naturally find it a strange text; to understand it, one must attempt to get inside it. The great difficulty is one of interpretation, and it is a twofold difficulty. First, we must attempt to accommodate ourselves to the original text, for its style is tied to the language and mindset of a particular people.[83] Hamann was extremely attuned to the difficulties of translation, and thus he emphasized that the reader of the Bible must submit himself or herself to the biblical style of thought. (Herder would take this as a principle to apply to *all* historical texts; Herder's stomach was, however, more capacious than that of Hamann, who preferred to season all texts with Christianity.) Second, the ultimate difficulty to overcome is the translation of divine ideas into human language. The strangeness of the text is due to its attempt to cross the infinite gulf between man and God; man can approach God only by allowing God to approach him. The text is at once supremely familiar in its personal significance and sensual imagery (evidence of divine condescension) and supremely alien (evidence of divine majesty).[84]

Now, a great deal could be said about this idiosyncratic justification of the scriptures, and we might equally say a great deal more on the figural relationship Hamann saw between the historical events of the Old Testament and his personal life story. But for our purposes it is enough to note how offensive he found the criticism of the bible in the name of the *Temple du Goût*. Voltaire, whose most characteristic device was to render biblical stories in as absurd a manner as possible, was naturally a prime target of Hamann's attack: 'Voltaire, the high priest in the temple of taste argues as convincingly as Kaiphas, and thinks more fruitfully than Herod.'[85] Baylean sceptics fare no better: 'The transmission of a divine message says as little as the appearance of a comet to a philosopher of today's tastes.'[86]

Taste is not good in itself, nor is it separable from other aspects of cognition. Hamann would have had no patience with Kant's mature aesthetic formalism: images without personal, passionate interest were as dead as idols.[87] The opening explosion of the *Aesthetica in nuce* makes it clear that art and beauty are not the subjects of Hamannian aesthetics: 'Not a lyre! – Nor a brush! – A winnowing fan for my muse to sweep the threshing floor of holy literature!'[88] The biblical image of the grain being separated from the chaff is the centre of this piece: Hamann would have us sweep away the bulk of aesthetic writing, allowing his readers, as he says in his concluding sentence, to 'hear the sum of his newest aesthetic, which is also the oldest: Fear God, and give glory to him.'[89] Aesthetics, for Hamann, entails sweeping away art in order to make way for revelation.[90] Enthusiasm for art is a product of a prosaic mind that separates form and content. The immediacy of aesthetic communication gives it a power that only religion can justify. Without piety, artistic enthusiasm is hedonism or idolatry.

Neither sublime nor beautiful, Hamannian aesthetics tend towards the ridiculous or ugly. He adorned the cover of his *Crusades of the Philologist* (which contains the *Aesthetica*) with a picture of Pan, and his numerous burlesque images, his allusive baroque excess, his love of dense apparent non sequiturs all evidence a conscious attack on the formal strictures of beautiful prose. This is not merely a stylistic device, but an indication of his view on the nature of beauty itself. Consider his review of Kant's pre-critical essay on the sublime and the beautiful. Hamann began with a relatively unremarkable comparison with Burke's work on the same question, but then made a strange non sequitur on Kant's section of the sublime and beautiful in men, complaining, 'But because the author's essay is supposed to touch only the sensory feeling, we suspect with some basis that in this section the five senses of men are entirely passed over. The great gusto for vessels anointed with devil's shit, of the king Demetrius Polio's contest *e regia glande*, touching the sublime of stinking things ... are exceptional examples of the peculiarities of human nature.'[91] Hamann was referring to a salacious anecdote in Bayle's *Historical and Critical Dictionary* entry on the prostitute Lamia, to whom King Demetrius attempted to give a perfume composed of his own semen.[92] Hamann was making several points with this unseemly story. First, of course, he was pointing out the relativity of taste – there was no accounting for what some people would find beautiful. But he was also postulating a higher, God's-eye view on beauty. In the *Aesthetica* he imagines that a 'Levite of the newest literature' will castigate him, saying, 'To readers of orthodox taste belong no common expressions nor unclean vessels.'[93] The 'Levite' establishes the boundaries of pure and impure, beauty and ugliness. Hamann's response is that nothing is inherently ugly or impure. This was not primarily a complaint about overly refined sexual mores – the spirit of the times was hardly one of repression. It was rather an argument for the sacramental nature of all sensory experience. Hamann insisted that earthly taste was relative; he championed anti-taste, and even the tasteless. He celebrated the beauty of an infant's 'authorship' – the dirty diaper.[94] There is a transfiguration of experience brought about by faith. As Hamann said of the *Sokratische Denkwürdigkeiten*, 'Because these little cakes are not to be chewed, but to be swallowed whole ... they are not made for taste.'[95]

Hamann summed up his indictment of the discourse of taste in *Leser und Kunstrichter*: 'Your morality [*Sittenlehre*] and your taste are grounded merely in painted goods, your way of living and way of writing are a whitewashed surface that tricks the eye and insults the sense ... But that critic whom Tiresias described with an unmistakable sign [i.e., Odysseus, i.e., Christ] will break the aesthetic bow of beautiful art in the valley of beautiful nature. Idols of porcelain and glazed earth are the ideas of our beautiful spirits; their cheeriest concepts that burst forth from the most delicate feeling and rush to the sentiments are as dirty as the stained clothes of a grape-stomper, whose eyes laugh like the doves who pull the wagon of Venus, whose coat is washed in the blood of winegrapes, and who has teeth like a dragon.'[96] The image of redeemer treading the winepress (from Revelations 19:15 and Isaiah 63:3), and God breaking the bow of his enemies (Jeremiah 49:35) gives a fair idea of Hamann's intent. (The 'critic whom Tiresias described' is a reference to book 9 of the *Odyssey*. Odysseus is the 'critic' – we have already seen Hamann's rendering of Odysseus into a Christ figure.)[97] As with wisdom and folly, beauty and ugliness know of a Pauline inversion. 'What delights men ... is a horror to God.'[98] When Nietzsche wrote that Hamann was 'very deep and fervent, but worthlessly in-artistic,'[99] he was unaware of the degree to which Hamann would have considered this description a compliment.

'Only a God Can Save Us'

If Hamann's theological aesthetics are anti-Platonic, anti-Nietzschean, and perfectly in opposition to eighteenth-century taste discourse, they might be considered to have greater affinities with Heidegger, and especially with his linguistic turn and his writings on poetry and art. Indeed, Heidegger had objections similar to Hamann's when he castigated 'modern subjectivism,' which 'immediately misinterprets creation, taking it as the sovereign subject's performance of genius.'[100] Heidegger also championed the aesthetic as a response to the instrumental reason that was so characteristic of Enlightenment thought. Finally, the historical contingency of Hamannian linguistic thought is at the root of a long trend in historicist thinking that has its most influential twentieth-century voice in Heidegger.

There is not space to do justice to this most interesting question here, but let us merely touch on the matter of whether Hamann 'dwells poetically' in a Heideggerian sense. Knut Martin Stünkel has begun to fill this hole in the scholarship.[101] Stünkel hits on many important similarities between Hamann's and the late Heidegger's treatment of language, placing great emphasis on Heidegger's anti-subjective argument about man's receptivity. But he admits in his conclusion that all comparison must be taken with a grain of salt, given the essentially Christian-theological nature of Hamann's thought. This is a point that cannot be stressed enough.

Heidegger famously declared philosophy and Christianity to be essentially distinct.[102] However, there are numerous similarities between Heidegger's writings and Christian theology. Heidegger writes of *alētheia*, normally translated as 'truth,' as the pre-Socratic concept of 'unconcealment' that stands before any thought. *Alētheia* and Being are pre-philosophic and are the subject of our most urgent questioning. Consider how he describes them in 'The End of Philosophy and the Task of Thinking': 'self-concealing, concealment, *lēthe*, belongs to *a-lētheia*, not as a mere addition ... but as the heart of *alētheia*.'[103] In other words, the truth of Being, the unconcealedness or revelation of what is most important to thought, is itself something hidden. What do we have here but the secular (or even pagan, since it claims to be pre-Socratic) appropriation of the old paradox (so dear to Luther) of the hidden God? Other theological motifs abound. Consider the Lutheran resonance in his doctrine of freedom: 'The freedom of the free consists neither in unfettered arbitrariness nor in the constraint of mere laws.'[104] The temptation to read him as rewriting Christian themes in pagan/philosophic guise is naturally increased by his baffling eschatological declarations in his later life.[105] Whether Heidegger advanced upon traditional theistic thought with his translation of the problems of religion into the non-theological language of the 'the truth of Being' – whether this new language offers greater clarity than anthropomorphic metaphors are questions that I leave unexplored. Certainly, some theologically inclined writers have turned to Heidegger as someone who can validate pious talk in an impious world (although Heidegger initially rejected this avenue).[106] Let it suffice for us to note that there is a most anti-Hamannian tenor to Heidegger's attempt to capture the meaning of Being. Hamann championed the concreteness of poetry; Heidegger used words with an abstract manner that would have made the most abject scholastic blush.[107]

But Heidegger's turn to *poiēsis* does indeed mirror Hamann's. Certainly, Heidegger lamented the turn to 'aesthetics' in which artworks are taken as a 'cultural activity.'[108] This mirrors Hamann's lament at the separation that created the realm of aesthetic autonomy. Like Hamann, Heidegger also condemned a certain metaphysical tradition for having produced the instrumental rationality that makes human beings into human resources.[109] But Heidegger's argument that one must confront technology in the realm of art would have been, for Hamann, the supplanting of one idol for another. Heidegger, we recall, did not condemn technology itself, but saw it as a necessary step towards a kind of freedom. This freedom would emerge in the aesthetic realm of poetry, which, like technology, entails making. Poetry speaks in a way that is different from prose in that poetry is not the vehicle for the mere communication of ideas. Poetry somehow can be revelatory and can avoid the instrumental nature of prosaic language.

'Art,' Heidegger writes (and poetry is the pre-eminent form of art), 'is ... a distinctive way in which truth comes into being, that is, becomes historical.'[110] This could be understood as a claim akin to Hamann's that something eternal is given expression in the historical world of becoming and appearance. The image (Van Gogh's painting of boots, for instance) tells us a great deal with immediacy – in Heideggerian terms, it shows us the 'unconcealment' (*alētheia*) of shoes' Being.[111] That is to say, something essential about temporal existence is revealed by the artwork, and it is equally preserved in a way that the actual shoes are not. Heidegger gives a fanciful description of the numerous associations to which a picture of shoes gives rise, and he insists that this is not a mere projection of the viewer onto the artwork, but something essential to the subject matter contained in the work.[112] Heidegger appears to be attempting to bridge a gap that Hamann thought was crossed only by divine condescension. 'The more simply and essentially the shoes are engrossed in their essence, the more directly and engagingly do all beings attain a greater degree of being along with them.'[113] Art does not give objective description (i.e., description of a mere object), but speaks its myriad specificities that find their meaning within the bounds of a historical life-world.

Just as Hamann saw Logos as the way in which God manifested himself to temporal beings, then, Heidegger was attempting to understand how Being is revealed in becoming. Heidegger was attempting to destroy the crystalline permanence of Platonic Being by insisting that Being has its being in beings. Or, to put it in English, he treated the Platonic ideas as themselves temporal. Heidegger did not wish to say that in the artwork 'something is correctly represented,' but rather, 'that beings as a whole are brought into unconcealment and held therein.'[114] Heidegger's method was to undermine Plato by investing in Platonic concepts a meaning that he attributed to the Greek language and to a primordial, pre-Socratic understanding of temporality in which Being is immanent in becoming.[115] There is a remarkable similarity here to Hamann's view of language's essential temporality and the manner in which thought is possible only within a tradition. Yet the difference between this Heideggerian view and Hamann's Christian treatment of the problem is not merely a difference of degree. For the Hamannian view of revelation retains its referent, the extra-temporal kingdom of God. If revelation, for Hamann, can take place only in the historical world, it remains supra-historical. Thus, Christian universals are available to people in sensuous form: scripture is symbolic representation of a transcendent reality.

Heidegger attempted to overcome traditional epistemology by treating art as a mode of uncovering what is concealed, and his emphasis on such themes as care, death, *Angst*, etc., have the same function as Hamann's argument for the priority of the passions and needs over conceptual systems. His anti-subjectivism also follows a pattern similar to Hamann's insistence on man's passivity and dependence, and the opacity of Heidegger's presentation carries a similar weight to Hamann's Lutheran/Pauline view of God's paradoxical concealment and revelation. But Heidegger reproduced the notion of Christian receptivity with a mixed language of romantic poets, pre-Socratic philosophers, and pagan religion. Heideggerian poetry becomes a strange phenomenon, uprooted from its spiritual and intellectual horizon of European religious history – deliberately uprooted from the onto-theological tradition that nourished it. It seems to damn creativity while raising an altar to it. 'Upon the earth and in it, historical man grounds his dwelling in the world.'[116] To struggle with Heidegger's paradoxical view of creative freedom is beyond the scope of this work, but I merely wish to contrast the revolutionary nature of Heideggerian poetry with the receptive conservatism of Hamannian Christocentrism. When he alleged that we need to wait for 'a god' to save us, Heidegger was articulating a need for revelation in a polytheistic religious language of his own devising. Hamann thought he knew which God he was waiting for, a belief that Heidegger would, quite correctly, have found unphilosophical.[117]

Neither Art nor Philosophy: Assessing Hamann's Foundational Aesthetics

Hamann opposed the Enlightenment fascination with taste and provided an immanent attack on the romantic and postmodern writers who have been said (incorrectly) to follow from him. Romantic writers transformed rather than rejected eighteenth-century fixations with taste and genius; the genius was not merely admirable, but was an earth-dwelling divinity. This movement found its conclusion in the Nietzschean divinization of subjective will. It had a somewhat more complex development in Heideggerian anti-subjectivism, but this view nonetheless retained the quasi-divinity of aesthetics. Both announced the need for an anti-Christian, pagan religion of art. Aesthetics became all-embracing, and existence became both palette and canvas. Hamann's poetic Christianity (not Christian poetry) objected at the outset to the Enlightenment's disenchantment of the world and gave grounds for rejecting its re-enchantment by aesthetic enchanters. His Lutheran insistence on man's powerlessness and his retention of the Christianized Platonism that placed the good beyond human evaluation allowed him to condemn the Enlightenment discourse of taste and to warn, as it were in advance, against the coming religion of art in which truth would become a matter of artistic transfiguration.

Poetry is often considered to be intoxicating. Plato famously described a poet as a kind of idiot savant who, under divine influence, babbles things without understanding them.[118] By this, Plato understood the poet as a champion in the realm of opinion and thus as a possibly dangerous force. It is the job of philosophers to control the poets' utterances by censorship (as is suggested for the ideal city of the *Republic*) or, more practically, rational interpretation (as is evidenced in Socrates' rigorous philosophical treatment of poetic utterances and commonly accepted myths). Because of the poetic nature of Greek faith, Plato dealt with poets and prophets with similar tactics. It is clear in both cases that they are intoxicated and intoxicating: the cold shower of *elenchus* is required. Hamann offered to fight firewater with firewater, a dubious proposition, as most alcoholics will confirm.

Edward Andrew has lamented the tendency for the Nietzschean aesthetic turn to undermine moral absolutes in the name of artistic evaluation.[119] Values are akin to tastes, superfluities that are little more than class signifiers. The dominance of values discourse in the social sciences (and in popular political discourse) undermines traditional moral language of the good and equally subverts discussion of fundamental needs. Andrew alerts us to the dangers of Nietzsche's inversion of the Platonic hierarchy between sense and reason. Hamann offers an interesting third position, both sharing Nietzsche's celebration of the sensory over the rational and rejecting the radical subjectivism that Nietzsche's move has tended to entail. In attempting to revive the medieval trope of the world as divine language, Hamann insisted upon the sensual, earthy, historically and culturally bounded nature of the understanding while at the same time retaining the universality and authority of the divine. Nineteenth-century romantics who read Hamann in explosive snippets understated the theocentric nature of his world view, and thus turned his fiery catchphrases ('poetry is the mother tongue of the human race,'[120] etc.) into slogans for the divinization of the poet. Hamann points to a Christian tradition in which the divine Logos is expressed in terms that are scarcely comprehensible to the philosophers. With this Hamann overturns the Enlightenment's antihistorical rational objectivity and its rejection of authority – the aesthetic (sensory) nature of the understanding must be interpreted through the lens of the Word. Taste, for Hamann, is the enemy of faith because it is a subjection of the aesthetic Word to human whim and evaluation. If Hamann is aesthetic, he is not a champion of the artist's will. Thus we see how Hamann sits on a little hill overlooking the trans-historical battle between Plato and Nietzsche.

The moral in Hamann emerges from the care for others that we develop in communion. The fundamental identity between human beings, their essentially communicative and relational nature, renders their highest aim that of communion with one another and God. They are powerless to achieve this in the absence of grace, and grace itself is the source of all interpersonal meaning. The moral significance of this outlook is the degree to which it renders impossible the objectification of others or of the world. To treat sense-experience and scripture with a 'poetic' eye allows one to see 'the profound meaning of transient actions'; one perceives 'a deity, where common eyes see a stone.'[121] Hamann's aesthetics are not the basis for treating existence as a spectator, or yet as a free creator, but rather as an interlocutor and lover. 'The more lively we bear in our breast this idea of the invisible God, the more capable we will be of seeing and tasting his kindness in his creatures, of observing and grasping it with our hands.'[122] Piety, then, does not become a manner of leapfrogging over our fellow creatures – it cannot be essentially otherworldly. The ethical is not a form different from the religious (in the manner of Kierkegaard), but resides within it. And they are both perceived through aesthetic (or sensory) revelation.[123]

Without the Bible, a Hamannian view of aesthetic language and mind's captivity in becoming might indeed become artistic and wilful. Or, at the very least, it would have something of the Heideggerian poetic to it, ushering in a pagan god of some sort. But what I have attempted to indicate is that his thought is entirely unthinkable without the 'word of God.' This sort of view raises alarm bells, however. We are often presented with the view that universal reason must provide us with some foundation or we will let loose radical irrational monsters. Others suggest that in the intersubjective realm of rational discourse itself lies something akin to (but not the same as) a foundation. Some fear (excessively but not groundlessly, I believe) that the alternative to rational argument is violence. But ultimately, the fear of radical individualism does not quite hit the mark with Hamann – no lovers of the word can be fully individualistic unless they think that the mental word is essentially private; none can be fully subjectivist if they think the Word is divine. One of the things I have attempted to indicate throughout is that Hamann's anti-philosophical 'philologism' is organized and systematic, but according to the organized system of religious revelation. The truth is in the text, but this is not some escape from the world; Hamann was not an amoral dandy or aesthete for whom life is art. For him, a 'rhapsody' stitches together bits of the world. It is fabric, not fabrication.

If we remove the divine word entirely, then the observation that all reason is contingent language becomes somewhat unsettling. Words become constructions from which we are freed once we deconstruct. Or, if freedom is not to our tastes, we can cheer the fact of our being trapped in the gilded prison of language. Or, alternately, we can go the Wittgensteinian route and make this a cure for the strange disease called philosophy. Then we enter into a pragmatic, post-metaphysical world that gets on with use because it no longer feels 'perplexity.' To put it bluntly, we risk relativistic aestheticism, reactionary conservatism, or pragmatism. Hamann's writings appear to flirt with all three of these things: his emphasis on individuality and creativity is easily mistaken for the first, his insistence on linguistic bounded-ness is taken for the second, and his periodic flirtation with naive intuitionism might be taken for the third. But these are all mistaken interpretations, for the view of God who *is* the Logos transforms all of these positions. For this reason, the theological impulse of Hamann's writing cannot be separated from his philosophical claims about language and cognition.

To assert the primacy of the divine word is well and good for a provincial, eighteenth-century Prussian, it will be objected, but we exist in a world in which the Christian Logos has lost any power it may have had. Yet if the death of God and the 'fact of pluralism' spell a serious challenge for Judeo-Christian symbolism today, they should not blind us to the significance of mytho-poetic symbolism in cognition. Sympathy with the Hamannian view of ourselves as constituted by our linguistic context can serve as an opening onto different structures of affective thought. Thus, we would be wrong to make the fact of pluralism the basis for disregarding the universal claims of such a parochial Eastern European writer; rather, attending to Hamann gives us insight into the nature of secularism and its challenges. For all that he differed radically from his teacher, Herder was indeed following an avenue whose possibility was opened by Hamannian reflection.

Even if one grants the accuracy of Hamann's view of the human mind, one is hardly in possession of a convincing defence of Christian symbolism. Nor, indeed, is one furnished with a particularly compelling defence of the very existence of a divine Logos. This is not surprising; his insistence on Christian figures is based on a faith that he did not think could be given universal justification. What Hamann defended with discursive argument was the *cogency* of the affective, metaphorical language in which faith is expressed. Ultimately I do not intend to provide an apology for religious/poetic speech, but to present Hamann's thought as a challenge to both Enlightenment reason and counter-Enlightenment aestheticism. It is a challenge that cannot be understood or appropriated by secular thought, either rationalist or irrationalist, which means that it is a challenge that resists being accepted by our *saeculum.*

In the crusades and counter-crusades of our world, there is a constant incapacity to communicate with one another because of these closed systems of thought. Hamann does not provide us with an ecumenical solution – indeed, the polemical nature of his thought, his ironic 'metaschematisms,' his provision of closed fists that we are obligated to open into flat hands are all evidence of a great problem for the religious consciousness in the secular city. Compelled to speak in the language of a babbler, faith struggles to make itself heard and *obeyed* in a world that is rightly suspicious of it. Imperious faith demands to be read, as it were, from the inside; imperious Enlightenment reason cannot make such a demand because it seeks only to exist outside, in the cold light of day. Hamann does not offer us a way forward; indeed, attending to his thought engenders a certain pessimism about the possibility of advancing. If Hamann's logos draws us together in a pre-subjective, pre-rational communicative context, so too does it clutter the path of communion with hermeneutic barriers, not the least of which is the existence or absence of a faith that it is not in our power to acquire.

11 Conclusion

We have followed Hamann somewhat closely, elucidating his political thought and paying particular attention to the importance of his insistence on the communicative – and thus social – nature of human beings, the resuscitation of myth, the importance of the affective and aesthetic elements in cognition, and the temporal access to meaning. We have discussed the limitations of public reason as a final locus for normative justification. We have also seen the way in which Hamann's historicization of thought remained anchored in a transcendent divinity, and we noted the distinct moral possibilities in his reconciliation of history and eternity. But we left off in chapter 10 on an ambivalent note – a note sounded throughout the work – pointing out the degree to which his Christocentric world view raised the possibility of insurmountable barriers between faith communities, and between believers and sceptics. Let us conclude our study, then, with some brief considerations on the possibilities of Hamann reception in a pluralistic world, for despite his numerous claims that appeal to modern counter-Enlightenment thought, his most important claims nonetheless present significant stumbling blocks, notably his defence of faith in general and his Christocentrism in particular. The fact of pluralism poses a problem for the reception of any thought situated fixedly in a religious tradition.

Having attempted, then, to understand Hamann's thought from the inside, let us step back and touch on some of the barriers for the reception of Hamann in a pluralistic world. I will conclude by suggesting that there are, beyond the more narrow confessional limits of Hamann's thought, important resources in Hamann's aesthetic, dialogical understanding of mind that ought to be harvested. To develop these resources in a way that is not dependent on a uniquely Christocentric – or even monotheistic – position is not the purpose of this book, which is the study of Hamann. Nor do I want to dilute Hamann's religious claims – I do not think that the ecumenical spirit is well served by ironing out confessional differences. But I suggest that Hamann's position, with its seemingly paradoxical reconciliation of transcendence and temporality, offers a powerful alternative to the enlightened and counter-enlightened offerings of the 'post-metaphysical' world.

We have seen that Hamann defended *Heilsgeschichte* by placing thought in the world, in concrete language and poetic images. His entire outlook was based upon the view that *meaning* is the necessary condition of all possible experience (if I may use a Kantian formulation). Meaning is temporal. Philosophical abstractions attempt to undermine such meaning by abstracting themselves right out of history. But this undermines the coherence of experience. The present exists for the perceiver in a historical continuum. It is cultural forms – languages, myths, stories, religious claims – that determine this meaning. Now, for Hamann this meaning was identified with the Logos of the fourth gospel, the Word that was God. And this Logos was elaborated for humankind in a prophetic tradition set down in the Bible, the text of texts. So Hamann saved the prophetic outlook from Enlightenment criticism with the view that mind was primarily poetic, imaginative, and thus tied to *stories*. But what Hamann never did – and never considered doing – was defend the preeminent place that he gave to the Christian story.

Even the most sympathetic reader of Hamann must run up against one of the greatest challenges for the religious mind in the late-modern world: the myriad stories that confront us. Voltaire delighted in the Chinese, who viewed the Abrahamic religions as quaint curiosities and whose history antedated the biblical story of Creation. The fact of religious diversity offered a delicious means of thumbing one's nose as the absurd pretensions of the Abrahamic faiths. Hamann never fully felt the force of this challenge. His anti-dogmatism and his capacity to read Christian revelation *in* other traditions provided him with a way out of the predicament, but he never fully squared the circle, and there remains in his thought the possibility of precipitous theological closure. This possibility is particularly evident in the instances where he insisted absolutely on a Christocentric reading of Torah or where he deployed Lutheran anti-Catholic rhetoric against Enlightenment philosophy.[1] Yet while we have seen that Hamann's Christianity was not something for which he offered philosophical justification, it is important to recall that Hamann was not some dogmatic snail, retreating into the comfort of his

Christian shell. He offered a way of seeing faith that opened up its myriad mytho-poetic meanings. If Hamann himself did not attempt to resolve the problems of pluralism, his insights are extremely valuable to those attempting to come to terms with the myriad faiths in the light of historical scholarship and the pluralistic world.

Before developing this point, however, it is worthwhile touching on one of the most disturbing elements of Hamann's politics – his attack on the Enlightenment discourse of toleration. In chapter 7 we noted a tension between Enlightenment privatization of religion that rejected the establishment of the state on any substantive transcendent foundation, and Hamann's conviction that the good (understood in a confessional manner) needed to be the foundation of political life. We have seen that in practice, Hamann championed a kind of established church and a universal toleration that went much further than that of Frederick the Great (whose anti-Semitic policies went hand-in-hand with the most enlightened discourse of religious toleration). I have expressed wariness at the dangers of Hamann's argument for tolerance as charity, but I have equally underlined the degree to which the insistence on humility and the fallibilism that accompanies his teaching render intolerance a great sin. There is a tendency in our public culture to see all exclusionary religious claims as the bases for intolerance, but this is a logically unjustifiable leap. One generally does not *tolerate* what one approves of, and we should demonstrate weak faith in the human capacity for charity to deny the possibility of civility or even friendship between people with radically different conceptions of the good. (At the risk of becoming anecdotal, I have had strong friendships with people who expressed the conviction that I will probably burn in the next life.) Nor should we take the self-congratulatory stance that the privatization of religion has eliminated exclusion, bigotry, or violence against minorities. In an age when people are being arrested without habeas corpus, closeted away in hidden prisons around the world and tortured on the basis of suspicion that they harbour dangerous beliefs and intentions, we should be wary of declaring the auto-da-fé immune to secularization.

The clash between Hamann and the Enlightenment discourse of tolerance is not a discussion about the merits of the policy of religious tolerance itself – it is a discussion about the justifications for tolerance and in particular about the perennial question concerning the relative merits of a politics founded on the priority of the right over the good. Hamann comes down firmly on the side of the priority of the good, and he comes down on the side of theorists sceptical of the procedural,

Kantian ideal. He perceived in the tolerance discourse of Frederick and Voltaire indifferentism at best and lightly veiled anti-ecclesiasticism at worst. Elsewhere, he decried it as the basis for 'armed neutrality,' indicating that such a policy might have little to do with a commitment to others. Tolerance as political secularization and tolerance as divine command to charity might entail similar policies (i.e., not persecuting religious dissenters), but they are competing ideals. It should go without saying that in pointing out the clash between these ideals I am not calling for the return of the Spanish Inquisition. One can praise the good over the right without thereby extolling the virtues of Mullah Omar and Pat Robertson.

But this does not allay our concerns about particularity. How can such a thick religious world view stand up to the vast wealth of religious and non-religious symbolic systems in the world? Must we see in its exclusive claims a monstrous assumption about the damnation of the other? When Hamann makes claims about the unique significance of the crucified God, he clearly cannot command widespread assent outside of Christian circles. What can such a position have to offer a wider audience? The question is basic – almost simplistic – but despite being entirely pertinent it is rarely posed. I have decried the attitudes of politeness or disdain that place the content of religious symbolism outside of serious discourse, and I have suggested that unless political theory can learn to engage with religious thought rather than merely treating it as an object of study it will remain crippled. But the problem remains: how can such thick and exclusive claims speak publicly, given that their very content resists the mores of publicity?

This is not merely a matter that affects the Christian and post-Christian world: if one looks to the Muslim world today, one sees a predicament similar to that of the Christian world in the face of the Enlightenment project. Historical scholarship and the fact of religious pluralism have forced a confrontation with the historicity of the prophet, his revelation, and the politics surrounding orthodoxy. As Muslims grapple with this interconnected world, they (with the other monotheistic faiths) are forced to confront the reality of symbolic multiplicity. And as in Christianity, a failure to come to terms with this tension breeds a type of dogmatism, as if shaken certainties can be buttressed through violent assertion. And the challenge is not confined to monotheistic traditions – to give just one example, the Hindu world is equally facing these difficulties and opportunities (although perhaps here there is a depth of ancient philosophical reflection on the reconciliation of unity and plurality). In these conflicts there is a kind of opening made by Hamann's thought itself. The plausibility of transcendent truths discovered by the mytho-poetic consciousness within history gives new life to the study of textual traditions.[2] I suggest that there may be ways of reconciling the polarities of universal and particular – ways based on Hamannian insights, rather than on some greater speculative unity of a Hegelian stripe, or on the privatization (subjectivism) of the good. Hamann himself did not pursue an ecumenical project – indeed, his tendency to project Christian typology at will undermines such a project. But there are resources within his thought that can serve us well in this ecumenical endeavour. Allow me to expand upon this by way of some reflections on the open and the closed in philosophy.

Hamann's arguments against public reason are not arguments against reason. But they are arguments against enshrining a mode of discourse – public reason – a mode of discourse at which *philosophes*, and most professional philosophers, excel. It is a mode of discourse that is necessary and useful – we make use of fictions such as the abstract public (and even the abstract writer). These fictions, added to the tone of objectivity, the move to universalization, and the relegation of imagery to a subordinate position of helper are all part of the mores that make the public realm function. They serve us very well, and when a writer deliberately flaunts the rules, we react with the same frustration that we would when encountering a deliberate breech of etiquette. Hamann's method – and particularly his stylistic extravagance – ought not to be taken as a model for the philosophy of the future. Indeed, Kant was somewhat justified in reacting with annoyance to the wave of idiosyncratic writing that took its cue from Hamann.[3]

If this aspect of Hamann's oeuvre has an anti-philosophical tenor, his insistence on the importance of the personal follows in the steps of Plato, for whom truth was not in some monological formula of words, but was rather experienced by an interlocutor in conversation. As much as I have indicated what Hamann took to be the limits of public reason, I have equally indicated that there are generalizable truth claims in his thought – claims about the nature of mind and claims that limit the reach of reason. If Hamann had the conviction that there is a place that unaided human reason cannot take us, this is a position that he buttressed with philosophical arguments about the limits of reason – arguments that are the very bases of the twentieth century's most powerful anti-metaphysical philosophical movements. Hamann's insights about the communicative basis of reality does not in itself demand of us assent to the theology of logos. As I have argued throughout, there are universalizable claims about the nature of mind in Hamann's thought – claims that can be translated into the public idiom of philosophical writing and subjected to analysis. But if some central elements of Hamann's thought can be made to conform to the norms of public reason, these claims themselves point to the limits of the impersonal, the public. The cogency of mystery is thus not some irrationalist call for leaps of faith, nor yet an example of emphatic speech whose purpose is to warm the hearts of the like-minded. It is an argument about the unanalyzability of the foundational phenomenon, communication. This phenomenon of communication, the logos, is, for Hamann, both thought and *being*. This is a field that we will have to 'plough with another heifer' than our discursive reason.[4]

Jürgen Habermas has recently expressed a clear view of the gulf between faith and discursive thought: 'At best, philosophy circles the opaque core of religious experience when reflecting on the intrinsic meaning of faith. This core must remain so abysmally alien to discursive thought as does the core of aesthetic experience, which can likewise only be circled but not penetrated by philosophical reflection.'[5] But it may be that reflection can speak of these 'cores' without thereby being irrational. The opaque core of all experience is what we must circle. Perhaps the insistence that all thought take the form of universalizable, public, discursive argument fails to attend to important elements of thought – fails, despite the best intentions of dialogical thinkers such as Habermas, to attend sufficiently to the communicative nature of thought. Perhaps there is a kind of reflection – and we might call it philosophy if we wish – that takes place in this interpersonal, culturally bounded, aesthetic (concrete, image-rich) realm. There are types of discourse that break the monopoly of 'nobody the notorious,' the public, but that are no less publicly significant.

Allow me to repeat a point I have made many times: Hamann's position was not subjectivist. In a sense, of course, all experience is *one*'s experience, but Hamann's argument – that which supported all of his thought – was that the subject is inconceivable alone. Solipsism is both morally and epistemologically insupportable. A kind of communication – the logos – is primordial. Readers of Hamann may point to the personal nature of his pietist conversion experience and see in it a mere subjective experience; Hamann would agree that there is a subjective (personal) element in one's relationship with God. But the communicative nature of existence is not based on some subjective experience, nor does it permit an extreme subjectivism. For a Hamannian, subjectivity and objectivity are two sides of the same coin: neither lends sufficient weight to the communicative nature of mind – and of reality itself.

This is not a matter, then, of asserting the authority of subjective will. Nor is it a matter of reasserting the authority of a closed religious system at the expense of other symbolic systems. But it is a matter of attuning ourselves to textual tradition, to context-specific symbolism, and to the *personal* and concerned nature of communication. Cultivating such an attunement might help us get *beyond* the battles between an intellectually stultifying (and morally obscene) religious dogmatism and a supercilious incredulity for which the ideas of transcendence or redemption are irrationalism or infantile wish-fulfilment. There are signs of advance from the most partisan defenders of impartiality. Reflecting on religion in the public sphere, Habermas has softened his tone on faith: 'Post-metaphysical thought is prepared to learn from religion, but remains agnostic in the process. It insists on the difference between the certainties of faith, on the one hand, and validity claims that can be publicly criticized, on the other; but it refrains from the rationalist presumption that it can itself decide what part of the religious doctrines is rational and what part irrational.'[6] This chastened faith in public reason is an important step. But I suggest that there is even more to be done than affording quiet respect for what offends against the ideal of publicity. We ought to look beyond the idolatry of the public, for if political life must be reduced to the mores of Kant's *Leserwelt*, the result will be a politics denuded of personality, of symbolic profundity, and, if one follows the Kantian logic, of strong claims concerning the good. Just as Hamann offers us some powerful resources for thinking about transcendence, and for reconciling it with our concrete, historical existence, so too might we be able to develop, from Hamannian insights, a politics where the concrete individual, in all her spiritual depth and in all the particularity of her commitments, is not alienated from the life of the secular city.

Fleshing out such a possibility is a task for another book. But for those who retain the idea of universality, the reconciliation of the particular and the universal remains one of our age's most pressing philosophical concerns. Whether such reconciliation can be accomplished in the realm of philosophy, with the medium of the concept, or in a concrete, historically bounded, aesthetic and interpersonal realm is a question raised by Hamann's thought. To say that this is a pressing concern might seem excessive – after all, such philosophical problems appear to pale beside material crises of global inequality, starvation amid plenty, and looming environmental catastrophes, to name just a few threats to human welfare. But the battles between the world's dogmatisms will only augment in the coming resource wars. How much more essential is it, then, to develop the intellectual tools needed to overcome the polarities of reason and textual tradition. How much more important is it to be able to cultivate a capacity for the sympathetic reception of the symbols of transcendence. Hamann does not reconcile the faiths; he does not offer any syncretistic faith. Nor yet does he point to a reconciliation of Enlightenment and its opposite. But attending to Hamann's thought on the aesthetic, *conversational* nature of existence opens us up to a vista of religious thought to which an enlightened eye is blind. The reconciliation of mytho-poetic traditions, in all their richness, is one of the more urgent intellectual challenges of our time. To address this problem with the tools of the Enlightenment is merely to exacerbate the problem by adding another dogmatism; to address it with radical subjectivism is to abandon the problem entirely. Thus, while I have expressed pessimism about a great synthesis, I nonetheless hold out the possibility that attendance to Hamann might awaken our receptivity. An attention to his thought can open up a possibility that Hamann himself never envisioned, the establishment of bridges between different horizons of meaning. For all his polemical rancour, then, Hamann might well be what he termed himself, a *metacriticus bonae spei*, a metacritic of good hope.

Notes

Preface

1 Bayer, ed., *Johann Georg Hamann*; Jørgensen, *Johann Georg Hamann*.
2 Blum, *La vie et l'oeuvre de J.G. Hamann*. This is an extremely accessible and lucid work whose scholarship has not staled with age. Also noteworthy (and more philosophical) is the work of the famous Islamist Henri Corbin, *Hamann*.
3 Alexander, *Johann Georg Hamann*; Berlin, *The Magus of the North*; Dickson, *Johann Georg Hamann's Relational Metacriticism*; O'Flaherty, *Johann Georg Hamann*); Smith, *Johann Georg Hamann*.
4 Among others, one might mention Bayer, *Zeitgenosse im Widerspruch*; Büchsel, *Biblisches Zeugnis und Sprachgestalt bei J.G. Hamann*; Gründer, *Figur und Geschichte*. Perhaps the most influential theologian to draw from Hamann (apart from Kierkegaard) is Hans Urs von Balthasar. See especially *The Glory of the Lord*, 3:239–78.
5 Blackall, *The Emergence of German as a Literary Language*; Dahlstrohm, 'The Aesthetic Holism of Hamann, Herder, and Schiller'; Hoffmann, *Johann Georg Hamanns Philologie*; Unger, *Hamann und die Aufklärung*.
6 Beiser, *The Fate of Reason*; Liebrucks, *Sprache und Bewußtsein*; Metzke, *J.G. Hamanns Stellung*; O'Flaherty, *The Quarrel of Reason with Itself*; Salmony, *Johann Georg Hamanns Metakritische Philosophie*; Swain, 'Hamann and the Philosophy of David Hume.'
7 Jørgensen, *Johann Georg Hamann*, 1. See also N 3:350/351.
8 Frederick II, *Oeuvres Primitives de Frédéric II*, 4:431–2.
9 Salmony concurs, despite ascribing to Hamann a 'metacritical philosophy'; Dickson prefers to consider Hamann a 'therapeutic' or 'edifying' philosopher, terms she derives from Richard Rorty (*Hamann's Relational Metacriticism*, 23).

I am suspicious of this category – therapy rarely erects edifices – and I am equally critical of Dickson's tendency to understate the Christocentric nature of Hamann's project. While Hamann does not tend toward terminological rigour, I have tended to take him at his word in his castigation of philosophy. Periodically he employs the term *philosophy* in a positive sense, suggesting that there might be some type of reformed philosophical activity of which he approves. But generally he indicates a conscious opposition to philosophy. I have chosen to draw out this opposition.

10 It is interesting that 'conservative' political culture has managed to unite rational and religious foundationalism. Witness the strange marriage of convenience between Straussians and right-wing Christian evangelicals. Or witness Pope Benedict's recent insistence that Christianity is essentially rationalist, inseparable from its Hellenic roots.

11 In addition to the two books by Oswald Bayer that we have already cited, we might mention *Vernunft ist Sprache*; Bayer and Knudsen, *Kreuz und Kritik*. Other writers with theological concerns are Hans Urs von Balthasar, Fritz Blanke, Elfriede Büchsel, Karlfried Gründer, Henri Corbin, Friedmann Fritsch, and Joseph Nadler.

12 Rawls, 'Kantian Constructivism in Moral Theory,' 518. This does have a Kantian air to it – certainly, Kant championed publicity and thought that common sense contained the core elements that philosophy refined.

13 There is a great deal of difference between Kant's suggestion that the moral law is latent in common sense and the Rawlsian attempt to take all the contentious philosophical problems out of political science as an area of study. Rawls is aware of this difference: *Political Liberalism*, xxvii.

14 A similar point is made by Beiner in his *Philosophy in a Time of Lost Spirit*, 17.

Chapter 1

1 Berlin, *Magus of the North*, 1.

2 Bayer, *Zeitgenosse im Widerspruch*.

3 O'Flaherty, *The Quarrel of Reason with Itself*. This is not unlike an interpretive move made in Rousseau scholarship that locates Jean-Jacques both with and against his contemporaries. Consider, among other monographs, Hulliung, *The Autocritique of Enlightenment*.

4 To list just two such instances, consider Pocock, 'Conservative Enlightenment and Democratic Revolutions'; Sorkin, 'The Case for Comparison: Moses Mendelssohn and the Religious Enlightenment'.' A surprising (and purposely paradoxical) phrase emerges in Hartz, 'The Reactionary Enlightenment.'

5 Schmidt, 'Inventing the Enlightenment,' 442. See also Schmidt's 'What Enlightenment Project?'
6 Schmidt, 'Inventing the Enlightenment,' 442–3.
7 Bahr, ed., *Was ist Aufklärung?* 9.
8 Pocock discards the definite article because he perceives several (or at least
   two) different projects of Enlightenment. Nonetheless, he finds the term
   conceptually useful. See *Barbarism and Religion*, 1:5–7. In retaining the definite article, I have not sought to refute Pocock's convincing claim that
   there were many different (and even conflicting) intellectual projects that
   can reasonably be considered under the luminous metaphor, but merely to
   downplay his fear that speaking in the singular will somehow give a false
   picture of a homogenous army of *philosophes* marching in lockstep. (Pocock's
   pluralization does not amount to a complete diluting of the term – unlike
   some, he is brave enough to give precise definitions, and, indeed, he does
   not reject the political philosophers' characterization of an 'Enlightenment
   project,' 1:295.) In general, I employ the article when referring to the historical phenomenon, and I omit it when referring to the trans-historical
   project. But since I take the two to be inseparable, I am not excessively
   careful about the distinction. I am pleased to note that Graeme Garrard follows a similar path in his *Counter-Enlightenments*, 5.
9 See Mendelssohn, *Jerusalem*, 96–7.
10 I choose to employ the term *enlightener* as an English equivalent for *Aufklärer*. The French equivalents would be *lumière* or, more accurately, *philosophe*.
11 Of course, all of these positions are caricatures, but they are not very far removed from reality. Dena Goodman cites one author who writes, 'The Enlightenment leads to Auschwitz; after Auschwitz, the Enlightenment is a
   bankrupt, discredited, blighted dialectic.' David Hollinger cites a colleague
   who blamed the Enlightenment for Charles Manson. See their articles in
   Baker and Reill, eds. *What's Left of Enlightenment?* 129, 7.
12 McMahon, *Enemies of the Enlightenment*, 13.
13 Burke, *Reflections on the Revolution in France*, 181–2. This is counter-Enlightenment rhetoric through and through. Nonetheless, I am in partial agreement with Pocock's characterization of Burke as an Enlightenment writer.
   As I will argue below, if we treat Enlightenment as a constellation of ideas
   rather than a group of people, we can more easily escape the problems
   with categorization. Burke was entirely enlightened in his epistemology,
   his views on commerce, and even his social psychology. His open championing of prejudice and tradition sets him apart from the movement, but
   his arguments for the utility of prejudice are not entirely removed from
   those of Voltaire.

14 'Mock on, Mock on, Voltaire Rousseau! / Mock on, Mock on – 'tis all in vain! / You throw the sand against the wind, / And the wind blows it back again.'

15 Muthu, *Enlightenment against Empire*, 183. Muthu does not mention Herder's view that the Turks are 'Asiatic barbarians' who do not belong in Europe, or his view that the Jews, with legal emancipation, will eventually be assimilated in Europe and cease to be a 'parasitic plant.' See Herder, *Ideen zur Philosophie der Geschichte der Menschheit*, bk 16, chap. 5, p. 370. As for Kant, one finds, contra Muthu, that even the older Kant thought that 'Negros' were inherently lazy. Kuehn, *Kant*, 344.

16 Muthu, *Enlightenment against Empire*, 265.

17 J.G Herder, 'Auch eine Philosophie der Geschichte zur Bildung der Menschheit,' in *Werke*, 4:15, 17, 38, 41, 105.

18 Muthu, *Enlightenment against Empire*, 257.

19 I do not wish to consider here Muthu's analysis of the three writers, despite my misgivings about his claim that, for Kant, 'humanity is cultural agency' (268).

20 Barnett, *The Enlightenment and Religion*, 26. James Schmidt makes a similar point in rebutting an author who attempted to characterize Enlightenment as reason's escape 'from the tutelage of religion.' Schmidt writes of Berlin pastors who taught an enlightened creed in their churches, in 'Projects and Projections,' 87. I would reply that the Enlightened pastors are far from Christian in a traditional sense – indeed, J.A. Eberhard, Frederick's court preacher, went so far as to champion Socrates over Augustine and Luther, and to argue for a rational piety. This group of pastors rather confirms Delacampagne's claim about Enlightenment's struggle with religion. Schmidt's suggestion that we ought to stop trying to give any definition to the concept of Enlightenment strikes me not only as going against his own practice (as I have indicated), but also as a hindrance to reflection. In any case, if we were to follow his advice we might wonder what purpose there is in keeping this floating signifier around at all. (If Schmidt were completely successful, he would have argued himself out of a job).

21 Schmidt, 'Projects and Projections,' 40.

22 Alembert, *Preliminary Discourse to the Encylopedia of Diderot*, 94. I am indebted to Edward Andrew for alerting me to this weakness in Horkheimer and Adorno's presentation.

23 Horkheimer and Adorno, *Dialektik der Aufklärung*, 100ff.

24 Jonathan Israel does us a useful service by drawing a sharp line between what he terms the 'radical Enlightenment,' which was happily iconoclastic, and the mainstream Enlightenment, which wished to limit the explosive effects of rational critique. *Enlightenment Contested*, 10–11.

25 Venturi, *Utopia and Reform in the Enlightenment*, 1, 16. Venturi places emphasis on republicanism in the Enlightenment.

26 Mill, 'Coleridge,' in *Dissertations and Discussions*, 338.

27 Schmidt draws our attention to this in 'Inventing the Enlightenment.' Garrard (*Counter-Enlightenments*, 11) confirms the lexicographic position, quoting *Webster's* definition of Enlightenment as 'untrammelled but frequently uncritical use of reason.' What is to be done when the age of critique is accused of being uncritical?

28 Diderot and D'Alembert, eds., *Encyclopédie*, 2:509–10.

29 Ibid.

30 See Kant, 'Was ist Aufklärung,' in *Was ist Aufklärung: Thesen und Definitionen*, 9–17. We will give much greater attention to this article and to Hamann's response to it later in the work.

31 'Befreiung vom Aberglauben heißt Aufklärung,' wrote Kant. *Kritik der Urteilskraft*, sec. 40, 158 (Reclam gives the page numbers out of the 1793 edition, consistent with the *Akademieausgabe*.)

32 Kant, *Kritik der reinen Vernunft*, A:x–xi.

33 Condorcet, *Esquisse d'un tableau historique des progrès de l'esprit humain*, 230.

34 Wokler, 'Enlightenment Project,' 303.

35 Bernhard Gajek, ed. *Johann Georg Hamann und die Krise der Aufklärung.* (Frankfurt am Main: Lang, 1988)

36 Unger, *Hamann und die Aufklärung*. Unger writes from the perspective of philology. It is clear that Berlin derived the bulk of his evidence from this rich text.

37 In this tradition I would place Hegel, Adorno, and even the late Foucault, who called for a perpetual *critique* of ourselves.

38 See the *Sokratische Denkwürdigkeiten*, N 2:64n13. Hamann's Protestant disdain for Aquinas's scholasticism is evident in his comparison of him to Molière's Thomas Dioforus, the jargon-ridden doctor in *Le Malade Imaginaire*. An adequate comparison with MacIntyre would be quite interesting, providing us with competing Catholic and Protestant reactions to modernity. Unfortunately, we cannot pursue this here.

39 See N 4:13–34. See also his early translation of Shaftesbury (N 4:131–91), or his paean to commerce and internationalism, the *Beylage zu Dangeuil* (N 4:225–42).

40 That Hamann had a certain amorous relationship with this man is clear enough (see Salmony, *Johann Georg Hamanns Metakritische Philosophie*). Whether his attachment was physical is less clear. He was under the protection of this man, who was also his lute teacher. He was most upset when he discovered that this man was 'kept' by a wealthy English aristocrat.

Hamann's actions and tone sound more like the result of jealousy than moral disapprobation. Possibly he experienced both. It must be said that there are erotic overtones in many of his friendships. When Berens enlisted Kant's help in the re-conversion of Hamann, Hamann referred to Kant as his '*Nebenbuhler*' and played with the rhetoric of a lovers' quarrel. He often employed the image of Socrates and Alcibiades, etc.

41 Hoffmann, *Johann Georg Hamanns Philologie*.

42 He bore a strange lifelong *idée fixe* about his mystical connection with Katharina (her thoughts on the matter are unknown to us, although she appears to have initially accepted Hamann's proposal of marriage). This was just one in a string of lifelong failures: he failed at business, he failed to attain his degree, he failed to secure a decent income for his family. He attacked the king but he failed to catch his attention.

43 Oddly enough, he did not marry in the church, but declared this a 'marriage of conscience.' The woman had been his father's caretaker.

44 One might be tempted to compare him to another apostle of the passions, Rousseau. The *philosophe* of Geneva broke with all his friends in bitter disputes. There is perhaps more than a mere difference of personality here. Another interesting point of comparison is their treatment of their children: Rousseau abandoned his, while Hamann lived perpetually at the door of poverty in order to care for his four children.

45 Herder, Kant, and Mendelssohn are notable examples. He vehemently attacked the Enlightened theologian and freemason Johann August Stark while at the same time taking him as his confessor! Schoonhoven and Seils, *Mysterienschriften erklärt*, 27. He held the curious view that polemic and friendship go together.

46 ZH 1:448 (to Kant). 'Dieser Name [Freund] ist nicht ein Leeres Wort für mich; sondern eine Quelle von Pflichten und Entzückungen, die sich auf einander beziehen.' See also ZH 1:417. 'Ich soll immer mit Freunden streiten.'

47 ZH 1:405. 'Freundschaft legt uns Hinderniße im Wege, die ich bey Fremden und Feinden nicht habe; und hiezu gehören neue Regeln.'

48 ZH 1:406. 'Sie machen mir noch ein theologisch Compliment, daß ich immer mit meinen Freunden streiten möge.'

49 It is amusing to see his tone in his letters to Kant, Herder, Jacobi, Lindner, Mendelssohn, et al., swing back and forth from almost excessive professions of affection to browbeating abuse.

50 ZH 1:445–6. For the translations of Hamann's letters to Kant I have used *Immanuel Kant: Correspondence*, 59. 'Ein philosophisches Buch für Kinder würde daher so einfältig, thöricht und abgeschmackt aussehen müssen, als

ein Göttliches Buch, das für Menschen geschrieben. Nun prüfen Sie sich,
ob Sie so viel Herz haben, der Verfaßer einer einfältigen, thörichten und
abgeschmackten Naturlehre zu sein? Haben Sie Herz, so sind Sie auch ein
Philosoph für Kinder. Vale et sapere AUDE!' I have reinstated Hamann's
Latin quotation from Horace rather than keep Zweig's translation lest the
reader miss the Kantian resonance. This is merely meant to be suggestive,
not to explain an origin; this letter predates Kant's famous article on Enlightenment by over twenty years.

51 ZH 1:447; *Correspondence*, 60. 'Die Natur nach den sechs Tagen ihrer Geburt
ist also das beste Schema für ein Kind, das diese Legende ihrer Wärterin so
lange glaubt … Ein Weltweiser liest aber die drey Kapitel des Anfanges
mit eben solchen Augen, wie jener gekrönter Sterngucker den Himmel. Es
ist daher natürlich, daß lauter eccentrische Begriffe und Anomalien ihm
darin vorkommen; er meistert also lieber den heiligen Moses, ehe er an seinen Schulgrillen und systematischem Geist zweifeln sollte.' The absurdity
of a dogmatic literalism is clearly articulated in N 1:11.

52 Kant, *Über Pädagogik*, in *Schriften*, A 111–12 (pagination derives from the
1803 edition).

53 Ibid., A:131–6.

54 ZH 1:450; Kant, *Correspondence*, trans. Zweig, 63. 'Die Natur ist ein Buch,
ein Brief, eine Fabel (in philosophischen Verstande) oder wie Sie sie nennen wollen. Gesetzt wir kennen alle Buchstaben darinn so gut wie möglich, wir können alle Wörter syllabieren und aussprechen, wir wißen so
gar die Sprache in der es geschrieben ist – Ist das alles schon genug ein
Buch zu verstehen, darüber zu urtheilen, einen Charakter davon oder einen Auszug zu machen. Es gehört also mehr als Physik um die Natur aus-
zulegen. Physik ist nichts als Abc.'

55 Indeed, we can be close to certain of Kant's feelings, since he did not respond. However, it is a remarkable testament to Kant that this would not
be the last time that he would exert himself on Hamann's behalf. Kant
would later help Hamann to get a job – no small favour.

56 ZH 1:378. 'Ich sehe die beste *Demonstration*, wie ein vernünftig Mädchen
einen Liebesbrief.'

57 ZH 1:379. 'Lügen ist die Muttersprache unserer Vernunft.'

58 Hegel, 'Über Hamanns Schriften,' in *Sämtliche Werke*, 20:253–4. 'Die Aufklärung, welche Hamann bekämpft, diese Aufstreben, das Denken und
dessen Freiheit in allen Interessen des Geistes geltend zu machen, wird, so
wie die von Kant durchgeführte, allerdings zunächst nur formelle Freiheit
des Gedankens, ganz von ihm verkannt, und ob ihm gleich mit Recht
die Gestaltungen, zu welchen es dieses Denken brachte, nicht genügen

konnten, so poltert er ganz nur so, um das Wort zu sagen, ins Gelag und ins Blaue hinein gegen das Denken und die Vernunft überhaupt, welche allein das wahrhafte Mittel jener gewußten Entfaltung der Wahrheit und des Erwachsens derselben zum Dianenbaume seyn können.' The 'Diana tree' or 'philosopher's tree' is a metaphor derived from alchemy. Hegel is playing upon a metaphor employed by Hamann himself (and quoted earlier in Hegel's essay).

59 Indeed, sec. 10 of the preface to the *Phenomenology of Spirit*, while possibly directed at Jacobi, would equally fit Hegel's characterization of Hamann.

60 Hegel, 'Über Hamanns Schriften': 'Hamann hat sich seinerseits die Mühe nicht gegeben, welche, wenn man so sagen könnte, sich Gott, freilich in höherem Sinne, gegeben hat, den geballten Kern der Wahrheit, der er ist (alte Philosophen sagten von Gott, daß er eine runde Kugel sei), in der Wirklichkeit zu einem Systeme des Staats, der Rechtlichkeit und Sittlichkeit, zum Systeme der Weltgeschichte zu entfalten, zu einer offenen Hand, deren Finger ausgestreckt sind, um des Menschen Geist damit zu erfassen und zu sich zu ziehen, welcher ebeno nicht eine nur abstruse Intelligenz, ein dumpfes konzentriertes Wesen in sich selbst, nicht nur ein Fühlen und Praktizieren ist, sondern ein entfaltetes System einer intelligenten Organisation, dessen formelle Spitze das Denken ist, das ist, seiner Natur nach die Fähigkeit, über die Oberfläche der göttlichen Entfaltung zuerst hinaus oder vielmehr in sie, durch Nachdenken über sie, hineinzugehen und dann daselbst die göttliche Entfaltung nachzudenken: eine Mühe, welche die Bestimmung des denkenden Geistes an und für sich und die ausdrückliche Pflicht desselben ist ...'

61 Dickson, *Relational Metacriticism*, 327.

62 Compare Löwith, *From Hegel to Nietzsche*, 25–6.

63 O'Flaherty, 'Magus of the North,' followed by Berlin's reply.

64 ZH 1:428. 'Ein Herz ohne Leidenschaften, ohne Affect ist ein Kopf ohne Begriffe ... Treiben sie die Verleugnung ihrer Vernunft und Phantasie nicht zu weit. Vernunft und Phantasie sind Gaben Gottes, die man nicht verwerfen muß.'

65 For example, N 4:458. The notion of Enlightenment as maturity (as in Kant's famous definition) is a commonplace of eighteenth-century progressive anthropology.

66 Cited in O'Flaherty, *Johann Georg Hamann*, 136.

67 Both the separation and fundamental connection of these two forms of rationality is expressed with clarity in Max Weber. Habermas gives a very helpful account of Weber's various uses of rationalization in *The Theory of Communicative Action*, vol. 1, chap. 2, sec. 1. For this distinction, see the

quotation on p. 168. Naturally, Habermas's wish to redeem communicative reason by separating it from instrumental reason is a thorough rejection of Hamann's dual attack. It remains the decisive question whether it is Hamann or Habermas who has disposed of the baby when emptying the bathwater.

68 It is, indeed, the type of question that is itself questionable. When philosophers speak about what we can *no longer* accept, their historicist utterance should raise alarm bells. The call to universalizability also raises a number of serious questions. That said, our concluding chapter will explore the possibility of Hamann reception in a pluralistic world.

69 In the *Malaise of Modernity*, he indicates a wariness toward both the 'knockers and boosters' of the modern project; in the *Sources of the Self*, he gives a similar warning about such reductive dismissal involved in this pro and contra attitude.

Chapter 2

1 Kant, 'Beantwortung der Frage, Was ist Aufklärung?' in *Was ist Aufklärung?* 9: 'der Ausgang des Menschen aus seiner selbstverschuldeten Unmündigkeit.' Other translators prefer *immaturity* or *minority*.

2 Ibid., 11–12.

3 Beyerhaus, 'Kants programm der Aufklärung aus dem Jahre 1784.' Despite the criticism that this article has received, I find it entirely convincing, especially when one compares the published writing of von Zedlitz, who was Kultusminister at the time.

4 Moses Mendelssohn, 'Über die Frage: was heißt aufklären?' in *Was ist Aufklärung*, 7. See also Mendelssohn, *Jerusalem*: 'The state may grant the individual citizen the right to pass judgment on the laws, but not the right to act in accordance with his judgment.' Mendelssohn avoids, however, Kant's collision case of the priest and the untrue doctrine by positing a distinct role for spiritual authority, but he concedes that truth and utility might collide, and that teachers of all sorts have to navigate this difficult water: 'I can conceive of a state of mind in which it is pardonable before the tribunal of the all-righteous Judge if one continues to mix into his otherwise salutary exposition of truths beneficial to the public some untruth that, perhaps, on account of an erroneous conscience, has been sanctioned by the state' (72). This is in some tension with Mendelssohn's claim, 'Reason's house of worship needs no locked doors' (88).

5 Lessing, *Die Erziehung des Menschengeschlechts & Ernst und Falk*, esp. Gespräch 2. This sort of dualism – Enlightenment, reason, and humanity for the literate, prejudice, obedience, and some degree of *l'infâme* for the people

– is a standard feature of the movement, noted even by the Enlightenment's most open admirers. See, for instance, Gay, *The Enlightenment*, chap. 10, p. 2. The Masonic ideal is illustrated beautifully in Mozart's *Zauberflöte*.

6 This is, most famously, the position of Habermas, *The Structural Transformation of the Public Sphere*.

7 This universal, however, becomes more a question of universalization within politico-cultural boundaries.

8 Such a comparison is bound to be confusing because of Kant's somewhat novel usage. Kant, we recall, refers to the 'public' as the extra-governmental realm of thought. Rawls refers to 'public' as that which speaks to the business of government. Thus, Rawls's public realm is akin to Kant's 'private' realm, in that both limit the possibilities for discussion on the basis of a practical need for stability.

9 The progress of humankind – a central Kantian concern – is touched on even in *Was ist Aufklärung*, when Kant speaks of Enlightenment as a process in which he and his age are engaged.

10 Perhaps the clearest Enlightenment antecedent of Rawls's project is Pierre Bayle, who attempted to overcome confessional squabbles by insisting that public arguments cannot rest on religious doctrines that are the very basis of contest. *A Philosophical Commentary*, 1:1. Bayle, however, does not admit to the plurality of truth and insists that *all* arguments must speak to the 'light of reason.' While he attempts to come to terms with conscientious differences of opinion, he is quite clear that comprehensive doctrines are to be debated. If he offers a pragmatic solution that speaks to the liberalism of fear, he does not exclude comprehensive doctrines from political discourse, but makes them the basis for his argument. Rawls's flight from substantive debate is thus somewhat a flight from the Enlightenment itself.

11 Rawls saw this difference clearly, in 'Political Liberalism,' 134–5.

12 The possible contradiction that one might find between this procedural reason and the absolute imperative of Kant's moral law is reconciled in Kant's optimistic philosophical eschatology that posits a time just over the horizon in which people will be Enlightened. Hamann rightly called him a 'cosmopolitan chiliast.'

13 Habermas, *Postmetaphysical Thinking*, 50.

14 Habermas, *Philosophical Discourse of Modernity*, 200. If this chapter places Hamann with the aesthetic response to Enlightenment, our final chapter will indicate his distance from the poetic postmodernity of Derrida and Rorty.

15 See Kant, 'Von einem neuerdings erhobenen vornehmen Ton in der Philosophie,' in *Was ist Aufklärung*, 113–22.

16 Kant, *Correspondence*, trans. Arnulf Zweig, 144.

17 For a more extensive treatment of this reaction, see Oswald Bayer, *Zeitgenosse im Widerspruch*. The letter, often cited by Hamann scholars, has attained a degree of canonization with its appearance in a small Reclam volume *Was ist Aufklärung*, 17–22, whose copious notes are invaluable. I have employed this edition. All other letters stem from Johann Georg Hamann, *Briefwechsel*, ed. Ziesemer and Henkel.

18 *Was ist Aufklärung*, 22. 'Was hilft mir das Feyerkleid der Freyheit, wenn ich daheim im Sclavenkittel.'

19 Ibid., 20. 'Why does the Chiliast treat this boy Absalom so cautiously? Because he counts himself among the class of guardians, and wishes, with this, to distinguish himself from the immature readers.' All translations are, unless otherwise cited, mine.

20 Ibid., 22. '*Anch'io sono tutore!* und kein Maul- noch Lohndiener eines Obervogts.' The '*anch'io*' is a play on the outburst attributed to Correggio when looking upon Raphael's painting, '*anch'io sono pittore.*'

21 N 2:353. 'Sie wissen … wie gern ich von solchen Dingen plaudern mag, die Kinder und den Gemeinen Mann angehen.'

22 N 2:202 (*Aesthetica in nuce*) 'wahrlich, wahrlich, Kinder müssen wir werden, wenn wir den Geist der Wahrheit empfahen sollen.'

23 N 2:171.

24 N 2:277. 'Socrates is on the throne, and truth reigns.' Here, as elsehwere, the spelling errors are in the original.

25 N 2:293, 297. *Glose Philippique.*

26 N 2:282. 'Come, Monsieur, let us approach the temple of *papier-mâché* that common sense and public reason owe to our philosophy. The reverences of a geometrician respond to all the enigmas of the tutelary Sphinx.'

27 N 2:220. 'neu aufgerichtete Scheidewand des Ex- und Esoterismus.'

28 N 3:221.

29 N 3:215. Incidentally, Hamann may have been following Augustine, who cites the same proverb in a similar way to describe his early attraction to certain heretical, esoteric teachings. *Confessions* 3.6.62.

30 N 3:48–9. 'Vielgeliebter Leser! ich heiße der Magus in Norden.' He was not to be confused with any 'Königlich-preußischen Geheimdienraths und ordentlichen Profeßors der Weltweißheit und Beredsamkeit auf der Universität Halle u.s.w.'

31 N 2:149. Of course, there is some irony in this description. He enjoyed mocking this title of the French literati, referring to them as 'Buchstabmänner' (men of the letter, as opposed to the spirit) (N 3:400).

32 Blanke, *Sokratische Denkwürdigkeiten erklärt*, 23–4.

33 N 2:87. 'WIR rathen Jedermann, wer nicht Lust hat seinen Verstand zu verderben, daß er diese unnatürliche Ausgeburt eines verwirrten Kopfes ungelesen laße.'

34 ZH 2:142 (to Mendelssohn). 'Die güldenen Tage sind meines Glaubens noch nicht da, daß Mardochai und der böse Agagite sitzen und sich einander zutrinken werden.' Mendelssohn appears to have found Hamann's jokes amusing, and he played along. Eventually, however, he tired of Hamann's style.

35 ZH 2:129 (to Mendelssohn). 'Ich habe Sie, Geschätzter Freund! bey der ersten Stunde unserer zufälligen Bekanntschaft geliebt, mit einem entschiedenden Geschmack. – Die Erneuerung dieser flüchtigen verloschenen Züge setze biß zu einer bequemern Epoke aus, die uns der *Friede* mitbringen wird. Weil der Charakter eines öffentlichen und privatautors collidiren, kann ich mich Ihnen noch nicht entdecken. Sie möchten mich *verrathen*, oder wie der Löw in der Fabel bey jedem Hahnengeschrey Ihre Grosmuth verleugnen. Fahren Sie fort mein Herr! mit der Sichel und Sie, mein Herr! mit der sharfen hippe – meine Muse mit besudeltem Gewand komt von Edom und tritt die Kelter alleine.' Hamann was referring to Isaiah 63:1–4, Revelation 19:15.

36 Notably, his most significant philosophical response to a text by Mendelssohn bears the pseudonym 'a preacher in the wilderness.' N 3:291 (*Golgotha und Scheblimini*).

37 Selis, *L'inoculation du bon sens*. Hamann cites a 1761 edition, so we can assume that the pamphlet was reprinted (unless, of course, Hamann erred).

38 N 2:151–6 (*Französisches Projekt einer nützlichen, bewährten und neuen Einpropfung*), and N 2:279–85.

39 Selis, *L'inoculation du bon sens*, 44.

40 Ibid., 46–7.

41 Indeed, we might speculate that Hamann's disdain for Helvétius was more than merely on the level of theory – Frederick's French tax collectors, whose domination of the department where Hamann worked struck the Magus as an odious imposition, had been the suggestion of Claude Adrien Hélvetius. See O'Flaherty, *Hamann's Socratic Memorabilia*, 31.

42 N 2:282.

43 From the *Göttingische Anzeige*, #68, 1762. 'Er hat eine dunkle und unbestimmte Schreibart, bey der man nur sehen kan, er wolle tadeln, nicht aber, was er statt des getadelten behaupte.' N 2:253. This review of the *Kreuzzüge* was reprinted by Hamann (with rebuttal) along with two other negative reviews.

44 Indeed, in reply to this reviewer's remarks, he twice had recourse to an epistle of Horace: 'Deme supercilio nubem, plerumque modestus /

Occupat obscuri specium, taciturnus acerbi.' N 2:253, 255. 'Unknit your brow; the silent man is sure / To pass for crabbed, the modest for obscure' (*Satires*, epistle 18, 143).

45 ZH 1:374. One of the articles in question was Diderot's treatise on beauty.

46 N 2:59–60. Some commentators have hinted at a similarity between Hamann's attack on the abstract public and Heidegger's discussion of the abstract '*Man*' or 'the they' from *Sein und Zeit*. See Metzke, *J.G. Hamanns Stellung*, 156, and Blanke, *Sokratische Denkwürdigkeiten erklärt*, 64. In this regard, one might also (more fruitfully) mention Kierkegaard's *The Present Age*, which contains a similar indictment of the abstract entity called 'the public.'

47 N 2:59. The allusion is to the Apocryphal *Bel and the Dragon*, 27. See O'Flaherty, *Hamann's 'Socratic Memorabilia,'* 105, and Blanke, *Sokratische Denkwürdigkeiten erklärt*, 66.

48 Ibid.

49 Bräutigam, *Reflexion*, 15. 'Hamann schreibt als Intellektueller für Intellektuelle. Sein Zielpublikum sind die Intellektuellen.'

50 Volker Hoffmann has shown the degree to which Hamann owes his style to a tradition of poly-historical study that has its origins in Renaissance humanism. *Johann Georg Hamanns Philologie*.

51 This is a point that is repeatedly stressed by Wolfgang-Dieter Baur in his *Johann Georg Hamann als Publizist*. Baur emphasizes both Hamann's opposition to the claim of objectivity on the part of the rational and to the notion that faith can be communicated 'like merchandise' (296). In addition to giving a thorough account of Hamann's newspaper experience, Baur also provides a very sophisticated analysis of Hamann's reaction to *Öffentlichkeit's* tyrannical possibilities.

52 See his commentary on the Bible from his period of conversion: *Tagebuch eines Christen*, N 1:5.

53 N 2:347. 'Schriftsteller und Leser sind zwo Hälften, deren Bedürfnisse sich aufeinander beziehen, und ein gemeinschaftliches Ziel ihrer Vereinigung haben.'

54 N 3:362 (Erste Fassung), 361–3 (Zweite Fassung). 'Um aber zu verstehen: Was geschrieben steht ... kommt es allerdings auf die Frage an: Wie liesest du?'

55 N 2:90. 'die Natur des Gegenstandes muß hier nicht allein, sondern auch das Gesicht des Lesers zu Rath gezogen werden.'

56 While many readers of Hamann have noted this, Gwen Griffith Dickson suggests most forcefully that this 'relational' aspect is the central idea of his authorship: *Relational Metacriticism*.

57 N 2:333. 'Der Kunstrichter, so lang er sich nicht merken läßt, daß er lesen und schreiben kann, läuft gar keine Gefahr mit einem Phylax [Guardian] verglichen zu werden. Zeigt er aber nur ein Ohrläpplein

seiner Geschicklichkeit; so hat er Selbstmord und Hochverrath an seinem Character schon begangen. Weil er sich die Thorheit gelüsten ließ, mit Autor und Leser einen Wettstreit einzugehen; zog er sich das Schicksal der lustigsten Jagd zu.'

58 N 2:61. 'Wo ein gemeiner Leser nichts als Schimmel sehen möchte, wird der Affect der Freundschaft Ihnen, Meine Herren, in diesen Blättern vielleicht ein mikroskopisch Wäldchen entdecken' (trans. O'Flaherty, *Hamann's 'Socratic Memorabilia,'* 143).

59 N 2:41. 'Ich fühlte mein Herz klopfen, ich hörte eine Stimme in der Tiefe desselben seufzen und jammern, als die Stimme des Bluts, als die Stimme eines erschlagenen Bruders, der sein Blut rächen wollte … Ich fühlte auf einmal mein herz quillen, es ergoß sich in Thränen und ich konnte es nicht länger – ich konnte es nicht länger meinem Gott verheelen, daß ich der Brudermörder seines eingeborenen Sohnes war.'

60 N 2:348. 'Wenn das Publikum ein Pfau ist; so muß sich ein Schriftsteller, der gefallen und die letzte Gunst erobern will, in die Füße und in die Stimme des Publici verlieben. Ist er ein Magus, und nennt die Antike seine Schwester und seine Braut, so verwandelt er sich in die lächerliche Gestalt eines Kuckucks, die der große ZEUS annimmt, wenn er Autor werden will.'

61 Commentators often quote from Hamann's letters: 'meine grobe Einbildungskraft ist niemals im Stande gewesen, sich einen schöpferischen Geist ohne genitalia vorzustellen.' ZH 2:415. See, for instance, Salmony, *Johann Georg Hamanns Metakritische Philosophie*, 114. Salmony provides one of the most extensive and instructive accounts of Hamann's 'grobe Einbildungskraft,' usefully reminding enthusiastic Hamannians that the Magus had a problematic relationship with his own pudendum – one that affected both theory and practice. Salmony actually goes a tad far in his speculation, but it makes for amusing reading.

62 N 2:61. 'Da Sie beyde meine Freunde sind; so wird mir Ihr partheyisch Lob und Ihr partheyischer Tadel gleich angenehm seyn.'

63 ZH 1:417–18. 'Ich soll mich also nicht mit Menschen überhaupt einlaßen, sonst würde ich ihnen unerträglich seyn. Ich soll immer mit Freunden streiten; in der *Situation* und Verhalten gegen sie bliebe ich erträglich. In dem Zusammenhange dieser Begriffe mag immerhin ein *sensus hermeneuticus* oder *mysticus* liegen, ich finde aber keinen *sensum communem* darinn.'

64 N 2:78.

65 Presumably, *Phaedrus*, 274c–277e. He also cited the *Gorgias*, though here it is sophistry in general that he is presumably decrying.

66 Plato, *Complete Works*: 'No sensible man will venture to express his deepest thoughts in words, especially in a form which is unchangeable, as is true of written outlines' (*7th Letter*, 343a). 'If Dionysius or anyone else … has written concerning the first and highest principles of nature, he has not properly heard or understood anything of what he has written about; otherwise he would have respected these principles as I do, and would not have dared to give them this discordant and unseemly publicity' (344d).

67 N 2:198. 'Rede, daß ich dich sehe!'

68 N 3: 289. '[Ich] überlasse es einem jeden, die geballte Faust in eine flache Hand zu entfalten.'

69 ZH 2:85 (to J.G. Lindner). 'Es fällt mir … ein, daß diejenigen nich so einfältig handeln, die für wenige als für viel schreiben; weil es das einzige Mittel ist die Vielen zu gewinnen, wenn man die Wenigen erst auf der Seite hat.'

70 ZH 2:85. There is a curiously Habermasian twist to this – Hamann was decrying the passivity with which the reading public ingested ideas. Hamann was basically attributing to Habermas's ideal public the characteristics that Habermas decries in the late-capitalist television-watcher.

71 ZH 2:85.

72 ZH 1:377 (to Immanuel Kant). 'Der eines andern Vernunft mehr glaubt als seiner eigenen; hört auf ein Mensch zu seyn und hat den ersten Rang unter das *seruum pecus* der Nachahmer.'

73 Kant, 'Beantwortung der Frage: Was ist Aufklärung?' in *Was ist Aufklärung*, 9, 'Habe mut, dich deines *eigenen* Verstandes zu bedienen!' Given Hamann's love of mimicry, one might be tempted to see his phrase as an ironic appropriation of Kant's famous dictum. This would, of course, be problematic, as Hamann's letter predates the famous article by over twenty years.

74 It should be noted that neither Kant nor Hamann was employing *Verstand* and *Vernunft* as precise terms of art in these contexts.

75 N 2:204. 'Das Buch der Schöpfung enthält Exempel allgemeiner Begriffe, die GOTT der Kreatur durch die Kreatur; die Bücher des Bundes enthalten Exempel geheimer Artickel, die GOTT durch Menschen dem Menschen hat offenbaren wollen' (trans. Dickson, *Relational Metacriticism*, 418).

76 ZH 1:379. 'Wenn zwey Menschen in einer verschiedenen Lage sich befinden, müßen sie niemals über ihre sinnliche Eindrücke streiten. Ein Wächter auf einer Sternenwarte kann einem in dritten Stockwerk viel erzählen. Dieser muß nicht so tum seyn und ihm seine gesunde Augen absprechen, komm herunter: so wirst Du überzeugt seyn, daß du nichts gesehen hast.'

77 N 1:298.

78 That such personal attunement is equally necessary for human communication should be evident. As Hamann wrote to a friend, 'Ich will nichts erklären. Ihr gutes Herz ist der beste *Exeget* meiner schweren Stellen; und Sie haben einen schnellen Zeugen an Ihrem Gewißen.' ZH 1:430.

79 N 2:72–3.

80 N 2:73. 'Die Unwissenheit des Sokrates war Empfindung. Zwischen Empfindung aber und einen Lehrsatz ist ein grösserer Unterscheid als zwischen einem lebenden Thier und anatomischen Gerippe desselben. Die alten und neuen Skeptiker mögen sich noch so sehr in die Löwenhaut der sokratischen Unwissenheit einwickeln; so verrathen sie sich durch ihre Stimme und Ohren. Wissen sie nichts; was braucht die Welt einen gelehrten Beweis davon?' (trans. O'Flaherty, *Hamann's 'Socratic Memorabilia,'* 167).

81 The latter term is used by O'Flaherty in his discussion of 'Empfindung.' Ibid., 100.

82 N 2:206. 'Ja, ihr feinen Kunstrichter! fragt immer was Wahrheit ist, und greift nach der Thür, weil ihr keine Antwort auf die Frage abwarten könnt' (trans. Dickson, *Hamann's Relational Metacriticism*, 420).

83 Z 1:420. 'Ein Mensch kann nichts nehmen, es werde ihm denn gegeben vom Himmel.'

84 N 2:73. 'Unser eigen Daseyn und die Existentz aller Dinge ausser uns muß geglaubt und kann auf keine andere Art ausgemacht werden' (trans. O'Flaherty, *Hamann's 'Socratic Memorabilia,'* 167).

85 N 2:73. The story is from Augustine, *The City of God*, 1.22.

86 N 2:72. 'Wenn die Schlange der Eva beweiset: Ihr werdet seyn wie Gott, und Jehova weissagt: Siehe! Adam ist worden als Unser einer ... so sieht man, daß einerley Wahrheiten mit einem sehr entgegen gesetzten Geist ausgesprochen werden können' (trans. O'Flaherty, *Hamann's 'Socratic Memorabilia,'* 165).

87 ZH 1:377 (to Kant). 'ich glaube wie Socrates alles, was der andere glaubt – und geh nur darauf aus, andere in ihrem Glauben zu stöhren.'

88 I can think of no substantive work on Hamann that omits a discussion of this point, but the most concise remain Berlin, *Magus of the North*, 31–5, and Metzke, *J.G. Hamanns Stellung*, 195–8.

89 Hume, *Enquiry concerning Human Understanding*, sec. 10, pt 2, p. 415.

90 ZH 1:380 (to Kant). 'daß man im Scherz und ohne sein Wißen und Willen die Wahrheit predigen kann, wenn man auch der gröste Zweifler wäre und wie die Schlange über das zweifeln wollte, was Gott sagt.'

91 N 2:150. See N 6:248 for the word's origin. 'Reversed imitation.'

92 The first reader to note the significance of *metaschematism* was Unger, *Hamann*, 1:501–5. Unger correctly noted that this principle is 'kaum weniger

als das einheitliche Organizationsprinzip, das dem auf den ersten Blick chaotischen Ideenwirrnis seiner Schriften die innere Form verleit.' Unger was also quite insightful when he suggested that Hamann's metaschematism indicates a kind of Neoplatonism. Many have taken Unger to task for this suggestion, and it is quite true that we should be wary of overstating the case. The 'ideas' that Hamann transfers to himself change radically with the transfer. Hamann would seem to take Christianity as far away from Plato as it can go. As Friedmann Fritsch says, for Hamann, 'Der Mensch ist das Maß aller Dinge, weil Gott, wenn er redet, menschlich redet.' See 'Die Wirklichkeit als göttlich und menschlich zugleich,' 73. But that said, there is a great affinity with Neoplatonic thought, and particularly its manifestation in the medieval view of the world as a book. The numerous anti-Platonic elements of Hamann's thought should not blind us to these affinities; when the Platonic forms are translated into expressions of God's will, Plato is naturally subverted, altered irreparably, but the relationship between being and becoming does not disappear in the transition to the relationship between divine and temporal. Chapter 10 elaborates upon this point.

93 O'Flaherty, *Hamann's 'Socratic Memorabilia,'* 4. See also Jørgensen, 'Nachwort,' in Hamann, *Sokratische Denkwürdigkeiten,* 177, and Blanke, *Sokratische Denkwürdigkeiten erklärt,* 17.

94 N 3:72.

95 The first thinkers to clearly articulate the centrality of typological thought in Hamann are Gründer, *Figur und Geschichte,* and Büchsel, *Biblisches Zeugnis und Sprachgestalt bei J.G. Hamann.* The latter makes use of Erich Auerbach's groundbreaking work in the study of medieval figuralism, a practice I have found fruitful to follow. See also Jørgensen, *Johann Georg Hamann,* 31–3.

96 Auerbach, 'Figura,' 72. An equally significant work on the issue of typology is Frye, *The Great Code.*

97 It is for this reason that Reiner Wild opts to employ the more general phrase 'figural thought.' *Metacriticus Bonae Spei,* 162.

98 O'Flaherty has provided a thorough discussion of Christian themes that Hamann found in history of Socrates, *Hamann's 'Socratic Memorabilia,'* 80–3, and the excellent table of biblical identifications, 207–8.

99 N 2:61n4.

100 N 2:65. 'vielleicht ist die ganze Historie mehr Mythologie ... und gleich der Natur, ein versiegelt Buch, ein verdecktes Zeugnis, ein Räthsel, das sich nicht auflösen läßt, ohne mit einem andern Kalbe, als unserer Vernunft zu pflügen' (trans. O'Flaherty, *Hamann's 'Socratic Memorabilia,'* 151).

101 N 2:175. 'Kann man aber das Vergangene kennen, wenn man das Gegen-
     wärtige nicht einmal versteht? – und wer will vom Gegenwärtigen richti-
     ge Begriffe nehmen, ohne das Zukünftige zu wissen?' See also N 3:398:
     'Was für ein Labyrinth würde das Gegenwärtige für den Geist der Beob-
     achtung seyn, ohne den Geist der Weissagung und seine Leitfäden der
     Vergangenheit und der Zukunft.' ['What a labyrinth the present would be
     for the spirit of observation without the spirit of prophecy and its guides
     of the past and the future.']
102 This emerges most clearly in the early biblical observations. N 1:5 'dies
     Wort [the Bible] ist der Schlüssel' to nature and salvation.
103 N 3:382–4. 'Geist der Beobachtung und Geist der Weissagung sind die
     Fittige des menschlichen Genius. Zum Gebiete der ersteren gehört alles
     Gegenwärtige; zum Gebiete des letzteren alles Abwesende, der Vergan-
     genheit und Zukunft. Das philosophische Genie äussert seine Macht
     dadurch, daß es, vermittelst der Abstraction, das Gegenwärtige abwe-
     send zu machen sich bemüht; wirkliche Gegenstände zu nackten Begrif-
     fen und bloß denkbaren Merkmalen, zu reinen Erscheinungen und
     Phänomenen entkleidet. Das poetische Genie äussert seine Macht da-
     durch, daß es, vermittelst der Fiction, die Visionen abwesender Vergan-
     genheit und Zukunft zu gegenwärtigen Darstellungen verklärt.'
104 N 1:12. 'Wie soll daher eine Erzählung beschaffen seyn, in der uns Dinge ver-
     ständlich und vernehmlich gemacht werden sollen, die so weit ausser dem
     ganzen Umfang unserer Begriffe abgesondert liegen.' ['How, then, should a
     story be created in which things that lie separate, so far out of the reach of
     our concepts, are to be made intelligible and distinct.'] See also N 2:171.
105 In a sense, the incarnation is the pre-eminent metaschematism, when God
     adopts a human figure.
106 N 1:10. 'Die Gründe dieser Wahl lassen sich ebenso wenig von uns erfor-
     schen, als warum es ihm gefallen, in 6 tagen schaffen, was sein Wille
     ebenso füglich in einem einzigen Zeitpunct hätte würklich machen
     können.'
107 N 2:197. 'Sinne und Leidenschaften reden und verstehen nichts als Bilder.
     In Bildern besteht der ganze Schatz menschlicher Erkenntnis und Glü-
     ckseligkeit' (trans. Dickson, *Hamann's Relational Metacriticism*, 411).
108 N 2:197. 'Der erste Ausbruch der Schöpfung, und der erste Eindruck ihres
     Geschichtschreibers; – die erste Erscheinung und der erste Genuß der Na-
     tur vereinigen sich in dem Worte: Es werde Licht! Hiemit fängt sich die
     Empfindung von der Gegenwart der Dinge an' (trans. Dickson, ibid.).
109 N 2:198. 'sinnliche Offenbarung' (ibid., 412).
110 N 2:198.

111   Ibid. 'Die verhüllte Figur des Leibes, das Antlitz des Hauptes, und das
      Äußerste der Arme sind das sichtbare Schema, in dem wir einher gehn;
      doch eigentlich nichts als ein Zeigefinger des verborgenen Menschen in
      uns' (trans. Dickson, *Hamann's Relational Metacriticism*, 412). Dickson's
      translation of *Schema* as 'habit' seems to be born of her desire to empha-
      size the continuity of the metaphor of clothing in this passage – a laud-
      able aim, despite the inexactness of the word. It is significant, however,
      that *Schema* and *Figure* are synonyms and periodically employed by Ha-
      mann as terms of art, as in *metaschematize.*
112   N 2:198. 'die erste Kleidung des Menschen war eine Rhapsodie von Fei-
      genblättern' (trans. Dickson, *Hamann's Relational Metacriticism*, 214).
113   Dickson, *Hamann's Relational Metacriticism*, 82.
114   N 2:198. 'Aber GOTT der HERR machte Röcke von Fellen, und zog sie
      an – unsern Stammeltern.'
115   N 2:198. 'durch den Umgang mit dem alten Dichter (der in der Sprache
      Kanaans Abaddon, auf hellenistisch aber Apollyon heist)' (trans. Dickson,
      Hamann's Relational Metacriticism 412).
116   N 2:197. 'Poesie ist die Muttersprache des menschlichen Geschlechts'
      (trans. ibid., 411).
117   N 2:199. 'Reden ist übersetzen – aus einer Engelsprache in eine Men-
      schensprache, das heist, Gedanken in Worte, – Sachen in Namen, – Bilder
      in Zeichen; die poetisch oder kyriologisch, historisch, oder symbolisch
      oder hieroglyphisch – und philosophisch oder charakteristisch seyn kön-
      nen. Diese Art der Übersetzung (verstehe Reden) kommt mehr, als irgend
      eine andere, mit der verkehrten Seite von Tapeten überein. *And shews the
      stuff, but not the workman's skill*' (trans. ibid., 413). Hamann cites an Eng-
      lish poet, the Earl of Roscommon.
118   The fact of our original separation from God indicates that human exist-
      ence is essentially permeated with metaphorical communication. Ha-
      mann's view should not be confused with any quietist, anti-linguistic
      mysticism. Human beings cannot (nor should they want to) escape lan-
      guage; rather, they should use language with due humility.
119   N 2:207. 'unnatürliche[r] Gebrauch der Abstractionen' (trans. ibid., 421).
120   N 2:206. 'Der Poet am Anfange der Tage ist derselbe mit dem Dieb am
      Ende der Tage' (trans. ibid., 420).
121   N 2:211. 'Die Geschichte des Bettlers, der am Hofe zu Ithaca erschien,
      wißt ihr; denn hat sie nicht Homer in griechische und Pope in englische
      Verse übersetzt?' (trans. ibid., 425). Dickson (440nww) suggests that the
      biblical reference is Philippians 2:7, '[Christ] took upon him the form of a
      servant.'

122 N 2:207. 'Versucht es einmal die Iliade zu lesen, wenn ihr vorher durch die Abstraction die beyden Selbstlauter α und ω ausgesichtet habt, und sagt mir eure Meynung von dem Verstande und Wohlklange des Dichters' (trans. ibid., 421. Despite its awkwardness, Dickson has defensible reasons for using the word *meaning* for *Verstand* here.)

123 ZH 1:309 (to J.G. Lindner). 'Jedes Buch ist mir eine Bibel.'

124 Berlin, *Magus of the North*, 78–9.

125 ZH 1:396 (to J.G. Lindner). 'Ein Lay und Ungläubiger kann meine Schreibart nicht anders als für Unsinn erklären, weil ich mit mancherlei Zungen mich ausdrücke, und die Sprache der Sophisten, der Wortspieler, der Creter und Araber, der Weißen und Mohren und Creolen rede, Critick, Mythologie, *rebus* und Grundsätze durch einander schwatze.'

126 Vico, with whom this theory has been associated, was one of the early authors to make systematic use of this notion, but he was by no means the only one (nor was his work very widely read in eighteenth-century France or Germany).

127 N 2:65. He implied that his *Sokratische Denkwürdigkeiten* might begin to do for Socrates what Blackwell had done for Homer.

128 Blackwell, *Enquiry into the Life and Writings of Homer*, 38.

129 Ibid., 43.

130 Bacon, *The Works of Francis Bacon*. See *De Sapientia Veterum*, 6:698. Hamann cites this passage in the opening paragraphs of the *Aesthetica*, N 2:197.

131 Jørgensen provides a marvelously concise discussion of Hamann's Bacon reception, 'Hamann, Bacon und die Hermeneutik,' in *Johann Georg Hamann und England*, 131–42.

132 There are several passages from the Lord Chancellor that served Hamann's purposes in his battles against Enlightenment biblical exegetes. Ibid., esp. 138–9.

133 Frye, *The Great Code*, 85. Another significant (and related) point of difference is noted by Gründer: 'Die Allegorese dagegen liest aus dem Text eine überzeitliche Wahrheit, die jede geschichtliche Wirklichkeit übersteigen soll.' *Figur und Geschichte*, 116. We have discussed the historical nature of typology.

134 Salmony, *Johann Georg Hamanns Metakritische Philosophie*, 221. 'Die 'Dunkelheit' des Magus kann nicht erhellt werden durch Systematisierung.'

135 See ZH 1:378 (to Kant). 'In meinem *mimi*schen Styl herrscht eine strengere *Logic* und eine geleimtere Verbindung als in den Begriffen lebhafter Köpfe.'

136 Hegel, 'Über Hamanns Schriften,' 20:203–75, esp. 254–9.

137 N 2:240. 'Philosophen, sind freche Buler [sic].' Alternately, *freche Buhler* could be rendered 'cheeky paramours' or 'impudent wooers' (of the sort that wooed Penelope, N 2:211).

138 Adorno, *Minima Moralia*, 86.

139 Adorno and Horkheimer, *Dialektik der Aufklärung*.

140 Hence his charge that LaFontaine understood the thought of animals better than of people. N 2:63 (*Socratische Denkwürdigkeiten*). See also his bitter lament that the Bible is often seen, in circles that prize LaFontaine fables, as a work without taste. N 2:187.

141 N 2:94. 'daß sie das Heiligthum der Wißenschaften gemein gemacht, die Poesie eines Originalgedankens in die flüßige Prose der Coffeekreyse und Spieltische ziemlich übersetzt.'

142 N 2:213. 'gestern und heute!'

143 N 4:259–63.

144 ZH 2:201 (to S.F. Trescho). 'Die Ungebundenheit der herrschenden Sitten und Freygeisterey muß durch die Freyheit der Preße theils sich selbst verrathen und in ihr eigen Schwerdt fallen theils die Macht der Unwissenheit verkürzen und den Anbruch des Tages beschleunigen, auf den wir alle warten.' See the same point in N 4:425n12.

145 In line with the liberal tone of the previous quotation, Hamann wrote two newspaper articles condemning censorship, noting that an author's 'thoughts will be tested by others' and if he has errors he will be laughed at. N 4:263. This view, in keeping with the Enlightenment's treatment of the public realm as a place for the refinement of ideas, is not in line with his mode of writing and his avowed rejection of public reason as a means to serious dialogue. Hamann wanted the freedom to print (and demanded it in terms similar to those of his enemies), but he did not hold out hope for public debate and critique.

146 N 2:171. 'Wenn also die göttliche Schreibart auch das alberne – das seichte – das unedle – erwählt, um die Stärke und Ingenuität aller Profanscribenten zu beschämen: so gehören freylich erleuchtete, begeisterte, mit Eyfersucht gewaffnete Augen eines Freundes, eines Vertrauten, eines Liebhabers dazu, in solcher Verkleidung die Strahlen himmlischer Herrlichkeit zu erkennen.'

147 N 2:211. 'Weder die dogmatische Gründlichkeit pharisäischer Orthodoxen, noch die dichterische Üppigkeit sadducäischer Freigeister wird die Sendung des Geistes erneuern, der die heiligen Menschen Gottes trieb ... Zu reden und zu schreiben' (trans. Dickson, *Hamann's Relational Metacriticism*, 425; I would render *Sendung* as 'transmission' here).

148 But humility towards heaven can still be pride on earth, and one can hardly imagine an author with more arrogance than the 'Magus of the North,' who claims God for his muse!

Chapter 3

1 Bayer, *Vernunft ist Sprache.*
2 ZH 5:108. 'Aber mein armer Kopf is gegen Kantens ein zebrochener Topf – Thon gegen Eisen.'
3 Baudler, '*Im Worte sehen,*' 179. Hamann scholarship is lamentably replete with this sort of thing. Kuehn, *Kant*, 239, cites a conversation that Hamann had with Kant on the subject of intestinal health. Kant, Hamann reported to a friend, 'is the most careful observer of his *evacuations,* and he ruminates often at the most inappropriate places ... The same thing happened today, but I assured him that the smallest oral or written evacuation gave me just as much trouble as his evacuations a posteriori created for him.'
4 ZH 4:294. He wrote to a friend after his first reading, 'Da der erste Theil zu Ende ist: so nehme ich mir jetzt die Mühe, mir ein Schema von seinem Inhalt auszuziehen und traue keinem Blick des Ganzen, so hitzig auch selbigem nachjage bey jeder Lectür, ohne eine nähere Zergliederung der Theile und des Einzelnen – um vielleicht das Werk recenzieren, aber nicht beurtheilen zu können – wenigstens nicht nach philosophischem Schrott und Korn. An solchen Kunstrichter wird es so nicht fehlen.' Kuehn, *Kant*, 239.
5 ZH 5:107. 'Das πρωτον ψευδος zu finden und aufzudecken, wäre für mich gnug' [sic].
6 Kant, *Kritik der reinen Vernunft* (hereafter *KrV*) B:xxx.
7 Bayer, *Vernunft ist Sprache*, 46.
8 Kant had helped get Hamann his job and had allowed Hamann's son to attend his university lectures for free.
9 N 3:283. See Hume, *Treatise of Human Nature*, vol. 1, bk 1, pt 1, sec. 7, p. 25.
10 Bayer cites Hamann's claim that this contains the 'orphic egg' of his work. Bayer, *Vernunft ist Sprache*, 216.
11 In a letter to Herder, he wrote, 'So viel ist gewiß, daß ohne Berkeley kein Hume geworden wäre, wie ohne diesen kein Kant. Es läuft doch alles zuletzt auf Überlieferung hinaus wie alle Abstraktion auf sinnliche Eindrükke.' ZH 5:376.
12 This might appear to anticipate Kant's *Critique of Judgment*, sec. 40, but there is no relationship between the Hamannian play on Shaftesbury's term and Kant's theoretical use of it. Indeed, by 'sensus communis'

Hamann here meant precisely the opposite of Kant: he meant the everyday
language of one's particular community. Kant's universalizing sensus communis refers to 'a power to judge that in reflecting takes account (a priori),
in our thought, of everyone else's way of presenting [something], in order *as
it were* to compare our own judgment with human reason in general and
thus escape the illusion that arises from the ease of mistaking subjective and
private conditions for objective ones.' Naturally, this common sense is common to everybody, and hence, in Hamann's view, nobody.

13   N 3:283. 'die Möglichkeit menschlicher Erkenntnis von Gegenständen der
Erfahrung ohne und vor aller Erfahrung und hiernächst die Möglichkeit
einer sinnlichen Anschauung vor aller Empfindung eines Gegenstandes.'

14   *KrV* A:1–2. As Bayer notes (*Vernunft ist Sprache*, 242), for Hamann all cognition is of objects. Hence the Kantian attempt to speak of elements of our
cognitive capacity that exist prior to empirical intuition is treated by Hamann as an attempt to do what Kant himself has noted is impossible, cog-
nizing outside of experience.

15   N 3:283. 'Auf dieser doppelten Un- Möglichkeit und dem Mächtigen Un-
terschiede analytischer und synthetischer Urtheile.'

16   Bayer, *Vernunft ist Sprache*, 248–50. See *KrV* A:760–1; A:ix–xii; A:388; and
passim.

17   Salmony suggests that the first stage is that of Descartes and Hume, the
second of Kant, and the third is the rational conclusion of this 'purism.' *Johann Georg Hamanns metakritische Philosophie*, 206–7. But he offers little evidence for characterizing these stages as the progression from Hume to
Kant and beyond, and one could easily place other philosophers in either
category. Hamann's target is the view of truth as an extra-historical, extra-
linguistic, unchanging realm. This is a charge that could apply equally to
numerous philosophers, including Descartes and Plato.

18   N 3:284. 'das einzige erste und letzte Organon und Kriterion der Vernunft,
ohne ein ander Creditiv als Ueberlieferung und Usum.' As Bayer notes
(*Vernunft ist Sprache*, 271), this makes a fine contrast with the *Prolegomena*
A45, where Kant argues that only in the answer to the question, how are
synthetic a priori possible? 'besteht das Creditiv, welsches sie [metaphysi-
cians] vorzeigen mußen, wenn sie im Namen der reinen Vernunft etwas
bei uns anzubringen haben.'

19   N 3:284. 'Je länger man nachdenkt, desto tiefer und inniger man verstummt und alle Lust zu reden verliert.'

20   N 3:284. 'Receptivität der Sprache und Spontaneität der Begriffe.' As Dickson points out (*Hammann's Relational Metacriticism*, 287, 529, n. y), this is an
interesting alteration of Kant's transcendental logic (A 50), in which the

philosopher claimed that 'Unser Erkenntnis entspringt aus zwei Grundquellen des Gemüts, deren die erste ist, die Vorstellung zu empfangen (*die Rezeptivität der Eindrücke*), die zweite das Vermögen, durch diese Vorstellungen einen Gegenstand zu erkennen (*Spontaneität der Begriffe*)' (italics mine). Hamann has collapsed Kant's 'cognition' (*Erkenntnis*) into 'reason,' and has turned Kant's 'impressions' (*Eindrücke*) into language. Language as an aesthetic (sensory) experience is emphasized. At the same time, the 'spontenaity of concepts' takes on poetic sense that was clearly unintended in Kant.

21 The similarity of this claim to that of Moses Mendelssohn in *Jerusalem* is striking; we will explore this argument in chapter 8.

22 N 3:285 (trans. Dickson, *Hammann's Relational Metacriticism*, 521. As usual, I will periodically translate myself, or employ others as I see fit. When unmarked, the translation is mine. Dickson's here is closest to the original. The translation by Kenneth Haynes in Schmidt, *What Is Enlightenment*, is slightly less accurate, though much more readable.) The original is as follows: 'Zwar sollte man aus so manchen analytischen Urtheilen auf einen gnostischen Haß gegen Materie oder auch auf eine mystische Liebe zur Form schließen: dennoch hat die Synthesis des Prädicats mit dem Subject, worinn zugleich das eigentliche Object der reinen Vernunft besteht, zu ihrem Mittelbegriff weiter nichts, als ein altes kaltes Vorurtheil für die Mathematik vor und hinter sich, deren apodictische Gewißheit hauptsächlich auf eine gleichsam kyriologische Bezeichnung der einfachsten sinnlichsten Anschauung und hiernächst auf die Leichtigkeit, ihre Synthesis und die Möglichkeit derselben in augenscheinlichen Constructionen oder symbolischen Formeln und Gleichungen, durch deren Sinnlichkeit aller Misverstand von selbst ausgeschlossen wird, zu bewähren und darzustellen.'

23 Philosophers might see some similarity between Hamann's argument and Quine's famous rejection of the analytic/synthetic distinction in 'Two Dogmas of Empiricism.' Although Quine begins with Kant, it is clear that Kant's analytic/synthetic distinction is *not* the subject of Quine's attack; rather, Quine treats the analytic as a priori and the synthetic as empirical. His argument refutes the 'boundary between synthetic statements, which hold contingently on experience, and analytic statements which hold come what may' (40). This was clearly not Kant's use. In Kantian terms, Quine calls into question the a priori itself. This aspect of the argument is akin to Hamann's claim, although Hamann would have rejected the pragmatic conclusion of Quine's argument.

24 *KrV* A:7–8.

25 *KrV* B:19 for his more explicit statement of the argument in A:164 / B:205.

26 Hume, *Treatise of Human Nature*, vol. 1, bk 1, pt 3, sec. 1. Hume appears to
    have changed his mind about geometry by the time he got to the *Enquiry
    concerning Human Understanding*, claiming that geometric propositions are
    certain. See sec. 4, pt 1. For our discussion, it should be noted that Kant
    and Hamann appear to have been working from different texts. Kant is of-
    ten said to have been concerned primarily with the *Enquiry*, but Hamann,
    who read fluently in English, considered the *Treatise* to be Hume's master-
    piece and always recommended it whenever the topic of Hume came up.
    Hamann also claimed to have made a convert of his friend, the philoso-
    pher Kraus, who, Hamann claimed, had learnt the work by heart. I do not
    know the degree of Kant's familiarity with the *Treatise*, but it is certain that
    many people around him prized the work.
27 The difference between the two is somewhat more complex than this brief
    statement. Indeed, the interpretation of Hume's 'demonstrative' arguments
    as analytic is up for dispute. However, the standard interpretation of
    Hume is that he accepted the analytic nature of arithmetic. Hamann wrote
    in a letter (ZH 4:294) that Kant was concerned 'um die mathemathischen
    Gewisheit festzusetzen und zu gründen, die Hume, mit Ausschließung der
    Geometrie, mehr auf Arithmetik einschrankt.'
28 Some might be tempted to see mathematics in Hume as a priori, thus un-
    dermining Hume's strict empiricist claim that all ideas are derived from
    sense impressions. However, despite his feeling that mathematics is certain,
    I see no reason to impute to him the view that mathematics contains a priori
    certainty. His account of how we attain certainty of mathematical proofs is
    most empiricist – we see the repeated assent of our fellow mathematicians,
    etc. (*Treatise*, vol. 1, bk 1, pt 4, sec. 1). We can consider a problem a priori, but
    our certainty and the certainty of mathematics appears to be as much born
    of habit as our certainty of causation. However, Hume is not entirely clear
    on this point and does appear to think that arithmetic is a priori.
29 Vaihinger, *Commentar zu Kants Kritik der reinen Vernunft*, 1:207.
30 The entire *Critique* rests on this passage, since the expansion of the a priori
    to include non-analytical judgments is the basis for undermining scepti-
    cism's claims. The degree to which this analytic/synthetic distinction de-
    pends on an observation of empirical psychology is a matter for debate.
31 In this, Hamann appears to share Hume's concern in the *Treatise*, vol. 1, bk 1,
    pt 3, sec. 1: 'It is usual with mathematicians to pretend, that those ideas,
    which are their objects, are of so refined and spiritual a nature, that they
    fall not under the conception of the fancy, but must be comprehended by a
    pure and intellectual view, of which the superior faculties of the soul are
    alone capable. The same notion runs through most parts of philosophy.'

32 *KrV* A:5.

33 *KrV* A:712–38.

34 Bayer, *Vernunft ist Sprache*, 300–3. The historian was one J.G. Wachter. In English the word is usually rendered 'curiologic.'

35 An empiricist might point to how a child learns basic arithmetic. The child begins by looking at physical objects. Two apples plus three apples makes five apples. Though he later learns to abstract from this origin, the entire system rests on his immediate sense impressions of the given.

36 If this appears fanciful or overly novel, we need look only to Berkeley's formulation: 'The theories therefore in Arithmetic, if they are abstracted from the names and figures, as likewise from all use and practice, as well as from the particular things numbered, can be supposed to have nothing at all for their object. Hence we may see how entirely the science of numbers is subordinate to practice, and how jujune and trifling it becomes when considered as a matter of mere speculation.' *The Principles of Human Knowledge*, in *Berkeley's Philosophical Writings*, 111–12.

37 N 3:285. 'misbraucht die Metaphysik alle Wortzeichen und Redefiguren unserer empirischen Erkenntnis zu lauter Hieroglyphen und Typen idealischer Verhältnisse, und verarbeitet durch diesen gelehrten Unfug die Biderkeit der Sprache in ein so sinnloses, läufiges, unstätes, unbestimmtes Etwas = X, daß nichts als ein windiges Saufen ... übrig bleibt' (trans. Dickson, *Hamann's Relational Metacriticism*, 521).

38 *KrV* A:251. 'Alle unsere Vorstellungen werden in der Tat durch den Verstand auf irgend ein Objekt bezogen, und, da Erscheinungen nichts als Vorstellungen sind, so bezieht sie der Verstand auf ein Etwas, als den Gegenstand der sinnlichen Anschauung: aber dieses Etwas ist in so fern nur das transzendentale Objekt. Dieses bedeutet aber ein Etwas = X, wovon wir nichts wissen, noch überhaupt ... wissen können, sondern welches nur als ein Correlatum der Einheit der Apperzeption zur Einheit des Mannigfaltigen in der sinnlichen Anschauung dienen kann, vermittelst deren der Verstand dasselbe in den Begriff eines Gegenstandes vereinigt' (trans. Kemp Smith).

39 Kemp Smith, *Commentary*, 406–7.

40 Ibid., 417.

41 Allison, *Kant's Transcendental Idealism*, chap. 3.

42 *KrV* A:346. With regards to the metaphysical subject, Kant makes the same claim in the same form. 'Durch dieses Ich, oder Er, oder Es (das Ding), welches denkt, wird nun nichts weiter, als ein transzendentales Subjekt der Gedanken vorgestellt = X, welches nur durch die Gedanken, die seine Prädikate sind, erkannt wird, und wovon wir, abgesondert, niemals den mindesten Begriff haben können.'

43 Incidentally, this is akin to Socrates' ad hominem against Protagoras in the *Theatetus* 161c: 'I was astonished that he did not state ... "Pig is the measure of all things" ... It would have made it clear to us at once that, while we were standing astounded at his wisdom as though he were a god, he was in reality no better authority than a tadpole.' Plato, *Complete Works*.

44 *KrV* A:xvii.

45 N 3:286. 'Nicht nur das ganze Vermögen zu denken beruht auf Sprache ... sondern Sprache ist auch der Mittelpunct des Misverstandes der Vernunft mit ihr selbst, theils wegen der häufigen Coincidenz des grösten und kleinsten Begriffs, seiner Leere und Fülle in idealischen Sätzen, teils wegen des unendlichen der Rede- vor den Schlußfiguren, und dergleichen viel mehr.' (I have not followed Dickson's translation here.)

46 Ibid. (trans. Dickson, *Hamann's Relational Metacriticism*, 522).

47 Kant, *Critique of Judgment*, para. 59, p. 226.

48 The young Wittgenstein was occupied with the problem of purifying language; the older Wittgenstein abandoned the project as erroneous and re-thought the problems of philosophy as one of competing 'language games.' Much linguistic philosophy was born of this turn. The natural sciences have also taken an interest in this aspect of cognition (one thinks particularly of the work of George Lakoff).

49 N 3:286. 'Laute und Buchstaben sind also reine Formen a priori, in denen nichts, was zur Empfindung oder sum Begriff eines Gegenstandes gehört, angetroffen wird und die Wahren, ästhetischen Elemente aller menschlichen Erkenntnis und Vernunft.' I employ *cognition* for *Erkenntnis* to retain the sense of the term in Kant's writing (Dickson's *Knowledge* is misleading).

50 Incidentally, those who feel that Kant's view of time and space is somehow undermined by the theory of general relativity might take comfort in such empiricist claims as Hamann's. I am reminded of a conversation with a physicist in which I expressed wonder that at high speeds 'time slows down.' The physicist chided me for speaking imprecisely: 'It is not "time" that slows down; *clocks* slow down.'

51 *KrV* A:51. 'Gedanken ohne Inhalt sind leer, Anschauungen ohne Begriffe sind blind.'

52 *KrV* A:51–2.

53 Alexander, 'Johann Georg Hamann,' 141–2. Alexander notes that Hamann's text in the *Metakritik* can be misunderstood as a misrepresentation of Kant, but he cites a letter to Herder indicating that Hamann had correctly understood Kant's proposition.

54 *KrV* A:x.

55　N 3:287. '... giebt uns die schlechte Busenschlange der gemeinen Volks-
sprache das schönste Gleichnis für die hypostatische Vereinigung der sinnlichen und verständlichen Naturen, den gemeinschaftlich Idiomenwechsel
ihrer Kräfte, die synthetischen Geheimnisse beyder correspondierenden
und sich widersprechenden Gestalten *a priori* und *a posteriori*, samt der
Transsubstantiation subjectiver Bedingungen und Subsumtionen in objek-
tive Prädicate und Attribute durch die *copulam* eines Macht- oder Flickworts.' *Ein Flickwort* is an expletive, but *ein Flick* is a patch. *Flickwerk* is
patchwork and indicates a bungled job. The *Machtwort* is, literally, a power
word. Thus, it is a decree in that it derives from a powerful person – in this
case a philosophical guardian.

56　Bayer, *Vernunft ist Sprache*, 352–3.

57　Martin Luther, 'The Pagan Servitude of the Church' (otherwise translated
as the 'Babylonian Captivity of the Church'), in *Selected Writings*, 270.

58　Ibid., 270.

59　*KrV* A:137.

60　N 3:287. 'Heere von Anschauungen in die Veste des reinen Verstandes hinauf– und Heere von Begriffen in den tiefen Abgrund der fühlbarsten
Sinnlichkeit herabsteigen, auf ainer Leiter, die kein Schlafender sich träu-
men läst' (trans. Dickson, *Hamann's Relational Criticism*, 533. Bayer's enthusiastic declaration that Hamann's brilliant metaschematism indicates his
possession of Demosthenes-like eloquence is dubious: the Greek orator did
not need 600 pages of exegesis).

61　N 3:289. 'im Geiste geträumt.' Dickson's rendering 'dreamt in his mind'
(525) does not convey the likely reference to Kant's work on Swedenborg.

62　Bayer gives the clearest explanation of this reference, *Vernunft ist Sprache*,
369–71.

63　N 3:288. 'Wörter haben also ein ästhetisches und logisches Vermögen.'

64　Hamann speaks of the 'seven letters' in the word *Vernunft*. Dickson translates this into the 'six letters' of the word *reason*. Smith, in *J.G. Hamann*,
220, clearly baffled by Hamann's arithmetic, translates the passage as
'in German the eight letters or two syllables of *Vernunft*.' The translator
in Schmidt's collection *Was ist Aufklärung* solves the puzzle with a
footnote suggesting that Hamann meant the seven different letters in
the word (i.e., the letter *n* would not be counted twice). This certainly
saves Hamann from the charge of having a new, warm prejudice against
mathematics.

65　N 3:289. 'Sollte es aber nicht möglich [seyn] aus dem Begriffe die Form seiner empirischen Anschauung im Wort herzuleiten, vermöge welcher Form
die eine von 2 Sylben a priori und die andere a posteriori steht oder daß

die 7 Buchstaben, in bestimmter Verhältnis geordnet, angeschaut werden? Hier schnarcht der Homer der reinen Vernunft ein so lautes Ja!'

66 *KrV* A:235–60.

67 *KrV* A:256.

68 *KrV* A:242–4.

69 *KrV* A:239.

70 Kant appears to agree with this point when he writes, 'Although all these principles, and the representation of the object with which this science occupies itself, are generated in the mind completely *a priori*, they would mean nothing, were we not always able to present their meaning in appearances, that is, in empirical objects. We therefore demand that a bare concept be *made sensible*, that is, that an object corresponding to it be presented in intuition … The mathematician meets this demand by the construction of a figure, which, although produced *a priori*, is an appearance present to the senses … The concept itself is always *a priori* in origin, and so likewise are the synthetic principles or formulas derived from such concepts; but their employment and their relation to their professed objects can in the end be sought nowhere but in experience, of whose possibility they contain the formal conditions' (A 240). Kant appears to be speaking about the need for empirically derived signs to discuss these formal necessities. Hamann's point is that the attempt to separate the formal necessities from the empirically derived signs is illicit, and the mother of numerous errors akin to those of the metaphysical traditions decried by Kant.

71 N 3:289. 'Diese letzte Möglichkeit nun, die Form einer empirischen Anschauung ohne Gegenstand noch Zeichen derselben aus der reinen und leeren Eigenschaft unsers äußern und innern Gemüths herauszuschöpfen, ist eben das … πρωτον ψευδος [preuton pseudos], der ganze Eckstein des kritischen Idealismus.'

72 N 3:289. 'Die Analyse ist nichts mehr als jeder Zuschnitt nach der Mode, wie die Synthese die Kunstnath eines zünftigen Leder- oder Zeugschneiders' (trans. Dickson, *Hamann's Relational Metacriticism*, 525).

73 Bayer has indicated the structural similarities between this sentence and the Pauline source of the term *metaschematism* in 1 Corinthians 4:6 (Bayer, *Vernunft ist Sprache*, 415).

74 It is thus slightly misleading to say with Reiner Wild that 'Hamanns metakritische Methode besteht also darin, die gegnerischen Positionen konsequent zuende zu denken und dadurch ihrer Unhaltbarkeit zu überführen.' *Metacriticus bonae spei*, 110.

75   Nadler's edition includes a final paragraph that was probably not intended to be part of the full work, although it can be read as a summation

of Hamann's attempt to synthesize Lutheran theological polemics with modern philosophical debates. Hamann repeats the claim, so often found in his writing, that 'the Jew had the word and the sign; the pagan, reason and its wisdom – (the result was a *metabasis eis allo genos* [a passing into another form], of which the most noble is transplanted in the little Golgotha).' (N 3:289). (See Dickson, *Hamann's Relational Metacriticism*, 534.) Not simply Kant, but philosophy itself is the target of the *Metakritik*. Both law and reason are tied to the 'word.' These halves are overcome – if we were Hegelian, we might say *aufgehoben*, but *transfigured* seems a more appropriate term – by the Christian Logos, the Word of the fourth gospel. Concepts, like laws, have letter and spirit, which are inseparable. Most interpreters omit this paragraph as the conclusion to the piece because they exist only on a handwritten copy by Hamann's son. In the original version, which was in a letter to Herder, parts of the lines exist in what is a clear reference to Hamann's other work, *Golgotha und Scheblimini*. Hamann, this evidence suggests, was merely referencing his more substantive treatment of the problem of language and philosophy. Bayer (*Vernunft ist Sprache*, 39–40) shares this view and prefers to treat the work as completed with the line about the 'balled fist.' That said, the opposition of Athens and Jerusalem and the Christological tone of this paragraph is fully consistent with Hamann's intentions.

Chapter 4

1 Alexander, 'Johann Georg Hamann,' 144.
2 Wittgenstein, *Philosophische Bemerkungen*, 1:9. 'Haben die Philosophen bisher immer Unsinn geredet?'
3 Simon, 'Immanuel Kant,' 234.
4 Ibid., 246.
5 Kant, *Kritik der Urteilskraft*, sec. 51, p. 204. 'Wenn wir also die schönen Künste einteilen wollen: so können wir, wenigstens zum Versuche, kein bequemeres Prinzip dazu wählen, als die Analogie der Kunst mit der Art des Ausdrucks, dessen sich Menschen im Sprechen bedienen, um sich, so vollkommen als möglich ist, einander, d.i. nicht bloß ihren Begriffen, sondern auch Empfindungen nach, mitzuteilen. – Dieser besteht in dem Worte, der Gebärdung und dem Tone.'
6 *KrV* A:312–13. Kant, *Critique of Pure Reason*, 308.
7 Note Kant's resemblance to Mendelssohn on this question.
8 Simon, 'Immanuel Kant,' 254.

9 *Critique of Judgment.* 'Unter dem sensus communis aber muß man die Idee eines gemeinschaftlichen Sinnes, d.i. eines Beurteilungsvermögens verstehen, welches in seiner Reflexion auf die Vorstellungsart jedes andern in Gedanken (a priori) Rücksicht nimmt, um gleichsam an die gesamte Menschenvernunft sein Urteil zu halten, und dadurch der Illusion zu entgehen, die aus subjektiven Privatbedingungen, welche leicht für objektiv gehalten werden könnten, auf das Urteil nachteiligen Einfluß haben würde.' *Kritik der Urteilskraft*, sec. 40, p. 157.

10 Kant, 'What Is Orientation in Thinking,' in *Kant: Political Writings*, 247 (italics in original). We will see in chapter 7 that this distinction between private thought and public speech is on somewhat shaky foundations in Hobbes, whose educational program in *Leviathan* indicates a belief that thoughts can indeed be controlled through a public control of language and discourse.

11 *KrV* A:xiv.

12 ZH 5:367 (#811, to Jacobi). 'Kant ist mir näher als Mendelssohn.'

13 N 3:279 (Hamann's unpublished review of the *KrV*).

14 In this, he is clearly a disciple of Hume, who wrote, 'There is no foundation for any conclusion *a priori*, either concerning the operations or duration of any object, of which it is possible for the human mind to form a conception.' *Treatise of Human Nature*, vol. 1, bk 1, pt 4, sec. 5.

15 N 3:32. 'Jede Erscheinung der Natur war ein Wort.'

16 N 2:199. 'Reden ist übersetzen – aus einer Engelsprache in eine Menschensprache.'

17 *KrV* A:253 / B:309, and passim.

18 Compare Augustine's *Confessions*, trans. Pine-Coffin, 12.4.282. 'How then could it [the abyss prior to creation] be described in such a way that even dull minds could grasp it, except by means of some familiar word?' Hamann is part of an old tradition of thought concerning the divine and human idioms.

19 One can see how others have made similar claims about our linguistic philosopher, Wittgenstein. See the brief aside in Ernest Gellner's delightful polemic, *Words and Things*, 113–14. Reiner Wild notes this similarity between Kant and Hamann in his study of *Entkleidung und Verklärung*, citing a handwritten document in which Hamann wrote, 'Alle relative Begriffe sind also nur denkbar, und haben keine andere Wirklichkeit, als die ihren Zeichen inhärirt, welche nichts weniger als das wirklich sind, was sie vorstellen und bedeuten, sondern bloße subjective Bedingungen und Hülfsmittel zur Bezeichnung und Bestimmung der Prädicate, welche sich so wohl nicht auf die Eigenschaften des Objects, sondern vielmehr auf unsere

Erkenntniß deßelben beziehen.' Wild, *Metacriticus*, 178–9. Hamann proceeds to give this a linguistic and prophetic significance, but the Kantian
tenor of this passage is remarkable.

20 N 3:27. 'Weil die Werkzeuge der Sprache wenigstens ein Geschenk der
alma mater Natur sind … und weil … der Schöpfer dieser künstlichen
Werkzeuge auch ihren Gebrauch hat einsetzen wollen und müssen: so ist
allerdings der Urspung der menschlichen Sprache göttlich. Wenn aber ein
höheres Wesen, oder ein Engel, wie bey Bileams Esel, durch unsre Zunge
wirken will; so müssen alle solche Wirkungen, gleich den redended Thieren in Aesops Fabeln, sich der menschlichen Natur analogisch äußern, und
in dieser Beziehung kann der Ursprung der Sprache und noch weniger ihr
Fortgang anders als menschlich seyn und scheinen.' See Numbers 22:28.

21 N 3:27. 'Alles Göttliche ist aber auch menschlich; weil der Mensch weder
wirken noch leiden kann, als nach der Analogie seiner Natur … Diese
communicatio göttlicher und menschlicher *idiomatum* ist ein Hauptschlüssel
aller unsrer Erkenntniß und der ganzen sichtbaren Haushaltung.'

22 Charles Taylor notes this post-Kantian aspect of both Heidegger and Wittgenstein in 'Lichtung or Lebensform: Parallels between Heidegger and
Wittgenstein,' *Philosophical Arguments*, 72–3.

23 N 3:28.

24 See, for instance, the *Aesthetica*, N 2:207: 'O eine Muse wie das Feuer eines
Goldschmieds … Sie wird es wagen, den natürlichen Gebrauch der Sinne
von dem unnatürlichen Gebrauch der Abstractionen zu läutern.'

25 N 3:191. 'so liegt der Grund der Religion in unserer ganzen Existenz und
außer der Sphäre unserer Erkenntniskräfte, welche alle zusammengenommen, den zufälligsten und abstractesten *modum* unserer Existenz
ausmachen.'

26 As Taylor says of transcendental arguments, 'Since they are grounded in
the nature of experience, there remains an ultimate, ontological question
they can't foreclose – for Kant, that of the things in themselves; for the
thesis of embodied agency, the basic explanatory language of human behaviour.' *Philosophical Arguments*, 33. And for Hamann, the nature of the
divine.

27 N 2:197. 'die erste Erscheinung und der erste Genuß der Natur vereinigen
sich in dem Worte: Es werde Licht! hiemit fängt sich die Empfindung von
der Gegenwart der Dinge an.'

28 N 2:198. 'eine Rede an die Kreatur durch die Kreatur.'

29 N 3:32. 'Alles, was der Mensch am Anfange hörte, mit Augen sah, beschaute und seine Hände betasteten, war ein lebendiges Wort; denn Gott
war das Wort.'

Chapter 5

1 *KrV* B:7.
2 *KrV* A:320.
3 *KrV* A:329.
4 *KrV* A:568–9.
5 *KrV* A:618.
6 *KrV* A:697 (trans. Kemp Smith).
7 *KrV* A:818–19.
8 Kant differentiates his position from the widespread, transcendent (as opposed to transcendental) natural religion. However, Kant's *Religion within the Limits of Reason Alone* indicates with great clarity the degree to which this difference does not alter the basic structure of eighteenth-century natural religion. Consider his discussion of the particular content of worship: 'Every church erected upon statutory laws can be the true church only so far as it contains within itself a principle of steadily approximating to pure rational faith (which, when it is practical, really constitutes the religion in every faith) and of becoming able, in time, to dispense with churchly faith (that which is historical), we shall be able to regard these laws, and the officials of the church established upon them, as constituting a [true] *service* of the church (*cultus*) so far as these officials steadily direct their teachings and regulations toward that final end (a public religious faith).' What for many would be considered the essential matter in worship is for Kant merely indifferent.
9 Bayer gives a more than adequate treatment of this in *Vernunft ist Sprache*, 56–62.
10 ZH 6:163 (to Jacobi). 'Kant macht Gott zum Ideal ohne zu wißen, daß seine reine Vernunft eben daßelbe ist.' Kant is thus part of a wider movement that Hamann condemns thus (N 4:283): 'Anstatt also die Schmach Christi und das Ärgernis seiner Nachfolge auf sich zu nehmen, sucht man das Kreuz zu vernichten, weil es ein leichtes ist, die Vernunft in einen Engel des Lichts und in einem Apostel der Gerechtigkeit zu verstellen.'
11 ZH 5:418 (to Herder). 'Statt der reinen Vernunft ist hier von einem andern Hirngespinst und Idol die Rede, dem guten Willen. Daß K. einer unserer scharfsinnigsten Köpfe ist, muß ihm auch sein Feind einräumen, aber leider! ist dieser Scharfsinn sein böser Dämon, fast wie Leßing seiner; denn eine neue Scholastik und ein neues Pabstum sind die beyden Midasohren unsers herrschenden *Seculi*.' *Seculi* or *saeculi* in Latin means 'of the century.'
12 Hume, *Treatise of Human Nature*, vol. 1, bk 1, pt 4, sec. 6, p. 239.
13 Ibid., vol. 1, bk 1, pt 4, sec. 7, p. 251.

14 Ibid., vol. 1, bk 1, pt 4, sec. 6, p. 239.

15 Ibid. vol. 1, bk 1, pt 4, sec. 6, p. 245.

16 Ibid. vol. 1, bk 1, pt 4, sec. 6, p. 248. In his moral inquiries, Hume avoids all the difficulties of metaphysically grounding identity in the distinction that he draws between 'personal identity, as it regards our thought or imagination, and as it regards our passion and the concern we take in ourselves.' The first is the subject of his epistemological inquiries in the first book of the treatise; the second appears to set aside the difficulties involved in the first, speaking of the self unproblematically.

17 'The whole of this doctrine leads us to a conclusion ... that all the nice and subtle questions concerning personal identity can never possibly be decided, and are to be regarded rather as grammatical than as philosophical difficulties.' Ibid. For the famous backgammon reference, see his conclusion to book 1 of the *Treatise*. Hume scholars will be more than familiar with this difficult point.

    Incidentally, the final chapter of the *Treatise* was translated in two installments by Hamann in the *Königsbergsche Gelehrte und Politische Zeitungen* in 1771 (N 4:364–70). The first instalment indicated the sum of Hume's doubts, and ended in the purest scepticism. Hamann did not put any author's name, but merely gave the heading 'Night Thoughts of a Doubter.' This is important not only because it demonstrates that Hamann had a continued interest in this seminal text, but also that Kant knew the *Treatise* to some extent long before beginning his first *Critique*.

18 One might argue that Kant was correct to assume this point. Hume's perplexity might well arise from our very inability to question this experience.

19 *KrV* A:106 (Kant, *Critique of Pure Reason*, trans. Kemp Smith).

20 *KrV* A:107 (trans. Kemp Smith).

21 *KrV* A:123 (trans. Kemp Smith).

22 The paralogisms are greatly shortened in the 1787 version, and they are altered somewhat. The general argument remains the same, however: the logical unity of apperception is not to be confounded with any knowledge of the self in itself. When rationalist metaphysicians speak of the soul as a simple substance, etc., they are mistaking the 'I think' as an object of consciousness, when it is, in fact, the mere unity of consciousness itself. It is always subject, never object. There is no space to enter into the arguments of the 'paralogisms.'

23 *KrV* A:346.

24 Consider the third paralogism's rejection of the proof of personality (A:363). This problem is put concisely at A397: 'Weil wir beim Denken überhaupt von aller Beziehung des Gedankens auf irgendein Objekt (es sei der Sinne

oder des reinen Verstandes) abstrahieren: so ist die Synthesis der Bedingungen eines Gedankens überhaupt (no. 1) gar nicht objektiv, sondern bloß eine Synthesis des Gedankens mit dem Subjekt, die aber fälschlich für eine synthetische Vorstellung eines Objekts gehalten wird.'

25 *KrV* A:680–4.

26 *KrV* A:644.

27 *KrV* A:672 (trans. Kemp Smith).

28 *KrV* A:329. The practical significance of the ideas is further outlined in the second section of the 'Canon of Pure Reason,' A:804–19 / B:832–47. Kant does not specifically address the 'person' in this section, but he does address the idea of God.

29 Kant, *Kritik der praktischen Vernunft*, A, 155. 'die Freiheit und Unabhängigkeit von dem Mechanismus der ganzen Natur.'

30 Compare the *Groundwork of the Metaphysics of Morals*, para. 65, and the *Rechtslehre* in *Metaphysik der Sitten*, 26 [223]. 'Person ist dasjenige Subjekt, dessen Handlungen einer Zurechnung fähig sind. Die moralische Persönlichkeit ist also nichts anders als die Freiheit eines vernünftigen Wesens unter moralischen Gesetzen (die psychologische aber bloß das Vermögen, sich der Identität seiner selbst in den verschiedenen Zuständen seines Daseins bewußt werden).' Here Kant makes explicit the two sides of the 'person.' We know from the *KrV* that the 'psychological' can be employed only as a regulative ideal and cannot be treated as a thing in itself.

31 *KrV* A:365. 'Indessen kann, so wie der Begriff der Substanz und des Einfachen, eben durch der Begriff der Persönlichkeit (so fern er bloß transzendental ist, d.i. Einheit des Subjekts, das uns übrigens unbekannt ist, in dessen Bestimmungen aber eine durchgängige Verknüpfung durch Apperzeption ist) bleiben, und so fern ist dieser Begriff auch zum praktischen Gebrauch nötig und hinreichend, aber auf ihn, als Erweiterung unserer Selbsterkenntnis durch reine Vernunft, welche uns eine ununterbrochene Fortdauer des Subjekts aus dem bloßen Begriffe des identischen Selbst vorspiegelt, können wir nimmermehr Staat machen, da dieser Begriff sich immer um sich selbst herumdreht, und uns in Ansehung keiner einzigen Frage, welche auf synthetische Erkenntnis angelegt ist, weiter bringt.' Kant, indeed, celebrated the separation of the two realms. Practical reason is given free reign in its own domain when speculative reason is kept within its proper bounds. (See the preface to the B edition.) Kant's procedure is somewhat reminiscent of Hume here, whose difficulties with personal identity appear to dissipate when he turns to practical philosophy in the second part of the *Treatise*.

32 ZH 5:265 (to Jacobi).

33 ZH 5:265 (to Jacobi). 'Er schuf den Menschen sich zum Bilde, zum Bilde
    Gottes schuf Er ihn – wir sind Seines Geschlechts.' This is a central point in
    the *Biblische Betrachtungen* (esp. N 1:13), the *Aesthetica in nuce* (N 2:198),
    and the *Sokratische Denkwürdigkeiten* (N 2:66).

34 Such lines as the following are a constant reminder of this point: 'meine
    grobe Einbildungskraft ist niemals im Stande gewesen, sich einen schöpfe-
    rischen Geist ohne *genitalia* vorzustellen' (ZH 2:415).

35 This is evident from his early 'biblical reflections' through to his latest let-
    ters and articles. N 2:164. 'nichts als die höllenfahrt der Selbsterkänntnis
    bahnt uns den Weg zur Vergötterung.' A good discussion of this can be
    found in Fritsch, *Communicatio Idiomatum*, 74–5, 115–21, 286–7.

36 ZH 4:6 (to Lavater). 'Selbsterkenntniß und Selbstliebe ist das wahre Maß
    unserer Menschenkenntniß und Menschenliebe.'

37 N 3:39. 'Gesetzt also auch, daß der Mensch wie ein leerer Schlauch auf die
    Welt käme: so macht eben dieser Mangel ihn zum Genuß der Natur durch
    Erfahrungen und zur Gemeinschaft seines Geschlechts durch Ueberliefe-
    rungen desto fähiger. Unsere Vernunft wenigstens entspringt aus diesem
    zwiefachen Unterricht sinnlicher Offenbarungen und menschlicher Zeug-
    niße, welche sowol durch ähnliche Mittel, nämlich Merkmale, als nach
    ähnlichen Gesetzen, mitgetheilt werden.'

38 He condemned Kant's a priorism, writing that this represented a leap
    'from Locke's *tabula rasa* to *formas et matrices innatas.*' But he continued,
    'Both err, and both are correct; but in what way and to what extent is also
    here *Rhodus et saltus.*' ZH 4:294. 'ein neuer Sprung von Lokes [sic] *tabula
    rasa* auf *formas et matrices innatas.* Beide irren, und beide haben recht; aber
    worin und wie weit ist auch hier Rhodus et saltus.'

39 N 2:123. 'Liebäugeln und Küssen der Liebe, diese beredten Leidenschaft,
    [dienen] zum allgemeinen Wörterbuche.'

40 N 2:66. 'Wie der Mensch nach der Gleichheit Gottes erschaffen worden, so
    scheint der Leib eine Figur oder Bild der Seelen zu seyn.'

41 N 2:199.

42 N 2:59. He quoted from Young's *Night Thoughts.*

43 Taylor, *Human Agency and Language*, 223. Or, as Clifford Ando (treating of
    Augustine's understanding of *Genesis*) writes, 'In the absence of a compre-
    hensible, objective reality there can be no semantically autonomous state-
    ments: all language becomes metaphoric.' 'Signs, Idols, and the
    Incarnation in Augustine's Metaphysics,' 33.

44 Taylor, *Human Agency and Language*, 223.

45 N 3:49.

46 In a letter to Kraus, he repeatedly referred to Kant as 'our Plato.' ZH 5:289–
    92. To Herder, he wrote, 'Ohne es zu wissen, schwärmt er [Kant] ärger als

Plato in der Intellektualwelt über Raum und Zeit.' ZH 4:293. We must recall that Hamann's choice of words was always dictated by his rhetorical
strategy at the time. Thus, his repeated accusation that Plato was a
Schwärmer (expressed first in the *Sokratische Denkwürdigkeiten*, N 2:61) is
not to be taken as in tension with his periodic self-designation as a
Schwärmer. In general, he enjoyed accusing philosophers of 'mysticism'
and enthusiasm. By now, we are quite familiar with this tactic.

47   N 3:32. 'Jede Erscheinung der Natur war ein Wort, – das Zeichen, Sinnbild und
Unterpfand einer neuen, geheimen, aunausprechlichen, aber desto innigern
Vereinigung, Mittheilung und Gemeinschaft göttlicher Energien und Ideen.
Alles, was der Mensch am Anfange hörte, mit Augen sah, beschaute und
seine Hände betasteten, war ein lebendiges Wort; denn Gott war das Wort.'

48   Augustine's radical alteration of Platonism is discussed in Veldhuis, *Ein
Versiegeltes Buch*, 27ff. 'Die große Veränderung gegenüber dem Platonis-
mus ist die Auffassung Augustinus,' die Exemplifizierung der Ideen in der
empirischen Wirklichkeit ergebe sich nicht notwendigerweise aus den Ide-
en selbst, sondern geschehe durch das freie Schöpfungshandeln Gottes.'

49   ZH 5:462. 'Jordani Bruni Principium coincidentiae oppositorum ist in
meinen Augen mehr werth als alle Kantische Kritik.' Commentators on
Hamann never fail to note that this concept has its origins in Nicolas of
Cusa, and not Giordano Bruno. See Metzke, *J.G. Hamanns Stellung*, 173.
Hamann latched onto this principle without looking into its origins.

50   N 3:27. 'Diese *communicatio* göttlicher und menschlicher *idiomatum* is ein
Grundgesetz und der Hauptschlüssel aller unsrer Erkenntniß und der ganzen sichtbaren Haushaltung.'

51   N 3:27. 'Daher hat bereits Protagoras den Menschen *mensuram omnium rerum* genannt.'

52   ZI I 5.271 (to Jacobi). 'Ursprüngliches Seyn ist Wahrheit; mitgetheiltes ist
Gnade.'

53   Hamann's clearest statements on the necessity for self-knowledge are in
the *Brocken*, N 1:300–2.

54   Metzke indicates this element of mystery with concision in *J.G. Hamanns
Stellung*, 167–70.

55   Being charged with more Platonism than Kant, however, would have sent
Hamann into apoplectic shock.

56   See Bayer, *Vernunft ist Sprache*, 347. 'Das πρωτον ψευδος, wodurch Gott,
Selbst und Welt als Dreigestirn von Ganzheitsvorstellungen in den
Ideenhimmel versetzt werden, anstatt sich als lebendige Kraft in der bzw.
als irdische Natur zu offenbaren, liegt für Hamann in Kants aus der
scheidekünstlerisch-puristischen Grenzziehung zwischen Sinnlichkeit und
Verstand bzw. Vernunft gewonnenem Anschauungsbegriff.'

57 N 3: 40. 'Weil das Geheimniß der Ehe zwischen so entgegen gesetzten Naturen als der äußere und innere Mensch, oder Leib und Seele, groß ist: so gehört freylich um zu einem faßlichen Begrif [sic] von der Fülle in der Einheit unsers menschlichen Wesens zu gelangen, eine Anerkenntnis mehrerer unterscheidender irrdischen Merkmale.'

58 N 1:302. 'Um die Erkenntnis unserer Selbst zu erleichtern, ist in jedem Nächsten mein eigen Selbst als in einem Spiegel sichtbar … Gott und mein Nächster gehören also zu meiner Selbsterkenntnis, zu meiner Selbstliebe.'

59 N 3:400.

60 ZH 6:162. 'Irren ist menschlich – aber unsere *infallible* Philosophen aspiriren zu einer mehr als menschl. Autorität, und fallen dadurch in transcendentelle Unwißenheit und Thorheit.'

61 Kant, *Metaphysics of Morals*, 16 (6:224 in the *Akademie-Ausgabe*).

62 Kant, *Groundwork of the Metaphysics of Morals*, 96 (p. 429 in the Academy edition). See also the *Kritik der praktischen Vernunft*, A155.

63 ZH 5:291 (to Kraus). 'Was hilft mir das Feyerkleid der Freyheit, wenn ich daheim im Sclavenkittel.' Incidentally, I have not engaged in a detailed exploration of the *Rechtslehre* because Hamann did not live to see that text.

64 Kant, *KpV*, A 155. 'Der Mensch ist zwar unheilig genug, aber die Menschheit in seiner Person muß ihm heilig sein.'

65 N 3:37–8. 'Diese Würde nun, gleich allen Ehrenstellen, setzt noch keine innere Würdigkeit noch Verdienst unsrer Natur zum voraus; sondern ist, wie letztere selbst, ein unmittelbares Gnadengeschenk des großen Allgebers.' This and the following citations are from a text whose target is not Kant, but Herder's essay on the origin of language. There are, however, numerous parallels to the *Metakritik* in this text.

66 ZH 5:434 (to Scheffner). 'Reine Vernunft und guter Wille sind noch immer Wörter für mich, deren Begriff ich mit meinen Sinnen zu erreichen nicht im stande bin, und für die Philosophie habe ich keine *fidem implicitam*. Ich muß allso [sic] mit Gedult die Offenbarung dieser Geheimniße abwarten.'

67 Kant, *Metaphysics of Morals*, 179, 180, 182.

68 N 3:38. Psalms 22:6.

69 N 3:38. 'Die Freiheit ist das Maximum und Minimum aller unsrer Naturkräfte, und sowol der Grundtrieb als Endzweck ihrer ganzen Richtung, Entwickelung, und Rückkehr./ Daher bestimmen weder Instinct noch *sensus communis* den Menschen; weder Natur- noch Völkerrecht den Fürsten.'

70 ZH 7:14. 'Sind Vernunft und Freiheit nicht die edelsten Gaben der Menschheit und beide zugleich die Quellen alles moralischen Übels?' In a youthful writing he had treated freedom as obedience to divine law, a view akin

to Luther's freedom but paralleling Kantian (and Stoic) freedom as obedience to law (N 1:307–8). The paradoxes of Christian freedom never received adequate treatment in Hamann's oeuvre.

71 N 2:38. 'Jeder ist sein eigener Gesetzgeber, aber zugleich der Erstgeborne
und Nächste seiner Untherthanen.'

72 ZH 4:416. 'Das Ideal seiner Selbstständigkeit ist für mein geschwächtes
Nervengebäude vielleicht zu überlegen, das in einer glücklichen Abhän-
gigkeit mehr Sicherheit und Ruhe findet. Fast scheint mir dieser Liebling-
sheld zu derjenigen Claße von Wesen zu gehören, welche eine
unbeschränkte Unabhängigkeit der rohen Natur gern mit den Ergötzlich-
keiten des geselligen Lebens verbinden möchte.'

73 N 3:38. 'Ohne das vollkommene Gesetz der Freyheit würde der Mensch
gar keiner Nachahmung fähig seyn, auf die gleichwol alle Erziehung und
Erfindung beruht; denn der Mensch ist von Natur unter allen Thieren der
gröste Pantomim.'

74 N 3:39. 'Die *stamina* und *menstrua* unsrer Vernunft sind daher im eigentlichsten Verstande Offenbarung und Ueberlieferungen, die wir zu unser Eigent-
hum aufnehmen, in unsre Säfte und Kräfte verwandeln und dadurch unsrer
Bestimmung gewachsen werden, die kritische und archontische Würde eines politischen Thiers theils zu offenbaren theils zu überliefern.'

75 N 3:37.

76 N 3:40.

77 N 3:224.

78 N 3:180.

79 The historical and concrete embodiment of people as opposed to abstract
personhood is an idea we are accustomed to finding in Hegel, or in contemporary critics of liberalism such as Michael Sandel, Charles Taylor, or
Edward Andrew.

80 Lo, 'A Critical Reevaluation,' 191.

81 *KpV*, A135–6.

82 N 2:93. 'Wer Menschen, als wären es Bäume, gehen gewahr wird und die
Schatten der Berge für Leute ansehen will, traut einem Schalksauge, oder
hat nicht Lust ein gesundes recht aufzuthun.'

83 In the first, a blind man in the process of being cured by Jesus first utters,
confusedly, 'I see men as trees, walking.' In Judges, the charge is made
against Gaal, 'Thou seest the shadow of the mountains as if they were
men.'

84 ZH 7:174. 'Geselligkeit ist das wahre Principium der Vernunft und
Sprache, durch welche unsere Empfindungen und Vorstellungen modifi-
ciert werden.'

85 Metzke, *J.G. Hamanns Stellung*, 224–5.
86 N 1:309. Quoted in Metzke, *J.G. Hamanns Stellung*, 224. 'Wie abscheulich würde der Mensch seyn vielleicht, wenn ihn der Leib nicht in Schranken hielte!'
87 Kant, *Religion within the Limits of Reason Alone*, 148.
88 N 1:300. 'So wie alle unsere Erkenntniskräfte die Selbsterkenntnis zum Gegenstand haben, so unsere Neigungen und Begierden die Selbstliebe. Das erste ist unsere Weisheit, das letzte unsere Tugend.'
89 N 1:302. 'Was für ein Gesetz, was für ein entzückender Gesetzgeber, der uns befiehlt, ihn selbst mit ganzem Herzen zu lieben und unsern Nächsten als uns selbst. Dies ist die wahre und einzige Selbstliebe des Menschen.'
90 N 1:301. 'Es ist die Frage nicht allein, wenn ich mein eigen Selbst ergründen will, zu wissen, was der Mensch ist? sondern auch, was der Stand desselben ist? Bist du frey oder Sclave? Bist Du ein Unmündiger, ein Wayse, eine Wittwe … Hieraus läst sich ersehen, auf wie viele *Facta* unsere Selbsterkenntnis beruht.'
91 Diderot, 'Suite de l'entretien,' in *Le neveu de Rameau*, 338–9.
92 Murdoch, *Sovereignty of the Good*, 80.

Chapter 6

1 ZH 5:71–2 (to Lavater). Quoted in Mendelssohn, *Gesammelte Schriften Jubiläumsausgabe*, 8:73: 'Je mehr ich lese, desto weniger ich versteh. Die Schuld liegt vermuthlich an mir. Daran scheint er mir aber ganz Recht zu haben, selbst ein Júde zu bleiben und seine Brüder beym Glauben ihrer Väter zu erhalten.'
2 This is a central aspect of Hamannian faith. For its most programmatic formulation, see the *Sokratische Denkwürdigkeiten*. N 2:73.
3 ZH 4:5. 'dass dieser Mann [Mendelssohn] wirklich ein Salz und Licht unter seinem Geschlecht ist, und all sein Verdienst und Würdigkeit verloren haben würde, wenn er unser einer geworden wäre.'
4 The term *Scheblimini* is a transliteration of a Hebrew phrase referring to Christ's place 'at the right hand of God.' Very few people understood the reference, and Hamann had to explain it to several of his friends in correspondence.
5 N 3:315.
6 Hegel considered this text to be 'ohne Zweifel das Bedeutendste, was er [Hamann] geschrieben.' Hegel, 'Über Hamanns Schriften,' in *Sämtliche Werke*, 20:243.
7 Mendelssohn, *Jerusalem*, 34.

8 N 3:303. 'einstimmig mit Hobbs die höchste Glückseligkeit in äußerlicher Ruhe und Sicherheit setzt.'

9 'Near-universal' because he did not go so far as to tolerate atheists. *Jerusalem*, 63. Alexander Altmann suggests that this is less than full intolerance, given Mendelssohn's insistence that the state ought to watch this 'from a distance.' Altmann, *Moses Mendelssohn*, 529n104.

10 Ibid., 36–7.

11 Hobbes, *Leviathan*, pt 2, chap. 17, p. 85. I have given the page numbers from the original 1651 edition (which the Penguin edition employs in brackets within the text).

12 Hobbes, *Leviathan*, pt 1, chap. 15, p. 80.

13 Mendelssohn, *Jerusalem*, 37. Arkush's translation is somewhat misleading, in that Mendelssohn wrote 'und so hätten wir abermals ein solennes Recht der Natur.' Mendelssohn, *Gesammelte Schriften Jubiläumsausgabe*, 8:107. Mendelssohn was clearly uninterested in maintaining Hobbes's strict distinction between *law* and *right* – by 'right,' here, he was implying more than a mere liberty, but rather a prescribed moral behaviour.

14 Warrender, *Political Philosophy of Hobbes*. Warrender caused a lengthy scuffle in twentieth-century Hobbes scholarship by arguing that Hobbes expounded a theory of moral obligation *that obtains in the state of nature*, and that he ought, therefore, to be considered among traditional natural law theorists.

15 Hobbes, *Leviathan*, pt 2, chap. 31, p. 193.

16 Leibniz, *Essais de théodicée*, 376.

17 Mendelssohn, *Jerusalem*, 40.

18 Ibid., 41.

19 Ibid., 44.

20 Ibid., 57.

21 Note that Mendelssohn is not advocating a complete separation of church and state – indeed, he sees the church as essential for the education of men.

22 Mendelssohn, *Jerusalem*, 45.

23 Ibid.

24 See Tuck, *Natural Rights Theories*, for a stimulating account of this problem in the history of rights discourse. I maintain some reservations about Tuck's genealogy, however, and about his interpretation of Hobbes and Locke.

25 This argument about appropriation being achieved by the mixing of one's labour with natural goods that were originally held in common was not taken directly from Locke, whose *Second Treatise on Government* Mendelssohn did not possess, but rather from Adam Ferguson's *Institutes of Moral Philosophy*. See Altmann's annotations to *Jerusalem*, 177.

26 Christian Freiherr von Wolff treats extensively of perfect natural rights and
    perfect natural duties, paying careful attention to the distinction between
    right as freedom and law as a binding. *Grundsätze des Natur- und Völkerre-*
    chts, sec. 46ff., sec. 80ff. Samuel Pufendorff, in *On the Duty of Man and Citi-*
    zen According to Natural Law, differentiates between perfect and imperfect
    rights, chap. 9, sec. 4. Hugo Grotius, in *The Rights of War and Peace*, em-
    ploys a slightly different distinction between perfect and imperfect rights
    and obligations. An imperfect right to a thing is a use-right (usufruct) in
    bk 1, chap. 1, sec. 5, pp.19–20. In bk 2, chap. 11, sec. 3, p. 134, imperfect
    obligations appear much closer to the Mendelssohnian conception of them
    – these are obligations that other parties have no right to compel. For all of
    these authors, natural rights entail natural obligations. Cicero differentiated
    between perfect and ordinary duties (not rights), *The Offices*, 1.3.4–5.
    Altmann elucidates the modern natural right teaching and its heritage
    in his commentary, *Jerusalem*, 174–6.
27 Mendelssohn, *Jerusalem*, 56.
28 Ibid., 57. Mendelssohn is not explicit about the causes of and the steps in-
    volved in the transition to civil society, largely because he does not wish to
    emphasize conflict. It is significant that his discussion of the origin of con-
    tract is based on an example of a transfer of right by means of a gift – be-
    neficence is his theme. It is a *sous-entendu* that the state will become
    guarantor of these (and all other) contracts, and thus that in the absence of
    the state, contracts will be morally valid but physically insecure.
29 Pufendorf, *On the Duty of Man and Citizen*, bk 1, chap. 5, sec. 23, p. 55.
    Pufendorf followed Grotius to some extent, although with significant
    alterations. Grotius had argued that in the state of necessity, property re-
    verts to a state of common ownership. This happens because one ought to
    presume that no one had willingly relinquished his right to self-preserva-
    tion (Tuck refers to this principle as 'interpretive charity'). Pufendorf re-
    jected this interpretation, noting a contradiction between Grotius's two
    contentions that (1) the goods in question revert to common property in
    the case of necessity, but that (2) they must then be repaid when the needy
    person has wealth. Further, he argued, Grotius had neglected to make a
    distinction between those who are needy through no fault of their own
    and those whose idleness has brought on their condition of dire necessity
    (*Of the Laws of Nature and Nations*, bk 2, chap. 6). This distinction, dubious
    as it may be, was essential for Pufendorf to retain both the right of neces-
    sity and the sanctity of property. In practice, Pufendorf did not think that
    many people were blameless in their own destitution. Naturally, the right

of necessity is entirely unproblematic for Hobbes – no one can be considered bound to a law that deprives him of his life.

30 Pufendorf, *Of the Law of Nature and Nations*, bk. 2, chap. 6, p. 6.

31 Morgan, 'Liberalism in Mendelssohn's *Jerusalem*,' 284–5.

32 Mendelssohn, *Jerusalem*, 52.

33 Ibid., 43.

34 Hobbes, *Leviathan*, pt 1, chap. 10, p. 41. 'Also Riches joyned with liberality, is Power; because it procureth friends, and servants.'

35 This is a move that Tuck locates in Pufendorf: 'Pufendorf provided a fundamental theoretical criticism of Hobbes ... According to him a Hobbesian "right" was simply *not* a right, since any right requires a definite obligation on someone else.' Tuck, *Natural Rights Theories*, 161.

36 Mendelssohn, *Jerusalem*, 35.

37 Ibid., 46. Alexander Altmann notes the similarity of this doctrine to Leibniz's *Essais de théodicée*. 'Sur l'ouvrage de M. Hobbes,' sec. 12: 'La justice ne dépend point des lois arbitraires des supérieurs, mais des règles éternelles de la sagesse et de la bonté dans les hommes aussi bien qu'en Dieu.' See Altmann, 'Moses Mendelssohn über Naturrecht und Naturzustand,' in *Die Trostvolle Aufklärung*, 176.

38 Mendelssohn, *Jerusalem*, 46. Edward Andrew has argued persuasively that this distinction between justice and charity is what sets modern rights doctrines most distinctly apart from the Thomistic heritage of natural right. *Shylock's Rights*, esp. chap. 2.

39 Mendelssohn, *Jerusalem*, 42.

40 N 3:293.

41 See Mendelssohn, *Jerusalem*, 45–6.

42 As Mendelssohn does, *Jerusalem*, 46.

43 N 3:294. 'Das Vermögen heißt sittlich, wenn es mit den Gesetzen der Weisheit und Güte bestehen kann: so sollte denn auch Weisheit mit Güte verbunden, Sittlichkeit heissen. Nennt man aber ihren Bund Gerechtigkeit: so sollte man mit gleichem Fuge ein Vermögen, das mit den Gesetzen der Weisheit und Güte bestehen kann, gerecht nennen. Sind ferner Macht und Recht auch schon im Stande der Natur heterogene Begriffe: so scheinen Vermögen, Mittel und Güter mit dem Begriffe der Macht gar nahe verwandt zu seyn, daß sie nicht bald auf Einerley hinauslaufen sollten. – Wo kommen aber die Gesetze der Weisheit und Güte her? Giebt es solche Gesetze; was hat man noch nöthig nach einem Licht und Recht der Natur zu forschen? Wären diese Gesetze nicht schon an sich das beste Recht der Natur?'

44 N 3:295. 'Wenn ich ein Recht habe, mich eines Dinges als Mittels zur
   Glückseeligkeit zu bedienen, so hat jeder Mensch im Stande der Natur ein
   gleiches Recht; gleichwie der Soldat, währendes Krieges, die Befugnis hat,
   den Feind umzubringen, und der Feind ihn. Oder sind die Gesetze der
   Weisheit und Güte so mannigfaltig, als mein und jedes andern Ich? Oder
   gehört auch das metaphysische Gesetz königlicher Selbst- und Eigenliebe
   zum Recht der Natur?'

45 Mendelssohn, *Jerusalem*, 46.

46 Ibid., 47.

47 N 3:295. '-und wird nicht die Freyheit dort, wie hier, ein Schlachtopfer sitt-
   licher Nothwendigkeit und des schrecklichen Muß nach den Gezetzen der
   Weisheit und Güte, in denen also auch schon ein Zwangsrecht liegt.'

48 N 3:298. 'Bey vollkommenen Rechten tritt an die Stelle des sittlichen
   Vermögens physische Gewalt, und bey vollkommenen Pflichten die
   physische Notwendigkeit mit Gewalt erpreßter Handlungen. Mit einer
   solchen Vollkommenheit bekommt das ganze speculative Recht der Natur
   einen Riß, und läuft in das höchste Unrecht über.'

49 N 3:302. 'Zwangspflichten, deren Vollkommenheit darinn besteht, daß sie
   mit Gewalt erpreßt werden können, scheinen gleich nahe an die Verbind-
   lichkeit der Furcht zu gränzen.'

50 See Andrew, *Shylock's Rights.*

51 Mendelssohn had said the same thing of ancient Judaic theocracy – it admits of no generic term: 'This constitution existed only once; call it the *Mosaic constitution*, by its proper name.' *Jerusalem*, 131.

52 N 3:297. 'Ist es Weisheit und Güte, einem jeden das Seinige zu geben und
   zu lassen? Freylich in dem einzigen Fall, wo es kein ander Recht zum Eigentum giebt, als die Weisheit und Güte des Gebers. Dieser Fall ist aber
   nur der einzige in seiner Art. Wie schickt sich nun ein Geschlechtswort für
   ein einziges Ding, das sich mit nichts schichtet, und mit nichts unter eine
   Rubricke zu bringen ist? Leibnütz hatte also Recht für jenen einzelnen Fall,
   von dem nur in einer Theodicee die Rede seyn kann.'

53 N 3:296. 'die sich einander niemals widersprechende Gesetze der Weisheit
   und Güte sich wider Wissen und Willen des Theoristen unter seinen Händ-
   en entzwyt, und eine neue Verbindung durch Gerechtigkeit nöthig haben.'

54 Ibid. 'Wie sollte die Gerechtigkeit ... ihre eigene unwandelbare Einheit für
   Zwey ausgeben, die so verschieden unter sich sind, als sie selbst von beyden ist.'

55 Ibid. 'Wegen dieser Collisionsfälle zwischen positiven und negativen Befug-
   nissen, zwischen Selbstgebrauch und leidiger Abhänigkeit vom Wohl-
   wollen weiserer Selbstbraucher im Stande natürlicher Unabhängigkeit,

erscheinet aus dem Gehirn der Theoristen, gleich einer Maschinenpallas, das Gesetz der Gerechtigkeit! – Was für ein Aufwand mystischer Gesetze, um ein kümmerliches Recht der Natur aufzuführen, das kaum die Rede werth ist, und weder dem Stande der Gesellschaft noch der Sache des Judenthums anpaßt!'

56 N 3:297. 'denn Pflichten und Gewissen scheinen für den Rechthabenden ganz entbehrliche Begriffe, unbekennte Grössen und qualitates occultae zu seyn.'

57 Mendelssohn, *Jerusalem*, 48.

58 N 3:300. 'Ist aber das Ich, selbst im Stande der Natur, so ungerecht und unbescheiden, und hat jeder Mensch ein gleiches Recht zum Mir! une Mir allein! – so laßt uns fröhlich sein über dem Wir von Gottes Gnaden, und dankbar für die Brosamen, die ihre Jagd- und Schooßhunde, Windspiel und Bärenbeißern unmündigen Waysen übrig lassen!'

59 N 3:295. 'Ist es aber Weisheit un Güte, unser – ich weiß nicht; ob vollkommenes oder unvollkommenes? – Recht auf Mittel der Glückseeligkeit, und das schmahle Vermögen unserer Habseeligkeit noch durch Gesetze zu beschneiden und zu verstümmeln?'

60 Schreiner, in *Golgotha und Scheblimini erklärt*, reminds us of Mendelssohn's unambiguous statement: 'Not all property is merely conventional.' *Jerusalem*, 47.

61 N 3:299. 'Giebt es aber einen gesellschaftlichen Contract: so giebt es auch einen natürlichen, der ächter und alter seyn, und auf dessen Bedingungen der gesellschaftliche beruhen muß. Dadurch wird nun alles natürliche Eigentum wiederum conventionell, und der Mensch im Stande der Natur von ihren Gesetzen abhängig, d.i. positiv verpflichtet eben denselben Gesetzen gemäß zu handeln, denen die ganze Natur und vornehmlich des Menschen seine, die Erhaltung des Daseyns, und den Gebrauch aller dazu gehörigen Mittel und Güter zu verdanken hat. Der Mensch, als Pflichtträger der Natur hat demnach am allerwenigsten ein ausschließendes Recht und verhaßtes Monopol auf seine Fähigkeiten, noch auf die Producte derselben, noch auf die unfruchtbare Maulesel seiner Indüstrie, und traurigere Wechselbälge seiner usurpierenden Gewaltthätigkeit über die seiner Eitelkeit unterworfene Creatur wider ihren Willen.' I have rendered *Wechselbälge* as 'bastards' – literally, the words translates as 'changeling' and refers to a monstrous birth of unnatural origin. *Bastard* is perhaps too weak a word, but it does carry on the metaphor of an unholy offspring. The *Wechselbalg* can also be a monstrous creature substituted by a demon for the mother's real child. Hamann implies that this earthly justice is a monstrous substitute for the divine.

62 It is not natural in any sense typical of natural rights discourse – on the contrary, it is based in theological premises. Let us recall that Hamann's engagement with the language of 'natural contracts' is typical of his tendency to parody the idiom of his opponents.

63 One is naturally reminded of Luther's somewhat unsavoury 'Suffering, suffering, cross, cross, is the right of a Christian, and none other.' Cited in Wannenwetsch, 'Luther's Moral Theology,' 124.

64 N 3:306.

65 When Hamann wrote *Golgotha* he had not read Hobbes for many years. He wrote in 1784, 'Ich besitze weder Spinoza noch Hobbs, die ich beyde vor 20 Jahren mit wahrer Andacht gelesen und ihnen mehr zu danken habe, als Schaftesbury u Leibnütz.' ZH 5:264. However, upon rereading *de Cive* and *Leviathan* in 1785, he concluded, 'ich bin beruhigt, daß Mendelssohn seinen Mann gefunden.' ['I am confident that Mendelssohn has found his man.']

66 N 3:313. 'Doch nach einer andern Dogmatik sind wenig nehmen und doppelt geben keine Gesinnungen noch Handlungern *deterioris conditionis –*'

67 N 3:313.

68 As one who never faced the real threat of religious persecution or civil war, Hamann was perhaps somewhat hasty in decrying those of Hobbesian timidity. Nonetheless, he was probably quite honest in his closing remarks, 'Andächtiger Leser, was geht mich und dich der Friede an, den die Welt giebt? Wir wissen gewiß, daß der Tag ges HERRN wird kommen, wie ein Dieb in der Nacht.' N 3:318. He goes on to contrast divine with earthly peace.

Chapter 7

1 Mendelssohn, *Jerusalem*, 40. Arkush's somewhat cumbersome rendering of the concise German nouns has the virtue of clarity.

2 Ibid., 42.

3 Ibid., 72.

4 Ibid., 89.

5 Ibid., 89–90.

6 Ibid., 97.

7 Ibid., 98.

8 See Altmann's commentary in Mendelssohn, *Jerusalem*, 206–8.

9 Ibid., 99.

10 I emphasize Hobbes, although Spinoza could equally be mentioned here. The view that Jewish revelation was merely the revelation of *law* exists in Hobbes, but had a more thorough development in the works of Spinoza,

an equally great influence on Mendelssohn, who wrote that Hobbes was to politics what Spinoza was to metaphysics: both were insightful but were led to unreasonable extremes by their own theories. The argument about false prophets has a forerunner in *Leviathan*, pt 3, chap. 32, p. 197; pt 3, chap. 36, pp. 230–1.

11 Hobbes, *Leviathan*, pt 1, chap. 11, p. 51. I leave the question of whether Hobbes himself shared this natural inclination.

12 Ibid. pt 2, chap. 31, p. 187.

13 Ibid., pt 1, chap. 7, p. 32.

14 Mendelssohn, *Jerusalem*, 93.

15 Ibid., 62.

16 Ibid., 73–4.

17 He does not enter into the question of who shall own meeting houses, synagogues, etc., but we get the impression that these things are merely owned by worshipers, and are not the possession of the church qua church, just as a minister might be remunerated for his time spent preaching, but ought not to receive a salary for teaching the faith, for his vocation ought to be entirely born of inner convictions, not external bribes.

18 Mendelssohn, *Jerusalem*, 59–60. Now, a problem clearly arises here – some charitable soul might, as had often been done, agree with Luke 14:23, that if people are unwilling to come to the religious feast, one should 'compel them to come in.' After a bite or two, they might begin to eat with more gusto. Indeed, such a practice would appear to be condoned with Mendelssohn's claim that it is a citizen's duty to lend an ear. But for now let us brush this objection aside by suggesting that Mendelssohn's civic duty to lend an attentive ear is merely an imperfect one.

19 Levy, 'Hamann's Concept of Judaism and Controversy,' 328.

20 Mendelssohn, *Jerusalem*, 89.

21 Ibid., 138–9.

22 Ibid., 131.

23 Ibid., 129.

24 Hobbes, *Leviathan*, pt 3, chap. 42, p. 270.

25 Ibid.

26 A Spinozist would find this puzzling – if the theocratic state was no more, why should its civil laws continue to be in effect? Mendelssohn is perfectly consistent, however. His argument is that divinely revealed law only had *civic* authority under unique 'Mosaic constitution.' In the absence of that constitution, God's particular law for his people remains, but civil authority has no business enforcing it.

27 Hobbes, *Leviathan*, pt 3, chap. 42, p. 271.

28 Mendelssohn, *Jerusalem*, 133. Most commentators on *Jerusalem* note the degree to which Mendelssohn's view followed Spinoza up to this radical
break. Spinoza had famously argued that Mosaic law had become invali-
dated with the end of the commonwealth. Hobbes's view was somewhat
closer to Mendelssohn's, for the Malmesbury philosopher thought that the
Sinaitic covenant had never been destroyed. Nonetheless, he reduced the
content of that law to obedience to kings, thereby emptying it of any content differing from civil law!

29 Ibid., 35. 'Thomas Hobbes lived at a time when fanaticism, combined with
a disorderly sense of Liberty, no longer knew any bounds and was ready
to bring royal authority under its foot and subvert the entire constitution
of the realm … He believed … that the public welfare would be best
served if everything, even our judgment of right and wrong, were made
subject to the supreme power of the civil authority.' Mendelssohn was
probably correct. Though Hobbes argued strongly for the uniformity of
public worship, he had a Mendelssohnian moment when he noted that the
Romans had been quite successful 'tollerating any religion whatsoever in
the city of Rome it selfe; unlesse it had somthing in it, that could not consist with their Civill Government.' *Leviathan*, pt 1, chap. 12, p. 57. Equally,
Hobbes appears at the end of chapter 47 to support the independence of
different congregations such that people may imitate the early church and
'follow Paul, or Cephas, or Apollos, every man as he liketh best.'

30 N 3:308. 'Nein, die ganze Mythologie der hebräischen Haushaltung war
nichts als ein Typus einer transcendenteren Geschichte, der Horoskop eines himmlischen Helden, durch dessen Erscheinung alles bereits vollendet
ist und noch werden wird, was in ihrem Gesetze und ihren Propheten geschrieben steht.'

31 N 3:311. 'Diese zeitliche und ewige Geschichtswahrheiten von dem Könige
der Juden, dem Engel ihres Bundes, dem Erstgebohrnen und Haupt seiner
Gemeine, sind das A und Ω der Grund und Gipfel unserer Glaubensflügel.'

32 This equation of 'Jews and naturalists' was a reference to Mendelssohn's
treatment of Judaism as natural religion.

33 Mendelssohn, *Jerusalem*, 94.

34 N 3:304. 'Der charakteristische Unterschied zwischen Judentum und
Christentum betrifft also weder un- noch mittelbare Offenbarung, in dem
Verstande, worin dieses von Juden und Naturalisten genommen wird –
noch ewige Wahrheiten und Lehrmeinungen – noch Cerimoniel- und Sit-
tengesetze: sondern lediglich zeitliche Geschichtswahrheiten, die sich zu
einer Zeit zugetragen haben, und niemals wiederkommen – Tatsachen,
die durch einen Zusammenhang von Ursachen und Wirkungen in einem

Zeitpunct und Erdraum wahr geworden, und also nur von diesem Punct der Zeit und des Raums als wahr gedacht werden können, und durch Autorität bestätigt werden müssen.' For this last line, see *Jerusalem*, 127.

35 N 3:305–6. 'Moses der größte Prophet, und der Nationalgesetzgeber nur der kleinste vergänglichste Schatten seines Amts, welches er selbst zum bloßen Vorbilde eines andern Propheten bekannte, dessen Erweckung er seinen Brüdern und ihren Nachkommen verhieß, mit dem ausdrücklichen Befehl und Gebot Demselben zu gehorchen.' See Deuteronomy 18:15–18.

36 At N 3:316, Hamann suggests that Mendelssohn's view is equally offensive to Judaism.

37 N 3:306. 'Durch diesen letzten Gräuel der Verwüstung wurde Moses zum Pabst der entweihten Nation.'

38 N 3:304. 'Gleichwie daher Moses selbst nicht wußte, daß sein Antlitz eine glänzende Klarheit hatte, die dem Volke Furcht einjagte: so war auch die ganze Gesetzgebung dieses göttlichen Ministers ein bloßer Schleier und Vorhang der alten Bundesreligion, die noch bis auf den heutigen Tag unaufgedeckt, eingewindelt und versiegelt bleibt.' See 2 Corinthians 3:14. This is Hamann (and St Paul) engaging in confessional polemic.

39 See Schreiner, *Golgotha und Scheblimini erklärt*, 105.

40 N 3:306. 'das Christentum weiß und kennt keine andere Glaubensfesseln, als das feste prophetische Wort in den allerältesten Urkunden des menschlichen Geschlechts und in den heiligen Schriften des ächten Judentums.'

41 N 3:304. 'Autorität kann zwar demüthigen, aber nicht belehren; sie kann die Vernunft niederschlagen, aber nicht fesseln. Dennoch verschwindet ohne Autorität die Wahrheit der Geschichte mit dem Geschehenen selbst.' The last line is from *Jerusalem*, 93.

42 N 3:304. 'Daher heißt die geoffenbarte religion des Christentums, mit Grund und Recht, Glaube, Vertrauen, Zuversicht, getroste und kindliche Versicherung auf göttliche Zusagen und Verheißungen.'

43 Mendelssohn, *Jerusalem*, 118. 'alphabetical script makes men too speculative.'

44 N 3:306. 'Das Christentum glaubt also nicht an Lehrmeinungen der Philosophie, die nichts als eine alphabetische Schreiberey menschlicher Speculation, und dem wandelbaren Mond- und Modenwechsel unterworfen ist!'

45 Mendelssohn, *Jerusalem*, 83; N 3:298.

46 Despite Mendelssohn's brief disagreement with aspects of Lessing's *Erziehung des Menschengeschlechts* (*Jerusalem*, 95), *Jerusalem* basically adopted Lessing's claim that revelation was a distinct path to a truth that was available to reason alone. Hamann hit the nail on the head when he wrote, 'But ever since the gods of the earth created themselves as the very highest

philosophers, Jupiter (formerly *summus philosophus*!) has had to hide in the cuckoo-form of a pedagogue; and although Herr Mendelssohn appears, to some extent, to resent his eternal Friend [Lessing] for having presumed to imagine, from who knows not? which historical researcher, the divine education of the human race, he has nonetheless ... reformed the concept of Religion and Church into a public educational institution himself.' N 3:310.

47 Mendelssohn, *Jerusalem*, 98.

48 N 3:298. 'so weiß ich nicht, wo die Schwierigkeiten herrühren, sich einen Zusammenhang zwischen sittlichen Vermögen und Lehrmeinungen vorzustellen.'

49 Hobbes, *Leviathan*, pt 3, chap. 42, p. 271.

50 Ibid., pt 2, chap. 18, p. 91.

51 Mendelssohn, *Jerusalem*, 62.

52 Ibid., 62.

53 Ibid., 63.

54 It does not resolve the tension to argue, as has Alexander Altmann, that the emphasis be placed upon the fact that Mendelssohn was not justifying violent coercion here, but thought these things were to be controlled 'from a distance' (Altmann, *Moses Mendelssohn*, 529). This goes a long way towards defending Mendelssohn's humanity, but not towards reconciling the tensions within his argument. The same type of defence could equally be made for Hobbes, who clearly did not want to see England become the home of the auto-da-fé. Hobbes, too, thought that doctrine should be supervised from afar – that is, public preachers would be expected to conform their speech acts to legally established doctrines. Hobbes's views on what may be rationally expressed concerning the deity give us some sense of the limited natural religion that would exist in his ideal commonwealth where *Leviathan* would be read from the pulpits. Both Mendelssohn and Hobbes saw in religion an essential foundation for society; they merely differed on the degree to which diverse theological claims affect the basic moral teaching of universal rational religion.

55 Mendelssohn, *Jerusalem*, 40.

56 Shreiner points to Luke 17:37. I'd like to think Roman eagles are meant here.

57 N 3:303. 'Folglich sind Handlungen ohne Gesinnungen, und Gesinnungen ohne Handlungen aine Halbirung ganzer und lebendiger Pflichten in zwo todte Hälften. Wenn Bewegungsgründe keine Wahrheitsgründe mehr seyn dürfen, und Wahrheitsgründe zu Bewegungsgründen weiter nichts taugen; wenn das Wesen vom nothwendigen Verstande, und die Wirklichkeit vom zufälligen Willen abhängt: so hört alle göttliche und menschliche Einheit auf, in Gesinnungen und Handlungen. Der Staat wird ein Körper

ohne Geist und Leben – ein Aas für Adler! Die Kirche ein Gespenst, ohne
Fleich und Bein – ein Popanz für Sperlinge!'

58 It should come as no surprise that Kant thought very highly of *Jerusalem*.
See Kant, *Correspondence*, 204. Also, Kuehn, *Kant*, 319.

59 N 3:318. 'Was geht mich und dich der Friede an, den die Welt giebt?'

60 Mendelssohn, *Jerusalem*, 132.

61 N 3: 314–15. 'Die Schuldigkeit einem Jeden das Seine zu geben, dem Key-
ser seinen Zinsgroschen, und Gott die Ehre seines Namens: dies ist in seiner Augen "ein offenbarer Gegensatz und Collision der Pflichten." War es
aber Jesuitische Vorsicht, die Heuchler und Versucher bey ihrem rechten
Namen zu nennen? … Jener gerechte Bescheid voller Weisheit und Güte,
dem Kayser seinen Zinzgroschen und Gott die Ehre zu geben, war also
kein pharisäischer Rath zween herren zu dienen und den Baum auf beyden Achseln zu tragen.'

62 Levy, 'Hamann's Concept of Judaism and Controversy,' 306.

63 N 3:312. 'Dogmatic und Kirchenrecht gehören lediglich zu den öffentlichen
Erziehungs- und Verwaltungsanstalten, sind als solche obrigkeitlicher
Willkühr unterworfen, und bald eine grobe, bald eine feine äußerliche
Zucht, nach den Elementen und Graden herrschender Aesthetik. Diese
sichtbaren, öffentlichen, gemeinen Anstalten sind weder Religion, noch
Weisheit, die von herabkommt; sondern irrdich, menschlich und teuflisch
nach dem Einfluß welscher Cardinäle oder welscher Ciceroni, poetischer
Beichtväter oder prosaischer Bauchpfaffen, und nach dem abwechselnden
System des statistischen Gleich- un Übergewichts, oder bewaffnete Toleranz und Neutralität – Kirchen- und Schulwesen haben, wie Creaturen
und Misgeburten des Staats und der Vernunft, sich beiden oft eben so
niederträchtlg verkauft, als selbige verrathen; Philosophie und Politik
haben zu allen ihren gemeinschaftlichen Täuschungen und Gewaltthätig
keiten das Schwert des Aberglaubens und den Schild des Unglaubens
nothing gehabt, und so wohl durch ihre Liebe als durch ihren Haß die
Dogmatik ärger gemishandelt, denn Amnon die Schwester seines
Bruders Absalom – '

64 Mendelssohn, *Jerusalem*, 41, 57.

65 N 3:312. Italics mine. Hamann wrote *Misverhältnis*.

66 Schreiner, *Golgotha und Scheblimini erklärt*, 141. See 2 Samuel 13:1–19.

67 Mendelssohn, *Jerusalem*, 128. 'And his oneness is such as not to admit the
least division or plurality in either the political or the metaphysical
sense.'

68 N 3:315. 'ER und der Sohn ist ein Einiges Wesen, das so wenig im Politischen als Metaphysischen die mindeste Trennung oder Vielheit zuläßt und

Niemand hat Gott gesehen; nur der Eingebohrne Sohn, der in des Vaters Schooß ist, hat seine Fülle der Gnade und Wahrheit exegesirt.'

69 N 3:314. 'Ein Reich, das nicht von dieser Welt ist, kann daher auf kein ander Kirchen-Recht Anspruch machen, als mit genauer Noth geduldet und gelitten zu werden.'

70 N 3:264. 'Die Toleranz ist freylich die erhabenste christliche Tugend; desto mehr nimmt es mich aber Wunder, wie es unserm Jahrhundert eingefallen, sich in diese schönste himmelstochter der drey paulinischen Gratien so sterblich zu verlieben.'

71 Schoonhoven and Seils, *Mysterienschriften erklärt*, 114.

72 Altmann, *Moses Mendelssohn*, 640.

73 ZH 5:402.

74 Edward Andrew has suggested that the discourse of toleration is tied to possessive individualism and the liberal vocabulary of rights. He sees modern views of justice as emerging against the medieval Christian view of love that places the duty of charity above property right and that justifies religious persecution in the name of love. Thus he presents us with a troublingly ambivalent portrait of modernity and its opposite. The debate between Hamann and Mendelssohn follows Andrew's central narrative remarkably closely, despite Hamann's not thinking that charity legitimated persecution. See Andrew, *Shylock's Rights*.

75 N 3:164. 'Denn was die unerkannte philosophische und politische Sünde des Gallionismus anbetrifft: so ließe sich jetzo noch etwas mehr darüber sagen, als der Berühmte Berkeley zu seiner Zeit und in seinem Lande darüber geschrieben hat; wiewol auch dieses Unkraut zum Besten des edlen Weitzens der Toleranz und Providenz des großen Hausvaters bis zur Erndtezeit empfohlen bleibt.'

76 Hamann quotes from Berkeley, who had begun his *Discourse Addressed to Magistrates and Men in Authority Occasioned by the Enormous Licence and Irreligion of the Times*, by citing Acts 18:17: 'Gallio cared for none of those things' (Berkeley, *The Works of George Berkeley*, 4:477.) Gallio is the deputy of Achaia who refuses to implicate himself in doctrinal matters when the Jews accuse Paul of teaching an unlawful manner of worship.

77 A comparison with Carl Schmitt is pertinent on this point. Schmitt was equally troubled by the distinction between internal and external, and he claimed to be enamoured with Hamann's argument in *Golgotha und Scheblimini*. But while Schmitt was correct to note that Hobbes's distinction between inner conviction and our action is what particularly disturbed Hamann, his presentation of Hamann's text is quite misleading. Allow me to quote Schmitt with my response in italics:

Moses Mendelssohn's work was also the inducement for the publication of the first great and truly profound discussion of German wisdom and the Jewish tactic of drawing distinctions, namely, Johann Georg Hamann's *Golgotha und Scheblimini* (1784). [*I indicate in the appendix the inaccuracy of Schmitt's depicting Hamann as a fellow nationalist anti-Semite.*] The great, knowledgeable Hamann was aware of the meaning of leviathan and behemoth [*i.e., Hamann was aware of the mythical relationship that Schmitt has insisted upon. Of course, Hamann nowhere mentioned this, so it is difficult to know whether he was aware of it*]. He knew the leviathan to be a huge fish and a symbol of English character. [*This assertion is fishier than the English: there is no textual evidence for it anywhere in Hamann's oeuvre.*] Drawing on this knowledge, he characterized the moralistic bourgeois hypocrisy, the cant, as the 'caviar of the leviathan' in contrast to the 'Gallic paint' of cultural pretense. [*Hamann did condemn the 'caviar of leviathan,' but it was in an entirely different text. See the 'Sibylle über die Ehe,' N 3:202. Behemoth is not mentioned in this text.*] In reference to the state of Frederick the Great, he cited the passage from *The Book of Job* 40:18, that refers to the land animal behemoth. Demonstrating a sense of superiority over the conceptual skill of the enlightened Jew, he replied to him that state, religion, and freedom of conscience are three terms, words that signify everything and nothing and relate to other words 'as the uncertainty of men to the certainty of animals.' The behemoth is an animal to whom the poor and the dependent are thankful because the hounds of the great Nimrod leave them some crumbs. [*Here, Schmitt has Hamann characterizing the behemoth as leviathan's opposing number; there is no textual evidence to indicate that Hamann saw behemoth and leviathan as opposites. Hamann does indeed cite Job 40:18, but he does so to characterize the egoistic 'Nimrod in a state of nature' (N 3:300). That is, Hamann is characterizing the sovereign in Hobbes's* Leviathan, *who remains in a state of nature and against whom no claims of justice can be made.*] But, above all, what becomes clear here is what has become of Hobbes' leviathan: An externally all-powerful, internally powerless concentration of power that can only justify 'forced duties because of the binding force of fear' and of which the Jew, Moses Mendelssohn, in great anticipation of success, demands that because everyone must become blessed in his own way, it (the leviathan) concern itself as little as possible with the inner disposition of an individual, just as little as God, in contract, cares about the outer actions of man. (Carl Schmitt, *The Leviathan in the State Theory of Thomas Hobbes*, 60–1)

What Schmitt is doing here with his incredibly dishonest presentation is taking Hamann's complaint about the separation of inner conviction and outer action as an articulation of Schmitt's own lamentation about the 'Jewish' aim of 'castrating a leviathan that had been full of vitality' (70). Schmitt has correctly seen in Hamann a castigation of Mendelssohn's Hobbesian distinction between inner and outer, but Schmitt has failed to see that Hamann was condemning Mendelssohn for being *too* Hobbesian – Hobbesian in spite of himself. For Schmitt, Mendelssohn's and Spinoza's insistence on the freedom of conscience is a 'Jewish' exploitation of a weakness in Hobbes's system. Hamann, however, saw Hobbes's distinction between inner and outer as an intrinsic part of the same system. What Schmitt sees as an emasculation of the great fish Hamann sees as its pudendum. The separation of inner conviction from outer action is a method of rendering faith claims 'indifferent,' of neutralizing them (as Schmitt would say). According to Schmitt, 'He who focuses on drawing distinctions between the internal and the external has, by elevating that intellectual device, conferred superiority on the internal (over the external)' (61). But for Hamann the point is not that this separation paves the way to a liberal emasculation of the state, but rather that it raises the *external* to greater heights, rendering the internal meaningless in action. Mendelssohnian state indifferentism is in structure no different from Hobbesian Erastianism in that faiths are judged and regulated according to their utility. Liberal indifferentism is not a subtle perversion of Hobbesian Erastianism but is merely the other side of the same coin. If Hamann mocks the benevolent and moralistic language of Mendelssohn, he does not do it to celebrate but to *condemn* the Leviathan who hides behind the painted veil. Mendelssohn is not exploiting a weak link in Hobbes's chain of reasoning, he *is* Hobbesian – that is his error. Hamann's condemnation of the leviathan is the sort of thing that Schmitt associates with a weak sentimentalism.

Chapter 8

1 Mendelssohn, *Jerusalem*, 102.
2 Ibid.
3 Ibid., 103.
4 Ibid., 133.
5 Ibid., 104–5.
6 Ibid., 105.
7 Ibid.
8 Ibid., 107.

9 Hobbes, *Leviathan*, pt 1, chap. 4, p. 13.

10 Incidentally, Hobbes appears to have shared this supposition that the things themselves were the first signs: 'And it seems, there was a time when those names of number were not in use; and men were fayn to apply their fingers of one or both hands, to those things they desired to keep account of; and that thence it proceeded, that now our numerall words are but ten, in any Nation, and in some but five, and then they begin again.' *Leviathan*, pt 1, chap. 4, p. 14. Hobbes gave the distinct impression that *things* were originally employed as markers of more abstract ideas (the fingers were the signs of number).

11 Mendelssohn, *Jerusalem*, 107–8.

12 I employ the present tense here, for Mendelssohn saw this not as a singular historical development, but as a repeated pattern in world history. He was somewhat suspicious of the notion of universal progress. See *Jerusalem*, 95.

13 Ibid., 111.

14 Ibid.

15 Ibid., 116. Socrates is clearly the pre-eminent figure that Mendelssohn had in mind.

16 Ibid.

17 Ibid., 119.

18 Ibid., 101.

19 Ibid., 119.

20 Ibid., 66. Italics mine.

21 Pope, *Essay on Criticism*, pt 1, ll. 9–10.

22 Mendelssohn, *Jerusalem*, 67.

23 Ibid., 93.

24 Pope, *Essay on Criticism*, pt 1, ll. 19 20.

25 N 3:317. 'Zweifelsucht an Wahrheit und Leichtgläubigkeit des Selbstbetrugs sind daher eben so unzertrennliche Symptome, wie Frost und Hitze des Fiebers.'

26 N 2:198. 'Rede, daß ich dich sehe!'

27 N 3:286. 'das ganze Vermögen zu denken beruht auf Sprache.'

28 N 3:284 (trans. Dickson, *Relational Metacriticism*, 520). 'ohne ein ander Creditiv als Ueberlieferung und Usum.'

29 See his charge that Kant had a 'mystical love of form.' N 3:285.

30 These phrases are directly lifted from Mendelssohn's text, 109.

31 N 3:310. 'Mit einem solchen Krebsgange des Verstandes lässet sich ohne Flug der Erfindungskraft eben so leicht das Unermeßliche als meßbar, und umgekehrt denken – eben so leicht durch unmittelbare Bezeichnung der Sache die ganze deutsche Literatur nicht nur übersehen, sondern auch

verbessern von einem Imperator zu Pekin, als von einem taubgebohrnen Johann Ballhorn!'

32 Mendelssohn, *Jerusalem*, 108.

33 N 3:302. 'In einem Schauthal voller unbestimmten und schwankended Begriffe, ist der Ruhm nicht fein von grösserer Aufklärung! – besserer Entwickelung! – richtiger Unterscheidung! – und sublimiertem Sprachgebrauch des gesunden Menschenverstandes! – gegen die Zeiten und das Systems eines Hobbs.'

34 ZH 5:264–5. 'Bey mir ist nicht so wol die Frage: was ist Vernunft? sondern vielmehr: was ist Sprache? und hier vermuthe ich den Grund aller Paralogismen und Antinomien, die man jener zur Last legt. Daher kommt es, daß man Wörter für Begriffe, und Begriffe für Dinge selbst hält. In Wörtern u. Begriffen ist keine Evidenz möglich, welche blos den Dingen und Sachen zukommt. Kein Genuß ergrübelt sich – und alle Dinge folglich auch das *Ens Entium* ist zum Genuß da, und nicht zur Speculation.'

35 N 3:284. 'Je länger man nachdenkt, desto tiefer und inniger man verstummt und alle Lust zu reden verliert.'

36 N 3:306. 'Das Christentum glaubt also nich an … fortdauernder Handlungen und Ceremonien, denen man eine geheime Kraft und unerklärbare Magie zutraut!'

37 N 3:300. 'alle gesellschaftliche Verträge beruhen, nach dem Rechte der Natur, auf dem sittlichen Vermögen Ja! oder Nein! zu sagen, und auf der sittlichen Nothwendigkeit, das gesagte Wort wahr zu machen. Das sittliche Vermögen Ja! oder Nein! zu sagen gründet sich auf den natürlichen Gebrauch der menschlichen Vernunft und Sprache; die sittliche Nothwendigkeit, sein gegebenes Wort zu erfüllen, drauf, daß unsere innere Willenserklärung nicht anders als mündlich oder schriftlich oder thätlich geäußert, geoffenbart und erkannt werden kann, und unsere Worte, als die natürlichen Zeichen unserer Gesinnungen, gleich Thaten, gelten müssen. Vernunft und Sprache sind allso [sic] das innere und äußere Band aller Gesellichkeit, und durch eine Scheidung oder Trennung desjenigen, was die Natur durch ihre Einsetzung zusammengefügt hat, wird Glaube und Treue aufgehoben, Lüge und Trug, Schand und Laster zu Mitteln der Glückseeligkeit gefirmelt und gestempelt.'

38 ZH 7:174 (to Jacobi). 'Geselligkeit ist das wahre Principium der Vernunft und Sprache, durch welche unsere Empfindungen und Vorstellungen modificirt werden.' We have had cause to visit this quotation before, in chapter 5.

39 N 3:300. 'Est enim *primum*, quod cernitur in universi generis humani societate, eiusque autem vinculum est RATIO et ORATIO, quae conciliat inter se homines coniungitque naturali quadam societate.' My translation

is derived from Cicero's *Offices*, trans. Thomas Cockman, 1.16, p. 23. *Golgotha* is peppered with references to Cicero. This is because Hamann had recently received (and devoured) a recent translation of the *Offices* by Mendelssohn's fellow enlightener, Christian Garve. The similarities between Cicero's moral optimism and Mendelssohn's views were not lost on Hamann. Hamann's favourable remarks concerning Cicero here are not due to a Hamannian identification with that writer. Rather, Hamann's use of Cicero is another example of metaschematism, as well as a playful rebuke of his century by employing one of its favourite ancients. Lothar Schreiner does make the interesting suggestion, however, that Hamann's reference to Cicero at the beginning of *Golgotha* is meant to indicate the difference between an ancient doctrine of *duties* and a modern doctrine of *rights*. *Golgotha und Scheblimini erklärt*, 57.

40 N 3:300. 'Vernunft und Sprache sind also das innere und äußere Band aller Geselligkeit.'
41 Genesis 2:19.
42 Jeremiah 3:4. He means our being made in the divine image.
43 As in 'a mighty fortress is our God.'
44 As in Helvétius, or the machinery of government. Schreiner writes 'Steuermaschine' – tax machine. Schreiner, *Golgotha und Scheblimini erklärt*, 91.
45 N 3:301. 'Er spricht: so geschichts! – 'und wie der Mensch alle Thiere nennen würde, sollten sie heissen.' – Nach diesem Vor- und Ebenbilde der Bestimmtheit sollte jedes Wort eines Mannes die Sache selbst seyn und bleiben. Auf diese Ähnlichkeit des Gepräges und der Überschrift mit dem Muster unseres Geschlechts und dem Meister unserer Jugend – auf dieses Recht der Natur, sich des Worts, als des eigentlichsten, edelsten und kräftigsten Mittels zur Offenbarung und Mittheilung unserer innigsten Willenserklärung zu bedienen, ist die Gültigkeit aller Verträge gegründet, und diese feste Burg der im Verborgenen liegenden Wahrheit ist aller welschen Praktik, Maschinerey, Schulfüchserey und Marktschreyerey überlegen. Der Misbrauch der Sprache und ihres natürlichen Zeugnisses ist also der gröbste Meineyd, und macht den Übertreter dieses ersten Gesetzes der Vernunft und ihrer Gerechtigkeit zum ärgsten Menschenfeinde.'

I have written 'political arithmetic' for *welschen Praktik*; this is a play on words. *Welsch* generally refers to non-German speaking Latin peoples, notably the French and the Italians, but most specifically the French. *Welsche Praktik* is a term for reckoning, or arithmetic often employed in trade, akin to the 'arithmétique politique' that Hamann denigrated so much.

46 ZH 7:176. 'Noch weiß ich weder was Hume noch was wir beide unter
   Glauben verstehen – und je mehr wir darüber reden oder schreiben würden, je weniger wird uns gelingen diesen Qvecksilber fest zu halten.'

47 Many writers have noted the affinity between Hamann's arguments on
   language and those of the late Wittgenstein. The first author to explore
   Hamann from the perspective of twentieth-century philosophy of
   language was James O'Flaherty, *Unity and Language*. Reception of this
   piece (and O'Flaherty's other work on Hamann) was relatively cold
   in Germany, where Hamann scholars, traditionally philologists and theologians, thought it a work overly influenced by problems in the anglophone analytic community. Berlin borrowed from O'Flaherty without
   really pursuing the latter's reflections on language and reason. Ian Hacking gets to the heart of the matter, setting aside the theological and philological matters that do not concern him. See 'How, Why, When, and
   Where?' 121–39.

48 ZH 7:169. 'Verstehst Du nun,' Hamann asked Jacobi, 'mein Sprachprincipi-
   um der Vernunft und daß ich mit Luther die ganze φφie [philosophie] zu
   einer Grammatik mache[?]'

49 See the inversion of Descartes' 'cogito ergo sum.' ZH 5:448.

50 Compare Wittgenstein's oblique attack on Hume in the *Philosophische Untersuchungen*, sec. 481: 'Wer sagte, er sei durch Angaben über Vergangenes
   nicht davon zu überzeugen, daß irgend etwas in Zukunft geschehen werde, – den würde ich nicht verstehen. Man könnte ihn fragen: was willst du
   denn hören? Was für Angaben nennst du Gründe dafür, das zu glauben?
   … Welche Art des Überzeugens erwartest du dir?' Hamann's response to
   Jacobi contains just such a sceptical undermining of the sceptical question
   itself. It is important to stab through the heart the beastly misinterpretation
   of Hamann than turns him into a philosophical heir of Hume.

51 N 1:302. 'Wie das Bild meines Gesichts im Wasser wiederscheint, so ist
   mein Ich in jedem Nebenmenschen zurück geworfen. Um mir dieses Ich so
   lieb als mein eigenes zu machen, hat die Vorsehung so viele Vortheile und
   Annehmlichkeit in der Gesellschaft der Menschen zu vereinigen gesucht.'
   I have rendered *Mensch* as 'Man,' although there is, of course, no essentially gendered implication. The term *humans*, or *humanity* would evoke certain eighteenth-century cosmopolitan notions with which Hamann would
   be ill associated.

52 N 3:296. '"Last sie nur bauen," würde ein Ammoniter sagen, "laßt sie nur bau-
   en; wenn Füchse hinauf zögen, di zerrissen wohl ihre steinerne Mauern."'

53 ZH 6:229–30. 'und ich habe nichts weder mit dem lebenden noch todten
   Juden und Rabbi zu tun, mag ihn weder bekehren noch verurtheilen,

sondern die Berliner sind meine Gegner und Philister, an denen ich mich rächen [werde].'

54 Hamann's allusion is to Nehemiah 13:24: 'And their children spake half in the speech of Ashdod, and could not speak in the Jews' language, but according to the language of each people.' N 3:316.

55 I can find no support for Ian Hacking's claim (presumably an extension of Berlin's) that Hamann was 'contemptuous of most European Jews in his own time.' See 'How, Why, When and Where?' 85.

56 N 3:313. 'Ausschließende Selbstliebe und Neid sind das Erbe und Gewerbe eines jüdischen Naturalismus.'

57 Strauss, *Gesammelte Schriften*, 3:766. Strauss's typical deprecation of all things plebeian aside, the thrust at Hamann's character is not entirely unjustified – Hamann was immoderately polemical. It is, however, entirely improbable that a 1930s Hamann would have donned a swastika. More likely he would have written irate letters to Hitler comparing him to Baal (see our chapter on despotism). Hamann nowhere mentions Luther's anti-Semitism, so we don't know what he thought of this.

58 It is this tactic that made Hamann's *Golgotha und Scheblimini* amenable to Carl Schmitt, who saw in the work a 'profound confrontation between German wisdom and the Jewish tactic of drawing distinctions' (*The Leviathan in the State Theory of Thomas Hobbes*, 60). This is discussed (and quoted) in Vatter, 'Strauss and Schmitt,' 193. As we will see in chapter 9, Hamann was not a German nationalist. Nor (as we have indicated) was his intention in *Golgotha* to write an anti-Judaic polemic. It should be noted that Hamann made similar polemical comments about Catholicism, clothing Freemasons and even enlightened theologians in the garb of Catholics. I will not take the time to demonstrate how he managed this trick, but it enabled him to lend to his polemic Reformation overtones. I mention this because Schmitt does not appear to have perceived in Hamann a 'profound confrontation between German wisdom and Catholicism'! Schmitt's interpretation is also hard to square with Hamann's view that Herder was correct to deprecate Mendelssohn as 'too much of a classic philosopher of the German nation' (ZH 6:229). Schmitt was incorrect to characterize Hamann as the champion of German wisdom against liberal Jews. I have indicated above that Hamann does not emerge as an altogether admirable figure in his treatment of Judaism, but I have also indicated how much he differed from Schmitt's anti-Semitism. George Schwab attempts to rehabilitate Schmitt by insisting that Schmitt was not an anti-Semite, but merely had an 'exclusionary theology' rather than a Nazi theory of race (Schmitt, *The Leviathan*, xxii). This is hard to reconcile with Schmitt's comments on

Stahl-Jolson, who converted to protestant Christianity, but whom Schmitt characterizes as a perpetual Jew who was both confused and deceitful, using baptism as a ticket into German mainstream society (ibid., 70). Stahl-Jolson's theological views apparently mean nothing where his race is concerned – he could not become 'somebody other than he actually was' (ibid.). Schmitt claims in passing (with evidence from such expert sources on Judaism as Luther's *Table Talk*) that the medieval Jewish cabbalists consider it 'kosher,' metaphorically speaking, to 'eat the flesh' of the self-destroying heathens (ibid., 8–9). No, Schmitt's book on Hobbes contains a great deal of garden-variety anti-Semitism; there is nothing in Hamann's oeuvre that approaches such racist malice, and a good deal that condemns it.

59 Alexander, *Johann Georg Hamann*, 121. (N 1:319.)

60 Levy, 'Hamann's Concept of Judaism and Controversy,' 296.

61 ZH 7:467 (to Jacobi). 'Laß jeder seine Haut zu Markt bringen. Was geht uns die bürgerl. Verfaßung der Juden und der Negern an? Ihre Stunde ist noch nicht kommen.'

62 Hamann had an uncomfortable moment at the aristocratic Kayserling's house, where the guests, presumably garden-variety anti-Semites, expressed disapproval for this ennoblement of the Jews. ZH 5:312.

63 Thus, despite the misquotation, Levy's interpretation of Hamann's position is basically correct: 'These thinkers, unlike people such as Lessing and Dohm, were simply indifferent to the problem of the civil rights of Jews.' Levy, 'Hamann's Concept of Judaism and Controversy,' 296.

64 One further note: Levy does not mention that this is a citation of Christ's response to his mother at the marriage of Cana (John 2:4). Mary alerts her son that there is no wine and he replies, 'Woman, what have I to do with thee? mine hour is not yet come.' The curious rebuke is often viewed as an indication of Christ's insistence on the secondary importance of worldly concerns. Nonetheless, I will avoid speculation on this quotation, given the number of thorny issues it raises. For instance, in John 2:4, Christ is the subject of both sentences, 'what is it to *me*' and '*my* time is not yet come.' (Luther's translation is 'Weib was habe ich mit dire zu schaffen? Meine Stunde ist noch nicht komen.' And Luther offers the alternate in the margin, 'was gehet es mich und dich an?' Luther, *Biblia*.) Oddly, in Hamann's letter, the first sentence refers to Christians like Hamann and his correspondent (what is it to *us*?), yet in the second sentence the role of Christ has been given to the 'Jews and Negroes' (*their* time is not yet come).

65 ZH, IV, 5. 'Was Moses am brennenden Busche sah, der brannte ohne zu verbrennen, das ist für uns das Judenthum und Christenthum, und der Stifter beider ist nicht ein Gott der Todten, sondern der Lebendigen.'

66 ZH, VII, 175. 'Bey einer andern Philosophie, bey einer andern Religion, ist eine andere Sprache unvermeidlich, andere Vorstellungen, andere Namen für dieselbe Gegenstände, die jeder aus dem Gesichtspunct seiner Nothwendigkeit oder Freywilligkeit bezeichnet.'

67 N 3:305. For more exclusionary, confessional content, see N 3:383, where Hamann insists that the Jews were stuck with the dead letter of the law, not having attended to Christ as they ought.

68 ZH 1:377 (to Kant, trans. Arnulf Zweig in *Immanuel Kant*, 50). Hamann felt guilty about having expressed himself with such heat in *Golgotha*, and after Mendelssohn's death he regretted never having written to him to assure him that he thought Mendelssohn should remain 'true to the faith of Moses and the prophets.' Hamann actually had the momentary idea that he should write to Mendelssohn's son urging him to maintain the faith of his fathers and not to fall into the trap of rational religion. That is, he was going to write to Mendelssohn's son in the spirit of friendship but basically to keep up his battle against the father's rationalist creed. Hamann called this a 'foolish idea,' and the observer has to agree: a more idiotic idea can hardly be imagined. Hamann fortunately had enough sense to abandon this plan (ZH 6:227). That said, this desire for Mendelssohn and his family to retain their faith should remind us both that Hamann's battle was with rational theology, not Judaism, and that Hamann did not think eternal damnation was on the horizon for non-Christians. As he said to Jacobi of Mendelssohn after his death, 'He is now, on the other side, closer to the truth than both of us' (ZH 6:222).

Chapter 9

1 On the relationship between philosophers and kings, see Andrew, *Patrons of Enlightenment*, esp. 75–6, 180–3.

2 Burke, 'Thoughts on the Cause of the Present Discontents,' in Edmund Burke, *Pre-Revolutionary Writings*, 187.

3 N 3:29–30; ZH 6:259, 276.

4 ZH 6:235. Cited in O'Flaherty, *Johann Georg Hamann*, 136.

5 See Johnson, *Frederick the Great*, esp. chap. 2.

6 Aristotle does not employ the term *despotism* to indicate a political regime, for the reason that *despot* is a term that belongs essentially to the household. However, he defines *tyranny* as a 'monarchic rule of a master over the political partnership.' *Politics*, 1279b16–17. See also 1295a17. There are, he notes, certain milder forms of tyranny that are run according to law, and thus that border on monarchy (*Politics*, 1285a29ff.). Despotic rule is

reasonable only for slavish Orientals who live in what is essentially a great household.

7 Montesquieu, *De l'esprit des lois*, II.i.

8 Montesquieu, *Lettres persanes*.

9 He distinguished between legal despotism, 'établi naturellement et *nécessairement* sur l'évidence des lois d'un ordre essentiel, et l'autre *arbitraire*, fabriqué par l'opinion, pour prêter à tous les désordres, à tous les écarts dont l'ignorance la rend susceptible.' *Ordre naturel et essentiel des sociétés politiques*, 177. For most, the defining feature of despotism was its arbitrary nature.

10 Hobbes, *Leviathan*, pt 2, chap. 20: 'In summe, the Rights and Consequences of both *Paternal* and *Despotical* Dominion, are the very same with those of a Soveraign by Institution.'

11 Voltaire, *The A B C, or Dialogues between A B C*, first conversation, 98.

12 Ibid., third and fourth conversations, 106–19.

13 Fritz Hartung locates the origin of the term in the nineteenth-century historian W. Roscher. 'Der aufgeklärter Absolutismus,' 123.

14 Since we have quoted Montesquieu, it is worth noting that the author of *De l'esprit des lois* would have treated 'Enlightened absolutism' as a short step from despotism. Common to enlightened absolutists (and particularly striking in the figure of Joseph II) was the desire to undermine the aristocracy in the interests of centralization. Frederick II was aware of the administrative problems raised by this policy, and he did not push it too far, but the spirit of centralization was nonetheless clear in all of his writings. Montesquieu thought that the marginalization of the nobles was a despotic practice, but not all Enlightenment writers shared Montesquieu's liberal arguments about the need for power to be dispersed. Voltaire was fully capable of wedding his admiration of 'English liberty' to his celebration of Frederick. He even expressed the desire to have 'le Roi Prusse pour maître, et le peuple anglais pour concitoyen.' Quoted in Schröder, 'Siècle de *Frédéric II*,' 31.

15 Hubatsch, *Frederick the Great of Prussia*, 7–9.

16 Johnson, *Frederick the Great*, speaks of an 'administrative stalemate.' 32ff.

17 Frederick II, *Oeuvres Complettes*, vol. 8, chap. 26. Nonetheless, Frederick could probably appeal to his justification of 'les guerres de précaution' (p. 125), which are offensive but directed against a perceived threat. The lofty rhetoric of the *Anti-Machiavel* should not blind us entirely to its numerous passages that smack of *raison d'état*.

18 Ibid., 5:37–60.

19 Ibid., 5:43.

20 Ibid., 5:58.

21 Although we note that he waited a decade after the king's death to do so. In *Zum ewigen Frieden* he praised Frederick who 'wenigstens *sagte:* er sei bloß der oberste Diener des Staats,' 28 (italics in original).

22 Frederick II, 5:40.

23 Ibid., 57.

24 Ibid., 54.

25 Ibid., 46. Similarly, one thinks of Hobbes's doctrine of natural punishments.

26 Quastana, *Voltaire et l'absolutisme éclairé*, 29.

27 Frederick II, *Die politischen Testamente Friedrichs des Grossen*, 38. On the same page, he repeats his favourite line about being the 'first servant of the state.'

28 Ibid., 31.

29 Ibid., 32.

30 He held the firm belief, so common in the eighteenth century, that a healthy country was a populous country. However, Frederick increased his population at the same time as he occasioned the death of hundreds of thousands of his subjects: the conquest of Silesia did increase the number of his subjects.

31 Schieder, *Frederick the Great*, 216.

32 Sinn and Sinn, *Der Alltag in Preußen*, 324. This policy had to wait until the 1960s to be put into practice.

33 Ausubel, *Superman*, 760–1.

34 It should be said that Frederick's vaunted tolerance was not peculiar to him; different degrees of religious toleration had been embraced by different regimes for economic purposes for quite some time. Frederick wrote of the Jews, 'Les juifs sont de toutes ces sectes la plus dangereuse, à cause qu'ils font tort au négoce des Chrétiens, et qu'ils sont inutiles à l'État. Nous avons besoin de cette nation pour faire un certain commerce en Pologne, mais il faut empêcher que leur nombre n'augmente, et les mettre, non pas à un certain nombre de familles, mais à un nombre de têtes, et resserer leur commerce, les empêcher de faire des entreprises en gros, pour qu'ils ne soient que détailleurs.' *Die politischen Testamente Friedrichs des Grossen*, 31. Desperate though he was for people, he forbade most of his Jewish subjects to have children.

35 Lessing in a letter to Nicolai (1769), in Frederick II, *Friedrich II*, 50–1.

36 Frederick II, 'Sur l'éducation,' in *Oeuvres Complettes*, 7:228.

37 As Fritz Hartung notes, 'es läßt sich nicht leugnen, daß der persönliche Anteil Friedrichs an der Pflege des Schulwesens in Preußen auch nach 1763 sehr gering gewesen ist.' 'Der aufgeklärte Absolutismus,' 135; Lentin, *Enlightened Absolutism*, xvi.

38 Hartung, 'Der aufgeklärter Absolutismus,' 134–5.
39 Even Peter Gay, the *philosophes*' greatest champion, notes this point, although he does not describe it as part of the Enlightenment project, but rather as a 'failure' that is 'the central weakness in the philosophes' political thought.' In his view, the heroes of the eighteenth century did not go where their program logically should have led them. One wonders if the fault belongs to their limitations or to Gay's interpretation. See *The Enlightenment*, 522.
40 Frederick II, *Oeuvres Complettes*, 3:200. 'Examen de l'essai sur les prejugés.'
41 Ibid., 3:255.
42 Sinn and Sinn, *Der Alltag in Preußen*, 279.
43 Frederick II, *Oeuvres Complettes*, 3:190.
44 Ibid., 3:195. Schoolmasters must be 'especially careful that the common people remain attached to religion and do not steal and murder.' Quoted in Melton, *Absolutism and the Eighteenth-Century Origins of Compulsory Schooling*, 115.
45 Holborn notes in *A History of Modern Germany: 1648–1840* that Frederick devoted only 2 per cent of public expenditure to his court, compared to the 6 per cent of Maria Theresa (197). However, if one allows for the desperate financial position of Prussia in the first twenty years of his reign and the comparatively high amount of military spending, Frederick's opera house or his 1500 jewel-encrusted snuff boxes appear somewhat decadent, as does his massive palace built just when the country was suffering the worst possible devastation after its 'success' in the Seven Years' War. Mitford, *Frederick the Great*, 151.
46 N 2:297. This vitriol is a play on Revelation 2:9, 3:9.
47 Frederick had written, 'que nous ayons des Médicis, et nous verrons éclore des génies.' *Oeuvres Complettes*, 7:352.
48 He wrote, 'Voici mon principe: si nous ne pouvons pas gagner par nos exportations, diminuons nos pertes par tous les articles que les mains d'hommes peuvent ouvrager.' *Die politischen Testamente Friedrichs des Grossen*, 125.
49 N 2:317. Hamann's piece 'Le kermes du nord ou la cochenille de pologne' bears the latin epigraph from Psalm 22, 'I am a worm and no man.' It is clear who Hamann thought would be squeezed! Kermes is a type of worm or caterpillar used in the manufacturing of dye.
50 Schieder, *Frederick the Great*, 196–212.
51 If he thought that it was perfectly enlightened to retain concern for the balance of payments, this should merely serve as a reminder that the Enlightenment, as a movement, had not settled on the question of the means to the

accepted end. Indeed, Frederick's views were probably mainstream enlightened opinion. Daniel Brewer describes mercantilism as the *Encyclopédie*'s primary economic doctrine. *Discourse of Enlightenment*, 31.

52 Frederick II, *Die politischen Testamente Friedrichs des Grossen*, 123.

53 Frederick II, *Oeuvres Complettes*, 6:306.

54 ZH 6:326. 'Unser Salomo soll sich sehr erholen – desto beßer für mich. Den Zusammenhang oder der Harmoniam praestabilitam dieses Windes mit meiner Muse weiß ich mir selbst nicht zu erklären.' See also 423.

55 ZH 4:253. 'daß de *Salomon du Nord* ein Nebenbuler des Magus in Norden geworden.'

56 This brief list is from Quastana, *Voltaire et l'absolutisme éclairé*, 27.

57 Orbilius was Horace's grammar teacher who whipped his students. The name has become synonymous with the brutal teacher. N 6:277.

58 Literally, an 'oil idol.' This term was used by reformers (especially Luther) to mock Catholic priests, who were anointed with oil.

59 Nadler, *Johann Georg Hamann*, 375.

60 N 5:225–42. This was his supplement to a translation he made of the writer Dangeuil.

61 ZH 4:389. 'Ohne einen allergnädigsten Widerruff des Verbots pollnische Ochsen einzuführen laufen wir Gefahr in 8 oder 14 Tagen kein Fleisch mehr in der Stadt zu haben.'

62 Aside from the widespread rumours of Frederick's homosexuality, or the scandal of prince Henry's lavish expenses occasioned by his male lover, Frederick in general was reputed to be indulgent of lax sexual mores. He slept with his favourite greyhound, whom others nicknamed 'Mme De Pompadour,' and he was widely seen as indulgent of every type of vice. Coming upon a soldier in chains, Frederick inquired into the man's crime. He was informed that the soldier had been found *in flagrante delicto* with his horse. Frederick thought the punishment inappropriate: 'Fool – don't put him in irons, put him in the infantry.' Mitford, *Frederick the Great*, 153, 149. Anecdotes aside, we might note that at the beginning of Frederick's reign there were three whorehouses in Berlin; at the end, there were over a hundred. See Sinn and Sinn, *Der Alltag in Preußen*, 150. This was probably a result of having one-sixth of the adult male population in uniform (see Frederick's *Testament politique*, 139). However, although large armies and prostitution tend to be related, Frederick William also had an enormous army, so there was clearly some other factor accounting for the increase, and Hamann may not have been wrong to think that the tone of the court was responsible for altered mores.

63 Hamann seduced (or was seduced by) his ailing father's caretaker and nurse. He remained with her, she bore him four children, and they led a relatively respectable bourgeois life together, but he never married her. The reasons remain obscure.

64 Nadler, *Johann Georg Hamann*, 375.

65 Kant, *Briefwechsel*, 5–6. He didn't receive it.

66 Fink-Langlois, 'Le Kermes du nord ou la chochenille de Pologne,' 207. '[Es ging] Hamann wahrscheinlich darum, sowohl auf der sozialen wie auf der nationalen Ebene den Minderwertigkeitskomplex der Deutschen zu bekämpfen.'

67 Cited in Nadler, *Johann Georg Hamann*, 376. 'Mein Patriotismus ist aus ebensoviel Liebe als Haß meines Vaterlandes zusammengesetzt.'

68 Ibid. 'Aus Neigung hab ich mein Vaterland niemals geliebt, aber je länger, je mehr aus Mitleiden.'

69 ZH 6:235. 'Es war dem Herzogtum keine solche Schande von Pohlen abzu-hängen, als es dem Königreich ein Unglück ist von der Politik der Chal-däer im deutschen römischen Reich.' Nadler finds this passage most revealing, *Johann Georg Hamann*, 375.

70 Johnson, *Frederick the Great*, 200–9; see also Hubatsch *Frederick the Great of Prussia*, 144–6.

71 Johnson, *Frederick the Great*, 200, 204.

72 ZH 4:463, 469. We should recall that 'arithmétique politique' was not a Ha-mannian neologism, but the term used to refer to the practical science of political economy. Hamann would, however, express rage at the view that politics could be arranged in a mathematical manner. This was not an es-sentially counter-Enlightened position, however. Let us recall the wide-spread opposition to 'esprit de systèmes.' Diderot's encyclopaedia entry on 'arithmétique politique' expresses similar reservations about the hubris of the physiocrats.

73 ZH 5:3. The Malachi citation is the following: 'Behold, I will send you Elijah the prophet before the coming of the great and dreadful day of the LORD: And he shall turn the heart of the fathers to the children, and the heart of the children to their fathers, lest I come and smite the earth with a curse.'

74 ZH 5:18. 'weder Stimme noch Antwort noch Aufmerken von Baal.'

75 ZH 5:61. Frederick was constantly trying to find productive work for the numerous invalid soldiers created by his wars.

76 N 3:52.

77 N 3:300.

78 ZH 3:24. He specified that his 'Au Salomon Prusse,' which was originally titled 'L'Apocalypse du Salomon du Nord!' was intended 'für das

Schlafzimmer des Neugebornen Königes von Preußen.' He was most
upset that he could find no publisher for this, the clearest of his anti-
Frederickian writings.

79 N 2:289.

80 ZH 3:62. The writer was Karl Gottlieb Guichard (whom the king called, af-
fectionately, 'Quintus Icilius') an author on military history. See N 6:160–1.
The 'Ecce' to which he refers was part of the *lettres perdues*. It consists of a
few pages in which Hamann revealed himself, enumerating his expenses
and indicating how much he had lost in the service of the king. It is a most
bizarre document, for reasons we have not the space to enter into here.

81 ZH 3:256.

82 Kant, 'Was ist Aufklärung,' in *Was ist Aufklärung*, 9–17.

83 ZH 5:290. 'Wozu verfährt der Chiliast [Kant, whom Hamann accused of a
Kosmopolitischplatonischen Chiliasmus] mit diesem Knaben Absalom so
säuberlich? Weil er sich selbst zu der Claße der Vormünder zählt, und sich
gegen unmündige Leser dadurch ein Ansehen geben will.'

84 Ibid., 291–2. See Matthew 18:3, 'Except ye be converted, and become as little children, ye shall not enter into the kingdom of heaven.' 19:14; Mark
10:14; Luke 18:16, as well as various references to children of God.

85 Recall Hamann's earlier conflict with Kant over the education of children.
ZH 1:444–54.

86 In this passage, Hamann championed Plato's egalitarianism in Book V of
the *Republic*, and he defended his daughters against the guardianship of
Kantians, who elevate bachelorhood to a universal maxim. Nonetheless,
we ought not to turn Hamann into a hero of emancipation, as he implies
elsewhere that there is a natural hierarchy in the household. He spent his
life with a peasant woman, and the difference in their station seemed to
have suited him perfectly. In addition, he certainly did not give the same
type of literary education to his daughters as he gave to his son (who was
taught French, Greek, Latin, Polish, Italian, English). For a Königsberg citizen who had something interesting to say about gender, see the work of
the mayor, Theodor von Hippel, who called for the complete civic emancipation of women.

87 Psalms 111:10; Proverbs 1:7, 9:10.

88 ZH 5:291. 'Meine Verklärung der Kantschen Erklärung läuft darauf hinaus,
daß wahre Aufklärung in einem Ausgange des unmündigen Menschen
aus einer allerhöchst selbst verschuldeten Vormundschaft bestehe. Die
Furcht des Herrn ist der Weisheit Anfang – und diese Weisheit mach uns
zu feig zu lügen und faul zu dichten – desto muthiger gegen Vormünder,
die höchstens den Leib tödten und den Beutel aussaugen können – desto

barmherziger gegen unsere unmündige Mitbrüder und fruchtbarer an guten Werken der Unsterblichkeit.'

89 ZH 7:464. 'Jeder thue seinem Beruff Gnüge aud Liebe der offentl. Ordnung und allgemeinen Ruhe.'

90 Kant claimed explicitly that philosophers should not *be* kings, but that they should be allowed to debate openly such that their principles would be available as a light to kings. *Zum ewigen Frieden*, 52.

91 Recall that the tension between the Platonism of the divine Logos and the radical anti-Platonism of Hamann's linguistic theory are one of the more interesting tensions in his thought.

92 Hegel, 'Über Hamanns Schriften' in *Sämtliche Werke*, 20:256–7. But Hegel did not appreciate the forays into personal matters such as the joke about the FOOI FOOI: 'The I of the particular will leads him to the consequence, to the thought of the monarchical principle, but his stressful Accise-existence makes him turn this into farce.' If we do want to roll our eyes at Hamann's references to Naboth's vineyard, etc., we must nonetheless insist once again on the gulf separating Hegel's attempt to embrace the particular within a greater Enlightenment and Hamann's treatment of such a rationalism as impious and unwarranted.

93 N 3:284. See Daniel 5:25–8. The prophet Daniel interprets the words written on Belshazzar's wall, 'MENE MENE TEKEL, UPHARSIN' as 'God hath numbered thy kingdom, and finished it … Thou art weighed in the balances, and art found wanting.'

94 N 3:284. 'jenen allgemeinen und zum Katholicismo und Despotismo nothwendigen und unfehlbaren Stein der Weisen, dem die Religion ihre Heiligkeit und die Gesetzgebung ihre Majestät flugs unterwerfen wird.' The form of this phrase is drawn from the famous footnote in the preface to the first crtitique in which Kant speaks of his 'era of critique.' See Kant, *Kritik der reinen Vernunft* (Stuttgart: Reclam) A:xi.

95 N 3:314.

96 N 4:417.

97 N 2:356. His reference to *Émile* here is more of an aspersion on Enlightened education than a mature reflection on Rousseau. There is a great deal in *Émile* with which Hamann ought to have agreed. Nonetheless, the natural religion expressed by the Savoyard vicar, despite its insistence on the inner voice, must have appeared to Hamann as much closer to the empty deism of the *philosophes* than to his own biblically centred faith.

98 Blum, *La vie et l'oeuvre*, 362. N 3:192.

99 N 2:356. 'Jedem Vater des Vaterlandes und jedem Mitbürger sollte die Erziehung am Herzen liegen … Nicht nur die üppige Mammons- und

sclavische Waffendienst, ihr künstlischer Fleiß und Adel, sondern auch die Chimäre der schönen Natur, des guten Geschmacks und der gesunden Vernunft haben Vorutheile eingeführt, welche die Lebensgeister des menschlichen Geschlechts und die Wohlfart der bürgerlichen Gesellschaft theils erschöpfen, theils in der Geburt ersticken.'

100 Frederick II, 'Essai sur l'amour propre,' 341–54.

101 Ibid., 345–6.

102 N 4:358. Trans. Sheridan, *Satires of Juvenal*, 29. The citations are identified in Baur, *Johann Georg Hamann*, 172–80. Baur's treatment of this review is excellent, and his work on Hamann's newspaper writings is unsurpassed.

103 N 4:358. 'Unser Kopf ist weder glücklich genug organisiert noch unsere Einbildungskraft so herkulisch … daß wir durch alle Labyrinthe, Widersprüche, Zweideutigkeiten, Mißverständnisse, Einfälle, Vorurtheile, Spitzfindigkeiten, Zweifel, Einwürfe, Dunkelheiten, Räthsel, Geheimnisse u.s.f. der Selbstliebe bis zu dem wo nicht metaphysischen, doch politischen Heiligthum der Tugend hindurch dringen können. So wie wir also mit Empfindungen einer dankbaren Bewunderung den denkwürdigen Versuch des weisen Gesetzgebers mitgetheilt haben; … Wohl dem Volk, das [sic] alle heroische und plebeje Tugenden des Clima, des Organismus und der Industrie in Unendliche zu vermehren sucht! aber wohl dem Volk, dessen Fürst ein Philosoph und Adept ist, der ihren Honig, ihre Wolle und ihr Obst durch ein großmüthiges: Sic vos non vobis in das blinde allgemeine Glück des Staats und güldener oder seidener Zeiten zu verwandeln weiß.' 'Sic vos non vobis' may be translated as 'you [do this] but not for yourselves.' Nadler gives the reference to Virgil: 'so you don't make your honey for yourselves, you bees.' N 6:353.

104 N 4:358. Persius, *The Satires of A. Persius Flaccus*, Satire III, ll. 35–8, p. 57.

105 N 2:206. 'Ist der Bauch euer Gott: so stehen selbst die Haare eures Hauptes unter seiner Vormundschaft. Jede Kreatur wird wechselsweise euer Schlachtopfer und euer Götze.'

106 N 3:240. 'Er treibt das Vorurtheil des Altertums und der Gewohnheit aus durch Vorurtheile der Eigenliebe, Neuheit oder der eigene Erfindung.'

107 Early in his fight with Behrens, he had summed up his disapproval of the epicurean basis of commercial cosmopolitanism: 'Er [Behrens] liebt das Menschliche Geschlecht wie der Franzmann das Frauenzimmer, zu seinem bloßen Selbstgenuß und auf Rechnung Ihrer Tugend und Ehre.' ZH 1:375. Commercial cosmopolitan love of humanity is not real love.

108 N 3:222. 'Das grosse politische Schneidergeheimniß Menschen zu machen und zu verklären, wär's auch durch eine Wendung des lumpigten

Christentums zum Unterfutter der purpurnen Selbstliebe, nach dem
güldnen Naturgesetz der Sparsamkeit, um durch schnelle, zuverläßig,
ausgebreitete und dauerhafte Eindrücke von Meteoren und Antithesen
dem Zeus gleich zu sein.'

109 N 3:316. 'Statt Tempels, Schulen, die dem Geburtsort des Erhöhten ähn-
lich sind!'

110 N 3:202. 'Todter und unfruchtbarer Wohlstand, scheinheiliger Pharisäer
unsers Jahrhunderts! Deine moralische und bürgerliche Vorurtheile, und
der hohe Geschmack oder Tand ihrer Verdienste ist nichts als Caviar des
Leviathans, der hoch in den Wellen des Luftkreises [Ephesians 2:2]
herrscht.' The passage in Ephesians is the following: 'Time past ye
walked according to the course of this world, according to *the prince of the
power of the air*, the spirit that now worketh in the children of disobedi-
ence / Among whom also we all had our conversation in times past in
the lusts of our flesh, fulfilling the desires of the flesh and of the mind;
and were by nature the children of wrath, even as others.'

111 N 3:158. Elfriede Büchsel identifies the passage from which this cento is
derived, *Über den Ursprung der Sprache*, 104.

112 N 2:49.

113 N 2:293.

114 N 2:60. 'Nach dem heutigen Plan der Welt bleibt die Kunst Gold zu
machen also mit Recht das höchste Project und höchste Gut unserer
Staatsklugen.'

115 Matthew 6:28–9 'And why take ye thought for raiment? Consider the lilies of the field, how they grow; they toil not, neither do they spin: / And
yet I say unto you, That even Solomon in all his glory was not arrayed
like one of these.'

116 N 2:79. 'Einer Frau, welche die Haushaltung eines Philosophen führen …
ist freylich die Zeit zu edel, Wortspiele zu ersinnen und Blumen zu reden.'

117 Early on, Hamann laid out this opposition to his friend Lindner, describing the practical absurdity of the prophets' tirades in the eyes of the corrupted people. ZH 1:412.

118 Frederick II, *Oeuvres Complettes*, 6:306.

119 N 2:294.

120 N 2:293.

121 ZH 6:533. 'Trotz seinem guten Willen eines Anti– wurde er durch ein
Schicksal u Misverständnis ein Metamachiavell.' Elsewhere he decried
'the antimachiavellian eloquence of Demosthenes and the silver quincy.'
N 3:32. Plutarch reports that Demosthenes, who had spoken loudly
against one Harpalus, was one day curiously silent on the matter. He

claimed that he had a quincy (tonsillitis); the townspeople knew that he had been bribed by Harpalus, and called it his 'silver quincy.' The implication is clear: Frederick dropped his virtuous rhetoric just as soon as he saw that he might profit from an unjust action.

122 As Voltaire said, 'Il parut bientôt que Frédéric II, roi de Pruss, n'était pas aussi ennemi de Machiavel que le prince royal avait paru l'être.' *Mémoires*, 32–3.

123 Schieder, *Frederick the Great*, 260.

124 Frederick II, *Oeuvres Complettes*, 8:113.

125 N 3:55. Frederick's verse is as follows: 'Si quelque jour il vous prend fantaisie / D'imaginer un ragoût de momie, En l'apprêtant de ce goût sûr & fin, / Et des extraits produits par la chymie; / L'illusion, le prestige & la faim / Nous rendront tous peut-être antropophages [sic].' And later, 'ses [Noel's] mets exquis amorçant les Prussiens, / Les ont changés en Epicuriens.' Frederick II, *Oeuvres Complettes*, 1:277.

126 N 3:143–4. 'Weil aber der Begriff des Geistes, vermöge der neusten philosophischen Offenbarungen, in einem guten Löffelvoll Grütze besteht, den jeder *homunculus* eines starken und schönen Geistes unter seinem goldenen Haarschädel oder seiner silbernen Glatze mit sich führt, und durch das Monopol seiner Grütze, die schon an sich lichtscheue Geisterwelt zu Contraband macht, um mit den Kräften der gegenwärtigern Körperwelt desto baarer wuchern zu können: so erlauben Sie mir ad imitationem großer Farren und weißer Ochsen.' I omit the lengthy remainder of the sentence to save the reader trouble. Note that 'wuchern,' which I have translated as 'grow' has a double meaning – it can also refer to usury.

127 Hobbes's anti-Machiavellian argument that the reduction of superstition would augment the fear of the sword was not confined to him. Bayle made a similar claim (with slightly more ambiguous purpose) in the *Pensées diverses*, vol. 1, sec. 131–2. Frederick himself thought that the 'brutish,' by which he meant the religious, were more obstinate. Frederick II, *Oeuvres Complettes*, 3:255. 'l'expérience prouve que plus le peuple est abruti, plus il est capricieux et obstiné!'

128 N 3:27.

129 N 2:282.

130 See Frederick's eulogy in La Mettrie, *Man: A Machine*, 8–9.

131 N 3:320.

132 N 3:22. 'Wäre ich ein gehaltiger *Accademico* … so würde es mir leicht seyn, die Physiognomien menschlicher Zungen mit den Stimmen der Thiere zu vergleichen.'

133 Today, we might complain about the inordinate amount of government money being spent on Hamann studies.

134 Perhaps Hamann was too hasty in condemning all who received patronage. For an interesting meditation on this problem, see Andrew, *Patrons of Enlightenment*. One cannot charge Hamann with hypocrisy here, however. The bulk of his talents lay in the literary world, but Hamann refused to pursue a literary or university career, despite the help and encouragement that Kant was willing to give. He felt that this path would make him subservient to the intellectual fashions of his century, and he preferred to retain the independence of his personal study. He did, however, accept gifts from some admirers late in his life (which he spent on the education of his daughter), and thus cannot be said to have existed in complete economic independence.

135 N 2:365. See also N 3:310, on the 'Imperator zu Pekin.'

136 ZH 4:260. 'Den Orbil der Litterature Tudesque habe zweymal im Original und ebensoviel mal in Uebersetzung gelesen. Was Sie vom *Despotismo* des Geschmacks sagen, ist wirklich seine Absicht, den welschen einzuführen. Alles soll ein Leisten, ein Schuh seyn, Fabrike u Heerdienst einer Eitelkeit, und seines Götzens Mäusim. Das philosophische Antichristentum ist an die Stelle des Päbstischen getreten, und die Philosophie ist der Koran des Lügenpropheten und seines Islamismus.'

137 See, for instance, N 3:107.

138 N 3:100. 'Stumme Gräuel und Seelenmord!' This passage refers not to Frederick's proposed reform, but to a proposition to rationalize German spelling by removing unpronounced *h*'s.

139 N 3:231. 'Ohne Sprache hätten wir keine Vernunft, ohne Vernunft keine Religion, und ohne diese drey wesentliche Bestandtheile unserer Natur weder Geist noch Band der Gesellschaft.'

140 Ibid.

141 ZH 4:409. 'Alle unsere Philosophen mit ihrer englischen Beredsamkeit sind nichts als Parasiten und Pantomimen, alle unsere Kunst- und Scharfrichter nichts als Nicolaiten, alle unsere Reformatoren der Justitz, der barmherzigen Plusmacherey des Glaubens im Handel und Wandel, nichts als Balhorne im Abc und EinmalEins.' I render 'Balhorne' 'ignorant, presumptuous meddlers': Ballhorn was a printer and book editor who had 'corrected' a book, giving it numerous significant mistakes. The name was proverbial for someone who made something worse in attempting to improve it.

142 See Hubatsch, *Frederick the Great*, 216–7. Also Mitford, *Frederick the Great*, 281. The case involved a miller who sued a local magnate for having

dammed the river on which his mill lay, thereby destroying his livelihood and rendering him unable to pay his rent. The case had gone through several courts, with each finding in favour of the noble landowner. Frederick decided to make an example of these corrupt judges who had so unjustly cheated Arnold. Subsequent investigation discovered that Arnold's mill was upstream from the diversion of water.

143 I quote from an English translation. Anonymous, *Royal Matins*, 23. The book is of uncertain authorship, although it has been attributed both to Voltaire and (what seems more likely) to Benedetto Patono, a Prussian officer. Büchsel argues that Hamann was taken in by the prank; Hamann certainly chose to treat the text as authentic. Considering the boldness of some of Frederick's authentic writings, one could forgive a reader for being fooled by this satire. Nonetheless, the piece is a little too obvious, and we need not necessarily accept Büchsel's evidence. Büchsel quotes from a 1765 letter to Herder, 'Daß unser König *les Matinées* und einen Auszug des Bayle ausgegeben, wird Ihnen bekannt seyn,' but fails to quote the rest of the sentence: 'aber noch nichts davon gesehen.' ZH 2:332. See Büchsel, *Über den Ursprung der Sprache*, 186.

144 See Unger, *Hamann und die Aufklärung*, chap. 17, n. 86. (see also 2:215). Unger notes that Cocceji's reforms had recently occurred, and that there were numerous reforms of the marriage laws. These new laws were quite humane and indicated a certain tolerance of 'suicide, adultery, incest, sodomy, blasphemy, fornication.' This merely reinforced Hamann's conservative view that the state was educating its citizens for libertinage. However, the aspect of the argument that I wish to emphasize here is the anti-legalism of Hamann's response to the *Corporis Juris Fridericiani*.

145 N 3:200.

146 N 2:293. For his reaction to Montesquieu, see N 3:158, where he treats Montesquieu's *Spirit of the Laws* as typical of the works that undermine divine law in the name of human law.

147 One is tempted to speculate that Hamann's 'marriage of conscience' was an example of him living up to the spirit of the law, and not the letter. Presumably he thought that he had circumcised his heart.

148 N 3:200. 'Weil der Ehstand der Köstliche Grund und Eckstein der ganzen Gesellschaft ist: so offenbart sich der menschenfeindliche Geist unsers Jahrhunderts am allerstärksten in den Ehgesetzen.'

149 See note 121. Frederick would have thought the first charge bizarre. He was an eighteenth-century Trudeau, who thought the state had little place in the bedrooms of the nation. If Hamann's argument here has a modern corollary, it would probably be that of social conservatives who are

obsessed with the liberalization of marriage laws and consider the state's increasing permissiveness to be an attack on the institution of marriage itself. However, on the subject of homosexuality, Hamann was somewhat ambiguous, for while he loved to laugh at Frederick's love of the flute, he himself had probably had a homosexual affair in London, and he defended Socrates' love of young men. N 2:68.

150   N 3:29–30. See Hamann, *Ausgewählte Schriften*, 145n37. The first part of the sentence is from the *Matinées Royales*. Hamann's scattered references to Frederick's homosexuality are treated as 'arbitrary imputations' by O'Flaherty, *The Quarrel of Reason with Itself*, 142. These were, however, not arbitrary, and they were terribly common. Voltaire popularized this rumour in his *Mémoires*. Voltaire (who was writing in order to avenge himself on the king) was not content with making Frederick a sodomite, preferring to ascribe to his royal highness the greater indignity of a catamite (43). One might be tempted to ascribe this to Voltaire's preference for the pagans over the Christians. In any case, Voltaire's text was widely circulated. Herder wrote to Hamann about it in 1784, but did not send a copy for fear that the Prussian post would intercept it and that Hamann would be severely punished (ZH 5:195). Like many, Herder was sceptical of the king of Prussia's vaunted toleration.

151   N 3:164.

152   N 3:29–30.

153   N 3:117. Isaiah Berlin entirely misses the point in his treatment of Hamann's monism. He correctly notes, 'The notion of confining [God] to his "sphere," of creating frontiers against his worship, is a blasphemy and self-deception.' But he then concludes, 'If this leads to confusion of private and public, to interference and intolerance, Hamann does not mind at all: toleration of differences is a denial of their importance.' *Magus of the North*, 47. If this were Hamann's feeling, one wonders why he defended Mendelssohn's decision not to convert to Christianity. ZH 5:71–2; ZH 4:5. More importantly, Berlin has completely missed the point of Hamann's opposition to the Enlightenment discourse of tolerance. Hamann argued that it was both hypocritical (as it hid conscious political decisions about the education of the populace) and intolerant of faith claims (since it leapt invariably to the accusation of fanaticism). He thought that the Enlightenment defence of tolerance was a 'Trojan horse' that would break into the city of God in order to deliver it to its enemies. N 3:226. Hamann thought that tolerance was a Christian duty (see chapter 7). He championed an established religion, but he emphasized the tortuous relationship between the sword and the cross to such an extent that he questioned

whether the sword could ever do anything but abuse or neglect faith. Thus, the Christian in society must hope to be *tolerated*, as he is always in opposition.

154 N 2:319.

155 Strässle, *Geschicht, geschichtliches Verstehen und Geschichtsschreibung*, 157–8.

156 Bayer, *Zeitgenosse im Widerspruch*, 134–5.

157 N 3:37.

158 N 3:32.

159 N 3:28. 'zwischen Fritz in der Purpurwiege und Fritz in *praesepio*.' Büchsel writes that *praesepio* is a symbol for poverty. (Büchsel, *Biblisches Zeugnis und Sprachgestalt*, 182) It is even more – it is the Latin for the 'swaddling clothes' in which the Christ child is wrapped, Luke 2:7. It goes without saying that Fritz is the standard nickname for Frederick.

160 Berlin, *Magus of the North*, 111; Blum, *La vie et l'oeuvre de J.G. Hamann*, 350. Blum's judgment is usually sound, but we cannot agree with his assessment that Hamann 'gémissait du désaccord qu'il avait entre ses devoirs de croyant et de sujet.' Hamann had little to say about resistance, and he was equally unforthcoming on the duties of obedience. But Blum makes the striking admission concerning his own argument that 'tout cela n'est que commentaire et déduction.'

161 ZH 4:295. In a letter to Herder he expresses the hope that 'Saul will fall on his sword' and cites Ezekiel 31, about the Pharaoh being cast down to hell. ZH 4:356. He expresses the wish that Jeremiah's prophesy will be realized. The prophecy reads, 'Behold, I will feed them with wormwood, and make them drink the water of gall: for from the prophets of Jerusalem is profaneness gone forth into all the land.' ZH 5:298. He speaks about the 'oil idol ... [and] his French scorpions against whom I have sworn a deadly hatred.'

162 ZH 7:464. 'Ich halte alle Regierungsformen für gleichgiltig, und bin gewiß daß alle Produkte und Ungeheuer der Gesellschaft wieder Natur Producte eines höheren Willens sind, den wir anzubeten und nicht zu richten Gewißen und Noth und Klugheit verpflichtet.'

163 ZH 7:464. 'Ein Republicaner liebe sein freyes Vaterland und der Unterthan eines Monarchen trage sein Joch ohne gegen den Stachel zu löcken.'

164 ZH 7:464. 'Hat der Hausvater mit dem Unkraute Geduld und Nachsicht: so mag ein jeder für seinen Acker und Garten sorgen.' The reference is to the parable of the wheat and the tares (Matthew 13:25–30). See his use of the same defence for toleration, N 3:232.

165 ZH 7:464. 'Alle Monarchen sind in meinen Augen Schattenbilder der güldnen Zeit, wo Ein Hirt und Eine Heerde seyn wird.'

166 Frederick II, *Ouevres primitives*, 429.

167 Note the play upon 'douteuse': instead of rendering it 'Zweifelhaft,' Hamann puts 'Zweideutig,' which, while having a similar connotation of 'ambiguous' or 'unknown,' clearly points to the dual nature of Christ, his humanity and divinity.

168 N 3:145. 'Wenn allso [sic] der Weg des Christentums noch immer eine Secte heißen soll; so verdient selbige vorzüglich als eine politische betrachtet zu werden. Der Held dieser Secte wurde bald nach seiner zweydeutigen Geburt für einen König erkannt. Er nannte selbst den Innhalt [sic] seines Theismi ein Reich der Himmel, und legte vor seinem heidnischen Richter, der das Urtheil der schmäligsten Todesstrafe an ihm vollziehen hieß, das gute Bekenntnis ab, daß sein Königreich nicht von dieser Welt sey; – denn welche irrdische Monarchie oder Republick kann sich einer solchen Ausbreitung und Dauerhaftigkeit, einer solchen absoluten Freyheit und despotischen Gehorsams, solcher einfachen und zugleich fruchtbaren Grundgesetze rühmen?'

169 N 3:146.

170 N 2:58.

171 The epigraph to *Wolken* is from Hamlet: 'The play's the thing, wherein I'll catch the conscience of the king.' N 2:85.

172 'For forms of government let fools contest / Whate'er is best administered is best.' Pope, *Essay on Man*, III: 303–4, in *Alexander Pope: Selected Poetry and Prose*, 155.

173 Cited in Lentin, *Enlightened Absolutism*, 10.

174 Sée, *Les idées politiques*, 148.

175 N 2:278. 'DESINE ERGO REX ESSE!' Here, he is citing from a story related by Francis Bacon about a king who refused to take an interest in the petition of a poor woman. This is her response. Hamann's concrete meaning is that the king's lack of response to his own petitions constitutes an abnegation of his responsibilities. But the tenor of the essay for which it is the epigraph is that the worship of *bon sens* is the true culprit.

176 Büchsel, *Die Hamann-Forschung*, 62. We have already encountered this 'metaschematism' in chapter 2.

177 ZH 7:464.

178 N 2:302. Edward Andrew points out that this was perhaps a joke on Louis XV, *le bien aimé*.

179 N 3:146. 'Das Mährchen des Himmelreichs mag daher immerhin, in Vergleichung aller übrigen Universalmonarchien und ihrer pragmatischen Geschichte, ein kleines Senfkorn seyn.' The parable of the mustard seed from Matthew 13:31–2 is as follows: 'Another parable put he forth unto

them, saying, The kingdom of heaven is like to a grain of mustard seed, which a man took, and sowed in his field: / Which indeed is the least of all seeds: but when it is grown, it is the greatest among herbs, and becometh a tree, so that the birds of the air come and lodge in the branches thereof.'

180 Wolin, *Politics and Vision*, 164.
181 ZH5:291.
182 ZH 3:18–9. 'sondern Blut und Feuer zu schreiben wie der Prophet Elias.' This advice was particularly amusing because Frederick's *Hofprediger*, J.A. Eberhard, was a great disciple of the Enlightenment and wrote a freethinking treatise granting divine justification to all pagan authors. Despite this tone, we should note that there is a certain lack of heroism in Hamann's temporal complaints, which touch mostly on the problems of the bourgeoisie. Hamann did not have to serve in the military and did not bear the burden of Frederick's bellicose foreign policy. Thus he never really delved into the problems of the peasants or the victims of war. However, given the audacity of his writings, he must be judged somewhat brave.

Chapter 10

1 Unger, *Hamann und die Aufklärung*.
2 Berlin, *Magus of the North*, 92.
3 Graubner, 'Theological Empiricism,' 382.
4 N 3:191–2. 'So wie alle Arten der Unvernunft das Daseyn der Vernunft und ihren Misbrauch voraussetzen: so müßen alle Religionen eine Beziehung auf den Glauben einer einzigen, selbständigen und lebendigen Wahrheit haben, die, gleich unserer Existenz, älter als unsere Vernunft seyn muß, und daher nicht durch die Genesin der letzteren, sondern durch eine unmittelbare Offenbarung der ersteren erkannt werden kann. Weil unsere Vernunft blos aus den äußeren Verhältnißen sichtbarer, sinnlicher, unstätiger Dinge den Stoff ihrer Begriffe schöpft, um selbige nach der Form ihrer innern Natur selbst zu bilden, und zu ihrem Genuß oder Gebrauch anzuwenden: so liegt der Grund der Religion in unserer ganzen Existenz und außer der Sphäre unserer Erkenntniskräfte, welche alle zusammengenommen, den zufälligsten und abstractesten *modum* unserer Existenz ausmachen. Daher jene mythische und poetische Ader aller Religionen, ihre Thorheit und ärgerliche Gestalt in den Augen einer heterogenen, incompetenten, eiskalten, hundmagern Philosophie, die ihrer Erziehungskunst die höhere Bestimmung unserer Herrschaft über die Erde unverschämt andichtet.'

5 Berlin, ever obliging in his provision of erroneous interpretation, shares
the existentialist thesis, attributing to Hamann these views: 'There exists a
pre-rational reality; how we arrange it is ultimately arbitrary.' *Magus of the
North,* 35. It is significant that Berlin is able to provide citation for the first
phrase; the information after the semicolon remains without evidence because it is false.

6 ZH 7:168 (to Jacobi). 'Nein Vernunft ist unsichtbar, ohne Sprache; aber
freylich ist sie der einzige Ausdruck der Seele und des Herzens zur Offenbarung und Mittheilung unsers Innersten.'

7 ZH 5:265 (to Jacobi). 'Unsere Vernunft muß warten und hoffen – Dienerin
nicht Gesetzgeberin der Natur seyn wollen.' In the *Aesthetica* he contested
radical subjectivity, charging his age's 'naturalists,' 'Nach Dero weitläufti-
gen Einsicht in physischen Dingen wissen Sie besser, als ich Sie daran erin-
nern kann, daß der Wind bläst, wo er will – Ungeachtet man sein Sausen
wohl hört; so ersieht man doch am wankelmüthigen Wetterhahn, von
wannen er kommt, oder vielmehr, wohin er fährt.' N 2:203.

8 Much more could be said about Hamann and existentialism. Writers like
Ronald Smith and Wilhelm Koepp have found existential aspects in Hamann precisely by ignoring the significance of Christian *Heilsgeschichte.*
Reiner Wild, in *Metacriticus bonae spei,* 186–7, has laid to rest Koepp's thesis
as 'das genaue Gegenteil des von Hamann Ausgeführten.'

9 There are numerous good reasons to avoid attributing anything resembling Platonism to Hamann. Nonetheless, some of the more 'dated' interpreters (Joseph Nadler and Rudolf Unger) did touch on this element of
Hamann's thought. Metzke attacks Unger's view by insisting on the historicity and dynamism of the Hamannian word. *J.G. Hamanns Stellung,*
128. Metzke is correct; Hamann is not thinking of 'Platonic ideas.' Our entire existence, including our ideas, is historical. God is transcendent and
reveals himself through expression and historical embodiment. But these
two realms, the divine/permanent and the human/historical, are not dis-
pensed with in Hamann's thought.

10 N 2:61. 'Die *Analogie* war die Seele seiner Schlüsse.'

11 N 2:139. 'Das menschliche Leben scheinet in einer Reihe symbolischer
Handlungen zu bestehen, durch welche unsere Seele ihre unsichtbare
Natur zu offenbaren fähig ist, und eine anschauende Erkänntniß ihres
würksamen Daseyns ausser such hervor bringt und mittheilet. Der blosse
Körper einer Handlung kann uns ihren Werth niemals entdecken; sondern
die Vorstellung ihrer Bewegungsgründe und ihrer Folgen sind die na-
türlichsten Mittelbegriffe, aus welchen unsere Schlüsse nebst dem damit
gepaarten Beyfall oder Unwillen erzeuget werden.'

12 Compare N 2:204. 'Das Buch der Schöpfung enthält Exempel allgemeiner Begriffe, die GOTT der Kreatur durch die Kreatur; die Bücher des Bundes enthalten Exempel geheimer Artickel, die GOTT durch Menschen dem Menschen hat offenbaren wollen.' N 1:300. 'Warum kann der Mensch sein eigen Selbst nicht kennen? Dies muß bloß in dem Zustande unserer Seelen liegen. Die Natur, die uns in lauter Räthseln und Gleichnissen von dem Unsichtbaren unterrichtet, zeigt uns an den Beziehungen, von denen unser Körper abhängt, wie wir uns die Beziehung unseres Geistes auf andere Geister vorstellen können.' N 2:64. 'Wie die Natur uns gegeben, unsere Augen zu öfnen; so die Geschichte, unsere Ohren. Einen Körper und eine Begebenheit bis auf ihre ersten Elemente zergliedern, heißt, Gottes unsichtbares Wesen, seine ewige Kraft und Gottheit ertappen wollen.' He dipped into the medieval *Quadriga*, N 3:367. 'Jede Handlung ist außer ihrer ursprünglichen und natürlichen materiellen und mechanischen Bezeichnung noch mancherley formeller, figurlicher, tropischer und typischer Bedeutung fähig, welche eben so wenig als handelnden Absichten und Gesinnungen 'begucket und betastet' werden können; sondern, wie alle intellektuelle und moralische Eindrücke, ohne sinnlichen Ausdruck, keiner Mittheilung noch Fortpflanzung empfänglich sind.'

13 Quoted in O'Flaherty, *The Quarrel of Reason with Itself*, 104. 'Die Wahrheit muß aus der Erde herausgegraben werden und nicht aus der Luft geschöpft, aus Kunstwörtern – sondern aus irdischen und unterirdischen Gegenständen erst ans licht gebracht werden durch Gleichnisse und Parabeln der höchsten Ideen und transcendenten Ahndungen, die keine *directi* sonder *reflexi radii* sein können, wie Du aus Baco anführst. Außer dem *principio cognoscendi* giebt es kein besonderes *principium essendi* für uns. *Cogito ergo sum* ist in diesem Verstande wahr.' O'Flaherty explains the reference to Bacon's comparison of 'three kinds of light rays: direct, refracted and reflected, corresponding to man's knowledge of God, nature, and man.' I have translated *Ahndung* (modern, *Ahnung*) as 'intuition' here, despite the fact that I normally reserve this term for *Anschauung*, given its preponderance in translations of Kant.

14 This type of irrationalism was condemned by Nietzsche thus: 'The ascetic self-contempt and self-scorn of reason decrees: There *is* a realm of truth and a realm of being, but it is precisely reason that is excluded from it!' cited in Jaspers, *Nietzsche*, 215.

15 Nietzsche, *Will to Power*, sec. 805.

16 Berlin, *Magus of the North*, 62–5.

17 Ibid., 66. It should be noted that Berlin takes some of the quotations out of context. For instance, he quotes Hamann as saying, '*children* are not full of

prudery, nor *savages*, nor Cynic philosophers' (62). Now, this quotation is derived from the *Versuch einer Sibylle über die Ehe*, and is much more nuanced than Berlin makes it appear. Hamann begins by questioning human shame at reproduction, but he does not entirely decry this shame. Rather he alludes to the curious passage in Genesis in which Adam began to feel shame. This certainly is not an attempt simply to liberate Adam from his guilt, and we can't take Hamann as siding with the Rousseauan noble savage or cynic philosopher! The full quotation, following this allusion to the Fall, is, 'It is not an inborn, general instinct, as is seen in the example of children, savages, and the cynic school, but rather, an inherited ethic [Sitte], and all ethics and mores are meaningful signs and markers employed for the preservation of original occurrences and the reproduction of conventional convictions.' N 2:200. I have not the space to interpret this passage, but merely wish to indicate Berlin's somewhat slippery use of the text.

18 N 2:208; N 3:201. One important point of similarity between Blake and Hamann is their common insistence on the 'spirit of prophecy' and its connection to the five senses. But Blake's poetic impulse storms heaven, where Hamann's take heaven to condescend to man. The difference is important, if easily overlooked by readers blinded by the 'prophetic' style. If Blake's 'business is to Create,' Hamann's is to receive.

19 N 3:202. 'sheinheiliger Pharisäer unsers Jahrhunderts! Deine moralische und bürgerliche Vorurtheile und der hohe Geschmack oder Tand ihrer Verdienste ist nichts als Caviar des Leviathans ... und die Schaamröthe eurer Jungferschaft, ihr schönen Geister! Ist gallicanische Schminke, Kreide, und insectendotter [literally 'insect-yolk,' i.e., colour used on make-up] aber kein adlich angeborner Purpur eines gesunden, vom Himmel geschenkten und belebten Fleisches und Blutes.' Certainly, Hamann's example demonstrates the inaccuracy of Nietzsche's claim that 'wherever on earth the religious neurosis has appeared we find it tied to three dangerous dietary demands: solitude, fasting, and sexual abstinence.' *Beyond Good and Evil*, para. 47.

20 N 3:197–203.

21 N 3:202. 'Ohne ein Schlachtopfer der Unschuld, bleibt das Kleinod und Heiligtum der Keuschheit unbekannt, und der Eingang dieser himmlichen Tugend undurchdringlich.'

22 It is as if Berlin had compared Luther and Diderot because both wanted to close down convents! Berlin failed to attend to the numerous places where Hamann cautions against such a reading of him. See, for instance, his distancing of himself from the libertines, N 3:201. But it is certainly true that Hamann overturned a long tradition of Christian suspicion of the body and sexuality. E. Schoonhoven cites from a letter to Jacobi in which

Hamann declares his view on marriage to be anti-Pauline, indicating his disagreement with Paul's celebration of virginity over marriage in 1 Corinthians. Schoonhoven and Seils, *Mysterienschriften erklärt*, 147; Alexander quotes the same letter in 'Sex in the Philosophy of Hamann,' 338.

23 N 3:39. See our chapter on the *Metakritik*.

24 N 2:201. 'Wagt euch also nicht in die Metaphysick der schönen Künste, ohne in den Orgien und Eleusinischen Geheimnissen vollendet zu seyn.'

25 N 2:206. We have seen his thoughts about Frederick's philosophical client, LaMettrie.

26 Nietzsche could not have been more un-Hamannian when he wrote, 'Chastity is merely the economy of an artist.' *Will to Power*, sec. 800. Nietzsche was Hamannian, however, when he wrote, 'There is no necessary antithesis between chastity and sensuality; every good marriage, every genuine love affair, transcends this antithesis.' *On the Genealogy of Morals*, Third Essay, sec. 2.

27 Nygren, *Agape and Eros*.

28 Nygren emphasizes the view that love 'seeketh not her own,' 1 Corinthians 13:5 (*Agape and Eros*, 641), but Hamann saw self-love as commanded in the law to love one's neighbour as oneself (Matthew 19:19, 22:39; Mark 12:31; Luke 10:27; Romans 13:9; Galatians 5:14; James 2:8; for Hamann's view, see chapter 5, also ZH 4:6). Certainly, the commandment (if it is not to be taken as a pure relativism) appears to imply the commandment to love oneself and the suggestion that there are correct and aberrant manners of loving oneself. Nygren disputes this interpretation (100–1), ascribing it to Augustine, 710, and shares Luther's view that the commandment was addressed to sinful man. Self-love, in this command, is actually condemned; to love one's neighbour as oneself is ultimately to cease to love oneself (712). (It should be noted that Nygren claims he is merely a scientific observer offering no 'value judgments,' but he defines his *agape* as *the* Christian love, despite his lengthy analysis of a thousand-year Christian tradition that saw the two types of love mixed together. We can safely disregard Nygren's – who was bishop of Lund – call for scientific objectivity.) A related tension between Nygren's view and Hamann's concerns particularism, which Nygren thought diminished the agape ideal (153, 730–1). Hamann saw the love of God in particular relations.

29 Kocziszky, *Hamanns Kritik der Moderne*, 134. This is precisely the mixing of loves that Nygren thought plagued Christianity for the millennium preceding Luther.

30 Dickson, *Relational Metacriticism*, 251. James O'Flaherty quotes from Walter Leibrecht thus: 'It is characteristic that Hamann never tries to distinguish

between *eros* and *agape*. Just as he believes that all creation derives solely from the love of God, so all man's behavior, if it is to be genuine and creative, must spring from love and passion.' 'Hamann's Concept of the Whole Man,' 260. Alexander equally insists that Hamann refuses to separate eros and agape, *Johann Georg Hamann*, 189.

31 See his passing denigration of the abstract character of Platonic love. N 4:441.

32 Recall that this is *not* an Augustinian dualism between evil body and good spirit; Hamann thought that body was in itself good, and rational abstraction was often the source of sin.

33 N 3:200–1.

34 Witness his defence, in spite of his views on the sacramental nature of marriage, of Herder's sister-in-law who wanted to divorce her loutish, alcoholic husband. Alexander, 'Sex in the Philosophy of Hamann,' 339.

35 N 3:202–3. 'und gleich einem treuen Schöpfer in guten Werken schloß er die Lücke der Stätte zu mit Fleish.'

36 N 3:202, 'Mitten im Wehrauch eines Schlummers sah ich jene Ribbe – und rief voll begeisterter habseliger Zueignung 'Das ist Knochen von meinen Knochen, und Fleisch von meinem Fleische.'

37 N 1:16. 'Wer sollte es glauben, wenn uns Gott nicht selbst gesagt hätte, daß die erste Welt ihn wund gemacht, seinem Herzen wehe gethan hätte; wer sollte es glauben, daß er seinen Ruhm in unserem Gehorsam und den Genuß seiner Herrlichkeit in unserer Gesellschaft und Theilnehmung findt.'

38 N 2:68. 'Ihre gesunde Vernunft … stieß sich daran, daß der Schönste unter den Menschenkindern ihnen zum Erlöser versprochen war, und daß ein Mann der Schmerzen, voller Wunden und Striemen, der Held ihrer Erwartung sein sollte.'

39 N 2:68. 'Man kann keine lebhafte Freundschaft ohne Sinnlichkeit fühlen, und eine metaphysische Liebe sündigt vielleicht gröber am Nervensaft, als eine thierische an Fleisch und Blut.' Hamann was referring here particularly to Socrates' attraction to his students. It is important to note that Hamann also praised Socrates for his self-restraint.

40 Nygren, *Agape and Eros*, 51.

41 Nietzsche thought that the metaphor of the soul as the bride of Christ was a mask for sensuality (*Will to Power*, 806); Hamann thought that sensuality was an image of the divine marriage. Both see the essential reality in a different place.

42 ZH 6:534 (to Jacobi). 'Freilich verliert *actio* und Handlung alle männliche Würde durch weibliche und kindische Passion oder Leidenschaft. Warum ist es aber in den verschiedensten Fällen wahr: wenn ich schwach bin, so

bin ich stark?' See 2 Corinthians 12:10. See also N 2:117. 'Glücklich ist der Autor, welcher sagen darf: Wenn ich schwach bin, so bin ich stark!'

43 N 2:208.

44 Ibid. 'Wenn die Leidenschaften Glieder der Unehre sind, hören sie deswegen auf, Waffen der Mannheit zu seyn?' James O'Flaherty has helped slay the misleading romantic interpretation: 'Hamann's idea that the passions are "Waffen der Mannheit" could, if the theological presuppositions were ignored, readily become a signal for the unbridled expression of emotion. This is, to be sure, what happened in the case of those adherents of the *Sturm und Drang* who looked to Hamann as their mentor. 'Hamann's Concept of the Whole Man,' 264.

45 Hamann did bequeath to the coming romantics an insistence on creativity, which he likened to a sexual power. But once again, this is not to be misunderstood as Promethean. This power of authoring or begetting was a product of man's divine nature, and creation itself was ultimately divine. Hamann loved to play on the word *spermologue*, one whose words impregnate. N 2:137; N 3:45, 144, 309. The term is derived from Acts 17:18 when Paul is in Athens: 'Then certain philosophers of the Epicureans, and of the Stoicks, encountered him. And some said, What will this babbler say?' Hamann gave the Greek word for *babbler* in capital letters, ΣΠΕΡΜΟΛΟΓΟΣ; he periodically employed the Vulgate's 'seminiverbius.' N 3:410. The image of the Stoics and Epicureans scratching their heads about Paul's bizarre speech is one that we have encountered before and it is the *Leitmotiv* of Hamann's entire oeuvre.

46 Nietzsche was clearly aware of Hamann, but did not study his works in any detail. He cited once from the *Sokratische Denkwürdigkeiten*, accepting Hamann's consolation for the loss of some ancient texts (although his motivation differs from Hamann's here). Friedrich Nietzsche, *Werke*, 3:359. His judgment of Hamann occurs in one letter of 1873: 'Sodann lese ich Hamann und bin sehr erbaut: man sieht in die Gebärzustände unsrer Deutschen Dichter- und Denker-Kultur. Sehr tief und innig, aber nichtswürdig unkünstlerisch.' Nietzsche, to Erwin Rohde, 31 Jan. 1873, *Sämtliche Briefe*, 4:121.

47 Nietzsche, *Beyond Good and Evil*, sec. 168.

48 N 3:213. 'Die Heimlichkeiten unserer Natur, in denen aller geschmack und Genuß des Schönen, Wahren und Guten gegründet ist, beziehen sich, gleich jenem Baum Gottes mitten im Garten auf Erkenntnis und Leben. Beyde sind Ursachen so wol als Wirkungen der Liebe. Ihre Glut ist feurig und eine Flamme des Herren; denn Gott ist die Liebe und das Leben ist das Licht der Menschen.' Incidentally, the Christian view in 1 John 4:48 that God is Love and the Gospel of John's claim that God is the Word are

somewhat difficult to reconcile with Platonism, which sees love (eros) and the Word (Logos) as means towards wisdom and the good. Hamann would see these phrases as analogies (God defines himself in terms of human attributes).

49 Hume, of course, would have found this move monstrously absurd. See the *Treatise of Human Nature*, vol. 1, pt 3, sec.10, where Hume expostulates against poetic enthusiasm.

50 Schmidt, *Die Geschichte des Genie-Gedankens*, 98–9.

51 N 2:74. 'Die Einbildungskraft, wäre sie ein *Sonnenpferd* und hätte Flügel der Morgenröthe, kann also keine Schöpferinn des Glaubens seyn.' Graubner draws our attention to this quotation as a foil to Hume, 'Theological Empiricism,' 381.

52 Fritsch, *Communicatio Idiomatum*, esp. 171.

53 Jünger, *Aladdin's Problem*, 11. For a treatment of the relationship between Jünger and Hamann, see the work of Jünger's friend Gerhard Nebel, *Hamann*, 76–88. Nebel indulges in endless superlatives, but friendship excuses.

54 Beck, *Early German Philosophy*, 381.

55 If the young Hamann behaved very much in the spirit of the Sturm und Drang, the older Hamann does not appear to have embraced the movement. Hamann made only one significant mention of *Werther* in his published work: there he joked that the many sufferings of young Werther were nothing compared to his extreme workload in the excise department! (N 3:141).

56 N 2:200. 'Virtuosen des gegenwärtigen Äons, auf welchen GOTT der HERR einen tiefen Schlaf fallen lassen! Ihr wenigen Edeln!' The reference is to Genesis 2:21, and Hamann continues in a typically obscure conceit to compare the virtuoso to Adam and to urge them not to produce Eve (whom Hamann compared to philosophy in the previous paragraph), but something worthy of the frightful, promised aeon to come.

57 Diderot, *Dictionnaire Encyclopédique*, vol. 3.

58 Allow a few examples. The OED cites Dryden, 'Extraordinary Genius's have a sort of Prerogative, which may dispense them from Laws.' Kant made the Genius the *giver* of rules. Lessing, in the same year as the *Sokratische Denkwürdigkeiten*, pronounced Shakespeare a true genius for having, in relative ignorance of ancient tragedy, come closest to its greatness. *Briefe, die neueste Litteratur betreffend* in *Werke und Briefe*m 4:500–1 (17th letter). Diderot's *Encyclopédie* article on *Génie* contrasts tasteful composition, which follows rules, to genius: 'Les règles et les lois du goût donneraient des entraves au génie; il les brise pour voler au sublime.'

59 Addison, *Essays from the Spectator*, no. 46, 200–1.

60 Gay, *The Enlightenment*, 2:210.

61 N 2:75. 'Was ersetzt bey *Homer* die Unwissenheit der Kunstregeln, die ein Aristoteles nach ihm erdacht, und was bey einem *Shakesspear* die Unwissenheit oder Übertretung jener kritischen Gesetze? Das *Genie* ist die einmüthige Antwort. Sokrates hatte also freylich gut unwissend seyn; er hatte einen Genius, auf dessen Wissenschaft er sich verlassen konnte, den er liebte und fürchtete als seinen Gott, an dessen *Frieden* ihm mehr gelegen war, als an aller Vernunft der Egypter und Griechen, dessen Stimme er glaubte' (trans. O'Flaherty, *Hamann's 'Socratic Memorabilia'*).

62 N 2:75. 'Ob dieser Dämon des Sokrates nichts als eine herrschende Leidenschaft gewesen und bey welchem Namen sie von unsern Sittenlehrern geruffen wird, oder ob er ein Fund seiner Staatslist; ob er ein Engel oder Kobold, eine hervorragende Idea seiner Einbildungskraft, oder ein erschlichner und willkührlich angenommener Begriff einer mathematischen Unwissenheit; ob dieser Dämon nicht vielleicht eine Quecksilberröhre oder den Maschinen ähnlicher gewesen, welchen die Bradleys und Leuwenhoeks ihre Offenbarungen zu verdanken haben; ob man ihn mit dem wahrsagendem Gefühl eines nüchternen Blinden oder mit der Gabe aus Leichdornen und Narben übelgeheilter Wunden die Revolutionen des Wolkenhimmels vorher zu wissen, am bequemsten vergleichen kann: hierüber ist von so vielen Sophisten mit so viel Bündigkeit geschrieben worden, daß man erstaunen muß, wie Sokrates bey der gelobten Erkenntniß seiner Selbst, auch hierinn so unwissend gewesen, daß er einem Simias darauf die Antwort hat schuldig bleiben wollen. Keinem Leser von Geschmack fehlt es in unsern Tagen an Freunden von Genie, die mich der Mühe überheben werden weitläuftiger über den Genius des Sokrates zu seyn' (trans. O'Flaherty, *Hamann's 'Socratic Memorabilia'*).

63 N 2:362. The full citation (with the reference to John 5:2) is the following: 'Ein Engel fuhr herab zu seiner Zeit und bewegte den Teich Bethesda, in dessen fünf Hallen viel Kranke, Blinde, Lahme, Dürre lagen und warteten, wenn sich das Wasser bewegte – Eben so muß ein Genie sich herablaßen Regeln zu erschüttern; sonst bleiben sie Wasser.

64 N 2:214. 'Der Geburtstag eines Genies wird, wie gewöhnlich, von einem Märtyrerfest unschuld'ger Kinder begleitet.'

65 N 2:98. 'In diesem göttlichen der Unwißenheit, in diesem menschlichen des Genies scheinet vermuthlich die Weisheit des Widerspruchs verborgen zu seyn, woran der Adept scheitert und worüber ein Ontologist die Zähne blöckt.'

66 There is a striking parallel in St Augustine, *Confessions*, 12.5.283. Thinking about the unfathomable 'formless matter' of Genesis, he writes, 'We may

think about it in this way [in sense images], but we must be content to know without knowing, or should I say, to be ignorant and yet to know.'

67 N 2:289. See Genesis 3:14. Isaiah Berlin is entirely mistaken to think that Hamann would have been in agreement with Diderot's paean to Genius in the *Salons*. (*Magus of the North*, 102.)

68 See Balthasar. *The Glory of the Lord*, 3:255–6.

69 ZH 7:166; also N 3:107.

70 ZH 5:95. 'Das ist die Natur der Leidenschaft, daß sie nicht am Dinge selbst, sondern nur an seinem Bilde hangen kann – und ist es nicht die Natur der Vernunft, am Begriffe zu hangen[?]'

71 Friedrich Nietzsche, *Die Geburt der Tragödie*, chap. V, p. 41. 'nur als aesthetisches Phänomen is das Dasein und die Welt ewig gerechtfertigt.'

72 N 2:347. 'die Kämmerlinge der schönen Künste … keine Auferstehung des Fleisches glauben können, weil sie hier schon ihren nichtigen Leib durch schöne Künste selbst verklären.'

73 N 2:209. 'Narciß, (das Zwiebelgewächs schöner Geister) liebt sein Bild mehr als sein Leben.'

74 Dickie, *Century of Taste*, 3.

75 N 4:133–91. Hamann declared that the article was largely a blather about Hutcheson. ZH 1:374.

76 We may think of Kant's disinterestedness or Smith's 'impartial spectator' as ideal versions of this tendency. The ideal of public reason itself rests on just such a disengaged perspective, as we noted in chapter 2.

77 N 2:164. '*Nil admirari* bleibt immer die Grundlage eines philosophischen Urtheils.' Naturally, we are reminded of the *Genealogy of Morals*, III.6.

78 N 2:164. 'alle Thaumaturgie reicht nicht zu, ein unmittelbares Gefühl zu ersetzen, und nichts als die höllenfahrt der Selbsterkänntnis bahnt uns den Weg zur Vergötterung.' (I translate this last word as 'justification,' in the religious sense. Were I to render it 'deification,' it would clearly give an inaccurate sense of Hamann's intent.) It should be noted that this insistence on direct feeling was placed in an attack on a negative review of Rousseau's *Julie*. Hamann was not a great Rousseauan, but he shared with the *citoyen de Génève* the view that inner feeling was superior to rational demonstration.

79 Hamann's treatment of aesthetic criticism as disengaged prefigures Kierkegaard's treatment of the aesthetic as essentially detached and observing. The aesthetic, in Kierkegaard, makes us spectators, not participants.

80 Hamann played upon the *querelle des anciens et modernes* by siding with the 'ancients,' by which he meant the Israelites, not the Greeks. He reacted to the burgeoning philhellenism of his contemporaries by calling for a return to the Old Testament. N 2:209.

81 N 1:10. 'Hat Gott sich den Menschen u dem gantzen Mschl. Geschlect zu offenbaren die Absicht gehabt; so fällt die Thorheit derjenigen desto mehr in die Augen die ein eigeschränkten Geschmack u ihr eigenes Urtheil zum Probestein des göttl. Worts machen wollen. Die Rede ist nicht von einer Offenbarung, die ein Voltaire, ein Bollingbroke, ein Schaftesbury annehmungswerth finden würden; die ihren Vorurtheilen, ihrem Witz, ihren moralischen, politischen … Grillen am meisten ein Genüge thun würde.' While using Nadler's pagination, I have employed Bayer's cleaned-up version of the *Biblische Betrachtungen* from *Hamann: Londoner Schriften*, 68. The ellipsis indicates a word that is corrupted and unreadable.

82 N 1:11. 'Diese Bücher sollten von den Juden erhalten werden; es musten also viele besondere Umstände dies Volk so nahe angehen.'

83 This point about the cultural relativity of poetic style is emphasized in the concluding remarks of the *Aesthetica* (where he compares Lithuanian cadences to those of Homeric Greek). N 2:215–16.

84 This is, or course, a circular argument, and Hamann was perfectly aware that he would not convince non-believers. 'People who trust their own insight enough to be able to do without a divine teaching would find faults in every other revelation, and have no need of one. They are the healthy who need no doctor.' N 1:10. 'Leute die dich Einsicht genung zutrau[en] um eines göttl. Unterrichts entbehr[en] zu könn[en] würd[en] in jeder andern Offenbarung Fehler gefund[en] hab[en] und hab[en] keine nöthig. Sie sind die Gesund[en] die des Artzes nicht bedürfen.'

85 N 2:205. 'Voltaire aber, der Hohepriester im Tempel des Geschmacks schlüßt so bündig als Keiphas, und denkt fruchtbarer als Herodes.'

86 N 2:68. 'Die Überlieferung eines Götterspruches will aber so wenig als ein Komet sagen für einen Philosophen von heutigem Geschmack.'

87 N 2:208.

88 N 2:197. 'Nicht Leyer! – noch Pinsel! – eine Wurfschaufel für meine Muse, die Tenne heiliger Litteratur zu fegen!' Nadler (II, 408) notes that the reference is to Matthew 3:12. Jesus' 'fan is in his hand, and he will thoroughly purge his floor, and gather his wheat into the garner; but he will burn up the chaff with unquenchable fire.'

89 N 2:217. 'Laßt uns jetzt die Hauptsumme seiner neusten Ästhetik, welche die älteste ist, hören: Fürchtet Gott und gebt Ihm die Ehre.' See Revelation 14:7.

90 Thus, I would quibble with Beiser's otherwise fine presentation when he writes that for 'Hamann, art is the highest form of knowledge, one which is far superior to even logic and mathematics.' *Fate of Reason*, 35. Hamann's aesthetic or poetic is *not primarily about art*.

91 N 4:290. 'Weil aber des Verfassers Entwurf nur das sinnliche Gefühl
berühren sollte, ahden wir mit einigem Grunde, daß in diesem Abschnitte
die fünf Sinne des Menschen gänzlich übergangen worden. Der hohe Gusto an Schüsseln, die mit T..f.ls Dr.ck gesalbt sind, des Königs Demetrius
Poliorcetes Wettstreit e regia glande, das Erhabene des Gestanks betreffend
… sind ausnehmende Beyspiele von den Besonderheiten der menschlichen
Natur.'

92 The entry is in Bayle's *Dictionnaire historique et critique*, 'Lamia.' Bayle re-
lates the story in Latin, indicating that it is too racy to be translated into
French. Hamann had further recourse to this story on the occasion of Frederick II's publication of an abridged version of Bayle's *Dictionary*. Lamia
was a prostitute and also a flute player. Part of the joke was merely drawing attention to the salacious publication that had been made through royal patronage. We have seen that Hamann also cited this joke elsewhere
when mocking Frederick's flute playing.

93 N 2:200. 'für Leser von orthodoxem Geschmack gehören keine gemeine
Ausdrücke noch unreine Schüsseln.' Hamann is alluding to Mark 7, Acts
10:28. In the *Sokratische Denkwürdigkeiten* Hamann notes the oddness to a
pagan mind of the saviour appearing in the form of a weak and suffering
little man.

94 Ibid.

95 N 2:60. 'Weil diese Küchlein nicht gekaut, sondern geschluckt werden
müssen ... so sind sie nicht für den Geschmack gemacht.'

96 N 2:346. 'Ihre Sittenlehre und ihr Geschmack gründen sich blos auf gemal-
te Güter, ihre Lebensart und ihre Schreibart sind eine getünchte Oberfläche, die das Auge täuscht und den Sinn beleidigt, ihre Kritik ein Mährchen
vom Schaumlöffel; – aber jener Kunstrichter, den Tiresias an einem untrüg-
lichen Zeichen (σημα μαλ αριφραδεζ) beschrieb, wird den ästhetischen
Bogen der schönen Künste zubrechen im Thale der schönen Natur. Götzen
von Porcellain und glasurter Erde sind die Ideen unserer schönen Geister,
ihre heitersten Begriffe die vom zartesten Gefühle entspringen und wieder
zu den Empfindungen eilen, sind schmutziger als das besudelte Gewand
eines Keltertreters, dessen Augen gleich den Tauben lachen, die den Wagen der Venus ziehen, der seinen Mantel im Weinbeerenblut gewaschen,
und Zähne wie ein Drache hat.'

97 Homer, *The Odyssey*, 174. More precisely, Tiresias tells Odysseus that he
will have to expiate his offence to Poseidon by carrying an oar deep inland
until he reaches such a place as has never heard of the sea. He will know
he has arrived because someone there will refer to his oar as a 'winnowing fan.' This will be an 'unmistakable cue.' We have here the symbol

of the winnowing fan separating the wheat and chaff (Luke 3:17) that Hamann used at the beginning of the *Aesthetica*, in which he also compared Odysseus to Christ. This is not one of Hamann's more transparent allusions, but I suppose it does illustrate his counter-Enlightened aesthetics of opacity!

98 N 2:146–7. 'Warum sollte sie, die eine Magd im Hause des HErrn su seyn gewürdigt wird, um sterbichen Geschmack buhlen[?] … was Menschen hingegen entzückt, ein Gräuel vor GOtt ist.' As Knut Stünkel points out, aesthetics is a 'Trojan horse' for Hamann, with which he storms the city of the tasteful in the name of his theological argument. 'Die Sprache bei Hamann und Heidegger,' 54n138. This Trojan horse strategy is, we have suggested, at the heart of 'metaschematism.' Hamann's aestheticism, then, does not differ from his other guises by which he undermines his opponents' positions.

99 See note 46.

100 Heidegger, 'The Origin of the Work of Art,' in *Basic Writings*, 200.

101 Stünkel, 'Die Sprache bei Hamann und Heidegger,' 26–55.

102 Heidegger, *Introduction to Metaphysics*, 8.

103 Heidegger, *Basic Writings*, 448.

104 Ibid., 330.

105 Many have drawn attention to Heidegger's decisive confrontation with Luther in the 1920s. See Buren, *The Young Heidegger*, chap. 8.

106 Heidegger, *Introduction to Metaphysics*, 8. He decries the 'pernicious opinion that, through a supposed refurbishment with the help of philosophy, a theology can be gained or even replaced, and can be made more palatable to the need of the age.'

107 Thus, Hamann would probably feel a certain limited sympathy with Carnap! This point might be given a polemical elaboration. Hamann's insistence on poetry was an attempt to avoid constructing word-castles that float high above the ground of experience. Heidegger cannot be said to have avoided confounding his own thought with reified abstractions. One can, of course, mention the disastrous silliness of describing the Germans as 'the metaphysical people,' and the accompanying nonsense about its destiny as a spiritual power (*Introduction to Metaphysics*, 41). Adorno was not entirely incorrect to castigate Heideggerian jargon. Consider Heidegger's attempt at a postwar explanation to a professor whom he had denounced to the Nazis: 'The present time, he wrote, "is a peril before which the past slips away. Sophocles has a saying about time that may help us think about the future: 'it leaves tasks unopenable and takes appearances back into itself'"' (Sheehan, 'Heidegger and the Nazis,' 40). I don't intend this to be

dismissive of the twentieth century's most important philosopher, but
merely to indicate his difference from Hamann. Hamann was obscure, but
with an eye to the concrete. Indeed, one of his prime motives for attacking
philosophy was his revulsion for those who attempt to hide their sins with
abstract terminology. Heidegger's moral lapses are not the best lens
through which to view his thought, but neither are they incidental to his
mode of expression and its periodic descent into pompous abstractions.
Heidegger speaks of his historical place and makes constant allusions to
political and ethical matters, but he shies away from directness because
'thinking that ponders the truth of being' 'has no result. It has no effect'
(*Basic Writings*, 259).

108 Heidegger, *Basic Writings*, 339.

109 Ibid., 'The Question concerning Technology,' 307–41.

110 Ibid., 202.

111 Ibid., 161.

112 *Basic Writings*, 161. Incidentally, there has been a brief debate occasioned
by the discovery that the painting described by Heidegger was actually
of Van Gogh's own shoes, not those of a peasant. Some might think this a
telling objection to Heidegger's insistence that he has not projected something onto the painting. An unconvincing attempt is made to refute this
suggestion in Kockelmans, *Heidegger on Art and Art Works*, 128–32.

113 Heidegger, *Basic Writings*, 181.

114 Ibid. Heidegger's expression is so difficult to decipher because he eschews
the subject-verb-object construction of everyday language. When we use
normal language we tend to reify the categories of subject-object that Heidegger wishes to avoid in his phenomenalism. The question that Hamann
would raise is whether such an attempt does not actually entail an alienation from the phenomena themselves. Another way of phrasing a Hamannian objection is that Heidegger's repeated insistence that truth 'happens'
attempts to retain objectivity, but escape the problem of agency. Hamann
saw truth as communicated from one being to another. Thus, he does not
use the language of things 'disclosing' themselves, truth 'happening,' the
world 'worlding,' etc. On the subject of opaque expression, Hamann and
Heidegger are both difficult to read, but for very different reasons.

115 Consider Heidegger's treatment of the Platonic ideas as appearances
linked to beings, not Being. *Platons Lehre von der Wahrheit*, 19–20. Or consider his views on truth expressed in 'The Origin of the Work of Art': 'But
truth does not exist itself beforehand [before the act of establishing],
somewhere among the stars, only subsequently to descend elsewhere
among beings. This is impossible for the reason alone that it is after all

only the openness of beings that first affords the possibility of a some-where and of sites filled by present beings. Clearing of openness and establishment in the open regions belong together. They are the same sin-gle essence of the happening of truth.' *Basic Works*, 186. Examples of this 'establishing' of truth are the grounding of a 'political state,' the sacrifice (presumably of a life), the act of philosophic questioning. I leave aside comment on this ontology of action and merely draw attention to the anti-Platonic nature of this truth.

116 *Basic Works*, 172. Further, 'The establishment of truth in the work is the bringing forth of a being such as never was before and never will come to be again.' Yet Heidegger insists in the same breath that this 'bringing forth' is 'rather a receiving and removing within the relation to uncon-cealment.' He at once treats the artist as a mere conduit of revelation (190) and as a creator.

117 In my brief treatment of Heidegger I have merely sought to compare his poetic turn to Hamann's aesthetic piety. There are numerous other areas that could reasonably be compared. For example, Heidegger's indictment of 'the They' in *Being and Time* has a great deal in common with Ha-mann's attack on the public 'nobody' in the *Sokratische Denkwürdigkeiten*. (One might even posit a direct lineage, through Kierkegaard's individualism.)

118 *Apology* 22c; *Phaedrus* 245a; *Ion* 533e.

119 Andrew, *Genealogy of Values*, xix.

120 N: 2:197

121 N 3:307.

122 N 2:207. 'Je lebhafter diese Idee, das Ebenbild des unsichtbaren Gottes in unserm Gemüth ist; desto fähiger sind wir Seine Leutseeligkeit in den Geschöpfen zu sehen und zu schmecken, zu beshauen und mit Händen zu begreifen.'

123 Kierkegaard derived a great deal from Hamann but ultimately differed from him in seeing excessive worldliness in Hamann's view. Like Ha-mann, Kierkegaard was preoccupied with the problem of history and the way in which Christianity entailed the entering of eternity into history. Kierkegaard was also troubled by the abstract public, and equally by the universalism of philosophy. The attack on Hegel in the *Concluding Unsci-entific Postscript* could have come directly out of the pages of Hamann. (And, indeed, in the *Philosophical Fragments*, Kierkegaard says as much of his argument's Hamannian overtones.) But Kierkegaard differed from Hamann in his separation of the aesthetic from the ethical and the reli-gious. What Hamann decried in taste and criticism Kierkegaard equally

deplored in the aesthetic, but Hamann retained a strong conviction in the divine nature of the world and our aesthetic (sensory) reception thereof. We can see this opposition clearly in their differing uses of Socrates. For Kierkegaard, Socrates does not lead to the religious disposition; for Hamann, he prefigures Christ. Hamann brought together much of what Kierkegaard separated, and he felt no need for leaping to the religious. Karlfried Gründer indicates Kierkegaard's view that Hamann's attempt to find truth in the sensory, in the low, the ugly, and the worldly was blasphemous. (Blanke and Schreiner, *Die Hamann-Forschung*, 50.) One might have wished that Hamann had addressed the type of problem that occupied Kierkegaard in *Fear and Trembling*. Faith that demands unethical action does not arise in Hamann's thought. Abraham's readiness to sacrifice Isaac receives no discussion in Hamann's biblical commentary. Hamann simply speaks of Abraham's life as a constant test of human obedience (N 1:35). Hamann exhibited a great deal more moral peace than most *Schwärmer*. His typical moral advice to people plagued by fear and trembling was the following (ZH 5:5): 'Ißt dein Brod mit Freuden, trink deinen Wein mit gutem Muth, denn dein Werk gefällt Gott. Brauche des Lebens mit deinem Weibe, das du lieb hast, so lange du das eitle Leben hast, das dir Gott unter der Sonne gegeben hat.'

Chapter 11

1 That said, Smith has emphasized the ecumenical nature of Hamann's friendship with the Catholic circle around the Princess Gallitzin, 'J.G. Hamann and the Princess Gallitzin.'
2 The project of Mohammed Arkoun is extremely suggestive, taking seriously the mythic and opening up monotheistic traditions to reflection that goes beyond the confines of religious and secular dogmas.
3 See Kant's 'On a Recently Prominent Tone of Superiority in Philosophy,' in Allison, *Theoretical Philosophy after 1781*, 425–45.
4 N 2:65.
5 Habermas, 'Religion in the Public Sphere,' 17.
6 Ibid.

Bibliography

Hamann, Primary Sources

Hamann, Johann Georg. *Ausgewählte Schriften*. Edited by Hans Eichner. Berlin: Nicolai, 1994.
- *Hamann: Londoner Schriften*. Edited by O. Bayer and B. Weissenborn. Munich: Beck, 1993.
- *Johann Georg Hamann Briefwechsel*. Edited by Walther Ziesemer and Arthur Henkel. 7 vols. Wiesbaden: Insel, 1955–79.
- *Sämtliche Werke*. 6 vols. Edited by Joseph Nadler. Vienna: Verlag Herder, 1949.
- *Sokratische Denkwürdigkeiten, Aesthetica in nuce*. Edited by Sven-Aage Jørgensen. Stuttgart: Reclam, 1998.

All Other Texts

Addison, Joseph. *Essays from the Spectator*. London: Routledge, 1886.
Adorno, Theodor W. *Minima Moralia*. Translated by E.F.N. Jephcott. London: New Left Books, 1974.
Adorno, Theodor W., and Max Horkheimer. *Dialektik der Aufklärung: Philosophische Fragmente*. Amsterdam: Querido Verlag, 1947.
Alembert, Jean Le Rond D'. *Preliminary Discourse to the Encylopedia of Diderot*. Translated by R.N. Schwab. Indianapolis: Bobbs-Merrill, 1963.
Alexander, W.M. 'Johann Georg Hamann: Metacritic of Kant.' *Journal of the History of Ideas* 27, no. 1 (1966): 137–44.
- *Johann Georg Hamann: Philosophy and Faith*. The Hague: Martinus Nijhoff, 1966.
- 'Sex in the Philosophy of Hamann.' *Journal of the American Academy of Religion* 37, no. 4 (December 1969): 331–40.

Allison, Henry E. *Kant's Transcendental Idealism*. Rev. ed. New Haven: Yale University Press, 2004.
– ed. *Theoretical Philosophy after 1781*. Cambridge: Cambridge University Press, 2002.
Altmann, Alexander. *Die Trostvolle Aufklärung*. Stuttgart: Fromman-Holzboog, 1982.
– *Moses Mendelssohn: A Biographical Study*. Alabama: University of Alabama, 1973.
Ameriks, Karl. *The Cambridge Companion to German Idealism*. Cambridge: Cambridge University Press, 2000.
Ando, Clifford. 'Signs, Idols, and the Incarnation in Augustine's Metaphysics.' *Representations* 73 (Winter 2001): 24–53.
Andrew, Edward G. *The Genealogy of Values: The Aesthetic Economy of Nietzsche and Proust*. Lanham, MD: Rowman & Littlefield, 1995.
– *Patrons of Enlightenment*. Toronto: University of Toronto Press, 2006.
– *Shylock's Rights: A Grammar of Lockean Claims*. Toronto: University of Toronto Press, 1988.
Anonymous. *Royal Matins or Prussia's Public Confession, in Five Mornings*. Translated by Anonymous. Cambridge: Archdeacon, 1768.
Aristotle. *Politics*. Translated by C. Lord. Chicago: University of Chicago Press, 1984.
Auerbach, Erich. 'Figura.' In *Scenes from the Drama of European Literature*, translated by R. Manheim, 11–78. Minneapolis: University of Minnesota Press, 1984.
Augustine. *The City of God against the Pagans*. Edited by R.W. Dyson. Cambridge: Cambridge University Press, 1998.
– *Confessions*. Translated by R.S. Pine-Coffin. London: Penguin, 1961.
Ausubel, Nathan. *Superman: The Life of Frederick the Great*. London: Routledge, 1932.
Bacon, Francis. *The Works of Francis Bacon*. 1857–74. Facsimile reprint of the Spedding, Ellis, and Heath edition. 14 vols. Stuttgart: Friedrich Frommann, 1963.
Baker, Keith Michael, and Peter Hanns Reill, eds. *What's Left of Enlightenment?* Stanford: Stanford University Press, 2001.
Barnett, S.J. *The Enlightenment and Religion: The Myths of Modernity*. Manchester: Manchester University Press, 2003.
Bathasar, Hans Urs von. *The Glory of the Lord: A Theological Aesthetics*. Vol. 3, *Studies in Theological Style: Lay Style*. Translated by A. Louth. Edinburgh: Clark, 1986.
Baudler, Georg. *'Im Worte sehen': das Sprachdenken Johann Georg Hamanns*. Bonn: Bouvier, 1970.
Baur, Wolfgang-Dieter. 'Die falschen Götzen macht zu Spott: Hamann als Publizist.' In Bayer, *Johann Georg Hamann*, 80–105.

– *Johann Georg Hamann als Publizist*. Berlin: de Gruyter, 1991.

Bayer, Oswald, ed., *Johann Georg Hamann: Der hellste Kopf seiner Zeit*. Tübingen: Attempo, 1998.

– *Vernunft ist Sprache: Hamanns Metakritik Kants*. Stuttgart-Bad Cannstatt: Frommann-Holzboog, 2002.

– *Zeitgenosse im Widerspruch: Johann Georg Hamann als radikaler Aufklärer*. Munich: Piper, 1988.

Bayer, Oswald, and Christian Knudsen. *Kreuz und Kritik*. Tübingen: Mohr, 1983.

Bayle, Pierre. *Pensées diverses sur la comète*. 2 vols. Paris: Société des textes français modernes, 1911.

– *A Philosophical Commentary on the Words of Jesus Christ: 'Compel Them to Come In, That My House May Be Full.'* Edited by John Kilcullen. Indianapolis: Liberty Fund, 2005.

Beck, Lewis White. *Early German Philosophy*. Cambridge, MA: Harvard University Press, 1969.

Beiner, Ronald. *Philosophy in a Time of Lost Spirit*. Toronto: University of Toronto Press, 1997.

Beiser, Frederick C. *The Fate of Reason: German Philosophy from Kant to Fichte*. Cambridge, MA: Harvard University Press, 1987.

Berkeley, George. *Berkeley's Philosophical Writings*. Edited by D. Armstrong. New York: Macmillan, 1965.

– *The Works of George Berkeley*. 4 vols. Oxford: Clarendon, 1901.

Berlin, Isaiah. *The Magus of the North*. London: Murray, 1993.

Beyerhaus, Gisbert. 'Kants programm der Aufklärung aus dem Jahre 1784.' *Kant Studien* 26, no. 1 (1921): 1–16.

Blackall, Eric A. *The Emergence of German as a Literary Language: 1700–1775*. 2nd ed. Ithaca: Cornell, 1978.

Blackwell, Thomas. *Enquiry into the Life and Writings of Homer*. 1735. Reproduced by Menston, UK: Scholar, 1976.

Blanke, Fritz. *Sokratische Denkwürdigkeiten*. Vol. 2 of the series *Johann Georg Hamanns Hauptschriften erklärt*. Gütersloh: Bertelsmann, 1959.

Blanke, Fritz, and Lothar Schreiner, series eds. *Johann Georg Hamanns Hauptschriften erklärt*. Gütersloh: Bertelsmann, 1956–63.

– *Die Hamann-Forschung*. Vol. 1 of the series *Johann Georg Hamanns Hauptschriften erklärt*. Gütersloh: Bertelsmann, 1956.

Blum, Jean. *La vie et l'oeuvre de J.G. Hamann, le 'Mage du Nord' 1730–1788*. Paris: Alcan, 1912.

Bräutigam, Bernd. *Reflexion des Schönen – Schöne Reflexion: Überlegungen zur Prosa ästhetischer Theorie – Hamann, Nietzsche, Adorno*. Bonn: Bouvier, 1975.

Brewer, Daniel. *The Discourse of Enlightenment in Eighteenth-Century France*. Cambridge: Cambridge University Press, 1993.

Büchsel, Elfried. *Biblisches Zeugnis und Sprachgestalt bei J.G. Hamann.* Basel: Brunnen, 1988.

– *Über den Ursprung der Sprache.* Vol. 4 of the series *Johann Georg Hamanns Hauptschriften erklärt.* Gütersloh: Bertelsmann, 1963.

Buffon, Georges Louis Leclerc, comte de. *Discours sur le style.* Castelnau-le-Lez: Éditions Climats, 1992.

Buren, John van. *The Young Heidegger.* Indianapolis: Indiana University Press, 1994.

Burke, Edmund. *Edmund Burke: Pre-Revolutionary Writings.* Edited by Ian Harris. Cambridge: Cambridge University Press, 1993.

– *Reflections on the Revolution in France.* Middlesex: Penguin, 1982.

Cicero. *The Offices.* Translated by T. Cockmann. Toronto: Dent, 1930.

Condorcet, Jean-Antoine-Nicolas Caritat, marquis de. *Esquisse d'un tableau historique des progrès de l'esprit humain.* Edited by Alain Pons. Paris: Flammarion, 1988.

Corbin, Henri. *Hamann: philosophe du luthéranisme.* Paris: Berg, 1985.

Dahlstrohm, Daniel, 'The Asethetic Holism of Hamann, Herder, and Schiller.' In *The Cambridge Companion to German Idealism*, edited by K. Ameriks, 76–94. Cambridge: Cambridge University Press, 2000.

Dickie, George. *The Century of Taste.* Oxford: Oxford University Press, 1996.

Dickson, Gwen Griffith. *Johann Georg Hamann's Relational Metacriticism.* Berlin: de Gruyter, 1995.

Diderot, Denis. *Dictionnaire Encyclopédique.* Edited by J. Assézat. Paris: Garniers, 1876.

Diderot, Denis, and Jean Le Rond D'Alembert, eds. 1757. Facsimile reprint, *Encyclopédie ou dictionnaire raisonné des sciences, des arts et des métiers.* Paris: Briasson, David, Le Breton, Durand. Elmsford: Pergamon, 1969.

– *Le neveu de Rameau suivi de six oeuvres philosophiques.* Paris: Gallimard, 1966.

Fink-Langlois, A. 'J.G. Hamanns französische Shriften übersetzt und erläutert.' In *Johann Georg Hamann und Frankreich*, edited by B. Gajek, 64–237. Marburg: Elwert, 1987.

Frederick II, King of Prussia. 'Essai sur l'amour propre envisagé comme principe de morale.' In *Histoire de l'Académie Royale des Sciences et des Belles-Lettres de Berlin* (1763), 341–54. Berlin: Haude et Spener, 1770.

– *Die politischen Testamente Friedrichs des Grossen.* Edited by Gustav Berthold Volz. Berlin: Hobbing, 1920.

– *Friedrich II, König von Preußen und die deutsche Literatur des 18. Jahrhunderts: Texte und Dokumente*, edited by Horst Steinmetz. Stuttgart: Reclam, 1985.

– *Oeuvres Complettes* [sic] *de Frédéric II, Roi de Prusse.* 1790.

– *Oeuvres primitives de Frédéric II, Roi de Prusse ou Collection des ouvrages qu'il publia pendant son règne.* 6th ed. Potsdam: des Associés, 1805.

Fritsch, Friedmann. *Communicatio Idiomatum*. Berlin: de Gruyter, 1999.
– 'Die Wirklichkeit als göttlich und menschlich zugleich.' In Bayer, *Johann Georg Hamann*, 52–79.
Frye, Northrop. *The Great Code*. London: Harvest, 1982.
Gajek, Bernhard, ed. *Johann Georg Hamann und Frankreich: Acta des dritten Internationalen Hamann-Colloquiums im Herder-Institut zu Marburg/Lahn 1982*. Marburg: Elwert, 1987.
– *Johann Georg Hamann und die Krise der Aufklärung: Acta des 5. Internationalen Hamann-Kolloquiums in Münster 1988*. Frankfurt am Main: Lang, 1990.
Garrard, Graeme. *Counter-Enlightenments: From the Eighteenth Century to the Present*. London: Routledge, 2006.
Gay, Peter. *The Enlightenment: An Interpretation*. Vol. 2, *The Science of Freedom*. New York: Norton, 1969.
Gellner, Ernest. *Words and Things*. London: Penguin, 1968.
German, Terence J. *Hamann on Language and Religion*. Oxford: Oxford University Press, 1981.
Goethe, Johann Wolfgang. *Sämtliche Werke*. 40 vols. Frankfurt am Main: Deutscher Klassiker, 1986.
Graubner, Hans. 'Theological Empiricism: Aspects of Johann Georg Hamann's Reception of Hume.' *Hume Studies* 15, no. 2 (1989): 377–86.
Grotius, Hugo. *The Rights of War and Peace*. Translated by A.C. Cambell. London: Dunne, 1901.
Gründer, Karlfried. *Figur und Geschichte: Johann Georg Hamanns 'biblische Betrachtungen' als ansatz einer Geschichtsphilosophie*. Munich: Karl Alber, 1958.
Habermas, Jürgen. *The Philosophical Discourse of Modernity*. Translated by F. Lawrence. Cambridge, MA: MIT Press.
– *Postmetaphysical Thinking*. Translated by W.M. Hohengarten. Cambridge, MA: MIT Press, 1992.
– 'Religion in the Public Sphere.' *European Journal of Philosophy* 14, no. 1 (2006): 1–25.
– *The Structural Transformation of the Public Sphere*. Translated by Thomas Burger. Cambridge: MIT Press, 1989.
– *The Theory of Communicative Action*. Translated by Thomas McCarthy. Boston: Beacon, 1984.
Hacking, Ian. 'How, Why, When, and Where Did Language Go Public?' In *Historical Ontology*, 121–39. Cambridge: Harvard University Press, 2002.
Hartung, Fritz. 'Der aufgeklärte Absolutismus.' In *Absolutismus*, edited by W.Hubatsch. Darmstadt: Wissenschaftliche Buchgesellschaft, 1973.
Hartz, Louis. 'The Reactionary Enlightenment: Southern Political Thought before the Civil War.' *Western Political Quarterly* 5, no. 1 (March 1952): 31–50.

Hegel, G.W.F. *Phenomenology of Spirit*. Translated by A.V. Miller. Oxford: Oxford University Press, 1977.

– 'Über Hamanns Schriften.' In *Sämtliche Werke*, edited by H. Glockner. Stuttgart: Frommanns Verlag, 1930.

Heidegger, Martin. *Basic Writings*. New York: HarperCollins, 1993.

– *Introduction to Metaphysics*. Translated by G. Fried and R. Polt. New Haven: Yale University Press, 2000.

– *Platons Lehre von der Wahrheit*. Bern: Franke, 1975.

Herder, Johann Gottfried. *Ideen zur Philosophie der Geschichte der Menschheit*. Berlin: Deutsche Buch-Gemeinschaft, 1924.

– *Johann Gottfried Herder Werke*. 10 vols. Edited by J. Brummack and M. Bollacher et al. Frankfurt: Deutsche Klassiker, 1994.

Hobbes, Thomas. *Leviathan*. 1651. Edited by C.B. Macpherson. London: Penguin, 1985.

Hoffmann, Volker. *Johann Georg Hamanns Philologie*. Stuttgart: Kohlhammer, 1972.

Holborn, H. *A History of Modern Germany: 1648–1840*. New York: Knopf, 1964.

Homer. *The Odyssey*. Translated by E.V. Rieu. London: Penguin, 1946.

Horace. *The Satires, Epistles and Poetry of Horace*. Translated by John Connington. London: Belle and Daldy, 1870.

Horkheimer, Max, and Theodor W. Adorno. *Dialektik der Aufklärung: Philosophische Fragmente*. Amsterdam: Querido Verlag, 1947.

Hubatsch, Walter. *Frederick the Great of Prussia: Absolutism and Administration*. London: Thames and Hudson, 1973.

Hulliung, Mark. *The Autocritique of Enlightenment*. Cambridge: Harvard University Press, 1994.

Hume, David. *An Enquiry concerning Human Understanding*. In *English Philosophers of the Seventeenth and Eighteenth Centuries: Locke, Berkeley, Hume*. New York: Harvard Classics, 1910.

– *Treatise of Human Nature*. 2 vols. Edited by A.D. Lindsay. London: Dent, 1974.

Israel, Jonathan. *Enlightenment Contested: Philosophy, Modernity and the Emancipation of Man 1670–1752*. Oxford: Oxford University Press, 2006.

Jaspers, Karl. *Nietzsche: An Introduction to the Understanding of His Philosophical Activity*. Translated by C.F. Wallraf and F.J. Schmitz. Baltimore: Johns Hopkins University Press, 1997.

Johnson, Hubert C. *Frederick the Great and His Officials*. Newhaven: Yale University Press, 1975.

Jørgensen, Sven-Aage. *Johann Georg Hamann*. Stuttgart: Metzler, 1976.

– *Johann Georg Hamann und England*. Edited by B. Gajek. Frankfurt am Main: Lang, 1999.

Jünger, Ernst. *Aladdin's Problem*. Translated by Joachim Neugroschel. New York: Marsilio, 1992.

Juvenal. *The Satires of Juvenal Translated with Explanatory and Classical Notes*. 1739. Translated by Sheridan. Facsimile reprint. New York: AMS, 1978.

Kant, Immanuel. *Briefwechsel*. Hamburg: Meiner, 1972.

– *Critique of Judgment*. Translated by Werner Pluhar. Indianapolis: Hackett, 1987.

– *Critique of Pure Reason*. Translated by Norman Kemp Smith. New York: St Martin's, 1965.

– *Groundwork of the Metaphysics of Morals*. Translated by H.J. Paton. New York: Harper, 1964.

– *Immanuel Kant: Correspondence*. Translated by Arnulf Zweig. Cambridge: Cambridge University Press, 1999.

– *Kant: Political Writings*. Edited by Hans Reiss. Cambridge: Cambridge University Press, 1991.

– *Kritik der praktischen Vernunft*. Leipzig: Reclam, 1878.

– *Kritik der reinen Vernunft*. Stuttgart: Reclam, 1966.

– *Kritik der Urteilskraft*. Stuttgart: Reclam, 1995.

– *The Metaphysics of Morals*. Translated by Mary Gregor. Cambridge: Cambridge University Press, 1996.

– *Metaphysik der Sitten*. Hamburg: Felix Meiner, 1966.

– *Religion within the Limits of Reason Alone*. Translated by T.M. Greene. New York: Harper & Row, 1960.

– *Schriften zur Anthropologie, Geschichts-philosophie, Politik une Pädagogik*. 2nd ed. Edited by W. Weischedel. Frankfurt: Suhrkamp, 1977.

– *Was ist Aufklärung? Thesen und Definitionen*. Edited by Ehrhard Bahr. Stuttgart: Reclam, 2000.

– *Zum ewigen Frieden*. Stuttgart: Reclam, 1981.

Kemp Smith, Norman. *A Commentary to Kant's Critique of Pure Reason*. 2nd ed. New York: Humanities, 1962.

Kierkegaard, Søren. *Concluding Unscientific Postscript*. Translated by D.F. Swenson and W. Lowrie. Princeton: Princeton University Press, 1968.

– *The Present Age*. Translated by A. Dru. New York: Harper, 1962.

Kockelmans, Joseph J. *Heidegger on Art and Art Works*. Dordrecht: Nijhof, 1985.

Kocziszky, Eva. *Hamanns Kritik der Moderne*. Munich: Alber, 2003.

Kuehn, Manfred. *Kant: A Biography*. Cambridge: Cambridge University Press, 2001.

La Mettrie, Julien Offray de. *Man: A Machine*. French-English ed. La Salle: Open Court, 1953.

La Rivière, Le Mercier de. *Ordre naturel et essentiel des sociétés politiques*. 1767. Évreux: Fayard, 2001.

Leibniz, Gottfried Wilhelm. *Essais de théodicée*. Edited by J. Brunschwig. Paris: Garnier, 1969.

Lentin, A., ed. *Enlightened Absolutism (1760–1790)*. Newcastle-upon-Tyne: Avero, 1985.

Lessing, G.E. *Die Erziehung des Menschengeschlechts & Ernst und Falk*. Stuttgart: Fries, 1958.

– *Werke und Briefe*. Edited by G. Grimm. Frankfurt am Main: Deutscher Klassiker, 1997.

Levy, Ze'ev. 'Hamann's Concept of Judaism and Controversy with Mendelssohn's "Jerusalem."' *Leo Baeck Institute* 29 (1984): 295–329.

– 'Johann Georg Hamann's Kontroverse mit Moses Mendelssohn.' In *Johann Georg Hamann und die Krise der Aufklärung: Acta des 5. Internationalen Hamann-Kolloquiums in Münster 1988*. Edited by B. Gajek, 327–44. Frankfurt am Main: Lang, 1990.

Liebrucks, Bruno. *Sprache und Bewußtsein*. Vol. 1, *Einleitung: Spannweite des Problems*. Frankfurt am Main: Akademische Verlagsgesellschaft, 1964.

Lo, Ping Cheung. 'A Critical Reevaluation of the Alleged "Empty Formalism" of Kantian Ethics.' *Ethics* 91, no. 2 (1981): 181–201.

Löwith, Karl. *From Hegel to Nietzsche*. Translated by D.E. Green. New York: Columbia University Press, 1991.

Luther, Martin. *Biblia: das ist die gantze Heilige Schrift Deudsch*. 1534. 3 vols. Frankfurt am Main: Röderberg, 1983.

– *Selected Writings*. Edited by John Dillenberger. Toronto: Anchor, 1961.

McMahon, Darrin. *Enemies of the Enlightenment*. Oxford: Oxford University Press, 2001.

Melton, James Van Horn. *Absolutism and the Eighteenth-Century Origins of Compulsory Schooling in Prussia and Austria*. Cambridge: Cambridge University Press, 1988.

Mendelssohn, Moses. *Gesammelte Schriften Jubiläumsausgabe*. Edited by A. Altmann et al. Stuttgart: Friedrich Frommann, 1983.

– *Jerusalem, or on Religious Power and Judaism*. Translated by Allan Arkush. Hanover: University Press of New England, 1983.

Metzke, Erwin. *J.G. Hamanns Stellung in der Philosophie des 18. Jahrhunderts*. Darmstadt: Wissenschaftliche Buchgesellschaft, 1967.

Mill, John Stuart. *Dissertations and Discussions*. London: Routledge, n.d.

Mitford, N. *Frederick the Great*. London: Hamilton, 1970.

Montesquieu, Charles Louis de Secondat. *De l'esprit des lois*. Paris: GF-Flammarion, 1979.

– *Lettres persanes*. Paris: GF-Flammarion, 1964.

Morgan, M.L. 'Liberalism in Mendelssohn's *Jerusalem*.' *History of Political Thought* 10, no. 2 (1989): 281–94.

Murdoch, Iris. *The Sovereignty of the Good*. London: Ark, 1985.

Muthu, Sankar. *Enlightenment against Empire*. Princeton: Princeton University Press, 2003.

Nadler, Joseph. *Johann Georg Hamann: Der Zeuge des Corpus mysticum*. Salzburg: Otto Müller, 1949.

Nebel, Gerhard. *Hamann*. Stuttgart: Ernst Klett, 1973.

Nietzsche, Friedrich. *Beyond Good and Evil*. Translated by W. Kaufmann. New York: Vintage, 1989.

– *Briefwechsel*. Edited by Colli and Montinari. Berlin: de Gruyter, 1978.

– *Die Geburt der Tragödie*. Stuttgart: Reclam, 1993.

– *On the Genealogy of Morals*. Translated by W. Kaufmann. New York: Vintage, 1969.

– *Sämtliche Briefe: kritische Studienausgabe in 8 Bänden*. Edited by Giorgio Colli and Mazzino Montinari. Berlin: de Gruyter, 2003.

– *Werke in Drei Bände*. Edited by K. Schlechta. Munich: Hanser, 1956.

– *Will to Power*. Translated by W. Kaufmann. New York: Vintage, 1968.

Norton, Robert E. *Herder's Aesthetics and the European Enlightenment*. Ithaca: Cornell University Press, 1991.

Nygren, Anders. *Agape and Eros*. Translated by P.S. Watson. Philadelphia: Westminster, 1953.

O'Flaherty, James. 'Hamann's Concept of the Whole Man.' *German Quarterly* 45, no. 2 (March 1972): 253–69.

– trans. *Hamann's 'Socratic Memorabilia': A Translation and Commentary*. Baltimore: Johns Hopkins University Press, 1967.

– *Johann Georg Hamann*. Boston: Twayne, 1979.

– 'The Magus of the North.' *New York Review of Books* 40, no. 19 (18 November 1993). http://www.nybooks.com/articles/2403.

– *The Quarrel of Reason with Itself: Essays on Hamann, Michaelis, Lessing, Nietzsche*. Columbia, SC: Camden House, 1988.

– *Unity and Language: A Study in the Philosophy of Johann Georg Hamann*. Chapel Hill: University of North Carolina, 1952.

Pascal, Roy. *The German Sturm und Drang*. London: Philosophical Library, 1953.

Persius. *The Satires of A. Persius Flaccus*. Translated by John Connington. Oxford: Clarendon, 1874.

Plato. *Complete Works*. Edited by J.M. Cooper. Indianapolis: Hackett, 1997.

Pocock, J.G.A. *Barbarism and Religion: The Enlightenments of Edward Gibbon*. Cambridge: Cambridge University Press, 1999.

– 'Conservative Enlightenment and Democratic Revolutions: The American and French Cases in British Perspective.' *Government and Opposition* 24 (1989): 81–105.

Pope, Alexander. *Selected Poetry and Prose.* New York: Holt, 1965.

Pufendorff, Samuel. *On the Duty of Man and Citizen According to Natural Law.* Translated by M. Silverthorne. Cambridge: Cambridge University Press, 1991.

– *Of the Laws of Nature and Nations.* Translated by Carew. London: Walthoe, 1729.

Quastana, François. *Voltaire et l'absolutisme éclairé.* Aix-en-Provence: Presses Universitaires d'Aix-Marseille, 2003.

Quine, Willard Van Orman. 'Two Dogmas of Empiricism.' *Philosophical Review* 60, no. 1 (January 1950): 20–43.

Rawls, John. 'Kantian Constructivism in Moral Theory.' *Journal of Philosophy* 77, no. 9 (September 1980): 515–72.

– *Political Liberalism.* New York: Columbia University Press, 1993.

– 'Political Liberalism: Reply to Habermas.' *Journal of Philosophy* 92, no. 3 (March 1995): 132–80.

Salmony, H.A. *Johann Georg Hamanns Metakritische Philosophie.* Basel: Evangelischer Verlag, 1958.

Schieder, Theodor. *Frederick the Great.* Translated by S. Berkeley and H.M. Scott. London: Longman, 2000.

Schmidt, James. 'Inventing the Enlightenment: Anti-Jacobins, British Hegelians, and the *Oxford English Dictionary.*' *Journal of the History of Ideas* 64, no. 3 (July 2003): 421–43.

– 'Projects and Projections: A Reply to Christian Delacampagne.' *Political Theory* 29, no. 1 (2001): 86–90.

– ed. *What Is Enlightenment? Eighteenth-Century Answers and Twentieth-Century Questions.* Berkeley: University of California Press, 1996.

– 'What Enlightenment Project?' *Political Theory* 28, no. 6 (2000): 734–57.

Schmidt, Jochen. *Die Geschichte des Genie-Gedankens 1750–1945.* Vol. 1, *Von der Aufklärung bis zum Idealismus.* Darmstadt: Wissenschaftliche Buchgesellschaft, 1985.

Schmitt, Carl. *The Leviathan in the State Theory of Thomas Hobbes.* Translated by G. Schwab and E. Hilfstein. Westport, CT: Greenwood, 1996.

Schoonhoven, E. *Johann Georg Hamanns Hauptschriften Erklärt.* Gütersloh: Gerd Mohn, 1962.

Schreiner, Lothar. *Golgotha und Scheblimini erklärt.* Vol. 7 of the series *Johann Georg Hamanns Hauptschriften erklärt.* Gutersloh: Bertelsmann, 1956.

Schoonhoven, Evert Jansen, and Martin Seils. *Mysterienschriften erklärt.* Vol. 5 of the series *Johann Georg Hamann:* Gütersloh: Bertelsmann, 1962.

– Vol. 5, *Mysterienschriften.* Edited by Evert Jansen Schoonhoven and Martin Seils. Gütersloh: Bertelsmann, 1962.

Schröder, Claudia. '*Siècle de Frédéric ii' und Zeitalter der Aufklärung.* Berlin: Duncker & Humblot, 2002.

Sée, Henri. *Les idées politiques en France au XVIIIe siècle.* Paris: Hachette, 1920.

Selis, N.J. *L'inoculation du bon sens.* London, 1762.

Sheehan, J. 'Heidegger and the Nazis.' *New York Review of Books* 35, no. 10 (June 1988): 40.

Simon, Josef. 'Immanuel Kant.' In *Klassiker der Sprachphilosophie: von Platon bis Noam Chomsky*, edited by T. Borsche, 233–56. Münich: Beck, 1996.

Sinn, Dieter, and Renate Sinn. *Der Alltag in Preußen.* Frankfurt am Main: Sociäts Verlag, 1991.

Smith, Ronald Gregor. 'J.G. Hamann and the Princess Gallitzin: An Ecumenical Encounter.' In *Philomathes*, edited by R.B. Palmer et al., 330–40. The Hague: Nijhoff, 1971.

– *J.G. Hamann: A Study in Christian Existence.* London: Collins, 1960.

– 'Vernunftkritik und Autorschaft. Reflexionen über Hamanns Kantkritik.' In *Acta des Internationalen Hamann-Colloquiums in Lüneburg 1976*, 135–69. Frankfurt am Main: Klostermann, 1979.

Sorkin, David. 'The Case for Comparison: Moses Mendelssohn and the Religious Enlightenment.' *Modern Judaism* 14, no. 2 (May 1994): 121–38.

Strässle, Urs. *Geschicht, geschichtliches Verstehen und Geschichtsschreibung im Verständnis Johann Georg Hamanns.* Bern: Lang, 1970.

Strauss, Leo. *Gesammelte Schriften.* Stuttgart: Metzler, 2001.

Stünkel, Knut. 'Die Sprache bei Hamann und Heidegger.' *Zeitschrift für systematische Theologie und Religionsunterricht* 46 (2004): 26–55.

Swain, Charles. 'Hamann and the Philosophy of David Hume.' *Journal of the History of Philosophy* 5 (1967): 343–52.

Taylor, Charles. *Human Agency and Language.* Cambridge: Cambridge University Press, 1985.

– *The Malaise of Modernity.* Toronto: Anansi, 1991.

– *Philosophical Arguments.* Cambridge: Harvard University Press, 1995.

– *Sources of the Self.* Cambridge, MA: Harvard University Press, 1989.

Tuck, Richard. *Natural Rights Theories.* Cambridge: Cambridge University Press, 1979.

Unger, Rudolph. *Hamann und die Aufklärung.* 2 vols. Halle: Niemeyer, 1925.

Vaihinger, H. *Commentar zu Kants Kritik der reinen Vernunft.* Stuttgart: Spemann, 1881.

Vatter, Miguel. 'Strauss and Schmitt as Readers of Hobbes and Spinoza on the Relation between Political Theology and Liberalism.' *New Centennial Review* 4, no. 3 (2004): 161–214.

Veldhuis, Henri. *Ein Versiegeltes Buch: Der Naturbegriff in der Theologie J.G. Hamanns.* Berlin: deGuyter, 1994.

Venturi, Franco. *Utopia and Reform in the Enlightenment.* Cambridge: Cambridge University Press, 1971.

Voltaire, *The A B C, or Dialogues between A B C*. In *Voltaire: Political Writings*. Translated by D. Williams. Cambridge: Cambridge University Press, 1994.
– *Mémoires pour servir à la vie de M. de Voltaire*. Edited by C.D. Brenner. Paris: Mercure de France, 1965.
Wannenwetsch, Bernd. 'Luther's Moral Theology.' In *The Cambridge Companion to Martin Luther*, edited by D. McKim, 120–35. Cambridge: Cambridge University Press, 2003.
Warrender, Howard. *The Political Philosophy of Hobbes*. Oxford: Clarendon, 1957.
Wild, Reiner. *Metacriticus bonae spei*. Frankfurt am Main: Lang, 1975.
Wittgenstein, Ludwig. *Philosophische Bemerkungen*. Frankfurt am Main: Suhrkamp, 1984.
– *Philosophische Untersuchungen*. Frankfurt am Main: Suhrkamp, 1982.
Wokler, Robert. 'The Enlightenment Project as Betrayed by Modernity.' *History of European Ideas* 24, nos. 4–5 (1998): 301–13.
Wolff, Christian Freiherr von. *Grundsätze des Natur- und Völkerrechts*. 1754. Facsimile reprint. Hildesheim: Olms, 1980.
Wolin, Sheldon. *Politics and Vision*. Toronto: Little, Brown, 1960.

Index